Financial and Human Resource Management in Organisations

SECOND EDITION

BBUS501

Compiled by:

Dr Petar Sudar
Nuala OSullivan
Julie Lister

UNIVERSITY OF WESTMINSTER

Westminster Business School

ISBN 13: 9781121954410

McGraw-Hill Custom Publishing

www.mcgrawhillcreate.co.uk

Published by McGraw-Hill Education (UK) Ltd an imprint of McGraw-Hill Education, 2 Penn Plaza, New York, NY 10121.

ISBN: 9781121954410

Financial and Human Resource Management in Organisations

SECOND EDITION

Contents

Credits

PART 1

Introduction

Part contents

CHAPTER 1

What is Human Resource Management?

By Christine Porter and Ania Przwieczerska

Chapter outline

Human Resource Management (HRM) is a philosophy of people management based on the belief that human resources are uniquely important to sustained organisation success, and the notion that an organisation gains competitive advantage[1] by ensuring that its employees are able to make use of their expertise and ingenuity to meet clearly defined corporate objectives (Price, 1997). The purpose of this chapter is twofold. Firstly, it seeks to outline the various roles that HRM plays within the organisation both at policy and practitioner level. The organisational problems that emerge in carrying out this role will be identified, with particular emphasis on the role of the line manager and the problems faced by the HR function in interfacing with line managers. Secondly, the chapter will serve as an introduction to the rest of the book, indicating the areas that are covered in the chapters that follow.

Learning outcomes

By the end of this chapter, you should be able to:

- Identify the potential contribution of HRM to the achievement of organisational objectives;
- Explain the role that the HR department can play in relation to the line manager;
- Identify HR practitioners' perspectives about the role that they need to play in an organisation;
- Explain the backgrounds of line managers, the likely impact of these backgrounds on the management of employees and the action that needs to be undertaken in order to make managers more effective;
- Explain the cultural basis of HRM and the extent to which changes may need to be made in the adoption of HRM tools to fit with different cultures;

---

[1] In not-for-profit organisations, a more relevant objective would be that of improving organisational effectiveness by achieving 'value for money'.

- ◆ Explain the contingency approach to the application of HR strategy and techniques;
- ◆ Identify the basis of conflict at work and the need for this to be taken into account when managing employees.

Introduction

HRM is a multidisciplinary activity based on ideas and theories drawn, for example, from sociology, law, psychology and economics. The subject has developed over the last 25 years to encompass fields of study that include organisation behaviour, personnel management and employee relations. It is viewed as involving all managers, especially general managers, and is therefore seen by many as broader in perspective than the subject matter of, say, personnel management. The extent to which this perception is founded on reality is discussed later in this chapter.

The term 'HR function' itself is a little ambiguous since it could relate to the activity of HR (or personnel management) throughout the organisation – wherever it is practised – thus including the activities of line managers as well as HR managers. It could also, however, just relate to the activities of the HR department. While the design of HR policies should be a joint effort involving both the HR specialists and line managers in an organisation, the implementation of human resource policies will be divided between the HR function and line management. There may be some difficulties in identifying the boundaries between these two sets of players and the extent to which either party are interested and willing to take responsibility for certain tasks. Much emphasis has been placed in the recent past on the strategic role of the HR department and HR practitioners do indeed need to take a corporate role and play an important part in the creation of organisational strategy, at least in relation to the extent to which the availability of skilled human resources will affect the achievement of these objectives.

The HR practitioner is part of the management team and their activities will impact on the relationship between the organisation and its employees. Despite interest in the extent to which HR is involved in the creation of strategies, HR practitioners also have an important role to play in administration and in the welfare of employees, although not necessarily as a buffer activity between management and unions. The relationship with line management and the need for line managers to be involved in the HR function is an important one and will be examined in greater detail in this chapter.

Historical perspective

HR began as a welfare and establishment function known as 'personnel management'. Personnel management was conceived of as being the practice of those in a specific department in the organisation. It was the duty of the personnel department to ensure that employees' health and safety needs were catered for. They also had to keep records of the numbers employed, dates of employment, holiday entitlement, rate of pay and training received. These aspects of the function are still important, in addition to the strategic approaches that HR could and should take and the need and desire for HR to be more involved in decision making at a corporate or strategy-making level.

The HR function has grown in importance with the growth of global competition. The increased pace of globalisation has meant that private sector organisations face far greater competition than in the past and one way of ensuring that they remain competitive has been to concentrate on their workforce. The need for skilled employees has increased, along with competition in the market place and the acquisition, retention and replacement of suitable employees has in itself become an even more skilled activity than in the past. Organisations are much more likely to recruit internationally than in the past but employees are therefore more likely to view the job market as global. As demand for skilled labour in the private sector has increased so has demand for skilled labour in the public sector. Both sectors require employees who are flexible and willing to respond to the ever-changing demands that organisations place on them. The public sector, non-governmental and quasi non-governmental organisations have all been under pressure. Public sector organisations have been required to make more effective use of their employees as the pubic expectations of service provisions have risen in excess of the financial resources available to meet these expectations.

The importance of the HR function has also increased in the UK with membership of the European Union, which has resulted in a plethora of statutes and directives that impact on the employment relationship (Ambler et al., 2004). UK government intervention in the workplace has also increased but much of this has been related to EU initiatives.

> 'The personnel function in firms has grown dramatically in recent years to cope with the expansion of regulation. The membership of the Institute of Personnel Management was 12,000 in 1979, and even as late as 1990 it was only 40,000. Today the grandly renamed Chartered Institute of Personnel and Development has around 120,000 members.'
>
> (Shackleton, 2005: 128–129)

The interventions in the employment relationship are also a response to changes in social norms about the protection of employees and the need, sometimes, for free enterprise to be restricted in order to promote the welfare of employees. Legislation has also increased the cost of employing people, therefore requiring the more efficient utilisation of human resources. This is in addition to the need for employers to be briefed about the details of legislation not just in order to avoid falling foul of the law, but because many of the provisions in employment statutes indicate levels of good practice that it is necessary for the employer to observe as a means of managing the workforce effectively.

The pace of economic change has quickened so that there is forever the problem of matching stock of skills with the requirements.[2] As this chapter is being written, Ernst & Young report that the UK economy is booming (*Sunday Times*, 2007), and there are low levels of unemployment. Despite the frequent scarcity of highly skilled employees in some areas, there is still a tendency among managers to treat employees as if they were the least significant and most easily malleable or

---

[2] Kersley et al. (2006: 107) suggest that skills are 'an increasing priority in British workplaces'. They also suggest that there is a large proportion of over-skilled employees and that these employees might be better utilised. This is backed up by research conducted between 1986–2001 (Felstead et al., 2002).

manipulated aspect of any change programme and for their needs and views on a situation not to be taken into account (see ACAS, 2004 for an analysis of the volume of case referrals).

Although the incidence of collective disputes has declined markedly since the peak of union recognition in 1979, the Workplace Employment Relations Survey (WERS) team point out (Kersley et al., 2006) that the focus has shifted to 'unorganised and individualised expressions such as grievances, Employment Tribunal claims and management-led sanctions including dismissals' (p. 207). Employees have increasingly higher expectations of their employers and may, if working in an area of skills shortage, be able to take their skills to another organisation. Their increased expectations partly relate to changes in education but also to increased expectations in terms of quality of life and a heightened view of themselves as 'the customer' and their importance in the market place (often encouraged by the marketing policies of the companies for whom they work). This increase will manifest itself in terms of negative attitudes towards authoritarian management, a desire for participation in decision making (particularly when they are subject to a programme of change), a need for improved physical working conditions and pressure for increases in pay and other rewards.

The move in the UK from a manufacturing to a service economy has meant that there is a greater than ever need for workers with a different skill base. The service economy has had to adapt to the requirement of a 24/7 service. With the rise in flexible working patterns, facilitated in some cases by new technology, has come further demand for services to be provided around the clock.

The HR function itself has in the past been slow to adapt to computerisation and to take advantage of the opportunities provided. However, that is changing with the increasing use of software to support HR activities in-house. Kettley and Reilly (2003) report that there is little independent evidence on the take-up of e-HR, which they describe as 'the application of conventional, web and voice technologies to improve HR administration, transactions and process performance'. According to IRS (2004a, 2004b), 90 per cent of organisations are using some form of e-recruitment packages to manage the process from advertising vacancies, through candidate applications to initial short-listing. Other software supports human capital management: this covers payroll, absence monitoring, staff development and providing data for human resource planning. Packages are also available to support employee learning and development needs via self-managed learning.

Models of human resource management

Globalisation and the greater need for organisations to be competitive on a global basis have meant that greater emphasis has been placed on the human resource. Delery and Shaw (2001) point out that human capital may be a source of competitive advantage. The advent of the knowledge worker has also meant that the human resource has been more valued. This led in the early 1980s to the development of models of HRM that emphasised the link with organisational objectives. It has always been the case that personnel (or HR) managers need to take into account organisational objectives when deciding on a package of employment policies. Similarly, organisations have always needed to consult with HR when devising corporate objectives, in order to ensure that their plans were feasible from the

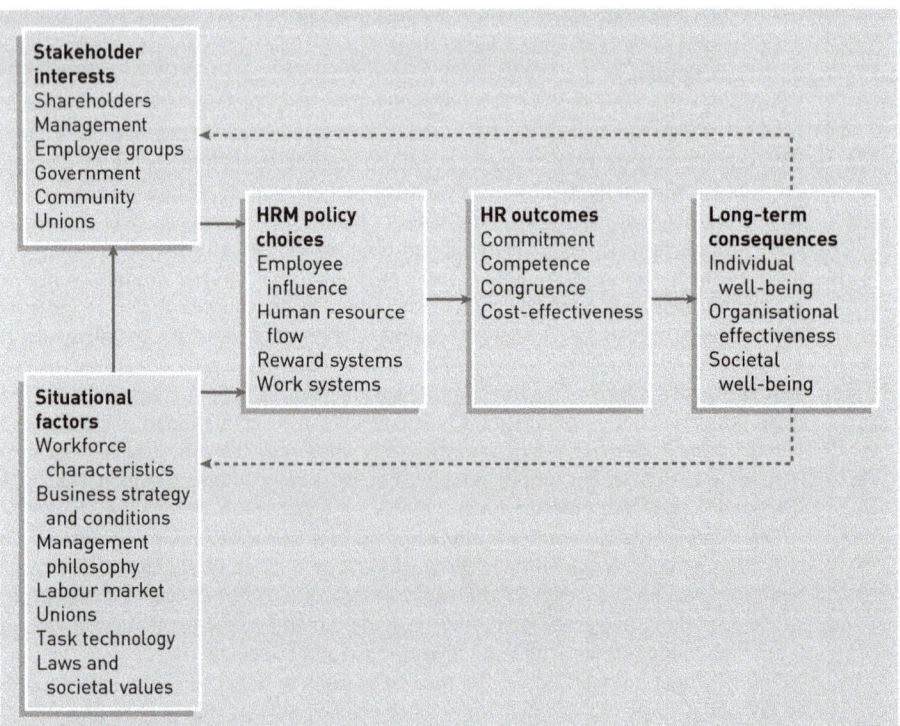

Figure 1.1 Map of HRM territory
Source: Beer et al. (1984: 16)

perspective of the labour resource. However, models of HRM written about in the 1980s were put forward as an innovative approach to managing people: an example of a repackaged idea, common in this area.

There were many models of HRM developed between 1984 and 1995. Two sub-divisions of models of HRM are emphasised – the 'hard' and 'soft' versions (Storey, 1992). Hard HRM emphasises employee costs and head count. Soft HRM emphasises employee participation, organisational capability and training and development.

A useful model for identifying the different interest groups within organisations is that of Beer et al. (1984), based at that time at Harvard University. As can be seen, the model of HRM reproduced as Figure 1.1 identifies the stakeholders and situational factors that will impact on the implementation of the HRM policies that an organisation devises and which therefore need to be taken into account. The model has the advantage that it appears to recognise that not all stakeholders will share the same interests and that because of this there could be conflict in implementing HRM practices. The model also encourages consideration of the need for policies and practices to be congruent with one another and for long-term consequences to take into account individual and societal well-being as well as organisational effectiveness.

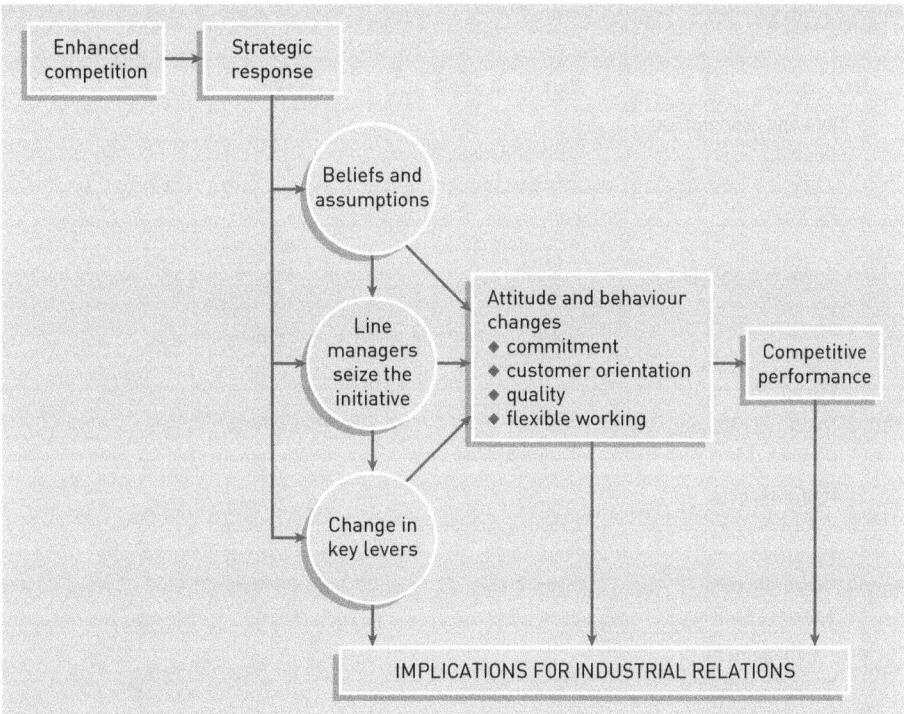

Figure 1.2 A model of the shift to HRM
Source: Storey (1992: 38)

Storey (1992) researched the transformation of organisations to the use of HRM instead of personnel management practices. From this research he created a model of the transformation, although he refers to it as an 'ideal type' – meaning that he has exaggerated the conception of how organisations have been transformed in order to make a point (see Figure 1.2). He identified 27 points of difference between the two terms human resource management and personnel management – these are summarised in Table 1.1.

Whether HRM exists as a separate approach to personnel management is open to debate. It is certainly true that many of the differences that are attributed to HRM (e.g. integration of HR with organisational strategy) can be identified as existing in organisations before HRM began to be discussed as a distinctive model.

Practitioners' perceptions of human resource management

As indicated above, despite the work of Storey and others, for some time academia (and to a lesser extent industry) has engaged in a debate on the differences, if any,

Table 1.1 Twenty-seven points of difference

Dimension	Personnel and IR	HRM
Beliefs and assumptions		
1 Contract	Careful delineation of written contracts	Aim to go 'beyond contract'
2 Rules	Importance of devising clear rules/mutuality	'Can-do' outlook; impatience with 'rule'
3 Guide to management action	Procedures	'Business need'
4 Behaviour referent	Norms/custom and practice	Values/mission
5 Managerial task vis-à-vis labour	Monitoring	Nurturing
6 Nature of relations	Pluralist	Unitarist
7 Conflict	Institutionalised	De-emphasised
Strategic aspects		
8 Key relations	Labour management	Customer
9 Initiatives	Piecemeal	Integrated
10 Corporate plan	Marginal to	Central to
11 Speed of decision	Slow	Fast
Line management		
12 Management role	Transactional	Transformational leadership
13 Key managers	Personnel/IR specialists	General/business/line managers
14 Communication	Indirect	Direct
15 Standardisation	High (e.g. 'parity' and issue)	Low (e.g. 'parity' not seen as relevant)
16 Prized management skills	Negotiation	Facilitation
Key levers		
17 Selection	Separate, marginal task	Integrated, key task
18 Pay	Job evaluation (fixed grades)	Performance-related
19 Conditions	Separately negotiated	Harmonisation
20 Labour management	Collective bargaining contracts	Towards individual contracts
21 Thrust of relations with stewards	Regularised through facilities and training	Marginalised (with exception of some bargaining for change models)
22 Job categories and grades	Many	Few
23 Communication	Restricted flow	Increased flow
24 Job design	Division of labour	Teamwork
25 Conflict handling	Reach temporary truces	Manage climate and culture
26 Training and development	Controlled access to courses	Learning companies
27 Foci of attention for interventions	Personnel procedures	Wide-ranging cultural, structural and personnel strategies

Source: Storey (1992: 38). Reproduced by kind permission of Blackwell Publishers.

between 'human resource management' and 'personnel management'. The central discussion revolves around whether these terms represent practices and approaches that are qualitatively different, or are merely alternative labels for applied principles that are fundamentally the same. Rarely, however, has this discussion sought to take account of actual HR/personnel practitioners' understandings of these issues and how, if at all, they describe what they do.

HRM/personnel management – the debate

Unpublished preliminary findings from research conducted by Przwieczerska in 2003 suggest that, notwithstanding the niceties of the academic debate, for some practitioners, HRM and personnel management are largely interchangeable terms, with the former representing little more than an Americanisation of the latter. However, others perceive a more substantive difference, with personnel management seen as denoting a more reactive set of activities, primarily concerned with the administration of employment and provision of employee welfare, while HRM is seen as more proactive, strategically driven people management, with the emphasis on eliciting performance. HRM is seen as a way of enhancing the profile and role of an otherwise low-status and misunderstood function. What often comes across is uncertainty about what the term entails and how it could be incorporated in an organisation's future development. Instead, it is not regarded in as much high esteem as other departments as its contributions are viewed as merely administrative, concerned with immediate workforce concerns rather than long-term plans.

Senior versus junior practitioners

Przwieczerska's research findings indicate that the terms HRM and personnel management seem to have different meanings for senior and junior practitioners. Senior practitioners emphasise HRM and its associated strategic role – that is, managing the performance of human resources in order to achieve the organisation's strategic goals. More junior practitioners, while recognising the theoretical distinctiveness of HRM, perceive what they are doing as primarily personnel management – the routine administration of pay, recruitment, appraisal, grievances and redundancy – without any evident sense of strategic purpose. In organisations where HRM does not appear to be regarded as highly as other departments, new HR managers are not allowed to put into practice their ideas and initiatives, and instead are pigeon-holed into what was previously titled personnel management roles. One very visible casualty of this restricted role is the training versus organisational development debate, discussed further in Chapters 15, 16 and 17.

Public versus private sector

The research conducted by Przwieczerska revealed signs of differences between the public and private sectors. Private sector practitioners appear to perceive their role more in terms of HRM, with an emphasis on strategy and performance, whereas public sector practitioners perceive their role more in terms of old-style personnel management, with a continuing emphasis on bargaining and employee welfare. It could be argued that this difference reflects the way the private and public sectors function.

pause for thought

Do you think that these perceived private/public sector distinctions described above will affect the potential for employee job satisfaction?

What were the reasons for you coming to this conclusion?

Models of HRM indicate the need to have HR practices that do not conflict with one another. For example, the simultaneous existence of practices such as performance-related pay that is based on an individual's performance and teamworking that obviously promotes the value of the team can be conflicting and therefore counter-productive. The lack of involvement of HR practitioners at board level very often militates against the development of strategy that takes account of the human resource realities in terms of the capacity of the organisation to undertake certain activities as the following example illustrates.

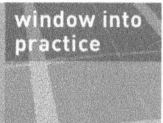

window into practice

A London-based children's charity decided to take over a number of nurseries in an ambitious programme of expansion. The charity did not involve the HR director in the decision to expand in this way and was therefore unaware that the employees in these other organisations had employment rights that made it difficult to make them redundant. The charity also lacked the managerial expertise to run a larger organisation. Before long they found themselves in severe financial difficulties and were lucky not to become bankrupt.

The extent to which strategic HRM is practised will vary from one organisation to another, and also from one country to another. There is, for example, far greater involvement of the function in Japanese and North American organisations. Japanese organisations in particular may have HR specialists who have worked for many years with the same company and are therefore very knowledgeable about the organisation. Any board member will need to have an understanding of the whole business in order to make a useful contribution to strategy development. For this reason, the professional examinations that HR professionals take to achieve chartered status include a strong general management component.

If HR directors have come from other organisations there may be a problem with adapting what worked in those organisations to the new situation. HR directors and other managers will need to take a contingency approach to the situation in which they find themselves.

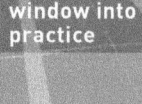

window into practice

The HR function has to earn its place on the board of directors

The new director of human resources at a well-established and respected research institute was pleased to be appointed to this job, especially since the role had been upgraded to a director level position. Previously he had worked for six years for a firm of management consultants who operated mainly in the private sector. His predecessor at the research institute had operated in what had been in reality an old style 'establishments'

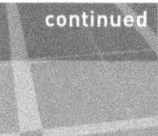

continued

department making sure that all the records were kept up to date and ensuring that everyone got paid on time. The predecessor had not been professionally qualified, unlike the new director.

The main problem that the new HR director identified was the over-involvement of the professional staff in the detailed work of their various units. Their loyalty appeared to be just to their discipline and not to their colleagues in other departments or the institute as a whole. He saw the professional staff as not being very deferential to authority and with a weak sense of corporate identity.

The HR director did not integrate with the organisation and became increasingly frustrated in his attempts to develop a modern human resource management function, which he thought was necessary to support the organisation in both the accomplishment of its strategic objectives and day-to-day operational effectiveness. He sought to implement a range of techniques that he saw as being 'best practice' but without identifying whether they fitted in with the culture of the institute. No attempt was made by him to identify the problems that line managers faced and when there was a real problem he was nowhere to be seen.

Eventually the HR director's post was down-graded since he was not perceived as contributing to organisational effectiveness.

The role of the HR manager

The role of the HR manager is seen to have changed over the years from that of a 'clerk of works' (Tyson and Fell, 1986) to that of 'strategic business partner' (attributed to Ulrich, 1998). A more strategic input for HR managers is seen as being an advance in the status of the profession. However, many of the roles identified still need to be undertaken simultaneously with that of a strategic input if organisations are to function effectively.

In 2003, Caldwell attempted to test out two models of the 'personnel manager's role' (that of Storey, 1992 and Ulrich, 1997) to identify the extent to which roles had changed now that 'HRM has increasingly become part of the rhetoric and reality of organisational performance' (Caldwell, 2003: 983). Storey (1992) draws on case-based research to inform his model that identified four different roles for HR managers: Advisors, Handmaidens, Regulators and Changemakers. These four roles were identified along two axes: *intervention* versus *non-intervention* and *strategy* versus *tactics* (see Figure 1.3).

HR managers as Advisors offer expertise and advice to line managers while operating in an essentially non-interventionist manner. Handmaidens provide specific services to management and, like those playing an Advisor role, are seen by Storey as being reactive. Regulators are interventionist, formulating policy and monitoring the implementation of it. Storey saw Changemakers as interventionists with a strategic agenda looking at the hard realities of business performance as well as the HR interventions designed to enhance employee commitment and motivation.

Ulrich's model, published five years later, also defines four roles along two axes. The two axes he calls *strategy* versus *operations* and *process* versus *people*. The four roles that he identified are: Strategic Partners to help successfully carry out

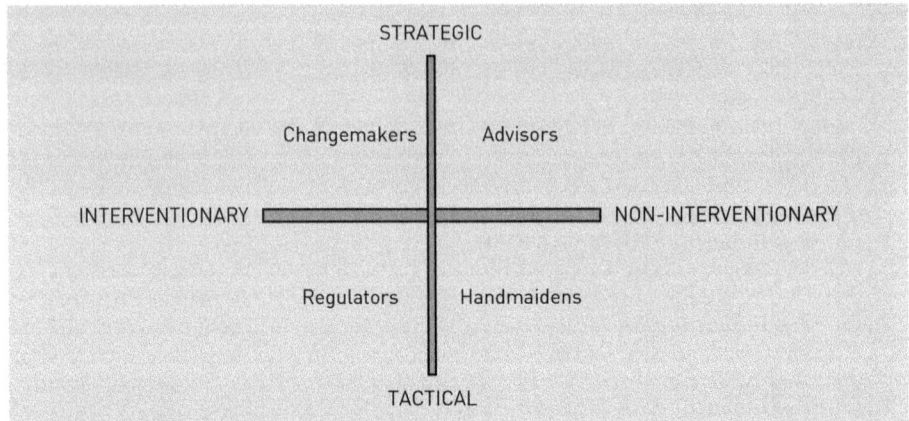

Figure 1.3 Storey's four roles of personnel managers
Source: Caldwell (2003: 986)

organisational objectives; Administrative Experts to constantly improve organisational efficiency by re-engineering the HR function and other work processes; Employee Champions to maximise employee commitment and competence; and Change Agents to deliver organisational transformation and cultural change (see Figure 1.4).

Caldwell (2003) comments that Ulrich's model is prescriptive and not based on research but is nevertheless a systematic framework for 'capturing the emergence of new roles'. The role definitions provided by Storey and Ulrich are useful in identifying the range of activities that HR professionals undertake. Caldwell sets out to identify changes in roles and contrasts Storey's typology with that of Ulrich to ascertain

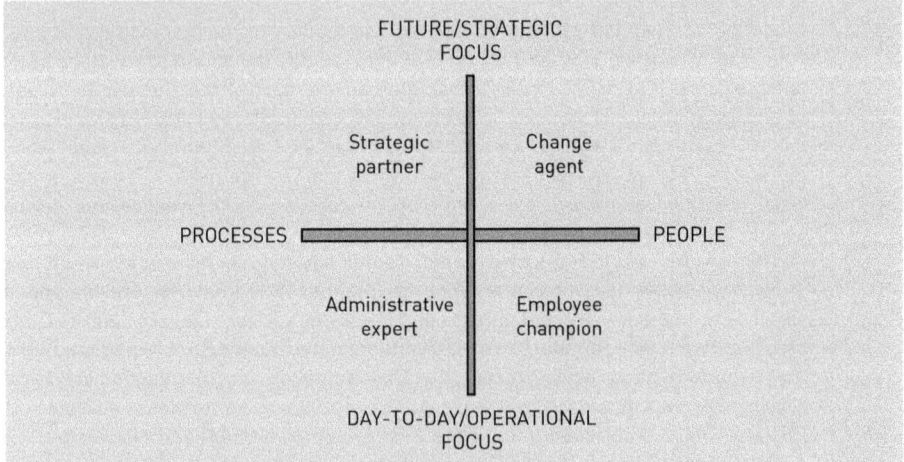

Figure 1.4 Ulrich's four roles of HR professionals
Source: Caldwell (2003: 987)

whether either model copes with the tensions he perceives between competing role demands. Caldwell finds that most of the respondents in a research survey had no 'main role' as categorised by Storey's matrix and that 'Ulrich's prescriptive vision promised more than HR professionals can really deliver'.

Caldwell (2003: 987) finds Ulrich's vision 'inspiring and sometimes disconcerting'. Ulrich claims 'HR professionals must become champions of competitiveness in delivering value or face the diminution or outsourcing of their role' (Ulrich, 1997: 17). As Caldwell points out (p. 1003), Ulrich's view of the HR role is unitary, i.e. there is an assumption that the employee aims and objectives and those of management coincide and that HR as a 'business partner' can deliver this collaboration without needing to manage conflict between employees and management. Managerial expectations of performance are ever increasing and demands made of the HR profession are likely to intensify in the future; Caldwell's implication being that HR is unlikely to ever totally fulfil these expectations given the competing nature of organisational requirements.

Some observers perceive a need for HR to be a presence within the workforce and to concentrate on guaranteeing 'employee well-being and satisfaction and work-life balance for all employees' (Francis and Keegan, 2006: 243). Francis and Keegan see the HR department as being 'guardians of employee well-being . . . who will ensure consistency of organisational justice for all employees.'

They comment that:

> 'the devolution of transactional HR work to the line combined with its relocation to service centres as well as the fact that business partners are largely oriented towards strategic issues means that employees are increasingly losing day-to-day contact with HR specialists and relying on line managers who have neither the time nor the training to give HR work the priority it needs.'

The following discussion is based on the assumption that HR exists to ensure that line managers take responsibility for employees by trying to ensure that those selected as line managers have the potential to take employees into account when carrying out their managerial role, giving managers the training and development necessary to ensure that they develop the skills to do this and setting up structures so that managerial performance can be monitored.

Division of responsibilities between human resource practitioners and line managers

As indicated above, some thought needs to go into the division of responsibilities between the HR department and the line manager. In this respect the distinction between 'manager' and 'supervisor' may not be a particularly useful one, so the following can be taken to refer to both managers and supervisors.

Problems in the division of responsibilities are incurred because of either line managers' unwillingness to carry out responsibilities or members of the HR department intervening in operational tasks, thus usurping the role of the line manager. In some organisations, problems will occur where the HR department is seen as perpetually thwarting the line management function in its efforts to carry out the operational role. Sometimes, line managers do need to be advised of the likely ill consequences of their decisions. HR practitioners may need to use their influencing skills to bring pressure to bear on a manager who persistently refuses to take advice and then leaves the HR department to sort out the ensuing situation. However, if HR professionals are able to show that much of the time they are there to facilitate the smooth running of the organisation, then they can be seen as making an overall positive contribution to the achievement of organisational objectives.

Areas where line managers have responsibility will include the following:

◆ **Human resource planning** – line managers would need to be involved in discussions on the development of their function. As discussed in Chapter 3, the HR department would need to advise on the human resource implications of any organisation development. As far as staffing levels for current and future activities are concerned, line managers would be in a position to know whether they are able to deliver a satisfactory service given their current staffing levels but would need to justify this in budgetary terms.

◆ **Organisational and job design and development in order to meet unit and departmental objectives** – HR professionals should have specialist skills and advice to give on organisational development and job design. They would need to work in close co-operation with line management over this. Chapter 17 discusses the organisational development issues from the perspective of the HR function.

◆ **Recruitment and selection** – the role of the HR department in relation to recruitment and selection is discussed in Chapter 7. HR should ensure that line managers have the necessary skills to draw up job descriptions and person specifications and carry out a selection interview, with due regard to equal opportunities legislation. Those in the HR department would be able to give guidance on legislative requirements and, together with line managers, can draw up a suitable advertising campaign.

◆ **Implementing equal opportunities** – HR practitioners would be involved in not only giving specialist advice about the state of legislation in this area but would also be able to indicate a range of policies that could be adopted in order to create an equal opportunities environment. However, the line manager would be involved in implementing these policies and ensuring that staff within their department adhere to them.

◆ **Performance management** – this includes objective setting and appraisal, both formal and informal. As is pointed out in Chapter 8, performance management is very much an integral part of the day-to-day responsibilities of the line manager. In a formal sense, performance management can be seen as an integrated system that is aligned with the corporate objectives, although performance management should occur in all organisations – whether they have adopted a formal, integrated system or not. The role of the HR manager in relation to performance management would be to participate in the development of any formal systems and to ensure that the line managers in the organisation have been developed in the skills of setting departmental and individual work objectives and of conducting appraisals.

◆ **Remuneration** – it is essential that line managers understand the basis on which the people in their department are being remunerated. If there are any queries about pay, the line manager will need to ensure that a good explanation can be given about the calculation of pay. It is also useful to know, when wanting to allocate work, exactly what impact this might have on actual remuneration. Similarly line managers may have to be involved if there are claims for upgrading; if nothing else, the manager needs to be aware of the impact on the rest of the department if an increase in pay is given. The actual reward structure will probably be designed by HR professionals, hopefully in discussion with line management. Chapter 9 explains the issues that the HR function will need to bear in mind, as well as trends in employee remuneration.

- **Training/coaching/mentoring** – HR professionals would be involved in creating an environment in which staff development needs could be identified, e.g. via a formal system of appraisal. The line manager and the individual employee would undertake the identification of staff development needs. HR practitioners might be in a position to give advice on the likely applicability of externally run programmes or deliver certain formal training programmes themselves. However, much of the day-to-day staff development will either be undertaken by the line manager in the role of coach or by the employee themselves, developing new skills on the job. Chapter 15 has a discussion on training and development and Chapter 19 on coaching.

- **Employee relations** – as explained in Chapter 12, those in the HR department will need to draw up procedures either unilaterally or in conjunction with staff representatives where these exist. These procedures will need to cover sickness absence, capability, discipline, grievance, disputes, health and safety, and redundancy. HR will need to ensure that line managers have knowledge and understanding of the procedures and an ability and willingness to implement them. Line management will undertake discussions with staff representatives on a day-to-day basis. Even if the board of the organisation is involved in deciding on pay increases without negotiation, there may be many negotiations taking place on a daily basis between the line managers and individual employees.

- **Disciplinary handling** – as is discussed in Chapter 12, the practice of handling disciplinary issues is often necessary to ensure that employees' behaviour matches that required to meet organisational objectives. As an HR manager you would need to ensure that managers have the skills not only to handle disciplinary issues themselves, but also to coach supervisors who report to them in how to handle discipline. If supervisors understand their role in dealing with problems before they escalate, then disciplinary issues can be dealt with at an early opportunity. By coaching supervisors rather than dealing with issues themselves, the manager can avoid acting down and undermining the supervisor. (For a more in-depth explanation of the role of the line manager in disciplinary handling, refer to the disciplinary pyramid in Rees and Porter, 2001: 296.)

HR managers have a major role in taking the lead in developing strategies related to the above areas that reflect the needs of the organisation as well as the values that the employees wish to aspire to. HR also has a role in ensuring that line managers have skills regarding the above (see Chapter 16 for a discussion on management development). Line managers will need to have access to 'bouquets' as well as 'brickbats'. Very often it is first line managers who have to hand out unpleasant tasks, reprimand staff or take awkward decisions. This is probably as it should be, since if these responsibilities are taken away from them the line structure could be undermined. However, they also need to be given the opportunity to hand out any 'goodies' that are available such as bonus payments or promotions or staff development opportunities (which are often seen in this light).

When implementing new policies and procedures, it is essential that HR and line managers work closely together. If they do not work together, new policies may be implemented that do not meet organisational needs and do not fit with the organisational culture.

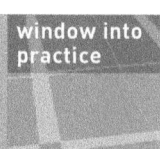

window into practice

One UK organisation introduced a system of job evaluation. Assuming that the technique was extremely robust, there was a lack of line manager input into the outcomes of the scheme. This resulted in some employees who had 'talked up' their jobs being over-promoted, leading to a sense of dissatisfaction among other employees who had not been promoted but felt that their jobs were equally demanding. This led to a large increase in the costs of employing people with no discernible improvements for organisational effectiveness. A similar result occurred in the UK's National Health Service, when doctors were asked to describe their jobs and on the basis of this were given increases in pay for no increase in service or productivity. Under a contract negotiated between the UK's Department of Health and the British Medical Association (which represents doctors in the UK), general practitioners received an uplift in pay of nearly 23 per cent on average in 2006 compared with 2003–04 for no apparent increase in services offered (*The Times*, 2007).

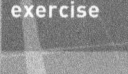

exercise

Make a presentation showing, with examples, the areas of the HR line manager's responsibilities and indicating what might happen if these are not aligned to organisational effectiveness.

The background of managers

The day-to-day responsibility for staff will rest with the line manager. It is also very often the case that the line manager will be implementing HR policies. Guest, writing about HRM in 1989, placed considerable emphasis on the role of the line manager as one of the central aspects of his model. This may have been a useful opportunity to emphasise the importance of line management, however, as McGovern (1999) points out, there is little empirical evidence that line managers' responsibilities have changed where HRM has been adopted compared with their role in organisations where models of 'personnel management' more reflect the norm.

For human resources to be effectively managed, the line manager needs to be willing to take responsibility for various aspects of staff management as well as have the skills and training to handle these situations. The background of many managers, particularly in the professions, is such that they either do not want to take on staff management activities or do not have the skills or training to undertake these activities effectively. However, in order to achieve departmental objectives they will need to devote more and more of their time to managing the people in their department, not just to implement HR policies as an end in themselves but in order to

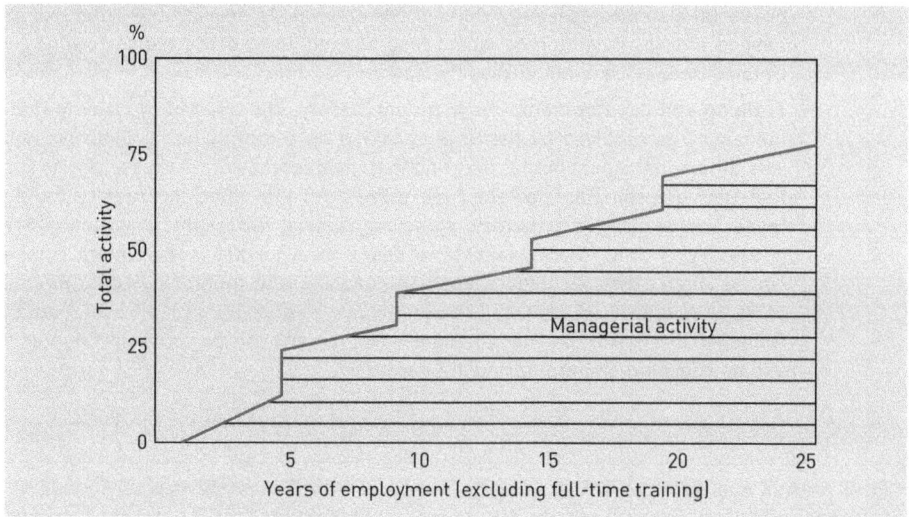

Figure 1.5 The managerial escalator
Source: Rees and Porter (2001: 5)

ensure that the human resources for whom they are responsible are effectively managed. The common path into management is illustrated by the so-called Managerial Escalator (Rees and Porter, 2001) – see Figure 1.5.

Looking at the above diagram (Figure 1.5), the horizontal axis gives an approximation of the amount of time that a manager will have been in management and the vertical axis indicates the percentage of working time that a manager at stages in his or her career is likely to need to spend on managerial activities. Many managers will have entered their chosen profession out of a sense of vocation and may be loathe to spend their time on activities that they do not perceive as related to their skills, expertise and training. Most managers in the professions will have had many years training related to their profession. However, the amount of training that they may have received to carry out what may be the greater part of their responsibilities could be counted in days, if not hours.

The HR department will need to help ensure that managers are effective in their jobs by observing four key action points:

♦ **Use of accurate role definitions and job titles** – very often managers are recruited to jobs that do not bear the name 'manager', nor are they given a job description that indicates the key areas of responsibility. Managerial jobs that do not bear the name manager include engineer, chief architect, nursing sister, head teacher, dean (of a university faculty) and bishop.

♦ **Recruitment and selection** – even if an accurate job description exists, managers are frequently recruited on the basis of spurious criteria that do not relate to the requirements of the job. For example, a head teacher may be appointed to manage a school on the basis that they were excellent at teaching. Once in post the new manager will find that his or her time will not be spent doing the activities on the basis of which they were promoted. This is not so problematic if the new post

Financial and Human Resource Management in Organisations, Second Edition

holder (a) also possesses the skills or the potential to develop the skills that are needed and (b) is willing to spend less of their time doing their previous job. Unfortunately, this is not always the case.

◆ **Training and development** – as mentioned above, the amount of training that a manager has received by the time of taking on the managerial duties may be very little and the post holder may find that the demands of their new job are such that they are reluctant to take time away from the office in order to develop these new skills. Nevertheless, some managerial development is likely to be necessary. If time is not available to spend on a formal management training course, then other techniques such as coaching and mentoring could be used to help the individual manager be as effective as possible in staff management. A deeper discussion on management development can be found in Chapter 16 and on coaching and mentoring in Chapter 19.

Developing the supervisor: Trouble in store

exercise

Fred Larkins is a forklift truck driver who has been with the company where you are warehouse manager for nine months. Fred's supervisor, Walter Smith, comes to see you towards the end of the working day and complains that he told Fred three hours ago to load a particular vehicle ready for the following morning. Walter further explains to you that when he had just asked Fred why he had not done as he had been asked, he had explained that he had been busy on other jobs and had not appreciated the urgency of the request. Walter added that Fred had failed to appreciate the urgency of a previous instruction about six weeks ago, which had led to a delivery crew getting away late and being caught in the morning rush hour traffic.

1. What would your objectives be in this situation, as the warehouse manager?
2. How would you seek to achieve these?
3. What impact might there be if you decided to speak to Fred yourself?

◆ **Monitoring and evaluation** – senior managers will need to monitor the performance of the more junior managers, and offer guidance where necessary if organisational objectives are not being met. The HR department will need to ensure that a system is set up so that this is carried out effectively, as well as being on hand to offer advice to management generally.

Write an email to the board of Warbings explaining why and how the four action points discussed above should be implemented.

exercise

Problem solving in human resource management

HRM is often the victim of fads as employers seek to find answers to their current problems, or rush to adopt a technique just because it is fashionable. Very often there is a lack of diagnosis of the causes of problems faced by the organisation

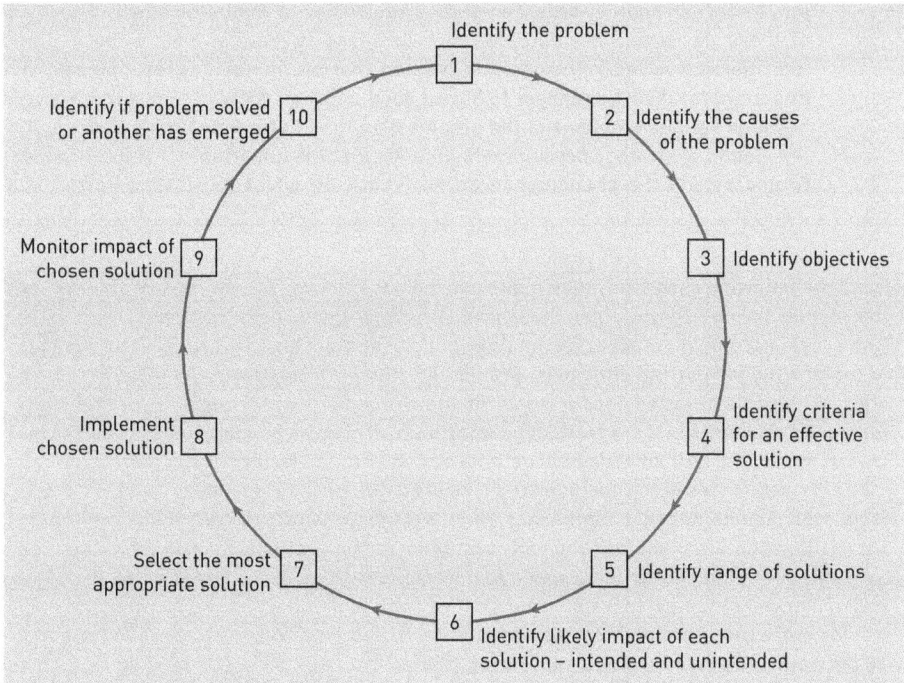

Figure 1.6 The problem-solving cycle
Source: Rees and Porter (2001)

(Watson, 2004). This lack of diagnosis may result in the adoption of inappropriate techniques. This can unfortunately mean that the problem besetting the organisation is not solved, although time, energy and organisational credibility will have been consumed, often resulting in a loss of face for the HR function. One way of overcoming this is to adopt a more structured approach to problem solving, as illustrated in Figure 1.6.

When problems are identified, the natural reaction is to implement a solution as quickly as possible. The problem-solving cycle puts more emphasis on diagnosing the causes of problems and of setting up criteria by which the chosen solution be judged. The latter stages of the cycle emphasise monitoring and evaluation, which may lead to the identification of further problems, and thus the need to continue with the problem-solving process. In analysing problems, a distinction needs to be drawn between symptoms and causes. It is also necessary to prioritise problems, since not all problems will be as important as others in terms of their impact.

Systems approach

When trying to identify the likely employee problems that may arise, managers may find it useful to take a systems approach. This emphasises the interconnectedness of organisational activity and the possibility that a change made in one area

Financial and Human Resource Management in Organisations, Second Edition

may impact on another area, sometimes known as the 'knock-on effect'. The impact of these decisions on employees may be more successfully identified if the HR manager is involved in the decision-making process. In many cases it may be more important for the HR manager to have a good understanding of the interrelationship between various functions of the organisation than to have an understanding of the fine points of strategy development. In any case it is important for the HR manager to understand the phenomenon of the 'knock-on effect' (Rees and Porter, 2001: 338–340).

exercise

Read the following case study then make two lists, the first delineating the problems and the second saying how you think these problems might have been rectified.

In a local evening newspaper, technological developments made it apparently possible to replace the former full-time print production staff with relatively unskilled part-time staff. While this reduced labour costs in the production department, it dramatically increased problems in the advertising department. This was particularly because of the loss of accumulated knowledge of customers' needs in the production department.

The consequences of this included the loss of customers. It also meant that the advertising staff had to spend a significant amount of time with the remaining customers for rectification work and dealing with customer complaints, thus cutting into the time available for selling advertising space to new customers. This in turn affected the commission payments made to advertising staff causing high labour turnover when the staff left for more lucrative jobs. The newspaper depended on advertising revenue for about 80 per cent of its income (Rees and Porter, 2006).

pause for thought

Can you identify any cases of organisations implementing new policies without thinking through the consequences?

Conflict at work

One aspect of HRM that is frequently overlooked is that, to improve organisational effectiveness, there may be a conflict with employee objectives. Many models of HRM do not make any allowances for employee representation and make assumptions that employees will automatically accept and co-operate with whatever changes management wish to make.

Managers' and employees' objectives in employee relations can be identified as shown in Table 1.2. There are two ways of examining the relationship between employers and employees: the unitary and pluralist perspectives. If the manager takes a unitary perspective this assumes that there is no difference between the objectives of management and employees. However, an examination of Table 1.2 demonstrates that managements' and employees' needs are often in conflict: managers wish to minimise unit labour costs and control change, whereas employees want to maximise the terms under which they are employed and also control change. A pluralist approach will take account of the likely conflict that may occur

Table 1.2 Management and employee objectives	
Management objectives	**Employee objectives**
◆ Cost-effective performance	◆ Maintenance and, where possible, improvement of terms and conditions of employment
◆ Control of change	
◆ Avoidance of stoppages and other sanctions	
	◆ Job security
	◆ Control of change
	◆ Avoidance of stoppages and other sanctions

Source: Rees and Porter (2001: 315)

when change is implemented, especially if it is likely to result in a worsening of terms and conditions of employment. This does not mean to say that employees must be allowed to dictate to management what change happens and what change does not, but it does mean that management will be more successful in implementing change if they think through the likely impact and make plans to deal with it. Further discussion about the impact of managerial styles on employee relations. can be found in Chapter 12

Conflict is often seen in this context as being a negative concept. The term is often seen as being synonymous with strike action. However, a strike, or application of other sanctions, will only occur as a means of trying to resolve the conflict when negotiations have broken down. Because of changes in the labour market, some employees have far less ability to impose sanctions than when there was a seller's market for labour. Changes that have affected certain employees' abilities to impose sanctions have included high levels of unemployment in some regions and occupations; a far lower level of trade union membership; a continuing diminution in trade union ability to impose sanctions; new technology – creating a buyer's labour market overseas; and more peripheral and part-time jobs.

However the ability of management to impose change, without consultation in some instances, still needs to take into account the importance of getting 'buy in' from the workforce and the likelihood that the implementation of new work practices is likely to be more effective if they have taken into account employee expertise.

Global applicability of human resource management techniques

HRM is generally conceived as if the principles on which it is based are universally valid. Additionally, HR textbooks often refer to HRM techniques as if they should be adopted by each and every organisation, within the UK as well as elsewhere, and that not to do so will automatically mean that a particular organisation will be deficient in some respect, not making the most effective use of its human resources. The concept of 'best practice' is often adopted to underline the message that there is one best way in which to manage human resources. However, the proposition that the practice of HR is converging around a common set of principles is not supported by all. Some HR practitioners are of the opinion that different techniques need to be adopted in different situations. Since organisations tend to reflect the societies in which they operate, it is necessary to be familiar with local conditions in order to identify the techniques appropriate for the situation in which they are operating.

A study carried out by Triandis (1994) indicates that 90 per cent of behavioural theories on which systems of HRM are based are derived from the US and UK. Frederick and Rodrigues (1994) point out that differences in culture exist not only between different societies but also between those operating in different economic systems, between different hierarchical levels within an organisation and between different types of organisations. This could mean that countries, which may be at different stages in their development, may have different requirements in terms of the HR policies that they will find useful and need to adopt. Employment systems reflect the context in which they operate. These contexts have historical, legal, socio-political/cultural dimensions.

Can you think of any overseas organisations that have had problems because they tried to impose the managerial culture of their 'homeland' on a UK-based part of their organisation?

pause for thought

Those who argue against the convergence thesis will point to the impact of history, legal system and laws, socio-political climate and societal culture upon organisations, resulting in differing organisational climates and HR requirements. Proponents of the convergence thesis will point to the impact of globalisation – technology; media; build up of global markets/trading blocs; and global travel – to back up their proposition that countries are becoming more and more alike.

An analysis of the assumptions on which HRM tools is based will indicate that not all HRM tools are appropriate for every situation. An analogous situation would be that of a physician who advocated a certain range of medicines without first conducting a diagnosis of the patient's condition. Legge (1978) points out that a physician will not only conduct a diagnosis as part of a professional approach to a patient but will also be on the look out for any symptoms that may indicate the onset of further bodily dysfunction and will advise the patient on lifestyle choices that could help to avoid future problems. She advocates such an approach among HR professionals and refers to the need for a contingency or best fit approach (Legge, 1978; Kinnie et al., 2005). A contingency approach will involve the HR practitioner analysing the situation in which they find themselves, diagnosing the causes of the problems they seek to address and proposing some solution that takes into account the dynamics of the situation and the actual causes of the problem. There is a further discussion regarding the appropriateness of 'best fit' compared with 'best practice' approaches in Chapter 3 of this book. Watson (2004) has an interesting discussion tracing the development of analysis in HRM and lamenting the quantity of normative and prescriptive thinking, which is relevant to this discussion.

In analysing the assumptions on which HRM is based, it is interesting to examine the cultural basis of HRM. It has been estimated that more than 90 per cent of the theories of how individuals think and behave in organisations reflect Western perspectives, primarily British and North American (Triandis, 1994). If the values underpinning the practice of HRM in various countries are analysed, however, it is clear that there is a great variation in the extent to which they match with the underpinning values of the UK and the US. Students from other countries may therefore be studying the subject from a UK or a US perspective and find that they are unable to recognise the premises on which the subject is based.

In the West, the management of human resources is second to the aim of achieving and maintaining the ultimate economic survival of an organisation. This has resulted in the US and the UK in the development of models of HRM to encourage a concentration on business objectives and the need for organisations to develop human resource policies which help the organisation to deliver those objectives. This contrasts with other, more paternalistic, cultures where the emphasis in the practice of HRM is not so much on the economic well-being of the company but to a greater extent on issues concerned with perceived obligations to individual employees, albeit often tempered by a fairly autocratic management style. In this context it is appropriate to mention that HRM in the US and the UK is much more likely to be based on a pluralist perspective, whereas in many developing countries both employers and employees take a unitary perspective: the assumption is made that organisational and employee objectives are the same (see Fox, 1974).

As well as differing views about organisational objectives, there are also differing expectations of the State. In EU countries there is an enhanced role for the State compared with the US. In PR China, for example, the role of the State is even more pronounced, as would be expected given the historical preponderance of State-owned enterprises. The role of the State in some economies is such that certain Western policies and procedures as used in the US or the UK are unlikely to be appropriate. For these and other reasons it is appropriate to take a contingency approach when implementing HR practices, rather than assuming that the techniques that are currently in favour in other countries will immediately be appropriate in another culture.

The future for HR across the world looks as if it will maintain its current importance. New markets are being created as previous dormant nations become economically more active. These markets include China, India and the former Soviet bloc countries in Central and Eastern Europe. As these economies expand, so will global competition become more intense and the need for skilled staff available as and when required become ever more important.

Current and future trends in HRM

Since HRM is concerned with delivering organisational effectiveness, it is likely that directors of organisations will continue to explore the extent to which the HR input in an organisation can most effectively contribute to this. The current debates about HR as a business partner, its contribution to the 'bottom line' and the extent to which this function can be outsourced will therefore continue. New labels may be invented to give added impetus to the debate but the concepts will be of a similar nature.

HR specialists will nevertheless continue to be called upon to reflect the concerns of society at large. For example, debates relating to societal well-being and the environment may have added impetus as the developed world takes on board the need to act as custodian of limited resources. The debate relating to ethics and HRM is continued in Chapter 2.

Summary

The role of HRM in an organisation is intended to help the organisation ensure that it meets its corporate objectives by the effective management of its employees. Both HR specialists and line managers carry out this role. HR specialists would need to help ensure that line managers are selected when they have both the desire and the skills to carry out their managerial activities. The practice of HRM is subject to many fashions and fads and it is important when applying HRM techniques to remember the importance of diagnosing accurately the causes of problems in an organisation in order that the most appropriate technique can be adopted. In addition, it is also important that the HRM technique adopted fits with the culture of the organisation.

Most HRM techniques are based on a unitary perspective. That is to say, they are based on the assumption that management and employees' objectives are the same. However, this is not always the case. HR techniques introduced to address organisational problems may have adverse consequences from an employee perspective. HR specialists and line managers therefore need to understand the employee perspective if they are to manage effectively and help employees realise their full potential in terms of the contribution they make to the organisation.

Review Questions

You may wish to attempt the following as practice examination style questions.

1.1   How do you think HRM contributes to the achievement of organisational objectives?

1.2   In what ways do HR managers in the public sector differ in their perceptions of their role from those HR managers in the private sector?

1.3   What HR skills do line managers need to make their work more effective?

1.4   Is HRM culturally dependent? Why did you give this answer?

References

ACAS (2004). Coming to the table with ACAS: from conflict to cooperation, *Employee Relations*, Vol. 26, No. 5, pp. 510–513.

Ambler, T., Chittenden, F. and Obodovski, M. (2004). *Are Regulators Raising Their Game? UK Regulatory Impact Assessments in 2002/3*, London: British Chambers of Commerce.

Beer, M., Spector, B., Lawrence, P.R., Quinn Mills, D. and Walton, R.E. (1984). *Managing Human Assets*, New York: Free Press.

Caldwell, R. (2003). The changing roles of personnel managers: old ambiguities, new uncertainties, *Journal of Management Studies*, Vol. 40, No. 4, pp. 983–1004.

Delery, J.E. and Shaw, J.D. (2001). The strategic management of people in work organisation: review, synthesis and extension, *Research in Personnel and Human Resource Management*, Vol. 20, pp. 165–197.

Felstead, A., Gallie, D. and Green, F. (2002). *Work Skills in Britain 1986–2001*, Nottingham: DfES Publications.

Fox, A. (1974). *Beyond Contract: Work, Power and Trust Relations*, London: Faber & Faber.

Francis, H. and Keegan, A. (2006). The changing face of HRM: in search of balance, *Human Resource Management Journal*, Vol. 16, No. 3, pp. 231–249.

Frederick, W.R. and Rodrigues, A.F. (1994). A Spanish organisation in Eastern Germany: culture shock, *Journal of Management Development*, Vol. 13, No. 2, pp. 42–48.

IRS Employment Review 792a (2004a). *Recruiters March in Step with Online Recruitment*, 23 January, pp. 44–48.

IRS Employment Review (2004b). *Answering the Recruitment Call Online*, 7 May, pp. 46–48.

Kersley, B., Alpin, C., Forth, J., Bryson, A., Bewley, H., Dix, G. and Oxenbridge, S. (2006). *Inside the Workplace: Findings from the 2004 Workplace Employment Relations Survey*, London, Routledge.

Kettley, P. and Reilly, P. (2003). *eHR: An Introduction*, Institute of Employment Studies Report 398, Brighton: IES.

Kinne, N., Hutchinson, S., Purcell, J., Rayton, B. and Swart, J. (2005). Satisfaction with HR practices: why one size does not fit all, *Human Resource Management Journal*, Vol. 15, No. 4, pp. 9–29.

Legge, K. (1978). *Power, Politics and Problem Solving in Personnel Management*, London: McGraw-Hill.

McGovern, P. (1999). *Strategic Human Resource Management*, Oxford: Oxford University Press.

Price, A.J. (1997). *Human Resource Management in a Business Context*, London: International Thomson Business Press.

Rees, W.D. and Porter, C.M. (2001). *The Skills of Management*, London: Thomson Learning.

Rees, W.D. and Porter, C.M. (2006). Corporate Strategy Development: the case for the incremental approach, Part 2 – implications for learning and development, Industrial and Commercial Training, Vol. 38, No. 7, pp. 354–359.

Shackleton, J.R. (2005). Regulating the labour market, in P. Booth (ed.) *Towards a Liberal Utopia*, pp. 128–143, Part 1, London: Institute of Economic Affairs.

Storey, J. (1992). *Developments in the Management of Human Resources*, Oxford: Blackwell.

Sunday Times (2007). *Booming Britain heads 'onwards and upwards'*, 21 January. *The Times* (2007). *Doctors' anger over plan to limit pay*, 20 January.

Triandis, H.C. (1994). Cross-cultural and organisational psychology, in H. C. Triandis, M. Dunette and L. Hough, *Handbook of Industrial and Organisational Psychology*, pp. 103–172, Palo Alto, CA: Consulting Psychologists' Press.

Tyson, S. and Fell, A. (1986). *Evaluating the Personnel Function*, London: Hutchinson.

Ulrich, D. (1997). *Human Resource Champions*, Boston: Harvard University Press.

Ulrich, D. (1998). A new mandate for human resources, *Harvard Business Review*, Vol. 76, pp. 124–134.

Watson, T.J. (2004). HRM and critical social analysis, *Journal of Management Studies*, Vol. 41, No. 3, pp. 447–467.

Further Reading

Boxall, P. and Purcell, J. (2003). *Strategy and Human Resource Management*, Basingstoke: Palgrave.

Leopold, J. (ed.) (2002). *Human Resources in Organisations*, London: FT/Prentice Hall.

Purcell, J. and Astrand, B. (1994). *Human Resource Management in Multi Division Companies*, Oxford: Oxford University Press.

Redman, T. and Wilkinson, A. (2002). *The Informed Student Guide to Human Resource Management*, London: Thomson Learning.

Useful Websites

www.cipd.co.uk – the official website of the Chartered Institute of Personnel and Development – the lead body for HR professionals

http://www.cipd.co.uk/subjects/maneco/general/rolefrntlinemngers.htm?lsSrchRes=1 – examines the role of the front-line manager in enacting and delivering HR processes

www.dti.gov.uk – the official website of the Department of Trade and Industry. A department of the UK government, the DTI collects and disseminates information and statistics relating to business and industry within the UK

www.humanresourcemanagement.co.uk – gives human resource information relating to both employers and employees

www.btinternet.com/~alan.price/hrm – a free source of worldwide human resource management in formation

www.hrmguide.co.uk – publishes articles and news releases about HR surveys, employment law, human resource research and related books and other publications

CHAPTER 2

Ethics and Human Resource Management

By Amanda Rose

Chapter outline

Standards, values, morals and ethics have become increasingly complex in a postmodern society where absolutes have given way to tolerance and ambiguity. This particularly affects managers in human resource (HR), where decisions will affect people's jobs and their future employment. This chapter explores some of the ethical dilemmas encountered in the workplace, discussing ethical behaviour and values that relate to HR. It looks at relevant ethical tools, such as utilitarianism and relativism in order to examine current practices in the workplace and their links to corporate social responsibility.

Learning outcomes

By the end of this chapter, you should be able to:

- Critically explore and evaluate the ethical nature of human resource management (HRM);
- Identify and define current ethical and moral issues confronting HR managers;
- Compare, contrast and critically appraise a range of approaches to ethical analysis;
- Critically appraise the relevance and usefulness of philosophical analysis to HR practice.

Introduction

HRM is a business function that is concerned with managing relations between groups of people in their capacity as employees, employers and managers. Inevitably, this process may raise questions about what the respective responsibilities and rights of each party are in this relationship, and about what constitutes fair treatment. These questions are ethical in nature, and this chapter will focus on debates about the ethical basis of HRM.

The ethical nature of human resource management

'All HR practices have an ethical foundation. HR deals with the practical consequences of human behaviour'.

(Johnson, 2003)

'The entire concept of HRM is devoid of morality'.

(Hart, 1993: 29)

Despite these moral appreciations of HRM, there is a strong tradition in business that insists that business should not be concerned with ethics. As Milton Friedman, a vociferous proponent of this position, has put it: *'The social responsibility of business is to its shareholders. . . . The business of business is business'* (1970).

The core concern of business – proponents of the market economy argue – is in attempting to secure the best possible return on any investment. Any dilution of this focus will lead to the corruption of what is a finely balanced system. Businesses that seek to be 'ethical' as well as profitable will probably fail economically, following which the whole community may suffer. Rather, let the *invisible hand* guide the market and all will prosper. Like some evolutionary force, the best will always survive. Wealth will trickle down from successful enterprises, and humanity will be best served. Any constraint on the freedoms of the market – be they motivated by ethical angst or vote-seeking government policy – will just mess everything up.

Notwithstanding the appeal of this position, a critique of business practice has continued to accumulate and assert itself, and to challenge the notion that business and morality have no meeting point. Concern has surfaced from a variety of sources: from consumer groups, political groups, religious and charitable organisations. Entrepreneurs, for example, Anita Roddick of The Body Shop (2000), academics and researchers (Winstanley and Woodall, 2000; Greenwood, 2002) and management professionals (Brown, 2003) have all expressed the view that standards of behaviour within business need to be evaluated, and improved.

A case can be made that negative consequences flow from poor ethical standards:

- ◆ While short-term goals may be achieved through the cut-throat tactics of free market principles, in the long run business will survive better if good standards of conduct are maintained;

- ◆ Ethical business creates a positive environment in which to buy and sell, as corruption, poverty and lack of respect for the environment generate problems for the business community in the long term;

- ◆ Finally, people neither hold moral values nor have religious beliefs to guide the conduct of their lives. Why should the area of business be exempt?

pause for thought   Do you think that ethical behaviour is relevant in today's business world? Why did you reach this conclusion?

Much of the recent focus on business ethics has been directed against financial corruption, especially a concern with accounting standards. The scandals involving Enron Corp. and WorldCom are two recent examples. But concern has been raised over a very broad range of issues, for example:

- Abuse of the world's physical resources, and the global ecological balance (Esso);
- Abuse of human rights (Shell/Nigeria);
- Animal rights (KFC, McDonald's);
- Aggressive treatment of competitors (Wal-Mart);
- Exploitative and unscrupulous marketing (Philip Morris) (Klein, 2000).

What other examples of unethical business practice have you heard about?

What have you experienced in an organisation known to you?

What is the difference between being fair and acting appropriately?

exercise

The unethical practice of HRM itself has also hit public attention:

- Off-shoring and exploiting 'cheap' labour markets;
- Using child labour;
- Reneging on company pension agreements;
- Longer working hours;
- Increasing work stress;
- The use of disputed and dubious practices in hiring and firing personnel.

It has been shown that just as consumers' perception of the ethics of a company can affect sales, so the views of its investors will affect its share price. Similarly, it has been suggested that poor standards of conduct emanating from the top management affect employee motivation and commitment to organisational goals (Schramm, 2004).

Ethics in the business environment

Concern with standards must be seen in the current context of business processes. We live in a complex society, which is both morally and culturally diverse.

Key drivers and features of this complexity can be identified:

- Globalisation of markets and labour forces ('McDonalidisation');
- Intensification of both competition and monopolies ('Coca Colonisation');
- Paradigmatic changes in technology and the application of ICT, creating new opportunities, but also new dilemmas over communication, surveillance and privacy;
- Rapidly increasing rates of product innovation, obsolescence and demand;
- Aggressive marketing and the use of celebrities by the media;
- An escalation of materialist values and the commodification of everything, even education;

◆ Increased isolationism, individuality and world-weariness, often demonstrated by cynicism, sarcasm and mockery, with a disregard for traditional values and any form of authority;

◆ A rise in secular concerns – but also a concern with a loss of spirituality.

Against this background, management style and management ideology has undergone great change. New organisational forms and new ways of managing, including the emergence of more flexible working patterns, have come into force. During this era, HRM has become more strategically focused and more concerned with facilitating the achievement of organisational goals.

Winstanley and Woodall (1996) highlight a number of ethical concerns about standards of HR practice, arising from this strategic focus. These include:

◆ Increased job insecurity – arising from 'flexible' work practices; short-term and temporary conditions of employment; fear of job loss due to outsourcing and off-shoring; increased stress; and a widening imbalance of power between management and workforce;

◆ Increase in surveillance and control – this ranges from the use of psychometric tests to electronic surveillance of work patterns through the application of ICT;

◆ Deregulation – freedom of the market place has been imposed by global regulators such as the World Trade Organizationl (WTO), and has led to what Storey (1993) has termed: 'impatience with rule' and 'can-do outlook' among line managers, which in practice may be seen to push HR into compromising 'good' practice, for business needs. In professional services organisations, for example, fee-earners may be challenged to decide between 'doing good' and 'doing well';

◆ Aligned to this is a decline in management integrity, leading to accusations of recourse to rhetoric and deceit among HR professionals. For example, the current emphasis on managing organisational culture and commitment of employees can be contrasted with a highly instrumental approach to the supervision of the employment contract.

In this current context, it becomes most relevant to examine the ethical dimension of HRM practice. In what ways can HRM be ethical and/or unethical? Are there guidelines and principles that all HR professionals ought to follow and adhere to? How can we judge what a good course of action might consist of in a specific situation?

However, it is simplistic to consider HRM as a coherent and unitary set of principles and practices. It varies from organisation to organisation, from culture to culture, and can be diverse both within and between industries and sectors. It has evolved in complex historical, economic and social contexts.

The current global operation of business creates extraordinary interactions of values and practice. HRM is a feature of both the public, private and voluntary sectors, and management practice differs accordingly. It is argued (Winstanley and Woodall, 2000) that HRM holds the moral 'stewardship' of organisations. It is interesting therefore to consider the special role of HRM in the generation of an ethical and moral climate in organisations in general.

Ethics and values

Organisations are bound by law to treat the people they employ fairly and not to discriminate against identified groups. Legislation is a codification of accepted moral principles, and acts to moderate standards within a community – 'the greatest good of the greatest number'.

But, conformity to all legal requirements does not necessarily ensure the best treatment of employees. The law itself may not be fair; it may not cover all eventualities; and it may not always offer a clear guide to action.

How far do you agree with the following list of HR objectives?
- **In recruitment and selection: ensure that all assessment measures are fair and just.**
- **In reward management: ensure fairness in allocation of pay and benefits.**
- **In promotion and development: ensure equal opportunities and equal access.**
- **Ensure a safe working environment for all employees.**
- **Ensure that procedures are not unduly stressful, and that the needs of employees' work-life balance are not compromised.**
- **When redundancies occur, to be fair and just in handling job losses.**
- **Deal effectively with all forms of bullying and harassment.**
- **In outsourcing and offshoring: ensure that contractors, consultants and franchisees are fair and honest in their dealings with employees, clients and customers.**

Ethics is a key branch of philosophy, concerned with analysing what is right or wrong in people's behaviour or conduct. Ethics and morality are terms that are often used interchangeably in discussions of good and evil. The term 'ethics' is usually applied to persons (ethics comes from the Greek *ethos*, meaning character) – and 'morality' to acts and behaviour (moral comes from the Latin *moralis*, meaning customs or manners).

Philosophy presents us with suggestions about the nature of morality and ethics. It also offers us a set of tools for analysing and exploring morality. Some main issues and approaches will now be discussed:

- Relativism and absolutism;
- Consequentialist approaches (e.g. utilitarianism);
- Non-consequentialist approaches (deontological or 'duty' ethics);
- The ethics of human rights;
- Virtue ethics;
- The *stakeholder* approach.

Cultural relativism

One core distinction when analysing morality is the issue of *relativism* – the idea that morality varies with culture, time and circumstances. The opposite position is that of *absolutism*, the notion that there are universal truths in morality that apply at all times and in all circumstances. In a global business world, this aspect becomes significant. When businesses operate globally, how far should they adapt company rules to local circumstances? Situational ethics can become problematical for organisations wishing to expand into new international markets.

exercise

The ethical concerns of personnel managers

A survey of over 1,000 US personnel managers (Danley et al., 1991) found that the most common areas causing ethical concern were: favouritism in hiring, training and promotion; sexual harassment; inconsistent disciplinary measures; not maintaining confidentiality; sex discrimination in promotion, and pay; and non-performance factors used in appraisals.

◆ How far do you feel these are culturally specific?

◆ Why did you reach this conclusion?

◆ Would personnel managers in different cultures agree with this list? Give reasons for your answer.

Consequentialist approaches (utilitarianism)

This approach was developed by Jeremy Bentham (1748–1832) and John Stuart Mill (1806–1873). Its main premise suggests that the morality of an act is determined by its consequences: people should do that which will bring the greatest *utility* (which is generally understood to mean whatever the group sees as good) to the greatest number affected by a given situation.

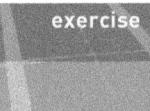

exercise

A company needs to make savings to survive a recession. They have a number of plants in the Yorkshire area, some of them in areas of above-average unemployment. All plants are equally profitable.

◆ Which plant should they close?

◆ Should they make their decision on purely economic grounds? Why?

◆ What if financial analysis doesn't produce an obvious choice?

◆ What should they then decide to do?

For example, military contractors may be faced with ransom demands for kidnapped employees. The UK government was embroiled in such a situation in 2004 in the case of a UK citizen who was taken hostage in Iraq. His captors demanded economic and political concessions to win his release. His family pleaded with the prime minister to meet these demands. The government argued that to do so would jeopardise the lives of many more UK subjects in Iraq and globally. In doing so, the government was appealing to utilitarian arguments.

Critics suggest that in practice it is very difficult to accurately determine what the maximal *utility* would be for all affected by a situation. People may not have the necessary information. The notion of utility is very vague. Are we thinking of the short or long term? These perspectives may lead to different conclusions. People may vary in their perceptions and requirements. What is the 'majority'? Can we accept a situation where the benefits of the majority might mean the exploitation, and suffering, of the minority? In this system, vast income disparity, or even slavery, might be condoned on the grounds that it maximised the benefits of the majority. Some very morally repugnant acts might be condoned on the grounds of utilitarianism.

Non-consequentialist or deontological approaches

This approach, associated with Immanuel Kant (1724–1804), is sometimes referred to as 'duty ethics'. Kant's aim was to establish a set of absolute moral rules, developed through the application of *reason*. He also put forward an acid test for evaluating the quality of moral rules and this is termed: the *categorical imperative*. This states that: 'I ought never to act except in such a way that I can also will that my maxim should become a universal law.' In other words, moral rules should follow the principle of *reciprocity*: do as you would be done by. This premise can be found in the moral principles of many religious systems, including Islam, Christianity, Judaism and Buddhism.

Kant further stated: 'Act in such a way that you always treat humanity . . . never simply as a means, but always at the same time as an end.' The defining characteristics of this approach are the universal *applicability* of principles to all humanity, and basic respect for humans.

A key notion for Kant was that of *intentionality*. It might well be that the outcome of an act leads to very bad consequences for people – for example, the closure of a site and subsequent job losses – but if one's aims and intentions are good, then the act is a moral one. It's all about motivation and meaning.

Goodpaster (1984) has attempted to develop a set of rules along Kantian lines for business practice:

1. Avoid and prevent harming others.

2. Help those in need.

3. Do not lie or cheat.

4. Respect the rights of others.

5. Keep promises or contracts.

6. Obey the law.

7. Be fair.

8. Encourage others to follow these principles.

Examine the rules of business practice developed by Goodpaster and the CIPD code of professional conduct, which can be found at the following site: www.cipd.co.uk/about/profco.htm.

◆ Which of these rules would you find:

  – easiest to follow?

  – hardest to follow?

Outline the reasons for your answer.

window into practice

The SHRM code of ethical and professional standards in HRM

Core principles

As HR professionals we are responsible for adding value to the organisations we serve and contributing to the ethical success of those organisations. We accept professional responsibility for our individual decisions and actions. We are also advocates for the profession by engaging in activities that enhance its credibility and value.

- As professionals we must strive to meet the highest standards of competency and commit to strengthen our competencies on a continuous basis.
- HR professionals are expected to exhibit individual leadership as a role model for maintaining the highest standards of ethical conduct.
- As human resource professionals we are ethically responsible for promoting and fostering fairness and justice for all employees and their organisations.
- As HR professionals we must maintain a high level of trust with our stakeholders. We must protect the interests of our stakeholders as well as our professional integrity and should not engage in activities that create actual, apparent or potential conflicts of interests.
- HR professionals consider and protect the rights of individuals, especially in the acquisition and dissemination of information while ensuring truthful communications and facilitating informed decision making.

The development of codes of good or ethical practice within organisations and professional associations stems from the deontological approach. However, the approach has been seen to present problems in its implementation, as follows:

- How do you judge that a rule is a good one?
- What, in the final analysis, is fair?
- Can we all agree?
- How should we proceed in cases where principles compete?
- And what about situations when avoiding harm to one person means harming another or where keeping a contract with one person or group leads to breaking it with another?

Hart (1993) has suggested that current HR practice falls short of Kant's categorical imperative. In tough business contexts, policies seem to support the premise that: 'We should behave towards our fellow human beings with the over riding objective of extracting added value' (p. 29).

Human rights

Another very influential view stems from seeing people as having basic *human rights*. In this view, there is recognition of a core set of human rights. Where a human right exists, there must also be a duty or *responsibility* to recognise, support and acknowledge that right.

John Locke (1632–1704) was one philosopher who emphasised and elaborated an ethics based upon human rights. He argued that it is not so much the application of reason to acts that is important to morality, but an *appreciation* of the fair and equal treatment of all people, enshrined in the recognition of basic human rights. For Locke, the key rights included freedom, and rights to property.

There have been many attempts to codify and elaborate human rights, including the declaration of the *Rights of Man* (1789), the *Universal Declaration of Human Rights* (1948) and the *European Convention on Human Rights* (1950). Recently, the UK has passed the *Human Rights Act* (1998) in an attempt to codify rights within British law. The full implications of this act for the business and employment arenas are currently being explored through case law and, undoubtedly, this will have major implications for HR practice.

Virtue ethics

Virtue ethics is an approach that is seen to originate with Aristotle (384–322 BC). It has recently regained prominence through the work of the philosopher Alasdair Macintyre (1981). Aristotle was not concerned to identify the qualities of good acts, or principles, but of good people. Acting as a 'good person,' Macintyre suggests, 'is the state of being well and doing well . . . a complete human life lived at its best' (pp. 148–149). For Aristotle, the virtuous man has to know that what he does is virtuous; a good man has to 'judge to do the right thing in the right place at the right time in the right way' (p. 150). This is not just the simple application of rules. The virtues include both intellectual and character virtues. Macintyre includes the need to *feel* that what one is doing is good and right; to have an *emotional* as well as a *cognitive* appreciation of morality is an essential component of virtue.

A key distinction between this approach and others is that it focuses on the issue of *agency* in ethical conduct. It suggests that neither good intentions nor outcomes, codes and the recognition of basic rights will necessarily ensure 'goodness'. In the final analysis, the effectiveness of an ethical system depends on the nature of the people who employ it. And are people essentially good or bad?

Stakeholder analysis

This approach has emerged from the area of applied business ethics, and proponents include Freeman (1998) and Weiss (1994). As discussed earlier, free market economics accords rights only to shareholders in the business enterprise. Stakeholder analysis offers an alternative view.

Stakeholder analysis sees morality as evolving within a community of equals, where rights and needs are recognised as residing within all individuals and groups that partake in business life. Organisations consist of many interwoven webs of relationships, rights and responsibilities. Many individuals and groups have a 'stake' in how an organisation performs, apart from just the shareholders and members of the board. Employees, customers, suppliers and the wider community should all be considered when decisions are made, and they should be consulted accordingly.

Financial and Human Resource Management in Organisations, Second Edition

exercise

Have a look at the Warbings case study.

Who are the various stakeholders in the organisation?

What rights and duties do you think they have concerning the activities of the company?

How could their concerns be raised and dealt with?

Winstanley and Woodall (2000) argue that this is a very useful approach for analysing ethical issues in HRM. Jones (1995) has presented evidence to suggest that companies that follow a stakeholder approach are actually more profitable. Greenwood (2002) finds this an underused approach in analysing the ethical aspects of HRM. She feels that it provides a framework which brings into relief both the macro (ideology) and micro (specific policy) aspects of HRM.

However, there are a number of practical problems with this approach. Firstly, companies must identify relevant stakeholders – and this is not always an obvious matter. Secondly, when stakeholders are identified, an organisation has a moral obligation to discover their views. This is not always easy. For example, 'the community' is a very vague term – who is included here? Will everyone in the 'community' have the same views? Can they all realistically be consulted? A company may, with the best of intentions, obtain a partial view of the wishes of its stakeholders that does not acknowledge the voices of several relevant diverse groups.

Corporate social responsibility and human resource management

Crowe (2002) defines CSR as, 'all the ways in which a company relates to society from purchasing to product disposal, from human resources to human rights'. The concept is generally used in management literature to refer to the responsibilities and relations between an organisation and the community within which it operates. This focuses attention away from individual practices and procedures, to the strategic direction and mission of the corporation as a whole.

One approach that companies can take to CSR is to include a 'social audit' in their annual reports. This was first recommended by Medawar (1978), and shows not just the financial performance of a company, but also details of its impact on both the environment and the community. It was reported in 2003 that 132 of the FTSE 250 companies now report their environmental performance, and 100 also report on social and ethical issues.

CSR can affect a company through the message it signals to potential recruits. Research conducted by Duncan Brown of the CIPD (2003) suggests that companies that adopt a policy of social responsibility tend to fare better in attracting new recruits – a key concern for UK companies in the current labour market. Eighty-eight per cent of participants surveyed said concordance of individual and organisational values was a key component in job choice.

Current CSR policies include an attempt to involve employees in voluntary community work. One-third of companies based in the City of London have community and volunteering programmes, covering an estimated 27,000 staff and providing charitable support worth an estimated £337 million (Heart of the City, 2002). Examples of companies that have implemented such schemes through the Business in the Community initiative include Walkers Snack Foods and IBM. Potentially, CSR can usefully form part of an employee development programme, and may benefit the community, employees and the organisation itself.

Corporations are unelected and unmonitored, and their involvement in charitable enterprises could be seen to compromise people's right to self-determination. Social critics, such as Klein (2000), have argued that corporations that involve themselves in community projects may be accused of promoting their own self-interest.

Tesco has spearheaded a 'Computers for Schools' campaign that gives shoppers in their stores tokens which can be exchanged for much needed IT equipment for schools. Many schools publicise this to parents – effectively asking them to shop at Tesco. This moral pressure is in Tesco's interests, and while the outcome may be positive and therefore applauded from a utilitarian point of view, it cannot be viewed as ethical from a non-consequentialist perspective. A similar discussion took place in the book and film *The Constant Gardener*, which explored the practice of a pharmaceutical company that killed healthy African adults in its clinical trials.

From a stakeholder perspective, CSR initiatives might seem to be the right approach, where companies acknowledge their responsibilities to their surrounding environment and community. But the critics of the approach would caution that a clearer analysis of the needs and interests of respective stakeholders needs to be undertaken in order to establish whether these are always beneficial, and ethically laudable. Employees and community members alike may be exploited through such initiatives. Both parties might benefit more from greater corporate governance in collaboration with national and international agencies or charities in the provision of social services. It might be better for companies to simply pay higher taxes.

Summary

Ethical conduct in business practice and HR procedures is no longer a matter of choice for UK companies. In 2000, the European Union included a requirement for social and environmental reporting in its fourth company law directive. The EU also voted in May 2000 to develop a label to endorse products made by companies that can demonstrate commitment and respect for human and trade union rights.

The current government strategy in the UK supports voluntary action, rather than legal requirement. The Department for Trade and Industry strategy is to encourage companies to sign up to best practice in CSR. The Confederation for British Industry has lobbied for this approach.

The DTI would seem to promote an approach of stakeholder analysis in recommending that company directors should consider the interests of multiple stakeholders in their strategy and action, including employees, customers, suppliers, the wider society and the physical environment.

There are a number of codes of practice to choose from:

◆ *The Global Compact*, launched by the United Nations in July 2000, encourages companies to incorporate nine human rights into their strategies and business dealings, and to consider a broad range of stakeholders in setting strategy;

- *The International Labour Organisation (ILO)* has prepared a Declaration of Fundamental Principles and Rights at Work (1998). This focuses on eliminating forced labour, child labour, freedom of association and the right to work free from discrimination;

- *The Organization for Economic Co-operation and Development (OECD) Guidelines for Multinational Corporations* cover standards of behaviour in employment and industrial relations; environmental impact; combating bribery; consumer interests; science and technology; competition and taxation.

Website addresses for these organisations can be found at the end of this chapter.

A deontological position would caution that if people are just mechanically following a guide, if they have no intention to act well, then their behaviour isn't strictly ethical. This is as true of the employee following company guidelines as of the management who devise them. For example, consider the role of both employees and directors in recent railway disasters in the UK.

A virtue analysis would suggest that the effectiveness of these codes depends on the goodness of the people who try to apply them.

HRM has a key interest in codes of behaviour, as it will most likely be the department called upon to implement and monitor them. A basic problem resides in the wider context. No matter how far HRM may work to improve the behaviour of professionals and aid in the implementation of codes of conduct that affect all employees, if businesses show little respect for any ethical or even legal considerations over and above the generation of profit, then the pursuit of an ethical HRM is essentially futile.

Review Questions

You may wish to attempt the following as practice examination style questions.

2.1   What is 'ethics'? How does it differ from 'morality'?

2.2   What is 'moral relativism'? Give an example from a business context.

2.3   'Corporate social responsibility without HR is just PR.' Do you agree? Why? Why not?

2.4   What is 'utilitarianism'? Give an example of a utilitarian argument in HRM.

2.5   List some human rights that are relevant to the work context.

2.6   What is the 'stakeholder' approach? List the key stakeholders in a typical work organisation.

2.7   Give an example of an ethical code of conduct? What are the key characteristics of a *good* code? How can they improve standards of behaviour?

2.8   What mechanism does HR have to ensure stakeholder participation in organisational decision making?

References

Brown, D. (2003). From Cinderella to CSR, *People Management*, Vol. 9, No. 16, p. 21.

CIPD (2003). *A Guide to Corporate Social Responsibility*, July.

Crowe, R. (2002). *No Scruples*, London: Spiro Press.

Danley, J., Harrick, E., Strickland, D. and Sullivan, G. (1991). HR ethical situations, *Human Resources Management*, Vol. 26, pp. 1–12.

Freeman, R.E. (1998). A stakeholder theory of the modern corporation, in Hartman L.P. (ed.) *Perspectives in Business Ethics*, pp. 171–181, Chicago: McGraw-Hill.

Friedman, M. (1970). The social responsibility of business is to increase its profits, *New York Times Magazine*, 13 September.

Goodpaster, K.E. (1984). *Ethics in Management*, Boston: Harvard Business Books.

Greenwood, M.R. (2002). Ethics and HRM: a review and conceptual analysis, *Journal of Business Ethics*, Vol. 36, No. 3, pp. 261–278.

Hart, T.J. (1993). Human resource management: time to exercise the militant tendency, *Employee Relations*, Vol. 15, No. 3, pp. 29–36.

Heart of the City (2002). Corporate social responsibility – City firms lead the way, at: http://theheartofthecity.com/html/news:htm.

Johnson, R. (2003). HR must embrace ethics, *People Management*, Vol. 9, No. 1, p. 10.

Jones, T.M. (1995). Instrumental stakeholder theory: a synthesis of ethics and economics, *Academy of Management Review*, Vol. 20, No. 2, pp. 404–437.

Klein, N. (2000). *No Logo*, Hammersmith: Flamingo.

Macintyre, A. (1981). *After Virtue*, London: Duckworth.

Medawar, C. (1978). *The Social Audit Consumer Handbook*, London: Palgrave Macmillan.

Roddick, A. (2000). *Business as Usual. The Triumph of Anita Roddick: The Body Shop*, London: Thomsons.

Schramm, J. (2004) Perceptions on ethics, *Human Resources*, Vol. 49, No. 11, p. 176, Society for Human Resource Management.

Storey, J. (1993). The take-up of human resource management by mainstream companies, *International Journal of Human Resource Management*, Vol. 4, No. 3, pp. 529–555.

Weiss, J.W. (1994). *Business Ethics: A Managerial Stakeholder Approach*, Belmont, CA: Wadsworth.

Winstanley, D. and Woodall, J. (1996). Business ethics and human resource management, *Personnel Review*, Vol. 25, No. 6, pp. 5–12.

Winstanley, D. and Woodall, J. (eds.) (2000). *Ethical Issues in Contemporary Human Resource Management*, Basingstoke: Macmillan.

Further Reading

Goodstein, J.D. (2000). Moral compromise and personal integrity: exploring the ethical issues of deciding together in organisations' business, *Ethics Quarterly*, Vol. 10, No. 4, pp. 805–819.

Legge, K. (2000). The ethical context of HRM: the ethical organisation in the boundaryless world, in Winstanley, D. and Woodall, J. (eds.) *Ethical Issues in Contemporary Human Resource Management*, pp. 23–39, Basingstoke: Macmillan.

McIntosh, M., Leipziger D., Jones, K. and Coleman, G. (1998). *Corporate Citizenship: Successful Strategies for Responsible Companies*, London: FT/Pitman.

Werther, W.B. and Chandler, D. (2006). *Strategic Corporate Social Responsibility Stakeholders in a Global Environment*, London: Sage.

Work Foundation (2002). *Corporate Social Responsibility: Managing Best Practice*, No. 98.

Useful Websites

www.dti.gov.uk – links to Department of Trade and Industry information on ethics and corporate and social responsibility. Also links to related sites identified by DTI

www.ilo.org – the International Labour Organisation (ILO) gives information about rights at work and social issues related to the workplace

www.globalcompact.org – The Global Compact is a United Nations initiative to identify and promulgate ethical business principles

www.bitc.org.uk – this is the website of Business in the Community, a network of 700 companies committed to operating on ethical business lines

www.tuc.org.uk – this is the official website of the UK Trade Union Congress. The website gives advice on ethical approaches to employment, welfare and society and work-life balance

www.businesslink.gov.uk – Business Link gives advice to business about corporate and social responsibility

http://www.csr.gov.uk – the UK government's site advising on corporate and social responsibility

www.nottingham.ac.uk/business/ICCSR/ research/paperseries.html – link to research papers produced by University of Nottingham's International Centre for Corporate and Social Responsibility

PART 2
Strategic aspects

Part contents

CHAPTER 3

Strategic Human Resource Management

By Christine Porter and Bill Spear

Chapter outline

This chapter is concerned with the concept of strategic human resource management (SHRM), the process of strategic planning in organisations and the impact of various HR practices on the achievement of organisational objectives. Therefore, the chapter starts with a discussion of the concept of strategic HRM. This is followed by an overview of some of the different approaches to strategy formulation. The chapter discusses the best practice and contingency approaches to integrating HR practices and explores some of the techniques that organisations can use when strategic planning. The chapter concludes with a discussion of the obstacles to integrating organisational strategy and strategic HRM and discusses the relevance of the strategy literature to the public sector and other not-for-profit areas of the economy.

Learning outcomes

By the end of this chapter, you should be able to:

- Identify the key features of SHRM;
- Explain the relationship between HRM and organisational strategy;
- Differentiate between the different approaches to organisational strategy and to SHRM;
- Identify the obstacles to the involvement of HR functions in strategic decision making.

Introduction

Senior managers in organisations very often do not take into account the HR perspective when planning the strategic direction of their organisation. Many HR departments (and also some teaching programmes) concentrate solely on the operational aspects of human resources. Very often there is too much thought of HR techniques as ends in themselves rather than as needing to mesh with broader objectives in organisation terms. However, strategic planning needs to take into account the human dimension: for example, organisational capacity, cultural issues and the interaction between the employees and the technical basis of the organisation. This chapter seeks to explain the relationship between corporate objectives and HR strategics, both in terms of the way that corporate objectives need to be set taking into account the HR realities as well as the contribution that 'bundles' of particular HR techniques can make to the achievement of organisational objectives.

Strategic human resource management

The purpose of strategic SHRM is to ensure that organisational objectives are adopted that reflect the reality of HR capability within an organisation and that human resources are managed in such a way that organisational objectives are met. The debate about the relationship between corporate and staffing decisions is not new. It has, in theory, however taken on increased significance as scarce resources have to be more tightly controlled and markets have become more competitive. As Tyson points out (1995: 15), 'the management of labour [with which SHRM concerns itself] is a fundamental process [from a societal point of view] because it creates the kind of society in which people live.'

The key feature of strategic HRM is the integration (or strategic fit) of HRM policies and practices with organisational strategy, ensuring that HRM is fully integrated into strategic planning at a senior level. There are numerous definitions of strategic HRM. Schuler (1992: 4) defines it as, 'all those activities affecting the behaviour of individuals in their efforts to formulate and implement the strategic needs of the business', and Bratton (in Bratton and Gold, 2003: 37) as, 'the process of linking the HR function with the strategic objectives of the organisation in order to improve performance'. Armstrong and Baron (2002) identified the main features of strategic HRM as:

- Integrating business and HR strategies;
- Contributing to the achievement of competitive advantage;
- Commitment to the organisation's mission and values;
- Culture of trust and commitment;
- People seen as an investment not a cost;
- Top management driven;
- HR policies and practices are mutually supportive;
- Line managers are responsible for implementing HR policies and practices;
- Unitarist employee relations.

While these features may be useful as an aide-memoire and help to give a basic understanding of the concept of strategic HRM, they merely represent a list of ideal criteria that in practice will be difficult to achieve simultaneously. In any case, SHRM is concerned with strategic choices that are very often not used uniformally with an organisation but may vary from one employee group to another within the same organisation.

There is often confusion between HRM and strategic HRM. Some writers see the two terms as synonymous (Mabey et al., 1998); others do not. Golding (2004) suggests that the confusion arises because embedded in the HRM literature is the notion of strategic integration of HRM with organisational objectives. It appears however that the discussion about whether HRM and SHRM mean the same thing is largely academic. It is the difference between the rhetoric of policy statements and the reality of action that is important. Senior HR professionals need to be involved from the beginning in board-level discussions which might have HR implications. HRM policies need to fit across policy areas and across departments. As mentioned in Chapter 1, line managers also need to follow appropriate HRM practices as part of their everyday work.

The evolution of strategic human resource management

The potential contribution of strategic HRM has been well documented from early academic theories of US business schools such as Harvard (Beer et al., 1984) and Michigan (Fombrun et al., 1984) to recent key texts such as that by Boxall and Purcell (2003).

While the HRM literature emphasises a strategic theme, some critical evaluation demonstrates that in practice HRM lacks integration with the objectives of the organisation. In 1989, Guest concluded that strategic HRM seemed to have had little or no impact on improving organisational performance. There appeared to be no increase in boardroom representation and little evidence of 'soft' HRM, although there was some evidence of increased line manager involvement in the management of people. Storey (1992), in a survey of 15 UK organisations, found that extensive change in people management practice was under way, driven by non-personnel specialists and focused on organisational restructuring, quality and culture. However, his findings revealed that despite the widespread adoption of some strategic HRM features that are essentially unitarist, many of the organisations in his survey retained their pluralist perspective. Legge (1995) suggests that while some changes have taken place in people management processes, this largely reflects the pragmatic response to opportunities and constraints in the environment rather than the implementation of coherent employment policies. The evidence of Marginson (1993) and Millward et al. (2000), referring to the lack of board-level representation, supports this. As one of the researchers noted at the time:

> 'if one of the defining characteristics of human resource management is the explicit link with corporate strategies, then this survey has failed to find it for the majority of companies'.
>
> (Marginson, 1993: 71)

The 2004 Workplace Employee Relations Survey (Kersley et al., 2006) used three indicators to ascertain whether employers are becoming more strategic in their approach to managing people. The three indicators are: (1) evidence of workplace strategy covering employee development; (2) strategy not covering employee development; and (3) no strategy. They found that 'across the economy as a whole there was little change [since 1998] in the percentage of workplaces incorporating employee development in their strategic business plans'. 'Furthermore [they continue], HR managers were less likely to be involved in the preparation of strategic plans in 2004 than in 1998, a trend discernible across all sectors of the economy [in the UK]' (Kersley et al., 2006: 67–68). Similar, if not even more profound, doubts about the strategic importance place by organisations on HR as a competitive tool across the EU generally were identified by Stavrou et al. (2004).

Despite the positive findings of some research (Guest et al., 2000a, 2000b; Boxall and Purcell, 2003), the reality appears to be that whereas many chief executives subscribe in principle to the concept of strategic HRM, the evidence of the practical implementation of SHRM is somewhat sketchy. A key reason for this gap between rhetoric and reality may be the difficulty that many organisations experience in being able to demonstrate a direct causal link between the implementation of strategic people management practices and the achievement of organisational objectives. It is very difficult to demonstrate that HR benefits organisational profits for a number of reasons: for example, a company may be very profitable simply because it is operating in a growing market. In the public sector there may be few worthwhile measures of an organisation's effectiveness, despite examples in the UK of where governments have attempted to do this – e.g. by drawing up league tables of schools and hospitals.

Nevertheless, the ethos behind this chapter is that planning and strategy are essential to the effective delivery of organisational objectives, which accepts the findings of research such as that by Koch and McGrath (1996) which showed that:

> 'Labour productivity . . . tend(s) to be better in firms that both formally plan how many and what kinds of labour they will need, as well as where employers systematically evaluate their recruitment and selection portfolios and practices . . .' (p. 350).

pause for thought   What else is important for determining whether an organisation achieves its objectives other than its management of labour?

The interface between human resource management and organisational strategy

To understand the interface between organisational strategy and SHRM, it is necessary to analyse the responses made by an organisation to the context within which it operates, as well as to examine the way in which the HRM techniques are employed. Such techniques are (a) likely to impact on the delivery of organisational strategy and (b) have the potential to have a negative impact on other aspects of HRM, as the following case study seeks to illustrate.

Mini case study: Recruitment and selection in a UK Bank

A large clearing bank in the UK decided to change its recruitment policies in response to changes in the market place. The bank had an HR department but the lead function within the organisation was banking and there was little or no emphasis on the importance of HRM in helping the organisation to achieve its objectives. Rather, it was felt that the organisation would be most effective by concentrating on banking specialists, who were very skilled in banking but largely untrained in managing people.

Previously banks had concentrated on the protection of their clients' deposits but after deregulation of the financial services sector it became possible to enter into other fields of financial activity, including the provision of mortgages and insurance policies. In addition, deregulation of financial services meant that building societies and overseas banks were able to operate in the same fields as UK banks. The UK clearing bank, along with others, therefore decided to put much more emphasis on sales and marketing in an effort to compete.

The traditional approach to recruitment and selection in the bank had been to create long career ladders, engaging most employees when they left school or university. An individual employee would then work their way up the organisation, as far as it was deemed that their capabilities would allow. Employees had been recruited using criteria related not only to whether they were numerate but also related to diligence and caution.

The new environment, however, required that employees were needed who were more extrovert, less cautious and more creative, willing to push the sales and marketing agenda. Not only did the recruitment policies change, but so did staff development and career planning. As priorities changed within the organisation senior employees with new skills profiles related to sales were brought in at higher levels in the organisation than previously. Unfortunately, this had a knock-on effect since these new employees had not worked their way through the various departments and therefore had less organisational knowledge than those who had followed the more traditional career paths. Not only did this mean these new employees were less effective in some senses, due to lack of organisational knowledge, there was also some resentment among the employees who had not been given the opportunity to leap over the heads of others.

To reinforce the new organisational objectives, a payment by results reward management system was introduced. In addition, employees were required to work in teams and small groups in a way that had not been felt to be appropriate before. Unfortunately, the individually based payment system did not fit easily with teamworking and it was some while before management realised the conflict between individual incentives and teamworking. The individual incentive scheme also had an adverse effect on client relationships, since employees were not being encouraged to spend time with people who simply had queries rather than wanted to purchase a mortgage or insurance policy.

The bank was restructured partly to take advantage of the new ways of working made possible by advances in information technology that enabled customers to carry out their own banking online or through Automatic Telling Machines (ATMs). Many branches of the bank were closed resulting in massive redundancies. Some long-standing employees were pleased to leave the bank's employment, however, because they felt that the new ways of working were not to their liking. Unfortunately, the bank subsequently discovered that too many people had been allowed to leave, thus resulting in public embarrassment for the bank as well as the loss of many long-serving and talented employees.

From the above case study, identify:

- the impetus for changes being introduced into this banking organisation.
- the impact of the changes on HRM practices.
- the contradictions that resulted and which could be attributed to an absence of SHRM.
- For what reasons might directors of this organisation not have wanted to adopt a strategic approach to HRM?

The banking case gives an example of a situation where a strategy was devised and implemented without discernible input from HR specialists. It also illustrates the role that HR can play in helping the organisation to achieve its objectives as well as the need to employ a range of HR techniques that complement one another. The emphasis in an organisation, at least as far as HRM is concerned, needs to be not just on the effectiveness of a particular technique at micro level but in the interaction between the 'bundles' of HR practices and their contribution to the achievement of organisational objectives.

Delivering strategic objectives

As well as being involved in devising strategy, the HR department can help the organisation achieve its objectives by advising on, and designing, a range of policies and practices. The banking organisation, in the case study above, used its recruitment process and redundancy packages as tools for changing the profile of the employees in the organisation, in response to changes in the statutory environment that altered the market place in which the organisation was operating. The bank could have also considered a programme of HR development, not only to develop the employees who were already 'on the books' but also to develop the management function and to ensure that the HR practices that were implemented, worked as effectively as possible. A stronger HR department could also have advised the organisation about the likely interplay between the various practices. For example, an individually based payment scheme means that individuals are encouraged to enhance their own performance. If employees perceive that an enhanced group or team performance potentially has a negative effect on their own pay, this may militate against them supporting the team effort. The simultaneous use of individually based payment by results systems and teamworking are therefore usually counterproductive.

The banking case study above illustrates how the following range of key HR techniques – HR planning, recruitment, redundancy, HR development and training and reward management – can help to deliver organisational strategy. They are explained in greater detail in the following chapters of this book.

What is organisational strategy?

Organisational strategy deals with fundamental issues that affect the future of the organisation, seeking to answer fundamental organisational questions such as:

Where are we now? Where do we want to be? How do we get there? Ideally, strategy matches internal resources with the external environment, involving the whole organisation and covering the range and depth of its activities.

The origins of strategy have a military connection going back hundreds of years. From the organisational perspective, strategy has taken an increased role in planning since the end of the Second World War. Chandler (1962: 7) provides a definition of organisational strategy as, 'the determination of the basic long term goals and objectives of an enterprise, and the adoption of courses of action and the allocation of resources necessary for carrying out these goals'. Organisational strategy means that an organisation will seek to organise both its *tangible* resources in the form of the core competencies of its staff, physical assets and finance, and also its *intangible* resources such as brand, image, reputation and knowledge, in order to deliver long-term added-value to the organisation.

Vocabulary of strategy

Strategy is a rather imprecise subject and the terminology used is very inconsistent in everyday operations and academic literature. Johnson et al. (2005) have offered general guidelines for the terms associated with strategy:

◆ **Mission** – overriding purpose and direction of the organisation in line with the values or expectations of the stakeholders.

◆ **Vision** – a desired future state; the aspirations of the organisation.

◆ **Objective** – statement of what is to be achieved and when (quantifiable if possible).

◆ **Policy** – statement of what the organisation will and will not do.

◆ **Strategic capability** – resources, activities and processes. Some will be unique and provide competitive advantage.

Features of strategy

Lynch (2003) suggests that the strategic decision-making process consists of a number of key elements that relate primarily to an organisation's ability to add value and compete in the market place. It should be:

◆ **Sustainable** – for the long-term survival of the organisation, it is important that the correct strategic decisions are made to ensure that the strategy is sustainable.

◆ **Deliverable** – strategy is at least partly about how to develop organisations, helping them evolve towards their chosen purpose.

◆ **Competitive** – a sustainable strategy is more likely to be achieved if it delivers competitive advantages for the organisation over its actual or potential competitors. There are many different ways in which this can be achieved, including differentiation (unique product); low costs; niche marketing (narrow market segment); superior quality or service; high performance; and culture, leadership and style of an organisation.

◆ **Exploit linkages between the organisation and its environment** – links that cannot easily be duplicated contribute to superior performance. The strategy has to exploit the many linkages between the organisation and the external environment, including suppliers, customers, competitors and government.

♦ **Visionary** – the long-term survival of the organisation depends on the ability of senior management to move the organisation forward beyond the current environment. This may involve the development and implementation of innovative strategies that could focus on growth or competition or a combination of both.

pause for thought   Think of an organisation you perceive as visionary. What is it that makes it a visionary organisation?

The strategic planning process

There are three aspects to the strategic planning process – strategic analysis, strategic development and strategic implementation:

♦ **Strategic analysis** is an assessment made by management of the current position of the organisation – *where are we now?* It includes the impact of the external environment on strategy – the political, economic, social, technological, legal and environmental issues; the identification of resources available to the organisation – physical, human, financial, and intangible assets such as knowledge, brand and image; expectations of stakeholders; and structures of power and influence.

♦ **Strategic development** is an assessment of *where do we want to be?* This is achieved by the generation of different strategic options, an evaluation of those options, and the selection of the most appropriate strategy for the organisation.

♦ **Strategic implementation** is an assessment of *how do we get there?* This is concerned with putting strategy into action and evaluating the outcomes in practice. For the implementation stage to be successful, the organisation requires a structure designed to deliver the required performance, deployment of the necessary resources and a constant awareness of the changing circumstances of the external environment.

Approaches to strategic planning

Strategy formulation is not always a neat, sequential process. Many organisations operate in conditions of extreme uncertainty, and the opportunity to analyse, develop and implement strategy sequentially is often not undertaken. Below are four approaches to strategy formulation – planned or prescriptive, emergent, comprehensive and incremental approaches.

Planned or prescriptive

Lynch (2003) describes the planned or prescriptive approach to strategy (also called the rational or classical approach) as a sequential implementation of the three core areas of strategy – analysis, development and implementation. It is possible to use the analysis to develop a strategy that is then implemented. The strategy is *deliberately* planned in advance and is *intended to be realised*.

Key assumptions of planned strategy include strategic fit with a stable external environment, top-down control with little employee involvement, where innovation is not generally encouraged, and where training and development is task orientated. Few organisations are in circumstances that meet these criteria in full.

Emergent

The reality for many organisations is that they operate in such uncertain and un-predictable environments that their intended strategies are not realised and other unintended strategies emerge. Lynch (2003) argues that the emergent approach takes a much more experimental view of the strategy choice and its implementation. It seeks to learn by trial, experimentation and discussion as strategies are developed. Strategies emerge as a pattern during the process of crafting and testing. There is no clear distinction in the emergent approach between the two stages of development and implementation.

Key assumptions of emergent strategy include an uncertain and unpredictable environment; an emphasis on learning and knowledge acquisition; employee involvement; and the encouragement of innovation and experimentation. Many organisations operating today have emergent strategies because of the uncertainty that exists in the current business environment, although managers often find it difficult to create an environment where learning, innovation and experimentation are encouraged.

Comprehensive versus incremental approaches

Organisations have a choice about whether they devise a comprehensive strategy which may involve radical change or whether a more cautious incremental approach is taken. The comprehensive strategy involves more risk taking and less possibility of taking a 'strategic retreat' if the new strategy turns out to be unworkable. In large organisations, it may be much easier to take an incremental approach, giving opportunities for confidence building as the strategy is implemented and greater freedom to alter course in a world where the pace of change is increasing and it may become apparent that the new strategy does not fit with the changes that are taking place (Rees and Porter, 2006).

♦ **How would you describe the approach to strategic HRM at Warbings Office Systems?**

♦ **What are the strengths and weaknesses of strategic HRM at Warbings?**

exercise

Models of strategic human resource management

Although there is some acceptance of the idea that strategic HRM should support the strategic direction of the business, there is no agreement on the best way of doing this. Two normative models epitomise the relationship between labour management and organisational strategy. The first is explored in the *best practice or universal* school. The second approach, where integration between strategic HRM and organisational strategy is an essential feature, is explored in the *contingency and configurational* schools.

Universal or best practice school

The *best practice or universal* school proposes that strategic HRM is composed of a single set of HR policies and practices that is suitable for all organisations in all circumstances. Universal or best practice HRM (also known as high-commitment or high-performance or high-involvement HRM) was originally identified in the early US models of HRM, many of which mooted the idea that the adoption of certain 'best' HR practices would lead to improved organisational performance, through improved attitudes and behaviours, lower levels of absence and turnover, higher levels of skills and, therefore, improved productivity, quality and efficiency. The models of best practice take many forms and there is no consensus on the 'correct' bundle of HR policies and practices. Furthermore it is difficult to demonstrate the link between best practice HRM and improved organisational performance.

It is difficult to accept that the universal or best practice school reflects reality because what works well in one organisation will not necessarily work well in another. HR techniques adopted may not fit the local customs, organisational or societal culture, management style or technology. The cultural basis of many techniques used in HRM was discussed in Chapter 1. Social traditions about the role of managers and their relationship with employees will determine which HR strategies are likely to be effective. Also important will be the relationship between employees, employee attitudes to work and the family and the importance of work in their lives. The interface between technology and social structures at work can also be important. Social factors may need to be taken into account at the technical design stage to avoid dehumanised working arrangements with the motivational problems that may arise as a consequence.

Contingency or best-fit school

Having learned what works and what does not work elsewhere, it is still up to the organisation to decide what may be relevant and what can be adapted to fit its own particular strategic and operational requirements. This view is consistent with the contingency or best-fit school, which advocates the need to fit HR strategy into its surrounding context. Boxall and Purcell (2003: 60) offer a view of the factors that they feel ought to be taken into account in a full assessment of the factors that can influence HR choices. These are outlined in Figure 3.1.

They point out that it is necessary to look for the 'best fit' between the organisation and the internal as well as the external environment. For this, the organisation will need to draw on the know-how of the HR professionals before making strategic decisions, as illustrated in the case study that follows Figure 3.1.

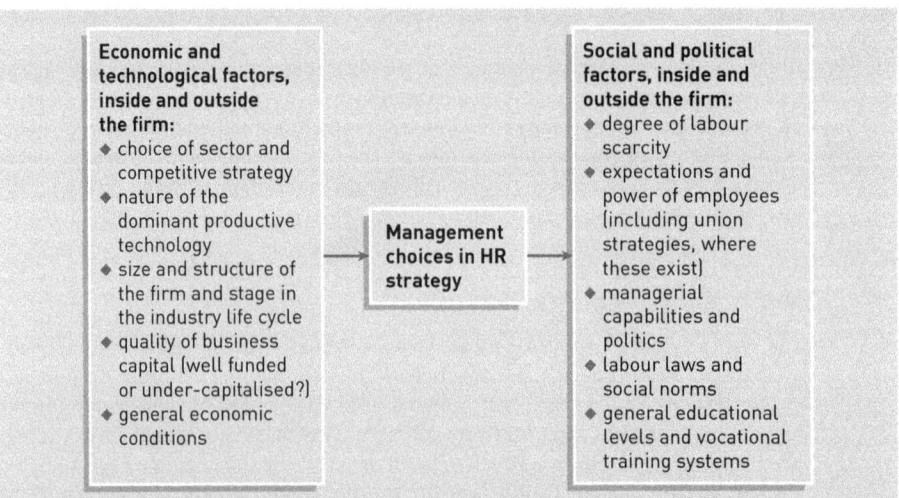

Figure 3.1 Major factors affecting management choices in HRM strategy
Source: Boxall and Purcell (2003: 60)

A national brewing company in the UK decided to build a large new brewery on a greenfield site in Merseyside. One reason for doing this was the government funding available for generating work in an area of high unemployment. Managers from the company's plant at Burton-on-Trent were transferred to help build and commission the new brewery. The engineering managers who were initially appointed to run the brewery were quite unused to the high degree of labour conflict that soon emerged and had great difficulty in handling it. This was because of the different regional culture in Merseyside: a key difference was the traditional antagonisms between management and employees in the area. The more amicable working relationships at Burton had not prepared the managers who had been transferred for this key aspect of their job. No one in the HR department had been consulted about the decision to make the move to Merseyside. Despite training and changes in managerial personnel, the conflict and costs persisted. When there was a need for rationalisation in the company, the new brewery, although the most modern, was the one to be closed. The labour relations issues were partly responsible for this decision (Rees and Porter, 2006: 229).

window into practice

There may be a tension in balancing external and internal environments as organisations seek to meet their objectives and a need to integrate organisational and employee needs, especially in highly competitive labour markets.

Resource-based approach

The resource-based approach argues for an exclusive form of 'fit' based on the theory that an organisation's resources are the key source of competitive advantage. In this context, it may be decided that the organisation should not try to achieve strategic fit with the external environment but aim to maximise its resources to create and dominate future opportunities.

Hamel and Prahalad (1994) have explored this view of strategy and suggest that it is a process for organisations to seek new opportunities over the long term while simultaneously maintaining the capacity to out-run competitors in the short term. The ability to achieve competitive advantage rests on the uniqueness of the resources; they must have value, be rare, be impossible to copy/imitate exactly and have no close substitutes.

The resource-based approach assumes that the core competencies in the organisation are unique; people are viewed as an investment and not a cost; that learning, knowledge sharing, innovation and experimentation are encouraged, and that employees are involved in decision making.

The debate as to which approach is most effective will continue, especially between those of the 'best practice' and 'best-fit' schools of thought. However, it seems appropriate to suggest that organisations should continue to analyse their environments, especially since these are fast changing and, as seems self-evident, not all HR techniques will be appropriate over time and from one situation to another.

pause for thought

◆ Distinguish between 'best practice' and 'best fit'.

◆ Which do you believe to be the most appropriate approach?

◆ What is your reason for coming to this conclusion?

Human resource management-related planning tools

To some, planning may seem to entail a bureaucratic process that ossifies the organisation and is more suited to stable than dynamic environments. However, if an organisation has done some planning, then it is easier to evaluate the effects of unexpected events on the situation than if little or no planning has taken place. There are several tools available to organisations that seek to plan their HR requirements. These include techniques of human resource planning (HRP) and balanced score-card. These two techniques are explained below.

HRP

HRP carried out effectively is inextricably linked with organisational strategy. Corbridge and Pilbeam's (1988: 33) model identifies four main components of HRP activity:

1. Investigation and analysis – both internal to the organisation and to the external environment.

2. Forecasting to determine an HR imbalance or 'people gap'.

3. Planning resourcing and retention activities.

4. Utilisation and control through HR policies, techniques and IT.

The techniques used in HRP have in the past often involved the creation of very elaborate mathematical equations, which gave a spurious accuracy to what is often a not easily quantifiable process. These techniques were probably more appropriate during periods of general labour shortages. Current problems, at least in the UK, are mainly of shortages of labour with specific skills, requiring an organisation to identify how they are going to fill these skills gaps, which may require employees to be flexible. This would especially be the case where an organisation has a superfluity of employees with skills that are no longer needed, thus indicating the need for retraining or the recruitment of people with generic skills.

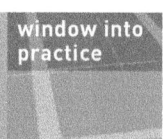

window into practice

A large petrochemical firm in the UK recognised the need for specialist and generic skills. Some graduates with specialist skills in petrochemical engineering were recruited to deal with the short-term needs. Graduates with a general engineering background were recruited and used in technical and managerial jobs, with a view to moving them around the organisation so that they developed a range of skills. The reasoning was that the organisation needed to be able to adapt to changes in the industry, and the latter group of generalists would more easily be able to fill the emergent jobs. This compares with the banking case study, where employees had previously only been recruited in a particular mould.

Previously referred to as manpower planning, HRP has developed from being a relatively narrow forecasting of organisational need for particular numbers of employees with particular skills to a much wider and more qualitative concern with business planning and organisational strategy.

As with strategic planning so with HRP, Boxall and Purcell (2003) have identified the need to involve all stakeholders in the process if the planning is to reflect the actual environment in which the organisation will be operating.

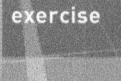

exercise

How would you explain the need for HR planning to be integrated into the overall organisational strategy?

Balanced scorecard

This is a managerial accounting technique developed by Robert Kaplan and David Norton, in two books (1996, 2001), that seeks to reshape strategic management. It is a process of developing goals, measures, targets and initiatives from the following four perspectives:

- Financial;
- Customer;
- Internal business process;
- Learning and growth.

Kaplan and Norton emphasise the notion that it is the strategy actually implemented that is important. Good operational systems are seen to be as important as a strategic plan. They recognise that although financial outcomes are important to shareholders, management needs to improve the organisational performance at operational level if a sound financial basis is to be created. Particular emphasis is placed on the role of HRM in helping an organisation to achieve its objectives. Boxall and Purcell (2003) criticise the model because they feel that it does not sufficiently emphasise the management of managers and the importance of team building for senior managers. They also point out that it does not recognise that some HR activities are carried out, not because they add directly to the profitability of the organisation, but for legal, social and political reasons.

pause for thought

What activities can you think of that are carried out by organisations for legal, social or political reasons?

Strategic planning as an iterative process

Strategic planning can be seen as a mechanistic process that takes place once every five years. As indicated above, however, there are other models. The development of strategy can also involve a more iterative process and be interwoven with operational issues. The following case study illustrates how contributions to strategy can occur as part of the interrelationship between the operational and the strategic.

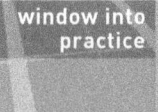

window into practice

At a healthcare trust in the UK it emerged at formal disciplinary proceedings that there was a pattern of similar types of failings in patient care, serious enough to warrant disciplinary action, including dismissal. The existence of the pattern was reported to the committee responsible for monitoring clinical governance. This enabled that committee to make a strategic intervention to try and determine the causes of these shortcomings and ensure appropriate remedial action was taken and that the strategic 'plan' was altered accordingly.

Integrating organisational strategy and human resource management

The banking case study (p. 45) is an example of a situation where input from the HR professionals at board level would have been useful so that workable strategies were conceived. There needs to be an HR input at the start of the decision-making processes when strategic issues are being considered. Unfortunately, all the evidence points to a paucity of board membership for HR directors in the UK. The Company Level Industrial Relations Survey found that only 30 per cent of companies with a thousand or more employees had an HR director on the executive board (Marginson, 1993). The function is more usually represented by the finance director who may be the only specialist on the board.

The difficulty in devising organisational strategies that are based on HR realities is not, however, just due to the fact that HR is often not consulted or not represented on the board or equivalent decision-making body. It is also due to other features of organisational strategy making. As pointed out by Rees and Porter (2006), there is an assumption that those who develop strategy welcome the prospect of open debate. However, debate can be hindered by personality clashes, rivalries and hidden agendas. Those taking part in the debate may have conflicting interests, although it may be assumed that there are none. These potential conflicts may not be taken into account when the issues are aired: senior managers are as likely as anyone else to take a unitary perspective and want to assume that what is being proposed is in the interests of all. The failure to identify potential conflicts of interest can also lead to naïve assumptions about the extent to which different objectives can be adopted, let alone the likelihood of complete agreement between the parties if a change in organisational culture is envisaged or deemed necessary. Therefore the resulting strategies may not be as appropriate as would be the case if the conflict of interests had been identified and taken into account by the decision makers.

The involvement of HR specialists in the formulation of organisational strategy has sometimes been inhibited by certain attributes of those in the HR profession. If HR specialists are to operate at a strategic level they must understand the nature and purpose of the organisation and be able to contribute to its future plans. Without such knowledge it is not possible for HRM to devise and implement policies and practices that will help the organisation achieve its objectives. Therefore, HRM specialists operating at a senior level must have considerable commercial acumen, understanding of organisational strategy, and awareness of strategic HRM if they are to comprehend the complex set of relationships that exist. Lack of organisational awareness on the part of HR professionals may be exacerbated by the fact that many HR departments are relatively small. In order to gain promotion HR managers may need to move frequently from one organisation to another, and even from one industry to another.

All managers, whether from an HR background or not, may be susceptible to promoting the latest HR techniques, ignoring the applicability of these techniques to the context in which the organisation is operating. Techniques may also be implemented without accurate problem diagnosis on the part of those involved (either in HR or among line managers). This, together with poor implementation, may result in the adoption of HR techniques that do not aid the achievement of objectives or that 'backfire', undermining the confidence that the senior management of the organisation has in HR.

The HR department may be weighed down with administrative responsibilities or in 'fire fighting', giving little time for thought about the wider organisational issues. Sometimes the problem of gaining acceptance of proposals made by HR can be attributed to the lack of facilitation skills demonstrated by those HR managers seeking to support operational managers but who are perceived as merely 'policing' management or erecting unnecessary obstacles. This may be due to ineptness on the part of practitioners in HR but it may also be due to the difficulty that managers from other backgrounds may have in understanding or having the patience to examine the 'soft' issues with which HR concerns itself. By the term 'soft' we are referring to the types of issues which are non-quantifiable but where judgement has to be made. Usually HR managers do not come from technical backgrounds and can

60   CHAPTER 3 STRATEGIC HUMAN RESOURCE MANAGEMENT

therefore be perceived as being outsiders when the cultures of many organisations, and the disciplines from which other senior managers come, are scientific, technical or medical.

Despite the promotion by the CIPD of HR managers as 'business partners', all too often strategy making is seen as being for 'really senior people' who do not want to share their thoughts with those whom they see as being more junior, or who have recently arrived in the organisation. Senior managers may find it more convenient to devise strategies in a vacuum rather than have 'cold water' poured on their plans by someone pointing out the shortcomings and deficiencies in their proposals.

pause for thought   What is your view of HRM? Why do you think that the HR function is not more influential in organisations?

Applicability of strategy to the public sector

One drawback of the strategy literature as far as the public and not-for-profit sectors are concerned is that the features of strategy discussed and the vocabulary employed appear to concentrate almost completely on the private sector. In some cases, the public sector (or that part of the economy that is heavily dependent on government funding for survival) will, however, have been encouraged to take a strategic approach to the management of the business. UK governments have sought to create a market, for example in the National Health Service and in education, which means that organisations in these sectors may indeed be in competition with each other for customers and the resources which follow. It is also necessary to take into account the importance of non-governmental organisations (NGOs) such as charities.

HR policies have been needed in these organisations to enable them to achieve the objectives that the new market economy has demanded. Employees in these sectors have suffered from downsizing, work intensification and a general reduction in resources per patient, per student or per client. This has been necessary to enable these organisations to be more business-like (although hospitals, schools and universities are not businesses in the accepted sense of the word). Many aspects of the strategic planning process described in this chapter will therefore be relevant to such sectors, even though the stakeholders may vary and there is no requirement to produce a profit in the conventional sense. Particular features of the public sector have been the need to give value for money, the creation of performance indicators and of course the need to balance their budgets. However, while there is a need for not-for-profit organisations to be business-like they are not businesses. They often have to operate in a sensitive political environment. In addition, there is always the danger that performance indicators and targets can be manipulated to create the appearance rather than the reality of progress. There is also the danger that simplistic accountancy models mean that much energy is expended into competing with other internal units rather than developing an integrated approach that meets the needs of the organisation as a whole. Nevertheless, it is not an option not to develop a strategic approach in the not-for-profit sector, providing such dangers are

recognised. These issues need to be considered before attempting to develop a strategic plan and it may be particularly appropriate for those in the HRM function to warn of the dangers of simply trying to copy the private sector.

---

pause for thought

How appropriate do you think the ideas in this chapter have been for public sector and other not-for-profit organisations?

What makes it difficult to adopt these ideas in such organisations?

Summary

In this chapter we have addressed the following:

♦ Key features of strategic HRM include integration with organisational strategy, contributing to the achievement of competitive advantage, a culture of trust and commitment, top management driven, line manager responsibility for implementing HR policies and practices, and unitarist employee relations;

♦ Organisational strategy deals with the fundamental issues that affect the future of the organisation. It integrates the functional areas of the organisation, covering the range and depth of its activities;

♦ There are three core areas of organisational strategy: strategic analysis, strategic development and strategic implementation. Although these areas are presented as occurring sequentially, they will be simultaneous in some circumstances;

♦ The planned approach to strategy assumes that the core areas are formulated sequentially and the emergent approach assumes that the core areas are interlinked;

♦ The best practice approach to HRM strategies assumes that the adoption of a core set of HR policies and practices would be suitable for all organisations. In contrast, the best fit approach advocates a contingency approach whereby policies and practices are adopted according to whether they fit the particular circumstances. The resource-based approach focuses on the organisation's resources as the basis for achieving competitive advantage;

♦ Features of organisational decision making that hinder the development of an appropriate strategy include the need for open debate unhindered by personality clashes, rivalries and hidden agendas;

♦ The lack of involvement of senior HR professionals on the board of directors together with the lack of understanding or interest in HR on the part of managers from other backgrounds will contribute to ineffective strategy formulation.

Review Questions

You may wish to attempt the following as practice examination style questions.

3.1 Consider an organisation with which you are familiar and analyse whether it has an organisation strategy. Would you say it has planned or emergent strategies or both? What has led you to this conclusion?

3.2 To what extent does the organisation strategy that you have identified concern itself with HR issues?

3.3 Is it evident that HR capacity was taken into account when the organisational strategy was developed?

3.4 What is the difference between the 'best practice' and 'best fit' approaches to strategic HRM?

3.5 What major obstacles to the integration of HR with organisation strategy can you identify?

· ·

References

Armstrong, M. and Baron, A. (2002). *Strategic HRM: The Key to Improved Business Performance*, London: CIPD.

Beer, M., Spector, B., Lawrence, P., Quinn Mills, D. and Walton, R. (1984). *Managing Human Assets*, New York: Free Press.

Boxall, P. and Purcell, J. (2003). *Strategy and Human Resource Management*, Basingstoke: Palgrave.

Bratton, J. and Gold, J. (2003). *Human Resource Management: Theory and Practice*, 3rd edition, Basingstoke: Palgrave.

Chandler, A.D. (1962). *Strategy and Structure*, Cambridge, MA: MIT Press.

Corbridge, M. and Pilbeam, S. (1988). *Employment Resourcing*, London: FT Pitman.

Fombrun, C., Tichy, N. and Devanna, M. (1984). *Strategic Human Resource Management*, Chichester: Wiley.

Golding, N. (2004). Strategic human resource management, in I. Beardwell, L. Holden and T. Claydon (eds.) *Human Resource Management*, 4th edition, London: Pearson.

Guest, D. (1989). Personnel and HRM: can you tell the difference?, *Personnel Management*, January, pp. 48–51.

Guest, D., Michie, J., Sheenan, M. and Conway, N. (2000a). *Employee Relations, HRM and Business Performance: An Analysis of the 1998 Workplace Employee Relations Survey*, London: IPD.

Guest, D., Michie, J., Sheenan, M., Conway, N. and Metochi, M. (2000b). *Effective People Management: Initial Findings of the Future of Work Study*, London: IPD.

Hamel, G. and Prahalad, C. (1994). *Competing for the Future*, Boston, MA: Harvard Business School Press.

Johnson, G. Scholes, K. and Whittington, R. (2005). *Exploring Corporate Strategy*, 7th edition, London: Pearson.

Kaplan, R. and Norton, D. (1996). *The Balanced Scorecard: Translating Strategy into Action*, Boston, MA: Harvard Business School Press.

Kaplan, R. and Norton, D. (2001). *The Strategy Focused Organisation*, Boston, MA: Harvard Business School Press.

Kersley, B., Alpin, C., Forth, J., Bryson, A., Bewley, H., Dix, G. and Oxenbridge, S. (2006). *Inside the Workplace: Findings from the 2004 Workplace Industrial Relations Survey*, London: Routledge.

Koch, M. and McGrath, R. (1996). Improving labour productivity: human resource management policies do matter, *Strategic Management Journal*, Vol. 17, pp. 335–354.

Legge, K. (1995). HRM: rhetoric, reality and hidden agendas, in J. Storey (ed.) *Human Resource Management – A Critical Text*, London: Thompson.

Lynch, R. (2003). *Corporate Strategy*, 3rd edition, London: Pearson.

Mabey, C., Salaman, G. and Storey, J. (1998). *Human Resource Management: A Strategic Introduction*, 2nd edition, Oxford: Blackwell.

Marginson, P. (1993). The multi-divisional structure and corporate control: explaining the degree of corporate coordination over decisions in labour relations, Papers in Organisation No. 12, Institute of Organisation and Industrial Sociology, Copenhagen Business School.

Millward, N., Bryson, A. and Forth, J. (2000). *All Change at Work: British Employment Relations, 1980–1998, as portrayed by the Workplace Industrial Relations Survey Series*, London: Routledge.

Pilbeam, S. and Corbridge, M. (2006). *People Resourcing – Contemporary HRM in Practice*, London: Pearson Education/Prentice Hall.

Rees, W.D. and Porter, C. (2006). Corporate Strategy Development and Related Management Development, Part I, *Industrial and Commercial Training*, Vol. 38, No. 6, pp. 226–231.

Schuler, R.S. (1992). Strategic HRM: linking people with the strategic needs of the business, *Organisational Dynamics*, Vol. 21, No. 1, pp. 18–32.

Stavrou, E., Brewster, C. and Charlambous, C. (2004). Human Resource Management as a Competitive Tool in Europe, Working Paper 0414, Henley Management College.

Storey, J. (1992). *Developments in the Management of Human Resources*, Oxford: Blackwell.

Tyson, S. (1995). *Human Resource Strategy: Towards a General Theory of Human Resource Management*, London: Pitman.

Further Reading

Leopold, J. (ed.) (2002). *Human Resources in Organisations*, FT/Prentice Hall.

Useful Websites

www.cipd.co.uk/search/default.aspx?q=hr%20strategy – links to the Chartered Institute of Personnel and Development resources relating to HR strategy

www.dti.gov.uk – links to Department of Trade and Industry information on ethics and corporate and social responsibility. Also links to other sites identified by DTI as being of related interest

www.humanresourcemanagement.co.uk – publishes articles and news releases about HR surveys, employment law, HR research and related books and other publications

www.btinternet.com/~alan.price/hrm – a free source of worldwide HRM information

www.hrmguide.co.uk – publishes articles and news releases about HR surveys, employment law, HR research and related books and other publications

PART 3
Resourcing

Part contents

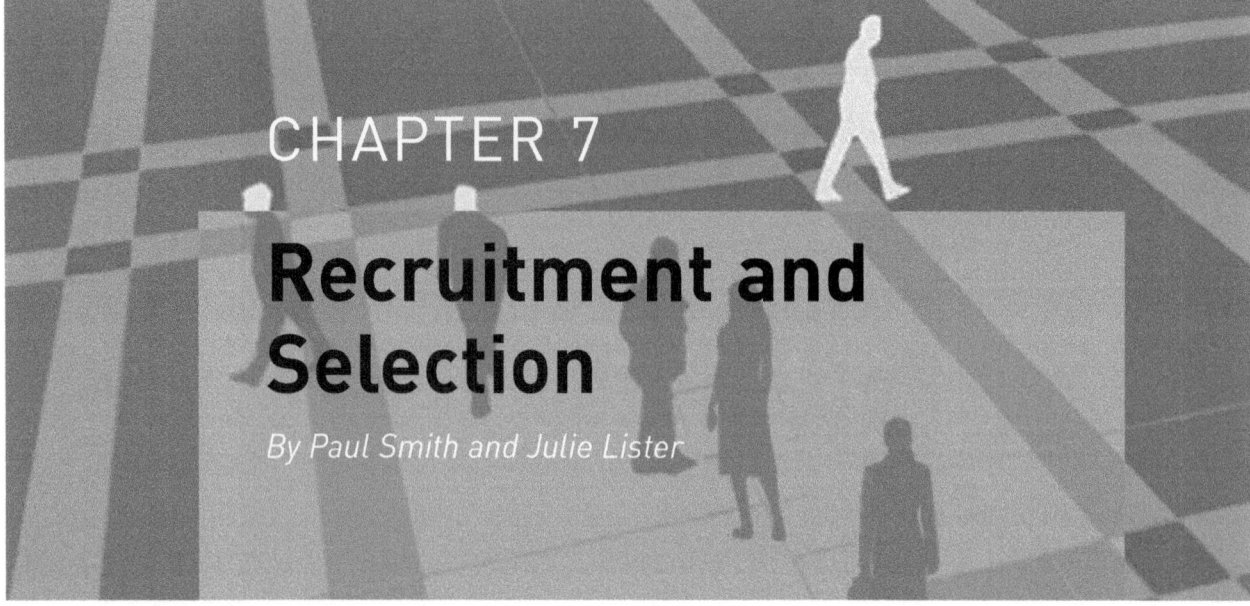

CHAPTER 7

Recruitment and Selection

By Paul Smith and Julie Lister

Chapter outline

This chapter introduces the theory and practice of recruitment and selection (R&S). The importance of recruitment and selection is highlighted and wider strategic and integrative issues are discussed. The psychometric approach is outlined, possible limitations of such an approach are considered and alternatives discussed. The application of theory is provided by practical examples.

Learning outcomes

By the end of this chapter, you should be able to:

◆ Describe the importance of R&S;

◆ Explain the role of R&S in relation to employee retention, and as part of a wider human resource (HR), and business, strategy;

◆ Link and integrate recruitment and selection with other areas of HRM;

◆ Analyse the contingent nature of R&S and the variety of approaches to R&S in practice;

◆ Evaluate different perspectives on the R&S process;

◆ Appraise the different methods of R&S.

Introduction

People resourcing in general, and R&S in particular, are crucial elements of HRM. It is axiomatic that organisations need people, and R&S provide the means to resource, or staff, the organisation. This chapter examines and critically evaluates R&S in the wider context of HRM and HR strategy.

Definitions

Beardwell and Wright (2004) point out that R&S are processes concerned with identifying, attracting and securing suitable people to meet an organisation's HR needs. The two terms are often used contiguously and where recruitment stops and selection begins is a moot point (Anderson, 1994). For the purposes of analysis, however, it is useful to separate the two; thus recruitment encompasses the first half of most definitions, selection the second. Recruitment is concerned with identifying and attracting suitable candidates, selection with choosing the most suitable. 'Selection represents the final stage of decision making in the recruitment process' (Cowling and Mailer, 1990: 46).

Marchington and Wilkinson (2005) argue that selection more often gets the focus of attention, particularly in relation to 'new' and 'sophisticated' selection techniques, with consequently less concern being given to recruitment or to other key aspects of resourcing such as HR planning and retention. This specificity of focus is however unjustified, given the interdependence of the different aspects of resourcing.

An examination of the different R&S methods also highlights the degree of overlap. Thus, while the drawing up of job descriptions and their use in the construction of job advertisements falls under the 'recruitment' heading, their use in formulating interview questions is part of selection. Job descriptions also play a role in wider aspects of people resourcing, such as in performance appraisal and job analysis.

Recruitment and selection: importance, links and integration

The importance of recruitment and selection (R&S) in HRM has already been alluded to: it provides the conduit for staffing and resourcing the organisation. An increasingly competitive and globalised business environment, coupled with the need for quality and customer service, has enhanced the importance of recruiting and selecting the right people and of being seen as an 'employer of choice' (Smith, in Porter et al., 2006: 19).

It can be argued that R&S form the axis on which all other HR issues turn. Dipboye (1994) argues that achieving a good fit between people and their jobs is a primary objective of HRM. As Marchington and Wilkinson (2005: 157) point out, the implications of poor selection decisions can be catastrophic for the business as a whole, in terms of the likelihood of disciplinary cases, retraining poor performers and dealing with labour turnover as a consequence. Selecting the right person or people for the task and for the organisation is paramount.

R&S and HRM

From the 1980s there were major changes in how the management of people was conceptualised and, to some extent, practised. HR became more assertive as to its role in organisations (Legge, 1995) due to an increasing awareness and evidence of the impact HR had on organisational success (Searle, 2003). The term 'Personnel Management' became increasingly subsumed by 'Human Resource Management', as explored in Chapter 1.

As part of such changes, R&S processes were recognised as critical components in successful change management (Iles and Salaman, 1995), providing a means of obtaining employees with a new attitude, as well as new skills and abilities.

In terms of models of HRM, R&S can be seen to form an important component of these. Examples include those of Beer et al. (1984), Fombrun et al. (1984), Guest (1989) and Storey (1992). Thus Beer et al.'s model has four key HR outcomes at its core: the competency of employees, their commitment, the importance of fit, i.e. congruence between the employee and the organisation's goals, and the cost-effectiveness of HR policies and practices. An organisation's R&S needed to act as enablers of these outcomes. Thus rather than *ad hoc* approaches to R&S, or methods which focused purely on the person–job fit, what was needed in a HRM approach, it was argued, were more sophisticated methods, which included consideration of prospective employee attitudes and their fit with the organisational culture.

Drawing on David Guest's work, Storey (1989: 11) provides a framework of HRM that encompasses three connecting elements: HRM aims, HRM policies and HRM outcomes. Aims would encompass high commitment, quality and flexible working for example; policies include those of selection on the basis of specific criteria using sophisticated tests.

Boxall and Purcell (2003: 85–86) point out that, in comparison with the physical, tangible assets an organisation possesses (such as plant and machinery), intangible or less tangible assets such as culture, skill and competency, motivation and social interaction are increasingly being seen as key sources of competitive advantage. 'Human resource advantage can be traced to better people employed in organisations with better processes' (ibid.). There are now many studies that seek to demonstrate this link between HRM policies and practices, including R&S, on the one hand, and performance, on the other, and these are reviewed in Marchington and Wilkinson (2005: 86–87).

Strategy and recruitment and selection

In terms of a strategic approach to the management of human resources, it is argued that R&S should form part of a wider resourcing strategy linked to organisational goals. Applying Porter's (1985) ideas on competitive strategy, Schuler and Jackson (1987) draw out the HR implications of these strategies; ideas that have been further developed by Sisson and Storey (2000). In relation to R&S, taking each of the three categories of competitive strategy, a firm adopting a cost-reduction strategy will, it is argued, have *ad hoc* methods of R&S and use agencies/subcontractors. Quality enhancement firms will show sophisticated methods of R&S, while firms in the innovation category will focus on core competences and transferable skills.

While such 'fit' models are subject to criticism, they do provide a useful reminder of the need to take contingent factors into account when deciding on relevant R&S approaches and thus form a useful alternative to best practice approaches.

HR policies and practices have also been linked to life cycle models (Schuler, 1989), i.e. matching appropriate HR to different stages of growth: Start-up, Growth, Maturity and Decline (or Renewal?). Thus, for example, during the early stages of a business, flexibility and informality are likely to be key. If and when new employees are needed, the ability to recruit and retain staff with the motivation to work long hours and engage in self-development is needed. Such a stage is likely to see formal procedures kept to a minimum.

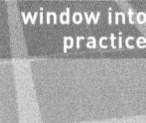

Recruitment and selection and the small business

Andrew Ferguson is the creator of Lifeshift. He has provided training and counselling for some 8,500 career-shifters. Most of these have as a result created a self-managed or self-employed career. The following excerpt from the appropriate section of his *Lifeshift Manual* demonstrates the requirements of the single-person firm or small business person when considering expanding by recruiting.

You and whose army?

You can't hope to manage a team until you can manage yourself. And once you can do that, perhaps you won't need a team! Or not just yet . . .

Recruitment guide

Before you set off down a track that can have some hefty time and money implications, check that you really need to. Is your To Do List cluttered with things you no longer need to do? Are there more efficient ways to do the job? Do you need an extra body, or just some time management? . . .

Cost justification

If you bring this person in, how will the business benefit? What value will they bring? And what costs are involved – recruitment, selection process, induction and further training, office space, salary, etc., NI, holidays, pension, cost of management time? Corporates reckon the real cost of a manager at five times their salary! Recruitment takes faith: you can rarely see in advance how you can afford it, and have to treat every appointment as an investment . . .

Where will you find your recruit(s)?

Recruitment is mostly done by networking . . . which is also the best way to find a job (and customers). Six out of seven jobs are never advertised. Can you promote/recruit internally (this is good for morale)? Do you have a file of past applicants? Are there any other strategies available? One good way is to ask current employees if they know anyone who'd be good . . .

Initial selection

Standard approaches are written for and by people from large organisations, and assume resources and constraints you simply don't have. . . . [In an interview] ask them to tell you about themselves, what they care about, what they would bring to the job and why they want it.

continued

The paper burden

Be aware what you're taking on when you become an employer, because you are effect-ively becoming an unpaid tax inspector. According to the Federation of Small Businesses (FSB), over 99 per cent of all government revenue is collected by employers. Employers currently collect and pay tax and NI. They also pay SSP, administer SMP and fund redun-dancy payments (Ferguson, 2001: 89–93).

Mr Ferguson usefully illustrates some of the considerations regarding R&S for the small business. Is a new employee absolutely necessary? What will be the costs involved in the recruitment and selection, and with subsequent employment? Approaches are also likely to be less formalised than in a larger organisation. It is recognised that recruitment by word of mouth, by 'asking current employees if they know anyone who'd be good', carries the risk of perpetuating any gender/ethnicity imbalance that exists in the workforce and can also lead to workforce cloning, which can squeeze out new ideas and innovation (see Chapter 14). However research suggests that it leads to the recruitment of employees who stay with the company for long periods. It is thought that this is because they already have an existing knowledge of the company through friends or relatives already employed, and that this provides them with a realistic job preview. This concept is explored further in the section on 'Recruiting to retain'.

Approaches to recruitment and selection

Textbooks on the subject aimed at a management audience tend to take a normative or prescriptive approach. This does not in itself make them worthy of criticism; they provide useful practical guidance on how to recruit and select staff. The problem occurs however when such advice is taken uncritically, or is used out of context.

The psychometric approach

The dominant paradigm of the last 30 years has been that of psychometrics. This approach is based on scientific rationality, and its application (by occupational psychologists) to candidate selection in particular. Selection, and the associated assessments involved, are treated as representing problems of measurement. In simple terms, which entails measuring individual differences so that people can be objectively matched to the requirements of a job. Such approaches, seeking object-ivity and fairness in selection decisions, can be viewed as laudable. The requirement still remains however that such tests be subject to scrutiny, in relation to their con-ceptual basis, and to their application in practice, and that alternative perspectives are also given due consideration.

The psychometric approach focuses on the measurement of individual differences. To enable this to be put into practice, a number of steps are taken, in a logical order. Thus R&S may be viewed as a systematic process. The psychometric approach is also closely aligned with that of rational decision making (Redman and Wilkinson, 2001: 24); decisions are made on the basis of some kind of assessment about the suitability of individuals who might fill a vacancy.

pause for thought   Do you think cultural biases influence which individual differences are measured?

Central to the psychometric approach are the concepts of validity and reliability. *Validity* refers to the extent to which what one is aiming to measure is actually measured. This is most often seen in terms of subsequent job performance. *Reliability* relates to consistency, thus if a selection measure were to be repeated, would it achieve the same results? Psychometric measures seek both high validity and high reliability.

Other ways of looking at R&S include regarding selection as a process of socialisation (to the organisation) and selection as socially constructed reality, i.e. as enacted within a wider societal framework and thus subject to the power and social structures inherent in that society. It must not be forgotten that R&S is a *two-way* process involving both the employer and potential employees, rather than simply being a matter of management prerogative.

The R&S process: a systematic approach

R&S as a process is set out in Figure 7.1. The steps in this process will be reviewed below, together with some discussion as to possible difficulties and shortcomings.

HR Planning

If R&S are not to be purely reactive and last minute, they need to be based on HR planning. This involves forecasting the demand for and the supply of labour, incorporating labour turnover and retention data (see Further Reading).

In relation to a consideration of HR planning, certain themes identified earlier in this chapter are pertinent. A competitive environment characterised by change provides a challenge for traditional planning approaches. Numbers and type of staff required may be subject to fluctuation, thus stressing the need for flexibility. Such flexibility requirements may encompass both numerical aspects (see Atkinson, 1984), i.e. hiring certain staff on atypical contingent contracts and functional, i.e. identifying prospective staff who are multi-skilled or have the ability to multi-task, or have the potential to do so.

Need requirement and job analysis

In terms of R&S *per se*, the first step is to decide whether a vacancy actually exists. When an employee leaves there may be alternative ways of filling the gap left by their departure, such as reorganisation, reassignment of tasks and automation.

The next step involves an analysis of the particular job. Job analysis refers to 'the process of collecting, analysing and setting out information about the contents of jobs' in order to determine the key tasks and roles (Armstrong, 1999: 190). Methods of job analysis include: observation of the person doing the job; getting

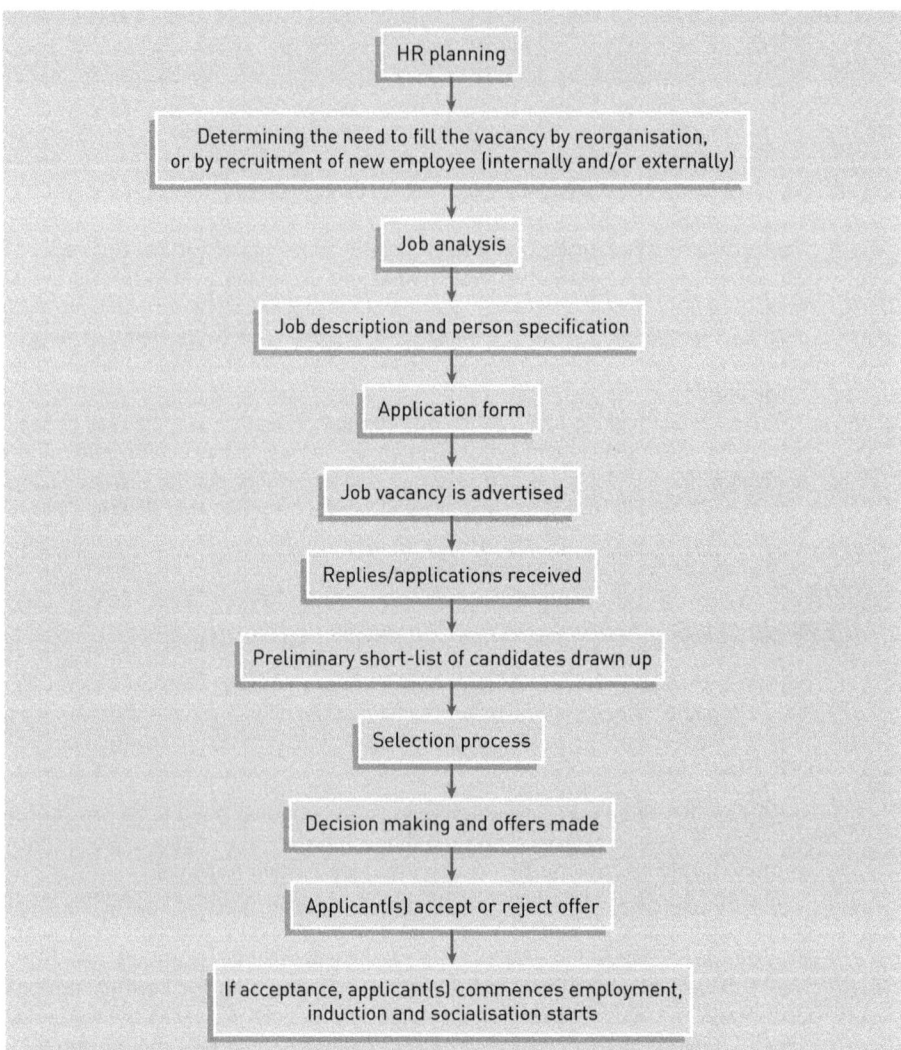

Figure 7.1 The R&S process

job-holders to record their activities in work diaries; interviewing the job-holder; questionnaires/checklists; critical incident; and repertory grid techniques (see Taylor, 2002a).

Criticisms of traditional job analysis include its focus on the job, rather than wider requirements, and that it collects information about the job as it currently exists, assuming that it will be similar in the future. Developments include future-orientated job analysis (Redman and Wilkinson, 2001), broader role analysis (Marchington and Wilkinson, 2005), and the identification of competences, i.e. behavioural indicators that have been identified as relevant to a particular context. The latter will be considered in more detail below.

Job descriptions and person specifications

These form the outcomes of job analysis and thus the same discussions apply. A job description provides information on the job, typically under relevant headings such as title, location, main purpose, responsibilities, working conditions and so on.

Job descriptions have been criticised for being outmoded and inflexible and frequently inaccurate. By specifying an employee's tasks and duties, the job description may inhibit the very sort of high performance 'working beyond contract' values and behaviours required in modern organisations. Indeed it is interesting to note that a recent CIPD survey on recruitment, retention and turnover (CIPD, 2005), found that the most frequent response of employers to recruitment difficulties was recruiting people who 'have the potential to grow, but don't currently have all that's required'.

Developments to the traditional job description have ranged from ensuring up-to-dateness by regular review, including some reference to the fact that duties may change from time to time and couching them in looser, more generic, terms. Another alternative is the depiction of 'key result area' statements (KRAs) that relate to the measures deemed critical for job performance, and accountability profiles that focus on achievement rather than a mere description of the job (Armstrong, 1995, 1999).

It must not be forgotten that in a tight labour market, where organisations face difficulties in recruiting, it could be the prospective employees who influence the job description – organisations may have to offer flexible roles that match the requirements of the individual.

While job descriptions outline tasks and duties, person specifications identify the personal attributes required of the job-holder. Such information is normally listed under relevant headings such as skills, knowledge, personality attributes, qualifications and experience. Such items can then be divided into 'essential' and 'desirable' characteristics to inform selection. Two traditional formats are Rodger's seven-point plan (1970) and Munro-Fraser's (1966) five-fold grading system. If used today, these are likely to require modification to avoid unfair discrimination and the use of categories that cannot be clearly linked to job requirements.

Person specifications rely heavily on personal judgement, so often such approaches have given way to a focus on competencies. Since these are, or should be, behavioural indicators, the need to make inferences about personal qualities is arguably removed.

Competency frameworks

Competences have been variously defined, but Roberts (in Beardwell et al., 2004: 206) has produced a definition that sees them in terms of 'the work-related personal attributes, knowledge, experience, skills and values that a person draws on to perform their job well'. Although such a broad definition encompassing such aspects as values raises the problem that the use of competences may include judgements about personal qualities and thus be subject to the same shortcomings as personal specifications, proponents argue that the focus of attention should be on the behavioural outcomes of these various characteristics.

In terms of their use in recruitment and selection, this involves the identification of a set of competences that are seen as important across an organisation or part of an organisation. Competences are person-based rather than job-based. The attributes of the top performers in the organisation are identified and profiled and the result is used to inform R&S. Commonly identified competences include: communication, achievement/results orientation, planning and organising, problem solving and teamwork. This approach has the scope for greater flexibility as it enables organisations to focus 'more on the qualities of the jobholder and the person's potential suitability for other duties as jobs change' than on the job itself (IRS, in Beardwell et al., 2004: 206).

The advantage of focusing on actual behaviour and outcomes means that there is no need to make inferences about personal qualities. However, in practice, competency approaches are often used in ways that specify not only outputs but also how these are or should be achieved (Redman and Wilkinson, 2001: 26). Generic competences on the personality or attitudinal end of the spectrum, as opposed to those that are skills-based, give greater scope for such personal judgements.

Criticisms of competency approaches include the view that they lead to an acquiescent workforce and 'cloning' (Taylor, 2002a: 106). It is also argued that they are backward looking in that they focus on past activities, and it has also been suggested that over-reliance on behavioural characteristics for recruitment or assessment purposes risks rewarding people for who they are, and not what they do.

Recruitment methods

The next step is to attract a pool of applicants from which to begin the selection process. Recruitment can be from both internal and external sources. In terms of external, the CIPD's Annual Survey (2005) estimates the average cost of filling a vacancy per employee as £3,950, rising to £4,625 if the associated costs of labour turnover are also taken into account. In total, nationally, this would run to in excess of £1 billion.

The types of recruitment methods used by organisations are listed in Table 7.1. The method chosen will be dependent on the type of vacancy and the organisation concerned. In simple terms, the method(s) used by a large well-known organisation seeking to recruit a new MD are likely to be different to those of a small business seeking an assistant to help out on Saturdays. There are also cost considerations to bear in mind and legal requirements, particularly, with regards to the latter, in the design and wording of advertisements.

exercise

At the warbings depots, drivers are primarily recruited via word of mouth. When vacancies occur, the drivers are asked if they know of anyone who might be interested and suitable. Only if this doesn't produce enough applicants are other recruitment methods used – primarily a specialist employment agency.

What are the advantages and disadvantages of such an informal word of mouth approach to recruitment?

Table 7.1 Recruitment methods

Recruitment method	% of organisations surveyed
To advertise vacancies internally:	
Intranet	70
Noticeboards	64
Team meetings	17
Staff magazine	13
To attract external applicants:	
Local newspaper advertisements	85
Recruitment agencies/search	80
Vacancies information (own website)	67
Specialist journals/trade press	59
National newspaper advertisements	55
Job centre plus	54
Speculative applications/word of mouth	52
Employee referral schemes	38
Links with schools/colleges/universities	35
Apprenticeships/work placements/secondments	32
Vacancies information (specialist website)	30
Posters/billboards/vehicles	14
Radio or TV advertisements	9
Other	7

Source: adapted from CIPD (2005)

In drawing up advertisements, the aim is to attract a reasonable number of suitably qualified applicants. Taylor (2002a: 134) refers to organisations deciding between a 'wide trawl' versus a 'wide net'. The aim of the wide trawl is to attract a large number of people – adverts are likely to be large and striking in appearance and be placed prominently. By contrast, the key aim of the net approach is to reach a relatively narrow audience and to encourage self-selection on the part of possible applicants. Advertisements in this category are likely to contain a lot of detailed information and be placed in specialist journals or on websites.

There are a number of different external agencies available that can be employed to undertake all or part of the recruitment process on behalf of employers. These include government and voluntary agents that encompass job centres, advertising and recruitment consultants, temporary employment agencies, headhunters and permanent employment agencies (Taylor, 2002a: 146).

window into practice

The recruitment consultant

David Carroll worked as a recruitment consultant before leaving to pursue postgraduate study. Here he gives a useful insight into the work of a recruitment consultant.

continued

The work of a recruitment consultant

The position of recruitment consultant can be broadly viewed as a sales role. It is typified by targeted objectives based on financial and non-financial activity to which rewards are linked, such as bonus, commission and promotion. The role is essentially focused on meeting the recruitment, and to some degree selection, needs of an external organisation in return for a pre-agreed fee. The fee is based on a percentage of a permanent salary (sometimes benefits also) or on a percentage margin of a contractor's pay rate.

A recruitment consultant's 'desk' is normally characterised by one of three areas:

◆ Firstly, on a contract/contingency basis, where the aim is meeting a short-term need of a client to cover incidents such as absence, a short-term project or an unexpected upturn in work. There is a need to fill the position quickly, normally between a few minutes and a few days. Candidates will, typically, be on the books and looking for work immediately. The placed candidate is paid by the recruitment agency/consultancy and a higher rate charged to the client.

◆ Secondly, on a permanent basis where the client's longer-term need is often due to replacing a leaver or to meet growth plans. The recruitment cycle is longer and the consultant's role will be more involved, generating fees on the basis of an agreed percentage of the basic salary/package.

◆ Thirdly, there is headhunting/campaign managed recruitment, which usually means exclusivity of business for the recruitment consultant. Positions are often at a higher level, such as director, or for specialist professional roles where there is a shortage of candidates in the market. Fees are generated at three key stages: accepting the assignment, producing a short-list for agreed interviews and on final placement. The percentage charge rate is also higher than for regular permanent recruitment fees.

Recruitment consultants are also generally specialised in niche markets and/or job types to enhance their area of expertise. This will focus their efforts towards certain types of jobs, for example secretarial/PA or architect positions and may be further focused within a geographical area and/or a market sector. The basic day-to-day key skills and competences used by a recruitment consultant include: finding positions, developing job descriptions and person specifications with the client, negotiating fees, advertising positions in selected media, resourcing, short-listing and interviewing candidates, undertaking reference and work eligibility checks, selling the client opportunity to the candidate and providing information on both the role and the company, arranging interviews, giving feedback and making offers and negotiating salary. Each of these processes has to be administered and is often performed within internal quality guidelines or by those set out by the REC.

(Information provided by David Carroll, 2005)

Electronic recruiting

Moving on from the use of external agencies, electronic recruitment methods are an increasingly important area. The use of e-recruitment is expanding, with 90 per cent of firms using some form of electronic recruitment at some stage of the process (IRS Survey, 2004). According to Marchington and Wilkinson (2005: 174), some of the main advantages of e-recruitment are:

- Reduced costs;
- Improved corporate image;
- Reduced administration;
- Wider pool of applicants;
- Shortened recruitment cycle;
- Improved overseas recruitment;
- Easier for applicants.

Among the main disadvantages are:
- Too many unsuitable applicants (because ease of application encourages speculative applications);
- Technical problems;
- Shortage of applicants;
- Expense.

And from the applicant's point of view:
- Slow feedback or follow-up;
- Insufficient job information;
- Concerns about personal security;
- Technical problems;
- Wish for human contact.

While e-recruitment is inappropriate in some circumstances (because it disadvantages certain socio-economic groups), it is likely to be the method of choice in others because candidates will perceive it as the most appropriate application method for that type of job. IT-related jobs are a good example of this. In such situations, employers can discourage more speculative applications by increasing the effort required – for example, by refusing to accept CVs and insisting on completion of online application forms.

Short-listing

Short-listing is the initial step in selection. It is done by comparing the information provided in the application form or CV with the selection criteria, as identified in the person specification. In theory, those who match the criteria will go on to the next stage of the selection process, although where there are large numbers of applicants recourse is likely to be made to the list of 'desirable' characteristics in addition to the 'essential'.

Selection

The psychometric approach aims to measure individual characteristics and match these to the requirements of the job in order to predict subsequent job performance. To achieve this, candidates who are successfully short-listed face a number of subsequent selection devices. These can be viewed as a series of hurdles to jump, with

Table 7.2 Accuracy of different selection methods (1.0 is perfect prediction)	
Selection method	**Accuracy**
Assessment centres (promotion)	0.72
Intelligence tests *and* structured interview	0.63
Intelligence tests *and* work sampling	0.60
Ability tests	0.56
Work sample tests	0.52
Intelligence tests	0.51
Structured interviews	0.51
Personality tests	0.40
Biodata	0.35
Typical interviews	0.26
References	0.26
Years of job experience	0.18
Years of education	0.10
Graphology	0.02
Chance prediction	0.00

Source: adapted from various sources, including Smith (2002)

the 'winner' being the candidate or candidates who receive the job offer. While this analogy undoubtedly reflects the attitude of many employers, it may be considered to be somewhat out of place in an already tight labour market that is set to tighten further in the face of prevailing demographic trends. Such traditional approaches take no account of the ultimate power of the chosen candidates throughout the process to turn down the offer of employment (Dale, 1995: 160).

Various selection techniques are available; the key factors influencing the choice of these is briefly reviewed now.

Accuracy

From the psychometric perspective, selection accuracy is defined in terms of the degree of match between predictor and subsequent job performance. It encompasses the notions of validity and reliability. Table 7.2 outlines the accuracy according to research studies of different selection methods measured on the correlation coefficient between predicted and actual job performance, with 1.0 being perfect prediction and zero being pure chance.

The type of job provides 'the most significant influence on the choice of selection methods for any one vacancy' (IRS, 1997, quoted in Beardwell et al., 2004: 217). Thus, for example, assessment centres tend to be reserved for managerial and graduate posts.

Such lists should be used with caution – they vary according to the research study or studies they are based on, and according to the specific example of selection method used for each category. Accuracy will also be dependent on the selection method being used correctly in a particular context. Bearing such health warnings in mind, however, they do provide an interesting basis for comparison and discussion. Intelligence tests, when combined with another specified method, score the highest. Of techniques used on their own, work sample tests offer the highest potential for accuracy. Intuitively this may not come as a surprise, since the best way to predict whether someone can do a job is to give them the job to do. Thus Pret a Manger, for example, requires candidates to undertake a day's on-the-job experience at one of their shops as part of their selection process (Beardwell et al., 2004: 220). Other examples of work sampling are in-tray exercises and role plays.

In terms of accuracy, interviews perform better if structured and carried out by trained interviewers, while assessment centres can score reasonably high for accuracy, depending on their design and the use they are put to. References score fairly low down on the scale, while graphology and astrology are close to zero.

Cost

Cost, in terms of direct money costs and indirectly in terms of time, is a major consideration when choosing selection methods. Thus, for example, assessment centres are resource-intensive and therefore tend to be used by larger organisations and for more senior jobs or for graduate-entry, particularly where there is a number of vacancies to fill at one time.

Selection methods

Mark Cook (1993) refers to the 'classic trio' of application form, interview and references. As Taylor (2002a) points out, what is interesting is that these traditional methods continue to dominate despite evidence that other selection tools offer greater accuracy.

The interview

The interview has been described as 'a controlled conversation with a purpose' (Torrington et al., 2005: 242) and continues to be an enduringly popular part of the selection process. As Table 7.2 demonstrates, the traditional (unstructured or informal) interview has a relatively low predictive validity, yet this is markedly improved by taking a structured approach, using trained interviewers, and combining the interview with other selection methods. Two structured interview techniques are behavioural and situational interviews. Both use critical incident job analysis to determine aspects of job behaviour that are key to effective performance (see previous section on 'Need requirement and job analysis').

Testing

As can be seen from Table 7.2, tests tend to score relatively highly in terms of accuracy, particularly in combination with another selection method when considering intelligence tests. Objectivity is viewed as a key advantage of tests over other selection methods such as the interview. The relevance of the test to the job applied for needs to be carefully considered, however, and questions have also been raised concerning unfair discrimination and bias (Torrington et al., 2005: 148).

Questions surrounding the use of personality testing include whether personality is open to such measurement, whether personality is constant, and whether the tests can be faked. Another fundamental question relates to the link to job performance – many jobs could be undertaken equally successfully by people of varying personalities. In counter-argument, certain basic personality requirements can be linked to some jobs: thus extraversion to salespeople and calmness to air traffic controllers. It has also been argued that, based on recent research, five basic building blocks of personality can be identified: extroversion/introversion, emotional stability, agreeableness, conscientiousness, and openness to new experiences.

Assessment centres

Assessment centres incorporate a variety of selection methods and work simulation, helping to potentially improve the accuracy of decisions. Job or role analysis is used to identify the behaviours and characteristics to be assessed. Assessment centres have been found to be one of the most effective means of selecting candidates (IRS, 2002). Drawbacks centre mainly around costs and resource issues.

Recruiting to retain

It is important not to lose sight of the ultimate business objective, which is to successfully recruit appropriately talented candidates who will continue working for the organisation for as long as the organisation wishes to retain their services. It therefore follows that strategies need to be adopted that, at best, support this objective or, at least, do not undermine it.

Central to the objective of recruiting and retaining is ensuring that the recruitment process (and the induction process) does not erode the goodwill of the chosen candidates. This is easy to do at all stages of a recruitment process that views the employer as the all-powerful party that 'awards' the job to the lucky winner. In *Successful Recruitment and Selection* (1995), Margaret Dale suggests that instilling a 'marketing' mindset in all staff involved in the recruitment process is one approach to ensuring that the favoured candidates do not de-select themselves. Every candidate should therefore be afforded the same courtesy given to potential clients, from the earliest stages of the process.

Taylor (2002b) stresses the importance of realistic job preview both to ensuring that the right candidate for the job is recruited, and that they stay with the organisation for a reasonable period of time. His approach is based on extensive research into the impact of realistic job preview conducted in the US (Wanous, 1992; Hom and Griffeth, 1995; Phillips, 1998). The concept of realistic job preview extends well beyond the obvious dangers of overselling jobs and glossing-over difficulties and disadvantages that will confront the new employee once they have joined and stresses the importance of giving candidates as realistic and complete a preview as possible – 'warts and all' – including creating opportunities for them to meet colleagues, see where they will be working and, if possible, be given an opportunity to sample the actual work.

The potential downside to this approach is readily apparent. The employment market in the UK is currently very tight, with a recent CIPD survey reporting that 85 per cent of employers are facing recruitment difficulties (CIPD, 2005). In such a competitive environment the leap of faith required to adopt such a frank and honest approach to advertising and recruitment may be seen as a step too far for many employers.

However, Taylor suggests that the advantages of realistic job preview far outweigh the disadvantages and notes that 'word of mouth' recruitment is a good way to provide this. He proposes that this is because employees have a more realistic impression of the company and the work prior to joining and that, even when they do experience disappointments, they have the support of family and friends who also work for the same employer.

window into practice

Recruitment and retention at Hertfordshire County Council

A few years ago Hertfordshire County Council (HCC) took the first steps towards a new and integrated approach to recruitment and retention, an approach that culminated in them winning both the Innovation in Recruitment and Retention and the Overall Winner awards in the prestigious *Personnel Today* Awards 2003.

In common with other public sector organisations, particularly those in the South East, HCC faces significant recruitment and retention challenges – living costs are high while unemployment is low. Many local people commute to London for work. There are also national skills shortages to contend with – for teachers, qualified social workers, engineers and planners. There are approximately 2,000 permanent posts to be filled each year, and £12 million a year is currently spent on temporary staff, not including teachers. The move to a different approach to recruitment was partly in response to such challenges, but was also driven by three more specific reasons.

Firstly, HCC were then using over 150 different agencies to supply temporary staff, leading to problems in control of standards, variability in mark-up by the agencies and inconsistencies in pay rates. In addition, despite the use of so many agencies, there were still difficulties in recruiting sufficient temporary staff.

Secondly, at the time the Council was undergoing significant change. It needed a method of retraining and redeploying staff to avoid redundancies. The need for a more flexible approach to working was also recognised.

Thirdly, the HR function at the Council wanted to modernise how recruitment was done and to shorten the recruitment cycle (the time taken to fill a vacancy). E-recruitment was seen as a means of achieving this.

The Recruitment Centre opened in 2000 in partnership with Manpower plc, providing a one-stop shop 24/7 service for managers and candidates alike. Job-seekers can register onto the database for both temporary and permanent posts. Recruitment is simpler, faster and less expensive. The Recruitment Centre provides fully integrated recruitment services – advertising, provision of all temporary staff, management of permanent recruitment and redeployment. Improvements include:

◆ Reduction in the number of temporary staffing agencies used. Major savings made and improvement in the quality of temps;

◆ Launch of an interactive website. Candidates can now apply for all vacancies online. 55 per cent of all applications are now made online;

◆ Line managers and applicants now have a single point of contact for all recruitment activities – temporary and permanent;

◆ A database of people wanting to work for the Council has been set up so that vacancies, when they arise, can be filled directly;

◆ The redeployment service helps to retain staff in whom a significant investment has been made;

continued

+ Improved management information provides a basis for further improvements and action;
+ Savings of £3 million in first five years.

The setting up of the Recruitment Centre accompanied other developments that had a positive impact on recruitment and retention, including: better management information to ensure actions, such as recruitment drives, are better targeted; flexible working options; and a commitment to training and development.

(Interview with Carole Grimwood, Assistant Director of HR, Hertfordshire County Council, 1 July 2005, available at www.hertscc.gov.uk)

Summary

The prime importance of R&S in HRM has been stressed. If people really are 'our most important resource' (Smith, in Porter et al., 2006: 4), then R&S provide the key drives to resourcing the organisation from which the other HR activities flow.

Differing approaches to, and perspectives on, the R&S process can be discerned: the psychometric stresses objectivity and accuracy; yet R&S in practice is often a mix of such objective views with the pragmatic, as evidenced by the continuing popularity of the application form, interview and references as selection devices. Moves away from selecting purely for 'a job' and towards using wider criteria such as those based on the attitudinal and 'the potential to grow' (CIPD, 2005: 2) provide their own challenges for objectivity. Different situations require differing approaches, as evidenced by our case study examples and windows into practice.

exercise

Making reference to Warbings, identify the main recruitment and selection problems. Identify and justify solutions to these.

Review Questions

You may wish to attempt the following as practice examination style questions.

7.1   Is good selection an art or a science? Discuss.

7.2   How would you account for the fact that the most popular selection methods (Cook, 1993; CIPD, 2005) are not necessarily the most accurate?

7.3   What do you understand by the term 'employer of choice'? Why is it argued that being such an employer is important in today's employment market?

7.4   Reflect on the approaches to recruitment and selection that have been introduced in this chapter. Under what circumstances might you propose a particular approach, and under what circumstances might you advise against it?

References

Anderson, A. (1994). *Effective Personnel Management: A Skills and Activity-based Approach*, Oxford: Blackwell Business.

Armstrong, M. (1995). *A Handbook of Personnel Management Practice*, 5th edition, London: Kogan Page.

Armstrong, M. (1999). *Employee Reward*, 2nd edition, London: CIPD.

Atkinson, J. (1984). Manpower strategies for the flexible organisation, *Personnel Management*, August, pp. 28–31.

Beardwell, J. and Wright, M. (2004). 'Recruitment and selection', in I. Beardwell, L. Holden and T. Claydon (eds.) *Human Resource Management: A contemporary approach*, 4th edition, London: FT/Prentice Hall.

Beardwell, I., Holden, L. and Claydon, T. (2004). *Human Resource Management*, Harlow: FT/Prentice Hall.

Beer, M., Spector, B., Lawrence, P., Quinn Mills, D. and Walton, R. (1984). *Managing Human Assets*, New York: Free Press.

Boxall, P. and Purcell, J. (2003). *Strategy and Human Resource Management*, London: Palgrave.

Chartered Institute of Personnel and Development (2005). *Recruitment, Retention, and Turnover: A Survey of the UK and Ireland*, Londo: CIPD.

Cook, M. (1993). *Personnel Selection*, 3rd edition, Chichester: Wiley.

Cowling, A. and Mailer, C. (1990). *Managing Human Resources*, 2nd edition, London: Edward Arnold.

Dale, M. (1995). *Successful Recruitment and Selection*, London: Kogan Page.

Dipboye, R.L. (1994). Structured and unstructured selection interviews: beyond the best-fit model, *Research in Personnel and HRM*, Vol. 12, pp. 79–123.

Ferquson, A. (2001). *Your Lifeshift Manual*, pp. 89–93, Breakthrough Publications, at: www.lifeshift.co.uk.

Fombrun, C., Tichy, M. and Devanna, M. (1984). *Strategic Human Resource Management*, New York: Wiley.

Fraser, J.M. (1966). *Employment Interviewing*, London: Macdonal Evans.

Guest, D. (1989). Human resource management: its implications for industrial relations and trade unions, in J. Storey (ed.) *New Perspectives on Human Resource Management*, pp. 41–55, London: Routledge.

Hom, P.W. and Griffeth, R.W. (1995). *Employer Turnover*, Cincinnati, OH: South-Western.

Iles, P. and Salaman, G. (1995). Recruitment, selection and assessment, in J. Story (ed.) *Human Resource Management: A Critical Text*, pp. 209–234, London: Routledge.

IRS (1997). The state of selection: an IRS Survey, *Employee Development Bulletin*, Vol. 85, pp. 8–18.

IRS Employment Review 749 (2002). *Focus of Attention*, pp. 36–41, London: IRS.

IRS Employment Review 792a (2004). *Recruiters March in Step with Online Recruitment*, pp. 44–48, London: IPS.

Legge, K. (1995). *HRM: Rhetorics and Realities*, Basingstoke: Macmillan Business.

Marchington, M. and Wilkinson, A. (2005). *Human Resource Management*, London: CIPD.

Phillips, J.M. (1998). Effects of realistic job previews on multiple organizational outcomes: a meta-analysis, *Academy of Management Journal*, Vol. 41, No. 6, pp. 673–690.

Porter, M. (1985). *Competitive Advantage: Creating and Sustaining Superior Performance*, New York: Free Press.

Porter, K., Smith, P. and Fagg, R. (2006). *Leadership and Management for HR Professionals*, Oxford: Butterworth-Heinemann.

Redman, T. and Wilkinson, A. (2001). *Contemporary Human Resource Management*, Harlow, FT/Prentice Hall.

Rodger, A. (1970). *The Seven Point Plan*, 3rd edition, London: National Institute of Industrial Psychology.

Schuler, R. (1989). Strategic human resource management and industrial relations, *Human Relations*, Vol. 42, No. 2, pp. 157–184.

Schuler, R. and Jackson, S. (1987). Linking competitive strategies with human resource management, *Academy of Management Executive*, Vol. 1, No. 3, pp. 207–219.

Searle, R. (2003). *Selection and Recruitment: A Critical Text,* Milton Keynes: Open University Press.

Sisson, K. and Storey, J. (2000). *The Realities of Human Resource Management*, Milton Keynes: Open University Press.

Smith, M. (2002). Personnel selection research, *International Journal of Organisational and Occupational Psychology*, Vol. 2, pp. 441–472.

Storey, J. (1989). *New Perspectives on Human Resource Management,* London: Routledge.

Storey, J. (1992). *Developments in the Management of Human Resources: An Analytical Review*, London: Blackwell.

Taylor, S. (2002a). *People Resourcing*, London: CIPD.

Taylor, S. (2002b). *The Employee Retention Handbook*, London: CIPD.

Torrington, D., Hall, L. and Taylor, S. (2005). *Human Resource Management*, Harlow: FT/Prentice Hall.

Wanous, J.P. (1992). *Organisational Entry: Recruitment, Selection and Socialisation of Newcomers*, 2nd edition, Reading, MA: Addison-Wesley.

Further Reading

Robertson, I. and Smith, M. (1999). Personnel selection, *Journal of Occupational and Organizational Psychology*, Vol. 74, No. 4, pp. 441–472.

Useful Websites

www.hrmguide.co.uk/hrm/chap8/ch8-links.html – guide to detailed process of recruitment and selection, particularly interviewing

www.agepositive.gov.uk/agepartnershipgroup/pages/top_tips_selection.htm – Age Positive's (government-sponsored campaign) advice on tackling age discrimination and promoting age diversity in employment

www.thetimes100.co.uk/theory/theory.php?tID=349 – *The Times* newspaper resource centre covering, inter alia, business studies teaching materials, particularly case studies

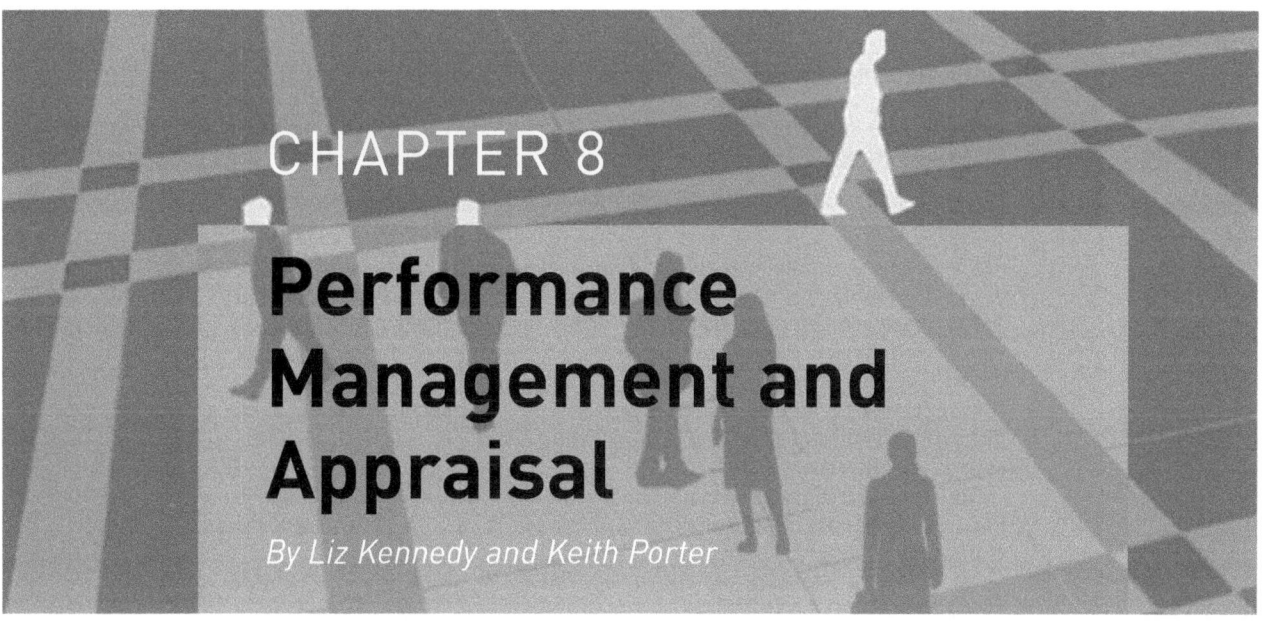

CHAPTER 8

Performance Management and Appraisal

By Liz Kennedy and Keith Porter

Chapter outline

Examining the strategic place of performance management (PM), this chapter looks at the ways in which PM can help an organisation achieve the vertical and horizontal integration of people management and development. It explores the practicalities of implementing PM and determines the purpose of performance appraisal while taking note of the relevant human resource management (HRM) issues that surround PM, such as competences and contingency pay.

Learning outcomes

By the end of this chapter, you should be able to:

◆ Explain the strategic role of PM;

◆ Demonstrate the link between PM and effective people management;

◆ Describe the different components of a PM process;

◆ Compare behavioural and output-based appraisal systems;

◆ Contrast the development and the assessment agendas;

◆ Identify the key factors associated with success in PM.

Introduction

The improvement of corporate and individual performance levels is a key priority for any organisation, but these are difficult to achieve. With greater recognition of the value added by competent and committed staff, performance management is increasingly seen as a key tool in most organisations (IRS, 2001). In this chapter we explore the nature of PM and its role within the organisation, as well as the key processes involved and the factors that contribute to its success or failure.

The strategic context

PM as an approach to effective people management

PM is sometimes mistakenly viewed as an event or activity that is somehow separate from the effective day-to-day management of people (Armstrong and Baron, 1998). There are two main reasons for this: firstly, the tendency to associate PM with performance *appraisal*; and secondly, the perception that PM is 'owned' (and enforced) by HR. Appraisal often conveys to employees' minds images of awkward confrontations at annual review meetings and pointless box-ticking exercises. Among small and medium-sized enterprises in particular, performance appraisal is seen as synonymous with PM.

The key to overcoming this confusion is to view PM not as an independent activity, but as a set of integrated processes aligning several elements of effective people management.

PM therefore needs to be placed very firmly in a management context. As Armstrong and Baron (2005) observe, it is a 'natural process of management' and management involves 'getting things done through the efforts of other people' (Mullins, 2002). So in many respects, PM *is* effective people management. Moreover, there is evidence to suggest that effective people management, enabled by a PM system, will lead to positive HR outcomes, such as employee commitment, competence and flexibility. These will in turn lead to quality and productivity, resulting in organisational success (Guest et al., 2000). As Porter et al. (2006: 13) note, this makes intuitive sense:

> 'Employees who are carefully recruited to suit the organisation and their roles, properly trained and developed, appraised and suitably rewarded, communicated to and involved . . . are more likely to put themselves out, to "go the extra mile" and demonstrate the sort of discretionary behaviours that are seen as crucial differentiators between "world class" high performance organisations and the rest.'

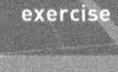 **exercise**   Make a list of all the ways organisations could maximise people's performance in the workplace.

Performance management and strategic alignment

This discussion about the nature of PM also highlights its role in achieving strategic alignment. This purpose is captured succinctly:

> 'Performance management is a strategic and integrated approach to delivering sustained success to organisations by improving the performance of the people who work in them and by developing the capabilities of teams and individual contributors.'

> (Armstrong and Baron, 1998: 8)

One of the distinguishing features of HRM is that it represents a strategic approach to people management. The practical question is how to achieve strategic fit. PM can provide the answer to this question by delivering both vertical and horizontal integration.

The potential of a PM system to support such alignment is illustrated by referring to the matching model of HRM (Fombrun et al., 1984); see Figure 8.1. Here, the key HR interventions of recruitment, reward, appraisal and development are mutually reinforcing and interact in a concerted way to enhance performance. 'Performance' in this case can be interpreted as whatever people need to do to achieve the organisation's business objectives. While there is both an underlying logic of this framework and also an attractiveness to HR practitioners striving to achieve 'strategic alignment' (Holbeche, 2001), the model raises some practical problems:

◆ How can business strategy be translated into a set of expectations about the ways that each individual must perform so that the organisation's objectives can be achieved?

◆ How can PM interventions be organised with the overall effect that every employee meets these expectations?

An effective PM system can address these problems.

Performance management systems

It is useful to think of PM as a 'system' (Kast and Rosenweig, 1985) – see Figure 8.1. Here, the PM system is a horizontally aligned (linked and mutually reinforcing) set

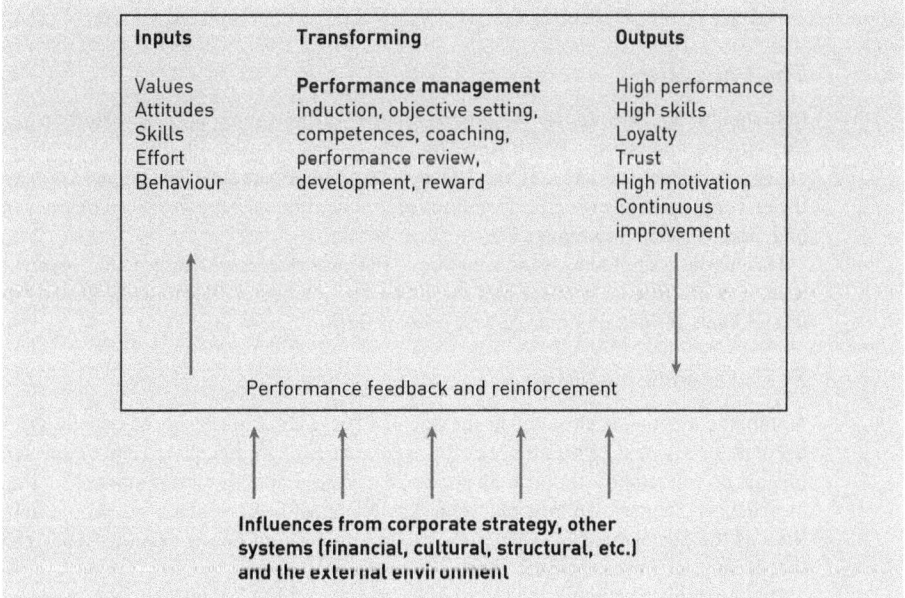

Figure 8.1 PM as a system

of PM interventions that converts existing values, attitudes and behaviours (inputs) into desired outputs, i.e. those values, attitudes and behaviours that are necessary to implement business strategy. The PM system is itself part of a wider organisational system with which it interacts. So, for example, employee reward will be influenced by the prevailing organisational culture and structure, as well as the financial system. This will in turn be influenced by external factors such as labour market conditions and the wider economic environment. But more significantly from the point of view of alignment, the PM system will be designed to ensure that employees' behaviour is directed towards delivering the business strategy.

PM is an *integrated* process that links individual employees and their teams to business objectives. It is *integrative* because an appropriately designed and implemented PM system represents a tool that organisations can use to align people both to the business plan and with each other, in a set of mutually reinforcing interventions, thereby adopting a strategic approach to the management and development of people. Having examined the managerial and strategic context of PM, it is now necessary to look at how PM itself works.

pause for thought

To what extent can a system of PM integrate the objectives of the individual and the organisation?

Why did you reach this conclusion?

The practicalities of performance management

The PM cycle

PM should be tailored to the needs of the organisation and operated flexibly (Armstrong and Baron, 1998). However, it is possible to identify a number of processes that form the basis of any PM system. Conventionally, PM is portrayed as a three-stage cycle involving performance planning, monitoring and review (Armstrong and Baron, 2005). See Figure 8.2.

This model is limited by its association of PM very closely with appraisal. Nevertheless, it is of value as it describes the three key phases of PM, thereby providing a useful basis for designing an appropriate system.

Performance planning

A planning meeting is often the first stage of a PM cycle. Objectives are usually set (or agreed) for the next 12 months, but these may be broken down into (often quarterly) targets or 'milestones' that can be reviewed and amended as circumstances change. In practice, the performance planning discussion will often take place at the same time as the performance review meeting, taking account of any development needs that have arisen over the past year.

The performance plan, negotiated by the employee and their line manager, performs a number of functions:

THE PRACTICALITIES OF PERFORMANCE MANAGEMENT   143

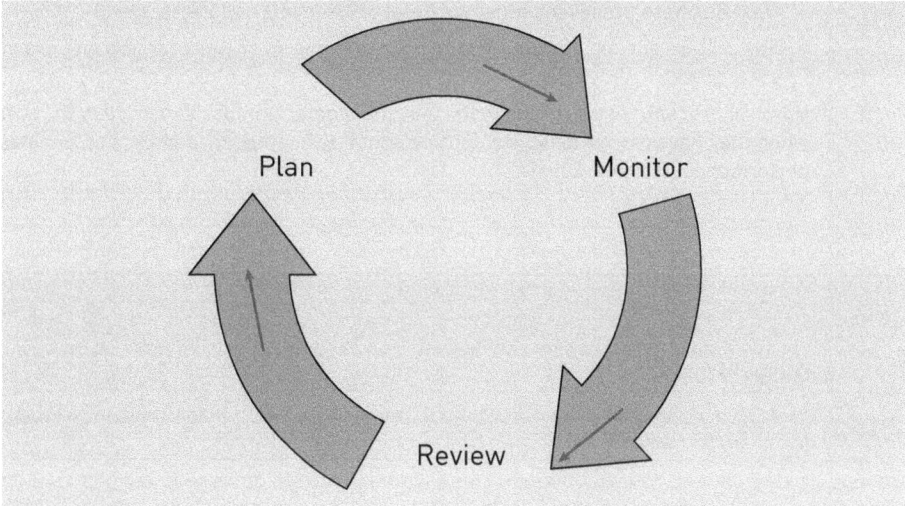

Figure 8.2 The PM cycle

♦ It represents a framework for future discussions about performance;

♦ It clarifies roles;

♦ It forms a basis for assessing progress in the future.

The essential requirement of the plan is the establishment of performance objectives.

Setting performance objectives

Employees may be given project or key task objectives. These should be designed to add value to the business and should not be merely a restatement of the individual's job description. It is important to align individual objectives with corporate strategy so that PM has an impact on business performance. It is conventional to refer to a cascading process, where corporate objectives are translated into functional objectives, team goals and, finally, into individual objectives. The aim is to establish a 'clear line of sight' between the individual's performance and the success of the organisation as a whole, although the further down the organisational structure, the more difficult it is to establish this link. Some organisations use 'balanced scorecards' in an attempt to create this clear line of sight.

First developed by Kaplan and Norton (1992), **balanced scorecards** are based on the argument that no single measure (e.g. short-term financial gains) provides a good indication of business success. Instead, a balanced selection of objective measures should be used based on the following questions:

♦ How should we appear to our shareholders? (the financial perspective)

♦ How should we appear to our customers? (the customer perspective)

◆ What business processes must we excel at? (the internal perspective)

◆ How will we sustain our ability to change and improve? (the learning and growth perspective)

However, recent research suggests that managers can lose their focus on costs when they have more measures to think about, with a negative impact on business performance (Pickard, 2006).

exercise

◆ Think about an organisation you know well. How (and why) could a balanced scorecard help the HR function?

◆ How do you think a balanced scorecard could help the management of Warbings improve performance?

Organisations usually seek to limit the number of performance objectives set for any individual, encouraging a sharper focus on a number of key goals that reflect business aims. The objectives themselves are usually formulated in line with the well-known 'SMART' model:

Specific – establishing clear expectations for the employee, possibly with the help of *key performance indicators* (KPIs) that help the individual establish when the objective has been met.

Measurable – measurable targets allow line managers to differentiate between levels of performance.

Achievable – clearly, setting daunting targets will result in demotivated employees. However, by the same token, objectives should be challenging ('stretch objectives'), placing the emphasis firmly on continuous improvement.

Relevant – employees' objectives should be relevant to their role and to the needs of the company. This implies the need to prioritise objectives by giving each respective target a weighting.

Timebound – setting a completion deadline for each objective allows for monitoring of progress and performance.

Performance planning as communication

Creating a clear line of sight between business goals and individuals' performance objectives is a communication process which, through the sharing of information about company strategy and decisions, makes employees feel trusted and involved and gives them a better understanding of their role (Fletcher, 2004). However, the 'cascading' principle implies top-down, one-way communication that can be viewed as indoctrinating and controlling (Marchington and Wilkinson, 2002). Communication is a two-way process with feedback loops that encourage involvement and reflection at lower levels to be fed back to senior management (Fletcher, 2004). However, research suggests that relatively few organisations have built-in provisions for upward feedback in their performance planning processes (CIPD, 2005).

THE PRACTICALITIES OF PERFORMANCE MANAGEMENT 145

To what extent do you think that feedback on performance can be damaging? Your answer should take into consideration organisational and individual aspects.	**pause for thought**

Competency frameworks

It has been suggested that, 'competencies are now taking a key role in describing the behaviours employees should demonstrate in achieving their goals' (IDS, 2005). By focusing on behavioural goals or competencies (the 'how') as well as on performance objectives (the 'what'), managers can get a more rounded view of an individual's performance. This realisation has lead many organisations to develop competency frameworks that help to align individual behaviour with the organisation's values and business strategy.

Developing management competencies is often the first stage of constructing a suitable framework to cover the whole organisation (IDS, 2001). Competencies are essentially explicit statements of the behaviours required of employees, at different levels and in various roles, to achieve business objectives. As well as promoting vertical integration, once the framework is in place it also provides a vehicle for horizontal integration (Miller et al., 2001). Specifically, a competency framework can support an organisation's HR strategy in the following ways:

♦ As a basis for recruitment and selection (e.g. competency-based interviewing);

♦ In performance planning and review;

♦ As a benchmark against which staff can be developed;

♦ As a basis for rewarding performance (competency-based and contribution pay).

In performance planning, individuals may focus on a specific number of competencies over the annual planning period, but the annual review is likely to take account of the employee's competency with reference to the whole framework (IDS, 2005).

Competency frameworks should reflect and support company values. Competency development fosters appropriate behaviours, which in turn reinforce organisational values and promote the creation of high performance cultures. The introduction of a competency framework into performance management is likely to be part of a deliberate strategy to bring about cultural change. As ever when implementing organisational change, employee involvement is important to ensure buy-in and staff will typically participate in developing competencies through focus groups and situational interviews, often (expensively) facilitated by consultants (Maloney, 2000). Another advantage of staff involvement is that the language in which competencies are couched is comprehensible to employees.

This leads us to the drawbacks of a competency-based approach to performance management. Woodall and Winstanley (1998) criticise competency frameworks on the following grounds:

♦ Competencies are static in that they describe the behaviours required by an organisation at a particular point in time and are not responsive to changing business conditions. Competency frameworks therefore require constant maintenance and regular updating to ensure that they evolve to keep up with new demands placed on them.

◆ Competency frameworks are bureaucratic and mechanistic. They can become unwieldy, and there have been cases of organisations developing hundreds of competencies (Miller et al., 2001). Thus a competency framework must be focused, providing just enough detail to ensure that competencies are meaningful and fit for purpose.

◆ Competencies stifle innovation and flexibility. Prescribing behaviours through a competency framework means that people are less likely to approach their roles creatively and develop original solutions to problems.

exercise Produce two slides showing the advantages and disadvantages of competency frameworks.

Development plans

The need for the organisation to support employees' own aspirations as well as its expectations of them has highlighted development as one of the key outcomes of PM. Thus one of the benefits of a PM system is seen to be the improved motivation and retention of staff. Personal development plans often form a vehicle for meeting employees' development needs and aspirations.

Development plans and goals are designed to meet individual growth and improvement, as well as meet the performance needs of the job. They encompass new skills needed to meet performance objectives, skills deficits highlighted in the last performance review and development to meet longer-term career aspirations.

Development goals need to be measurable, taking into account how skills and competencies will be acquired and applied in the workplace. Development planning itself often happens at the same time as objective setting and plans are usually included in the same performance agreement (IDS, 2005). It also reinforces the organisation's commitment to supporting employee development, but it should be noted that development can be achieved in ways other than through training.

Monitoring performance: supporting progress

We now turn to the second stage in the PM cycle – the monitoring of performance. The main implication of this is that managers should monitor employees' progress and support them throughout the year. Increasingly, managers are expected to hold either formal interim reviews, where objectives can be amended, or regular one-to-one meetings with employees, but some organisations take this a step further by establishing a coaching culture (Porter et al., 2006).

pause for thought Can you think of any occasions when individuals might resent their performance being monitored?

Do you think such feelings of resentment would have an impact on their subsequent performance?

Why did you reach this conclusion?

Developing managers as coaches

One of the main functions of these monitoring processes is to provide feedback to people to help them keep on target with regard to their performance plan. One way of achieving this is by line managers taking on the role of coach (Parsloe, 1999; IDS, 2005). Establishing such a 'high performance culture' requires managers to stretch high-potential staff, manage underperformers and motivate 'steady' workers.

For many organisations, creating a coaching culture requires both significant investment in developing managers as coaches and systems that provide incentives for them to focus on the development of employees. Organisations could include the responsibility for employee development in the managers' competency framework and performance objectives to reinforce this developmental focus.

Managing underperformance

window into practice

With staff survey results showing that employees rated their managers' ability to deal with underperformance as 'very poor', a television company decided it was time to tackle the problem. Managers from the company reported that dealing with poor or inadequate performance was one of their most difficult tasks. They particularly disliked dealing with issues that were personal to the employee, or tackling employees who had not received any feedback previously.

A number of interventions were put in place. The management team agreed the standard and level of performance that they were expecting, and clarified this to staff. Team away-days enabled staff to participate in setting team objectives in line with organisational goals, and to review codes of behaviour and ground rules. A revised performance management process made a particular feature of regular one-to-one feedback sessions on an ongoing basis, with clear objectives agreed at each session and followed up subsequently. Rather than relying on an annual appraisal, these regular meetings encouraged better relationships between managers and staff and allowed issues to be raised and resolved before they escalated into more serious performance problems. Focused goals that were reviewed each session took the place of yearly objectives that tended to be overlooked in the day to day work.

By using role plays with actors, managers and staff were trained in how to use these sessions in the most effective way, covering issues of: feedback; dealing with conflict; listening; and questioning skills. Procedures for dealing with discipline and lack of capability were also reviewed.

Overall, performance has improved, with employees reporting greater clarity about their roles and better communications with their managers.

pause for thought

In a recent survey of managers, nearly half of respondents stated that they would prefer to go to the dentist for root canal treatment than appraise their staff.

Why do you think this is?

Financial and Human Resource Management in Organisations, Second Edition

Performance appraisal

The purpose of performance appraisal

Performance appraisal – or performance review as it is increasingly being called (IRS, 2001) – is at the centre of the PM process. Despite attracting criticism, mainly due to the ineffective way in which it is often carried out, performance appraisal is used as a key element of PM by over 80 per cent of employers (IRS, 2001; Industrial Society, 2001; CIPD, 2005).

While performance appraisal comes in various different forms, it will typically involve a formal review of an employee's work over a set period of time – normally a year. Appraisals tend to have two parts – the first is looking back over the past year to review performance and objectives; and the second part is looking forward to set objectives and targets for the next year and to identify learning and development needs. It provides the opportunity for the employee and manager to sit down and have a dialogue about performance and development at least on a yearly basis.

Key aims for performance appraisal would include the following:

♦ *Improving performance* – in the absence of clear feedback, it is difficult for people to improve, at least in the way the organisation requires. Performance appraisal provides an opportunity for managers to reinforce good performance by praise and recognition. Identifying gaps in performance and providing appropriate learning opportunities also helps to improve performance. Equally important is the clarification of goals, roles and standards.

♦ *Motivating staff* – recognition, knowledge of results, feedback and agreeing SMART goals are all factors that contribute to improving motivation (Locke and Latham, 1990).

♦ *Allocating rewards* – the assessment of performance made in the appraisal interview can form the basis for decisions about allocations of pay and incentives.

♦ *Succession planning and career progression* – identifying those with potential and ensuring that they have the right development opportunities.

♦ *Improving communication between manager and managed* – providing a two-way channel of communication.

pause for thought

What is the main purpose of performance appraisal?

Since it is the subject of so much criticism, why is it commonly used?

While these are all laudable aims, many authors would argue that appraisal often has opposite effects. Taylor (2005) postulates that it can be concluded from the research that performance appraisal is less a panacea and more of a curse. Managers often find the process challenging, particularly when giving critical feedback, and are often expected to do this with little training.

Different approaches to performance appraisal

These can be categorised into two main types – those focused on **output** and those focused on **behaviour**.

Output-based assessment

Output-based assessment has its roots in the Management by Objectives movement originating in the 1950s. Performance is measured in terms of quantifiable results, either in terms of productivity or quality measures or, most commonly on the achievement of a series of specific objectives. With some jobs, such as salespeople, it is relatively easy to identify clear measures of performance that are intrinsic to the achievement of the role, but for others those aspects of the job which are most easily measured are often not the most significant. If this is the case, then employees can be encouraged to focus on the measurable, but less important aspects of their roles. What gets measured is often what gets done.

In a recent CIPD survey, 62 per cent of respondents used objective setting as part of their appraisal process (CIPD, 2005). This involves the appraisee and appraiser jointly agreeing objectives that are specific and measurable, and then reviewing the achievement of these objectives at the next appraisal session. Setting targets in this way not only encourages participation in the process but is a powerful way to increase motivation (Locke and Latham, 1990). The main criticisms of objective-based assessment revolve around the perceived difficulty of setting meaningful objectives for particular jobs; the relevance of these to the totality of the role; and the difficulty of using this approach to compare individuals one with another.

Behavioural assessments

It could be argued that the way a person fulfils their job role is as important, as the results that they achieve. An assessment of employee behaviour is therefore seen by many as an important aspect of an appraisal process. This will involve identifying the criteria that are important for the effective performance of the job, then rating the individual against those criteria. An appraiser would use evidence from direct observation of the employee, or by reports from others, to make a judgement about the appraisee's performance, and rate him or her accordingly.

A variety of different rating schemes are used but despite efforts to improve objectivity, behavioural assessment sometimes remains less objective than the output-based approaches. See the box below.

Behavioural and numerical rating scales

Numerical – individuals are rated on a number of different criteria and given a score on a scale from best to worst. Typical discussions are around whether to have odd or even scales, e.g. 1–5 or 1–4.

Intervals with **descriptions** – as above, but the scales are given verbal descriptions, e.g. outstanding, very good, good, fair, unsatisfactory, too early to judge.

As above, but directly related to **job requirements**, e.g. consistently exceeds requirements, occasionally exceeds requirements, meets requirements, fails to meet requirements.

> **Behaviourally based** scales – in this case, the key dimensions of the job are broken down into aspects of behaviour that relate to effective performance. Each of these is then rated, often using a numerical scale, for example:
>
> **Managing performance**
>
> 1. Agrees objectives and standards with teams
> Regularly 1 2 3 4 5 Rarely
> 2. Uses coaching skills and tools to improve performance
> Regularly 1 2 3 4 5 Rarely

There are advantages and disadvantages to both output and behaviour approaches. Because of this, organisations are increasingly moving towards a combination approach, involving the results-based approach of objectives with the development-based approach of the use of competencies (IRS, 2001; Fletcher, 2004). This is more likely to succeed in ensuring that performance expectations are based on a more rounded picture of the role.

Self-appraisal

An increasingly common approach to assessment involves a combination of downward-appraisal (manager-led) and self-appraisal (IRS, 2001; CIPD, 2005). Self-appraisal allows the appraisee to comment on their own achievements and contribute to their performance plan for the next period. This two-way process encourages participation and commitment, and allows the appraisee to take greater ownership of the process.

Multi-source appraisal: 360°

The use of multi-source feedback is growing, partly as a response to flatter organisational structures, and also in an attempt to introduce more consistency and breadth into the process. Evidence from a number of sources is more likely to provide a balanced picture of an individual's strengths and development needs. Multi-source feedback can range from simply asking peers or other managers to make comments, with examples, on an individual's performance, to the more sophisticated 360° feedback systems. These have grown in popularity, particularly for managerial staff, and look to continue to do so (Fletcher, 2004).

Common problems

Making a judgement about another person's performance, and giving them that feedback honestly is something that most people find challenging; they will often take steps to avoid, or to dilute, any critical feedback. Overcoming this is a critical challenge. Other common problems that occur with appraisals include:

♦ Lack of regular feedback – instead of tackling difficult issues at the right time, feedback is stored and given in one piece at the appraisal time;

- Collecting comprehensive evidence about performance – appraisers do not always work with the staff they are appraising, making it sometimes difficult to collect evidence about performance;

- Lack of follow-up;

- Time pressures;

- It is often viewed as a tedious routine;

- Filling out the forms and dealing with the paperwork becomes more important than the motivational aspects of the process;

- Focus on the negative – a large proportion of time in the appraisal spent talking about the things that have gone wrong rather than accentuating the positive aspects of performance;

- Inadequately trained appraisers;

- It can be complex to administer.

360° skills surveys

window into practice

The popularity of 360° or multi-input feedback has increased as organisations seek ways of creating more open environments, with a greater emphasis on continuous performance improvement. This process provides a snapshot of an individual's current impact and an assessment of their performance based on the perceptions of the members of their role set. It is particularly useful for development purposes.

QAS is a thriving and dynamic organisation, providing a range of address management and data accuracy solutions to organisations worldwide. Voted the most fun company to work for in the *Sunday Times* Best Company Awards of 2001, the challenge was to improve managerial proficiency – without losing the fun.

QAS strongly believes in growing its own talent. The vast majority of QAS managers joined as graduates and have grown and developed along with the company, many of them on a fast and steep career trajectory. Early in 2001, the company realised that, with international expansion plans in full swing, the depth of managerial capacity might prove to be a limiting factor on growth.

Making extensive use of 360° surveys and feedback, the bespoke management development programme that was implemented over the next two years was aimed at producing measurable improvements in managerial capability.

Key managerial competencies appropriate for QAS were defined by a team of managers and ratified by the board. A 360° management skills survey questionnaire based on these competencies was developed. The questionnaire had 47 questions, with a 1–5 rating scale, and three free-form questions at the end. A pilot group of 30 managers each selected ten people to complete the questionnaires using a combination of their managers', their peers' and their direct reports' feedback. They also completed a questionnaire themselves. Each manager had a review session, where individual development plans were agreed, based on the results of the survey. Common themes arising from the aggregated feedback were used to design six training modules, which were delivered over a period of a year. In addition, managers worked on their individual plans in a series of action learning sets.

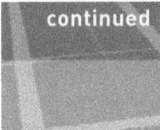
continued

Three months after the completion of the formal part of the programme, the managers took part in a repeat 360° survey to evaluate any change in the perception of their competency. Aggregated scores showed an improvement in 42 out of the 47 questions, while over two-thirds of the managers showed significant improvements – particularly in the areas they had highlighted in their development plans. Generally, participants reported that the 360° feedback was the most valuable part of the programme: not only was it revealing to see themselves as others saw them, but it enabled clear and focused development objectives to be set, which could be followed up during the rest of the programme.

Issues in performance management

Success factors in performance management processes

What makes the difference between a system that is regarded by all as a waste of time and one which delivers key benefits to the business and to individuals?

The 2004 survey on PM by the CIPD revealed a strong degree of consensus among respondents about the key issues associated with a successful system. Top of the list was management buy-in: it is seen as essential that line managers own the system and are well trained in how to use it. Most respondents felt that PM is only successful if it forms a 'continuous and integrated part of the line manager/employee relationship' (Armstrong and Baron, 2005).

Other important elements are:

♦ Alignment with business goals and objectives;

♦ Integration of the goals of the organisation with those of individuals;

♦ Objectivity and the importance of providing quantifiable measures of performance;

♦ Effective communication of the aims of the process;

♦ Regular evaluation of its effectiveness;

♦ A process that is simple and easy to use increases the likelihood of success;

♦ Effective follow-up with ongoing feedback;

♦ An explicit link to a personal development plan.

Critics of PM point to lack of consistency as a problem area (Grint, 1993) and organisations are increasingly using different techniques to attempt to overcome this. These include:

♦ Increased emphasis on line manager training and ongoing coaching;

♦ The provision of more objective feedback on performance;

♦ More input into the appraisal process by staff, including a greater emphasis on self-assessment;

♦ Scrutiny of managers' assessments by their peers;

♦ Increased use of multi-source feedback.

Cultural and structural fit

Organisations differ in structure and culture and, to be successful, PM systems need to reflect this. A large bureaucratic organisation, where consistency and formal rules are important, will probably need a more formal system. A more organic, project-orientated, organisation in a fast-moving environment will need to have a system that allows for change and flexibility.

Some commentators argue that the traditional hierarchical structure of management is no longer a feature of many organisations (Kettley, 1995). Instead, flexible teams and cross-functional projects are a reality of organisational life. With increasing de-layering, it is not always clear who is directly responsible for an individual's appraisal. The wider span of managerial control often gives them an unrealistic number of employees to appraise. Solutions to this include appointing 'performance managers' or 'team leaders' to undertake appraisal and ongoing feedback for staff and to act as a support for developmental purposes. Peer appraisal may also be seen as a solution.

Staff expectations and values will have implications for the type of PM system chosen and for the way it is operated. For example, a sales company where output is not only crucial but easily measured will be comfortable with a system that is based on quantifiable measures. According to Fletcher (2004), professional groups which are characterised by a high degree of independence, and where some elements of the work are less easy to quantify in any meaningful way, will require a more developmental, less hierarchical approach with a greater emphasis on quality.

pause for thought

How do you feel about being assessed by your tutor?

Do you feel the same way about being peer assessed?

Account for the differences, if any, in your feelings between the two methods of assessment.

The aims of PM fall into two main categories – assessing the past and improving the future. This leads us to a conflict at the heart of PM systems. Termed the evaluation agenda or the development agenda, writers such as Taylor (2005) argue that it is not possible to successfully fulfil both aims within the same process. The main reasons for this lie in employees' attitudes towards appraisal. If employees perceive the process to be evaluative, they are less inclined to be open about their performance gaps and development needs, feeling that this will count against them in the assessment process. The mutual trust that is necessary for an honest appraisal of strengths and weaknesses will be further undermined when an individual perceives that this will be used to inform decisions about rewards or redundancy. Fletcher (2004) argues that it is mainly top management who want the appraisal to be primarily assessment driven, while appraisers and appraisees want it to be development led. He suggests that the process is more likely to be successful if it is defined as development led, as this will be more acceptable to both appraisers and appraisees and will provide a strategy for improving performance. He also challenges the efficacy of appraisal as a vehicle for comparative assessments of individuals. In the CIPD survey (2005),

71 per cent of the sample agreed that the focus of performance appraisal should be developmental.

Many organisations overcome any difficulty by clearly distinguishing between these two aims, and by having separate meetings at different times, one to focus on development and one for the purpose of assessing the individual in order to allocate rewards. Fletcher (2004) proposes that the most effective method combines a results-orientated appraisal with a competency-based appraisal, allowing measurement of targets and goals to be combined with a focus on personal development.

Contingent pay

It is by no means essential for a PM system to include performance-related pay – indeed in the CIPD survey, only 42 per cent of all respondents had contingent pay, dropping to 29 per cent for the public sector. The IRS survey on PM (2001) reported a third consecutive yearly fall in the use of merit pay systems.

exercise   What are the arguments for and against using appraisal to link pay to performance?

Contingent pay is seen as desirable by organisations because it is fair and equitable to reward people differentially for their different contributions; it raises the importance of performance and by linking this to contribution, it motivates people to perform better. Yet according to the IRS Management Review (2001: 37), 'the slowdown in the take up of individual merit schemes has coincided with a mounting body of research that suggests performance pay does not actually deliver what its advocates claim.' Armstrong and Baron (2005: 106) question the relationship between contingent pay and motivation, quoting studies that show a negative rather than a positive impact.

However, if people are to be paid differentially in accordance with their contribution to the organisation, then an *accurate* and *fair* assessment of that contribution needs to be made. It is really important for organisations to have a robust performance management system in place before attempting to introduce any kind of contribution-based pay scheme. Employee satisfaction with the reward system depends on their estimate of the fairness of the process, and the accuracy of the measurement of their contribution, particularly in comparison to others. Often managers feel they are operating in a transparent and unbiased way, while employees feel the reverse.

While the 1980s and 1990s were dominated by the rise of performance-related pay schemes, in many organisations these are now being revised and converted into contribution pay schemes. Performance-related pay typically provides increases in the form of basic pay or a cash bonus usually linked to the achievement of agreed objectives. Contribution pay, on the other hand, includes an assessment of competency (inputs) as well as an assessment of performance (outputs), thus giving a more holistic picture. This gives a more balanced approach to pay and performance management, linking pay, career development and performance improvement to rewarding staff for their contribution to personal and business objectives.

Summary

In this chapter, we have explored the strategic role of PM systems in aligning both the efforts of teams and individuals with business objectives and the key HR interventions of reward, development and appraisal with each other. Our examination of the PM cycle has shown that appraisal is one vital but problematic element in a PM system and that to be effective, appraisal systems must be adapted to meet the structural and cultural needs of the organisation. Different approaches to appraisal are discussed in some detail, focusing on the increasing use of multi-source appraisal. The tension in appraisal between assessment and development was also highlighted, as were the issues associated with using appraisal as a vehicle for linking pay to performance. Finally, we considered the value of appraisal training for managers and their staff.

exercise

At the moment, Warbings does not have a PM system.

1. Make a case for the introduction of a performance management system into Warbings.

2. Which factors would you need to take into account when developing the system?

3. Which components would you include in the PM system?

W

Review Questions

You may wish to attempt the following as practice examination style questions.

8.1 How can a PM system help an organisation achieve both vertical and horizontal integration of people management and development?

8.2 What is the role of competencies in PM?

8.3 How can organisations ensure that line managers are more effective in managing the performance of their staff?

8.4 What are the pros and cons of having a direct link between PM process and pay?

8.5 What are the key success factors for PM?

8.6 What is the role of self-appraisal in PM?

References

Armstrong, M. and Baron, A. (1998). *Performance Management: The New Realities*, London: IPD.

Armstrong, M. and Baron, A. (2005). *Managing Performance: Performance Management in Action*, London: IPD.

CIPD (2005). Survey report, *Performance Management*, September.

Fletcher, C. (2004). *Appraisal and Feedback: Making Performance Review Work*, 3rd edition, London: CIPD.

Fombrun, C.J., Tichy, N.M. and Devanna, M.A. (1984). *Strategic Human Resource Management*, New York: Wiley.

Grint, K. (1993). What's wrong with performance appraisal? A critique and a suggestion, *Human Resource Management Journal*, Spring, pp. 61–77.

Guest, D., Michie, J., Sheehan, M. et al. (2000). *Effective People Management: Initial Findings of the Future of Work Study*, London: CIPD.

Holbeche, L. (2001). *Aligning Human Resources and Business Strategy*, London: Butterworth-Heinemann.

Incomes Data Services HR Study 706 (2001). *Competency Frameworks*.

Incomes Data Services HR Study 796 (2005). *Performance Management*.

Industrial Relations Services (2001). Performance management revisited, *IRS Management Review*, 20 January.

Industrial Society (2001). Managing performance, *Managing Best Practice 86*, at: www.theworkfoundation.com.

Kaplan, R. and Norton, D. (1992). The Balanced Scorecard – measures that drive performance, *Harvard Business Review*, January–February, pp. 197–221.

Kast, F.S. and Rosenweig, J.E. (1985). *Organisation and Management: A Systems Approach*, 4th edition, New York: McGraw-Hill.

Kettley, P. (1995). Is Flatter Better? Delayering the Management Hierarchy, Institute of Employment Studies, IES Report No. 290.

Locke, E.A. and Latham, G.P. (1990). *A Theory of Gaol Setting and Task Performance*, Englewood Cliffs, NJ: Prentice Hall.

Maloney, K. (2000). History repeating, *People Management*, July, pp. 23–25.

Marchington, M. and Wilkinson, A. (2002). *People Management and Development*, 2nd edition, London: CIPD.

Miller, L., Rankin, N. and Neathey, F. (2001). *Competency Frameworks in UK Organisations: Key Issues in Employers' Use of Competencies*, London: CIPD.

Mullins, L.J. (2002). *Management and Organisational Behaviour*, 6th edition, London: Prentice Hall.

Parsloe, E. (1999). *The Manager as Coach and Mentor*, London: CIPD.

Pickard, J. (2006). Scorecard system might not be so balanced, says research, *People Management*, April, p. 5.

Porter, K., Smith, P. and Fagg, R. (2006). *Leadership and Management for HR Professionals*, London: Butterworth-Heinemann.

Taylor, S. (2005). *People Resourcing*, 3rd edition, London: CIPD.

Woodall, J. and Winstanley, D. (1998). *Management Development: Strategy and Practice*, Chapters 4 and 5, Oxford: Blackwell.

Further Reading

Industrial Relations Services (2003). Performance management: policy and practice, *IRS Employment Review 781*, August.

Kearns, P. (2000). *Measuring and Managing Employee Performance*, Marlow: FT/Prentice Hall.

Purcell, J. et al. (2003). *Understanding the People and Performance Link: Unlocking the Black Box*, research report, London: CIPD.

Useful Websites

www.cipd.co.uk – the official website of the Chartered Institute of Personnel and Development – the lead body for HR professionals

www.dti.gov.uk – links to Department of Trade and Industry information on business performance and productivity

www.incomesdata.co.uk – Income Data Services studies on performance management and competency

www.irseclipse.co.uk – access to Industrial Relations Services reviews on HRM issues, including PM

www.teachernet.gov.uk – resources for teaching in PM and appraisal

www.theworkfoundation.com – access to studies on individual and business performance, including the Industrial Society past papers

PART 4

Reward

Part contents

CHAPTER 9

Through a Glass Darkly: problems and issues in reward

By Angela Wright

Chapter outline

The aim of this chapter is to explore some current developments in reward management and to discuss some key issues and questions around the effectiveness of reward systems. It discusses aspects of reward strategy, in particular the relationship between employee commitment and reward and the interrelationship between motivation and reward. It considers some aspects of market and internal equity issues and examines current developments in pay structures and pay systems and employee-centred reward, especially flexible benefits.

Learning outcomes

By the end of this chapter, you should be able to:

◆ Discuss reward strategy concepts, the relevance of motivation theory and aspects of employee commitment;

◆ Identify salary market issues;

◆ Explain some of the developments in employee-centred reward and in pay structures.

Introduction

Pay and benefits form one of the largest items of expenditure in any organisation and yet in many organisations there is a lack of evidence as to whether the particular pay and benefits practices are adding value or merely adding to costs. There is also often a lack of openness and transparency and poor levels of understanding of the way pay is managed. At the academic level, there is less specific research about the range of activities now termed 'reward management' than there is for some other aspects of people management. As Milsome (2005) summarises from the Reward Management Symposium 2005, reward practices are rarely based on evidence as to what produces good organisational outcomes and what does not. It is just as unusual for practices to be evaluated for their effectiveness.

Some strategic aspects of reward

Reward is underpinned by a mix of theoretical perspectives, drawn from different academic disciplines, principally economics, psychology and industrial relations, as well as the comparatively new perspectives drawn from human resource management. However when considering the strategic place of reward and its impact, the literature and theories of business strategy are of key importance. Within the strategy literature, reward features rather lightly and this has led to the growth in the US of quantitative studies looking for associations between high performance in organisations and specific human resource management (HRM) practices.

Reward strategy may be characterised as comprising the future imperatives of the organisation's approach to pay and benefits. The CIPD (2006), drawing on earlier work, identifies the key characteristics of a written formal statement of strategic intent for reward which:

- Defines broad objectives for reward;

- Is a framework for use by managers in making reward decisions;

- Is long term;

- Has clearly planned goals based on business objectives;

- Is flexible and able to be adapted when business circumstances change.

Lawler (1995) advocated that reward approaches should be tailored to fit the strategic business 'compass' of the specific organisation as a way of promoting change and enhancing performance. However, the CIPD (2006) reveals that only a minority of organisations has a formal reward strategy. Why do so few employers not adopt such a strategic approach to reward? One possible explanation is that there is no business strategy to align to, or, if there is one, it is so weak that it is not worth aligning a reward strategy to, reflecting perhaps the realities and complexities of modern organisations. However, reward could be treated in some organisations as part and parcel of human resource (HR) strategy.

Regardless of what organisations formally commit to writing, the idea that reward might have potential to positively influence organisational performance is compelling. One of the key problems is that the interrelationships between reward and other HR practices are difficult for researchers to determine. Gerhart (2000) concludes from his analysis of various studies assessing the influence of reward on corporate performance that there is evidence of relationships between organisational performance and pay strategy, but it is difficult to determine their precise nature. While key outcomes such as job satisfaction, recruitment/retention and employee performance seem to be associated with reward, the numerous US studies do not permit reward – as an influence on organisational performance – to be isolated from other causes.

pause for thought   Why do you think Gerhart concluded that it was difficult to determine the precise nature of the relationship between the way an organisation performs and its pay strategy? Do you think this relationship is important? Why did you reach this conclusion?

Theoretical perspectives

Best fit or contingency theory

This view suggests there are no universally good reward practices – what is appropriate in any one organisation is what works for that organisation. The contingency view suggests that HR practices need to achieve a 'best fit' by taking into account the circumstances and goals of the company. But, as Boxall and Purcell (2000) argue, there are many problems with this type of approach when we begin looking at practical situations, and the theory could be criticised as being too simplistic. Certain bad practices can be identified, which would add little to any organisation.

Best practice

The best practice school of thought proposes that certain HR practices are related to organisational success, regardless of the organisation's business context or strategy. But this approach has been criticised by Boxall and Purcell (2000) for providing uplifting, simple messages, while lacking credibility. What is 'best' in one set of circumstances will often not work in another, and it stretches credibility to assume that what works best for a multinational oil company can be applied to the local corner shop.

To what extent can reward practices be integrated into and with other HR practices in an organisation known to you?	**pause for thought** 

Pfeffer (1998) proposes that there are 'golden rules' in reward policy and practice, which hold good across all organisations. These essential rules in crafting a reward strategy are:

◆ Include 'large dose' collective reward;

◆ Accept that pay is not a substitute for a 'high trust' environment, 'fun' and 'meaningful work';

◆ Openness and transparency are vital, with a positive message about equity;

◆ Employers should use means other than pay to signal company values and to focus behaviour;

◆ Employers should use pay as only one element in building employee commitment.

Huselid (1995) and Macduffie (1995) suggest there are 'bundles' of HR practices that help to drive organisational performance, but the elements in the bundles may vary according to business sector. There is little evidence of particular pay or reward practices consistently appearing in these 'bundles', but in all the US studies performance-related pay tends to feature. The rationale for the universal applicability of these practices is that they lead to superior performance, since they draw upon the discretionary effort of individual employees. Marchington and Grugulis (2000) question the validity of such work.

In the search for the bundle of HR practices (including reward practices) that may or may not be associated with higher corporate performance, much of the earlier research has focused on policies and practices. Pfeffer (1998), among others, has indicated that 'shared compensation' schemes, for example long-term all-employee share schemes and gain-sharing schemes, are associated with higher productivity or performance. Few organisations opt for a gain-sharing arrangement (CIPD, 2005) under which employees themselves are fully involved in devising the (sometimes) modest bonus scheme, which rewards productivity improvements.

In order to achieve sustainable organisational improvements, Purcell's (2003) work identifies the importance of releasing the 'discretionary' efforts and voluntary co-operation of employees. The place of specific reward practices in supporting these developments is not clear. The role of front-line managers is seen as critical in translating all people management and development policies (including reward) into practice, and eliciting discretionary behaviour from individual employees. Hutchinson and Purcell (2003) further show that the crucial difference between low-performing and high-performing organisations comes from front-line leaders. CIPD's (2006) survey finds most of the respondents do not rate highly the reward decision-making or communication skills of their line managers, with only one-third of respondents saying they feel managers receive sufficient training in reward skills. Purcell and Hutchinson's later work (2007) shows that the day-to-day reward activities carried out by line managers are largely unregulated by their organisations, although such rewards, even though they may be at the symbolic rather than tangible level, are highly valued by employees.

Cox (2000) raises the idea of 'best process' as a central concept in which the emphasis is more on the quality of relationships between management and employees than with the actual reward practice applied. Essential elements of employee involvement and participation are seen as crucial, particularly in pay system development.

Also of relevance to reward is the newer research area of employee engagement, although this overlaps with more established areas of employee commitment and organisational citizenship behaviour. Robinson et al.'s (2004) study shows that the management of pay and benefits features in the spectrum of factors affecting employee engagement, but does not disentangle reward from the other aspects of HR practice and management.

West et al.'s (2005) study on rewarding customer service demonstrates a strong relationship between employee commitment and reward, and a relationship between employee satisfaction and commitment and reward.

Communication and transparency

Openness and a positive message about equity are vital to the effectiveness of managing pay. Writers, including Pfeffer (1998), support this view. The general principle of openness and transparency of pay policies and practices is also a key requirement under equal pay legislation (see Chapter 10), but few organisations would claim to have transparent pay systems. Apart from the legal rationale, there are other reasons for employers to think seriously about making pay transparency a much stronger focus of their policies:

- Pay delivers a strong message, quite separate from its purely monetary value. If time and expense have been applied to designing a reward system then employees must understand it if it is to influence their behaviour.

- Some studies have shown that employees misunderstand pay relationships. For instance they tend to overestimate the pay of lower level jobs and underestimate the pay of those in higher-level jobs. If pay differentials between one level of role responsibility and another are underestimated by employees, their motivational value is reduced.

- Employees whose organisations are open about pay tend to express greater satisfaction with their pay and the system used to determine it.

Salary market issues

Much has been made of the 'new pay' school of thought (Zingheim and Schuster, 2000), arguing that internal equity should no longer be a priority for employers and that 'market value' should instead predominate. Vocal critics of that controversial manifestation of internal equity in practice – job evaluation – suggest that notions about a job as a distinct concept to the individual job-holder is an outmoded concept in the context of a flexible, market-orientated approach to pay. Instead, new pay writers (Lawler, 1995) advocate a much stronger focus on competencies and skills as well as on salary market rates. One central problem in this is the 'pay market'. In classical terms the market does not operate unless people can move around between organisations freely. This may be too simplistic a view of the complexities of the modern labour market. Gomez-Mejia and Balkin (1992) observe that while the myth persists that the market wage can be accurately and scientifically measured, in fact there is a wide range of market pay rates available for each occupation.

This process of pay comparability takes into account earnings for similar level posts in comparable organisations or in the economy generally, in setting an appropriate level of pay, but this is not the same as the operation of a true market. What the 'right' pay level may be will depend on a number of factors, not least those people with whom employees themselves choose to compare themselves. Heneman and Judge (2000) conclude that there is insufficient evidence concerning the focus on particular 'referents' (i.e. who they choose to compare themselves with) to the exclusion of others.

For pay practitioners, the market and pay surveys are virtually synonymous. Surveys of course are useful, and as IDS (2005) shows there are increasing sources of pay data at the disposal of employers, mostly at a considerable cost. Salary surveys are of course subject to the same statistical quality criteria as other sample surveys. Some, it must be acknowledged, are of dubious quality. The checklist below lists some of the key questions that reward practitioners need to ask when assessing the potential value of any survey.

Checklist of pay data quality

How are data collected?

♦ *Recruitment salary surveys*. Are these simply surveys of people applying for jobs through a recruitment agency? If so, what evidence is there that the data are representative of people already in post – whose pay may be higher or lower than those active in the job market?

♦ *Sample surveys*. How is the sample derived? Is it structured, representative, opportunistic?

Sample sizes and job matching:

♦ Is sample size mentioned?

Check for company size in sample:

♦ How many small companies/large companies? Large companies tend to have higher pay than smaller ones so it is important to use a survey which has an appropriate and comparable set of organisations.

Job matching is vitally important; job titles alone give a poor degree of matching:

♦ What job matching techniques are used?

♦ If job evaluation is used, is the system used relevant for the organisation?

♦ If a basic ranking scheme is used for job matching, how relevant is this to the organisation?

Check participants/repeat participants:

♦ Some turnover in participants is inevitable but a sample that is completely different one year to the next can prompt questions about how useful the previous year's participants found the survey results in practice. (Some surveys are only available to those organisations that supply data.)

Table 9.1 is an extract from the government's *Annual Survey of Hours and Earnings*, a survey which has the advantage of a sample which is representative of the workforce, but which is perhaps less useful in providing useable data on executive pay levels.

Pay, motivation, reward and recognition

Few senior managers doubt that *money motivates*. From a theoretical point of view, however, the underpinning for such confidence is mooted. Academics' work on performance-related pay (PRP) has taken a largely sceptical stance, stressing both theoretical deficiencies and the preponderance of studies showing mediocre

Table 9.1 Extract from pay survey (annual pay – gross (£) for all employee jobsᵃ: UK, 2006)

Description	Code	Number of jobsᵇ (thousand)	Median	Annual percentage change	Mean	Annual percentage change	Percentiles									
							10	20	25	30	40	60	70	75	80	90
All employees		19,700	19,496	2.9	24,301	3.9	5,880	10,002	11,799	13,392	16,355	23,031	27,209	29,779	32,615	42,048
Managers and senior officials	1	3,083	33,423	3.7	46,057	6.1	15,406	21,000	23,211	25,250	29,444	38,400	45,323	49,837	55,188	77,635
Corporate managers	11	2,628	34,887	3.3	48,470	6.3	16,269	22,192	24,525	26,643	30,583	40,226	47,495	51,844	57,698	81,378
Managers and proprietors in agriculture and services	12	455	26,000	2.3	32,116	1.6	12,780	16,851	18,544	20,038	23,015	29,695	33,866	36,534	39,937	52,947
Professional occupations	2	2,689	31,631	2.8	34,303	2.5	13,169	20,311	23,044	25,124	28,741	34,500	38,032	40,079	43,000	53,392
Science and technology professionals	21	709	34,057	3.4	36,507	3.1	20,480	25,513	27,034	28,568	31,281	36,904	40,188	42,378	45,328	54,159
Health professionals	22	175	47,688	1.7	57,067	–0.6	x	23,608	27,466	33,044	40,251	57,021	73,163	81,132	91,919	111,668
Teaching and research professionals	23	1,257	29,731	0.8	28,421	1.4	8,378	16,785	19,583	22,015	26,333	32,320	34,807	36,499	38,250	43,359
Business and public service professionals	24	548	31,111	3.2	37,678	5.5	16,278	20,648	22,952	25,000	28,179	34,648	39,776	43,458	46,911	60,596
Associate professional and technical occupations	3	2,926	24,644	2.3	26,492	1.9	10,867	15,909	17,701	19,274	22,104	27,154	30,068	31,859	34,033	40,512
Science and technology associate professionals	31	443	24,057	1.6	25,401	1.8	12,706	16,821	18,185	19,518	21,790	26,580	29,366	30,764	32,687	38,796

Table 9.1 continued

Description	Code	Number of jobs (thousand)	Median	Annual percentage change	Mean	Annual percentage change	Percentiles									
							10	20	25	30	40	60	70	75	80	90
Health and social welfare associate professionals	32	977	21,661	4.1	21,199	4.3	8,538	13,065	14,758	16,298	19,173	23,792	26,120	27,488	29,043	32,611
Protective service occupations	33	351	31,003	2.0	31,352	1.9	19,856	24,521	25,812	26,695	28,488	33,568	36,875	38,375	40,017	43,724
Culture, media and sports occupations	34	220	22,757	−1.0	26,991	−2.5	4,805	12,086	14,359	16,568	19,608	25,687	29,414	32,536	35,731	46,013
Business and public service associate professionals	35	936	26,153	1.8	30,592	1.4	13,032	17,631	19,196	20,675	23,504	28,917	32,535	34,694	37,234	46,905
Administrative and secretarial occupations	4	2,704	15,219	3.9	15,867	3.7	6,453	9,109	10,464	11,700	13,672	16,915	18,889	20,043	21,472	25,452
Administrative occupations	41	2,174	15,485	3.7	16,095	3.8	6,715	9,591	10,995	12,139	14,018	17,196	19,126	20,250	21,630	25,388
Secretarial and related occupations	42	531	13,847	3.1	14,933	2.9	5,539	7,831	8,832	9,828	11,945	15,585	17,747	18,981	20,529	25,831
Skilled trades occupations	5	1,627	21,220	2.5	22,050	3.0	11,006	14,506	15,918	17,102	19,228	23,397	25,851	27,320	29,120	33,902
Skilled agricultural trades	51	102	15,944	4.3	15,802	4.9	7,926	11,982	12,497	13,358	14,579	17,006	18,290	19,008	19,979	x
Skilled metal and electrical trades	52	909	23,820	2.5	24,659	2.7	14,182	17,572	18,826	20,009	21,825	25,848	28,309	29,728	31,286	35,984
Skilled construction and building trades	53	311	21,204	3.6	22,221	5.0	12,866	15,960	16,991	18,073	19,652	23,000	25,290	26,450	28,062	32,317
Textiles, printing and other skilled trades	54	304	15,171	1.5	16,166	1.1	6,399	9,747	10,658	11,697	13,359	17,210	19,072	20,141	21,936	26,392

	Code															
Personal service occupations	6	1,558	10,992	3.2	11,667	3.2	3,993	6,230	7,041	7,841	9,433	12,716	14,431	15,362	16,424	19,656
Caring personal service occupations	61	1,253	10,590	2.9	11,122	3.1	3,949	6,210	6,977	7,717	9,176	12,239	13,876	14,811	15,743	18,442
Leisure and other personal service occupations	62	306	12,956	2.5	13,903	4.6	4,209	6,300	7,488	8,602	10,920	14,865	17,253	18,564	19,933	24,354
Sales and customer service occupations	7	1,463	8,535	1.0	9,956	0.3	3,329	4,679	5,223	5,775	6,985	10,325	12,113	13,211	14,417	17,919
Sales occupations	71	1,189	7,903	−0.3	9,422	−0.7	3,167	4,456	4,944	5,436	6,526	9,495	11,245	12,186	13,384	17,065
Customer service occupations	72	274	12,206	3.7	12,274	4.4	4,575	6,343	7,144	8,082	10,314	13,788	15,497	16,355	17,222	19,737
Process, plant and machine operatives	8	1,503	19,274	2.6	19,934	2.6	10,748	13,529	14,529	15,568	17,398	21,354	23,484	24,700	26,174	30,074
Process, plant and machine operatives	81	882	19,059	1.9	20,069	2.8	10,906	13,346	14,308	15,171	17,010	21,230	23,594	24,908	26,690	30,689
Transport and mobile machine drivers and operatives	82	621	19,528	3.4	19,742	2.3	10,252	13,882	15,013	16,015	17,874	21,484	23,347	24,431	25,654	29,008
Elementary occupations	9	2,146	11,129	3.9	11,870	3.4	2,548	4,277	5,201	6,284	8,701	13,369	15,684	16,980	18,507	22,188
Elementary trades, plant and storage related occupations	91	691	15,517	2.6	16,185	2.7	8,313	11,082	11,944	12,685	14,100	16,919	18,711	19,789	20,964	24,712
Elementary administration and service occupations	92	1,455	7,829	4.4	9,820	4.2	1,995	3,260	3,938	4,519	6,035	10,191	12,775	14,399	16,119	20,643
Not Classified		:														

Key	
	CV <= 5%
	CV > 5% and <= 10%
	CV > 10% and <= 20%
x = unreliable	
	CV > 20% or unavailable
.. = disclosive	
: = not applicable	
- = nil or negligible	

a Employees on adult rates who have been in the same job for more than a year.

b Figures for Number of Jobs are for indicative purposes only and should not be considered an accurate estimate of employee job counts.

KEY – The colour coding indicates the quality of each estimate: jobs, median, mean and percentiles but not the annual percentage change.

The quality of an estimate is measured by its coefficient of variation (CV), which is the ratio of the standard error of an estimate to the estimate.

Source: adapted from Office of National Statistics, *Annual Survey of Hours and Earnings* (2006).

effectiveness in practice. Indeed, Sisson and Storey (2000) claim that, should one ignore the substantial body of evidence casting doubt on the links between pay and performance, the case for PRP is very plausible. Reward practitioner studies (for example, CIPD (2006)) continue to show the value that managers place on the ability to reward performance, within their organisations (Armstrong and Barron, 2005). The CIPD's and other studies show that performance pay remains in use in many organisations.

Theoretical support for performance pay is equivocal. Research casts doubt about the motivational effectiveness of using pay linked to performance. There remains a polarisation of views – managers, HR specialists and consultants 'believe' in what they may regard as the self-evident and practitioner-led case for PRP but most academic writers are sceptical of the value of the practice. Even at its best, however, performance pay may gain only employee compliance, not their long-term commitment. For example, performance may be more effective in helping to build immediate sales of a specific new product than in longer-term new product development generally.

Drawing on Legge's (1995) work, Perkins and Sandringham (1998) argue that instrumental approaches such as performance pay are essentially negative and may not lead to the sort of attitudinal change that is necessary for a 'strategic' level of commitment and high performance. There is as yet little systematic evidence of the specific role reward can play in attitudinal change.

Assumptions that money is the main motivator relate back to Taylorist scientific management principles of the early twentieth century, in which workers were set narrow tasks and paid under a 'piecework' arrangement for work done or output achieved.

From the motivation perspective, pay and benefits form *extrinsic* motivation; that is, they are external to the individual. Such rewards can include praise and promotion prospects as well as monetary rewards.

Both process - and cognitive-motivation theories are relevant to a discussion of reward. Maslow's *hierarchy of needs* and Herzberg's *two-factor theory* models are well known (if somewhat discredited, Rynes et al., 2005), but the *process theories of motivation* have attracted more attention. These theories focus on the psychological processes involved in motivation, and on individuals' perceptions of their working environment. For example, *expectancy theory* – devised by Vroom (1964) and extended by Porter and Lawler (1968) – emphasises that pay and benefits may motivate people if there is a direct relationship between effort and reward, but individuals must be able to control the factors which influence the level of that reward. It leads reward practitioners to incorporate the principle of *line of sight* in the design of pay systems, where employees can see clearly that they can control the criteria which will lead to better rewards. See Figure 9.1.

Basic formula

$F = V \times I \times E$

- F is the Force of the individual's motivation
- V is the Valence or value the individual perceives the outcome to have
- I is Instrumentality – the extent to which performance is seen by individuals to be linked to rewards which they value

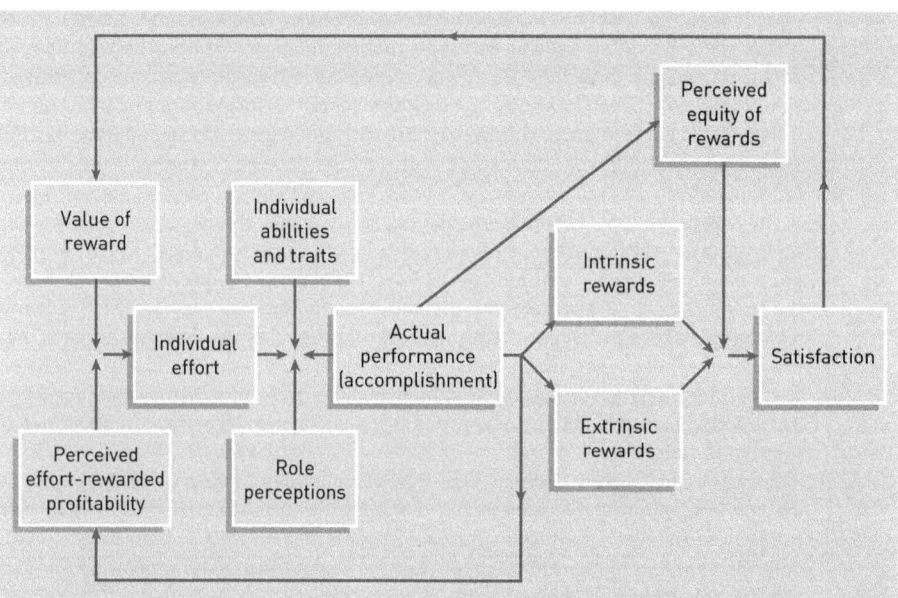

Figure 9.1 Expectancy theory
Source: Huczynski and Buchanan (2001)

The degree of motivational value of a reward is heavily constrained in the eyes of its potential recipient by a number of factors. Both *expectancy theory* and *equity theory* can help us to understand these situational factors. Under Adams's equity theory (1965), employees are seen to compare their reward with others in relation to their input and to determine whether they are equitably rewarded, relatively under-rewarded, or over-rewarded.

Organisational justice theories (Greenberg, 1987) are potentially of considerable relevance to the management of reward. Perceived fairness can be considered from three points of view:

- **Distributive justice** – the perceived fairness of the outcome.

- **Procedural justice** – fairness of how the rewards are allocated or decisions made.

- **Interactional justice** – relating to the nature of the interpersonal relationships.

Bowen et al. (1999) has shown the direct relevance of *fairness* in reward decisions to the quality of service provided by employees to the organisation's customers. On the other hand, the work of Folger and Konovsky (1989) show that although perceptions of *distributive* justice are associated with employee levels of pay satisfaction, it is *procedural* justice that is more strongly associated with employee commitment.

Locke and Latham's (1990) *goal setting theory* suggests that individuals are more likely to achieve agreed goals that they believe are achievable. This led to the development of the SMART concept in setting performance goals – SMART goals are Specific, Measurable, Achievable, Realistic and Time-bound.

Mini case study: 'McDonaldising' pay

McDonald's, notable for paying low wages, maintains its edge in a competitive market. David Fairhurst, vice-president, McDonald's UK, explained that the company is 'not a career destination for everybody', although 75 per cent of managers start as 'crew members'. The proportion of McDonald's employees who regard their pay as 'fair' is 30 per cent higher than the retail average, according to a comparative survey, and pride in working at McDonald's is 6 per cent higher than the average. The basic wage for new staff is at, or just above, the normal minimum wage (NMW), and the company offers a package of rewards including flexible working, with the company emphasizing the concept of *total reward*. For both 18- to 21-year-olds and those aged 22 and above, the McDonald's current minimum rate is exactly the same as the NMW (£4.25 an hour and £5.05 an hour, respectively). But for 16- to 17-year-olds, the lowest rate of £4 is a full pound above the state's 16- to 17-year-old development rate. After training, McDonald's pay rates rise incrementally: the top rate for hourly paid staff over 18 is £8.70. In their first year, all crew members have two pay reviews. After an initial 21 days' probation, crew member benefits include a free meal allowance and paid holidays (four weeks pro rata). Those who stay for three years also get additional benefits. There is private healthcare, and, for the committed, long service awards at three, five, 10 and even 15, 20 and 25-yearly intervals (those who stay a quarter-century get a £750 voucher). Others may be more interested in discount cards on holidays, computers, shoes, holidays and DVD rentals, and even a 15 per cent discount from HSS, a tool hire outfit.

Two performance reviews in the first year are designed to promote people quickly, provided they can convince restaurant managers of their abilities. There is also an additional bonus system for high-performing teams – any restaurant that figures in the top 10 per cent in a league table run by the director of operations wins a 50p-an-hour bonus.

60 per cent of staff is under 21. For 25,000 of its UK workforce, McDonald's is a first job and a first taste of non-academic learning. When critics scoff at the way the company celebrates those who 'graduate' from its programmes, it is possible that these initiatives are perceived differently by teenagers who may be staying in a fancy hotel for the first time. Moving into management job roles can attract a salary of over £30,000.

Fairhurst sees reward as extending to 'values issues' such as recognition, citizenship, personal growth and respect. Everything the company does, he argues, is aimed at affirming these values. These can be relatively trivial things – ensuring the use of 'please' behind the counter, for example, or name badges emblazoned with 'proud of you'. Innovations include a 'family contract', which enables different members of the same family to take shifts for each other.

'Reward is only rewarding if it is meaningful to individuals,' Fairhust says.
'We do our utmost to ensure that the behaviours that deliver great customer service get noticed and rewarded.'

(Adapted from: Fast Forward, *People Management*, 9 February 2006, and McDonald's fights 'McJob' tag, *People Management*, 23 February 2006, p. 19)

Based on your reading of this case study, and the theories on motivation and organisational justice:

* What is the company seeking to achieve?
* What is your assessment of how well the rewards meet those aims?

Developments in pay structures

Pay structures are developing as employers seek a balance between the highly flexible approaches which typically lack transparency and the more defined structures, which may be difficult to operate in an active salary market climate. Other key factors affecting current developments are *equal pay for work of equal value* and the link between career and pay systems. There are four main types of pay structure:

◆ **A spot salary structure** – in which there is a single rate of pay for the job and no range of pay through which individuals can progress their pay. Such a system has the advantage of transparency but relies critically on those setting the rates to make the appropriate choice in the context of a moving pay market.

◆ **A narrow-banded or graded salary structure** – in which there is a restricted level of pay progression – typically on the basis of assessment of individual performance, or pay progression may be service-related. Such systems are easy to understand but with long-serving staff run the risk of a high proportion of people being stuck at the top of the structure and feeling they have no way of progressing their pay

◆ **Broad-banded structures** – in which the range of pay in a band is significantly wider than in a conventional graded structure. The band width may be 100 per cent or even more. Broad bands or grades make it difficult to explain to people why some earn more than others (and this has dangers from an equal pay perspective). However, they give greater scope for employees to recognise individual performance or competencies, and to respond flexibly to salary market conditions.

◆ **Job family systems** – in which there are separate pay structures for different occupational groups. These seem simpler to explain to employees; they are responsive to the specific pay market for the respective occupations, and they help in linking pay to career progression. But, again, there may be equal pay dangers where different occupational groups are gender segregated, as is likely in UK organisations, and they may lead to 'silo' thinking and competition rather than co-operation between functions in the organisation.

An e-reward survey (e-reward.co.uk, 2006) claimed that *career families* are the latest manifestation of grade structure development: just 6 per cent of respondents had them while 17 per cent had job families. Career families consist of jobs in a function or occupation, such as marketing, operations, finance, information technology (IT), HR, administration or support services, which are related through the activities carried out and the basic knowledge and skills required, but in which the levels of responsibility, knowledge, skill or competency needed differ. In a career family structure the various career families are also identified and the successive levels in each family are defined by reference to the key activities carried out and the knowledge and skills or competencies required to perform them effectively. Typically, career families have between six and eight levels as in broad-graded structures, although some families may have more levels than others. Unlike job family approaches, career family structures have a common grade and pay structure. Jobs at the same level in each career family are deemed to be the same **size**, and the pay ranges in corresponding levels across the career families are the same. In effect, a career structure is a single graded structure in which each grade has been divided into families.

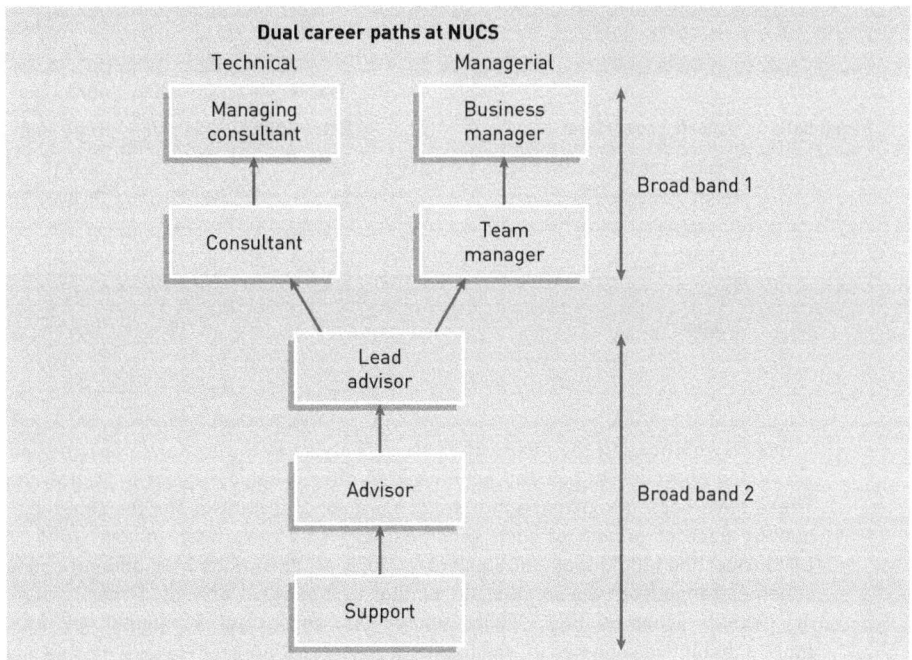

Figure 9.2 Norwich Union: career family pay structure
Source: adapted from *IDS HR Study 814*, January 2006

Norwich Union Central Services (NUCS) designed a new pay structure following a merger. The company wanted a simpler approach than its previous system, aiming to make career progression more transparent and give employees a clearer view of where they fitted into the organisation. The career family structure was developed and includes 22 separate job families – from chauffeurs to switchboard staff.

There are three elements to the pay system – career families, broad salary bands and the use of generic roles/groups. Within the majority of career families jobs are aligned to one of seven generic groups – managing consultant, business manager, team manager, lead adviser and support – see Figure 9.2.

Broad salary bands are used. The salary market is surveyed and for each generic group in each family, a salary entry point, 'low point' and 'high point' are set, as shown in Table 9.2.

Towards a more employee-centred approach to reward

In the last quarter of the twentieth century pay determination in the UK became increasingly individualised, although as Brown et al. (1998) suggest, there often continued to be a standardised approach to the setting of pay and benefits in many organisations, even though collective bargaining with trade unions had been reduced. At the same time there was a growing acknowledgement that employers may need to respond to the increasingly diverse needs and lifestyles of today's workforce.

Table 9.2 Example of a career family at NUCS: facilities management

| Broad band | Generic group/level | Market salary guides at 1 April 2005 | | |
		Entry point	Low point	High point
1	Business manager/managing consultant	26,800	33,500	45,000
	Team manager	18,400	23,000	30,000
	Consultant	17,350	21,700	29,000
2	Lead advisor	13,200	16,500	19,600
	Advisor	10,080	12,600	14,500
	Support	9,250	11,300	12,000

One way of meeting the needs of diverse lifestyles in the context of a more individualised approach to pay and benefits is to offer a flexible benefits programme. These have been in existence in a small number of organisations for some years but the pace of growth of such schemes seems to have been modest, with the CIPD reporting (2007) that just 8 per cent of UK organisations have schemes. Such schemes range from the small scale, similar to those that are now termed 'voluntary benefits schemes' (IRS, 2005) – whose cost and extent is minimal – to much more substantive schemes in which employees get a significant level of choice as to the benefits they receive. This may include 'buying ' or 'selling ' holiday entitlement; extending medical insurance or pension benefits; and the possibility of choosing a range of lower cost benefits.

Mini case study: Flexible benefits at AstraZeneca

AstraZeneca implemented a total reward package system incorporating flexible benefits, when UK company Zeneca (formerly part of ICI) merged with Swedish firm Astra. The new company, which employs 10,000 people in the UK, brought together two financially and culturally disparate reward systems by this means. The 'total reward' scheme encompassing flexible benefits is called AZAdvantage. Under it, employees are allocated a fund comprising a reference salary and a budget for spending on various benefits.

An employee can opt to change the mix of salary and benefits as they wish. Although all staff are given core benefits, including annual leave, private healthcare and pension, they are also able to choose from a menu of other benefits, so their package is individually tailored.

The range includes lifestyle options such as extra holiday and retail vouchers; health benefits such as dental cover; financial options such as enhanced retirement benefits; and other options, including insurance.

Each benefit has a pricing structure and offers savings for the employer either through tax and national insurance efficiencies or through corporate discounts. The scheme is administered via an intranet site and a service centre run by the company's consultants.

(Adapted from Manocha, 2002)

Flexible benefit plans also have the advantage of involving employees in selecting the benefits that best suit their current *and* future lifestyles. Various quantitative studies (Hong et al., 1995; Baughman et al., 2003; Dale-Olsen, 2005; Tsai, 2005) indicate that benefit programmes may have positive effects on productivity, motivation and employee retention. Hence it might be argued that offering people a choice over which benefits to receive could have further positive business outcomes (Barringer and Milkovich, 1998). Organisations may also be able to limit benefit costs and exert greater cost control with a flexible programme compared with a standardised package. The Employee Benefits survey (2003) indicates self-reported positive outcomes from organisations that had such schemes. These outcomes include:

- Showing employees the value of their benefits;
- Aiding recruitment;
- Improving retention;
- Harmonising benefits;
- Reinforcing company culture;
- Improving/maintaining staff motivation;
- Aiding 'employer of choice' status;
- Reducing/removing status symbols;
- Reducing/containing the cost of reward.

Although there is little academic research in this area, Barber (1992) reports improved employee satisfaction with benefits and Hillebrink et al. (2003) report potential motivational effects from the possibility that flexible schemes offer the opportunity to 'buy time'.

As with other aspects of reward, there is at present no systematic evaluation of whether flexible benefits add organisational value and are worth the work involved in setting up and maintaining schemes. Considerable research is needed in this and other areas of reward.

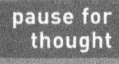

pause for thought   'Through a glass darkly.' How does this phrase relate to remuneration systems? Why did you reach the answer you did?

Summary

In managing pay and reward in organisations, gaining trust, commitment and employee engagement within particular situational contexts is vital, but the factors that critically influence this complex set of relationships are only partially understood. Current issues in reward focus on developments in managing – as well as designing – reward systems, but some long-standing problems such as gender pay inequality are still to be solved.

Review Questions

You may wish to attempt the following as practice examination style questions.

9.1   What do you understand by the term reward strategy? How would you set about devising a strategy for an organisation?

9.2   In what circumstances can pay motivate?

9.3   Devise a PowerPoint slide show to explain to senior managers the benefits of greater openness and transparency about pay.

References

Adams, J.S. (1965). Inequity in social exchange, in L. Berkowitz (ed.) *Advances in Experimental Social Psychology*, New York: Academic Press.

Armstrong, M. and Baron, A. (2005). *Managing Performance: Performance Management in Action*, London: CIPD.

Barber, A.E., Dunham, R. and Formisano, R. (1992). The impact of flexible benefits on employee satisfaction: a field study, *Personnel Psychology*, Vol. 45, pp. 55–75.

Barringer, M.W. and Milkovich, G. (1998). A theoretical exploration of the adoption and design of flexible benefit plans: a case of human resource innovation, *Academy of Management Review*, Vol. 23, No. 2, pp. 305–324.

Baughman, R. et al. (2003). Productivity and wage effects of 'family-friendly' fringe benefits, *International Journal of Manpower*, Vol. 24, No. 3, pp. 247–259.

Bowen, D. et al. (1999). How being fair with employees spills over to customers, *Organisational Dynamics*, Vol. 27, No. 3, pp. 7–23.

Boxall, P. and Purcell, J. (2000). *Strategy and human resource management*, Palgrave Macmillan.

Brown, W. et al. (1998). The individualisation of employment contracts in Britain, research paper for the Department of Trade and Industry, Centre for Business Research Department of Applied Economics, University of Cambridge.

CIPD (2005). *Reward Management Survey 2005*, London: CIPD.

CIPD (2006). *Reward Management Survey 2006*, London: CIPD.

CIPD (2007). *Reward Management Survey 2007*, London: CIPD.

Cox, A. (2000). The importance of employee participation in determining pay system effectiveness, *International Journal of Management Review*, Vol. 2, No. 4, pp. 357–375.

Dale-Olsen, H. (2005). Using linked employer–employee data to analyze fringe benefits policies: Norwegian experiences, Institute for Social Research, Norway, paper presented at Policy Studies Institute Seminar, July.

Employee Benefits/MX Financial Solutions (2003). Flexible benefits research 2003, *Employee Benefits*, April, pp. 4–9.

Folger, R. and Konovsky, M.A. (1989). Effects of procedural and distributive justice on reactions to pay raise decisions, *Academy of Management Journal*, Vol. 32, No. 1, pp. 115–130.

Gerhart, B. (2000). Compensation strategy and organisational performance, in S. Rynes et al. (eds.) *Compensation in Organisations: Current Research and Practice*, San Francisco, CA: Jossey–Bass.

Gomez-Mejia, L.R. and Balkin, D.B. (1992). *Compensation, Organizational Strategy and Firm Performance*, Cincinnati, OH: South-Western Publishing.

Greenberg, J. (1987). A taxonomy of organisational justice theories, *Academy of Management Review*, Vol. 12, pp. 9–22.

176 CHAPTER 9 THROUGH A GLASS DARKLY

Heneman, H.G. and Judge, T.A. (2000). Compensation attitudes, in S. Rynes et al. (eds.) *Compensation in Organisations: Current Research and Practice*, San Francisco, CA: Jossey-Bass.

Hillebrink, C. et al. (2003). Choosing time or money: a study into employees' decision-making regarding flexible benefits, paper presented at the HRM Network Conference, Twente, Netherlands, November.

Hong, J.-C. et al. (1995). Impact of employee benefits on work motivation and productivity, *International Journal of Career Management*, Vol. 7, No. 6, pp. 10–14.

Huczynski, A. and Buchanan, D. (2001). *Organizational Behaviour: An Introductory Text*, 4th edition, Harlow, Essex: FT/Prentice Hall.

Huselid, M. (1995). The impact of human resource management practices on turnover, productivity and corporate financial performance, *Academy of Management Journal*, Vol. 38, No. 3, pp. 635–672.

Hutchinson, S. and Purcell, J. (2003). *Bringing Policies to Life: The Vital Role of Front Line Managers in People Management*, Executive Briefing Report, London: CIPD.

IDS (2005). *Directory of Salary Surveys 2005/06: IDS Executive Compensation Review*, London: Incomes Data Services.

IRS (2005). Voluntary benefits: saving in the workplace, *IRS Employment Review*, Vol. 818, Pay and Benefits, 25 February.

Lawler, F. (1995). The new pay: a strategic approach, *Compensation and Benefits Review*, July–August, pp. 14–22.

Legge, K. (1995). *Human Resource Management: Rhetoric and Realities*, Basingstoke: Macmillan.

Locke, E.A. and Latham, G.P. (1990). *A Theory of Goal Setting and Task Performance*, Englewood Cliffs, NJ: Prentice Hall.

Macduffie, J. (1995). Human resource bundles and manufacturing performance: organizational logic and flexible production systems in the world auto industry, *Industrial and Labor Relations Review*, Vol. 48, No. 2, pp. 197–221.

Manocha, R. (2002). Pick 'n' mix, *People Management*, 7 November, p. 45.

Marchington, M. and Grugulis, I. (2000). 'Best practice' human resource management: perfect opportunity or dangerous illusion?, *International Journal of Human Resource Management*, Vol. 11, No. 6, pp. 1104–1124.

Milsome, S. (2005), Symposium report, Reward Management, 13 July, organised jointly by e-reward and CIPD.

Perkins, S.J. and Sandringham, S. (eds.) (1998). *Trust, Motivation and Commitment: A Reader*, Oxford: Strategic Remuneration Research Centre.

Pfeffer, J. (1998). *The Human Equation: Building Profits by Putting People First*, Boston: Harvard Business School Press.

Porter, L. and Lawler, E. (1968). *Managerial Attitudes and Performance*, New York: Richard Irwin Inc.

Purcell, J. et al. (2003). *Understanding the People and Performance Link: Unlocking the Black Box*, research report, London: CIPD.

Purcell, J. and Hutchinson, S. (2007). *Rewarding Work: The Vital Role of Line Managers*, Change Agenda, London: CIPD.

Robinson, D. et al. (2004). The drivers of employee engagement, IES Report 408, London: Institute of Employment Studies.

Rynes, S. et al. (2005). Personnel psychology: performance evaluation and pay for performance, *Annual Review of Psychology*, Vol. 56, pp. 571–600.

Sisson, K. and Storey, J. (2000). *The Realities of Human Resource Management*, Buckingham: Open University Press.

Tsai, M.-C. (2005). Evaluating sociologists in Taiwan: power, profession and passerby, Department of Sociology, National Tapai University, Taiwan.

Vroom, V. (1964). *Work and Motivation*, Chichester: Wiley.

West, M. et al. (2005). *Rewarding Customer Service? Using Reward and Recognition to Deliver Your Customer Service Strategy*, research report, London: CIPD.

Zingheim, P. and Schuster, J. (2000). Total rewards for new and old economy companies, *Compensation and Benefits Review*, Vol. 32, No. 6, pp. 20–23.

Further Reading

Corby, S., White, G. and Stanworth, C. (2005). No news is good news? Evaluating new pay systems, *Human Resource Management Journal*, Vol. 15, No. 1, pp. 4–24.

Forth, J. and Millward, N. (2000). The determinants of pay levels and fringe benefit provision in Britain, discussion paper No. 171, National Institute of Economic and Social Research.

Guest, D. (2002). Human resource management, corporate performance and employee wellbeing: building the worker into HRM, *Journal of Industrial Relations*, Vol. 44, No. 3, pp. 335–358.

Pfeffer, J. and Veiga, J.F. (1999). Putting people first for organisational success, *Academy of Management Executive*, Vol. 13, No. 2, pp. 37–48.

Rynes, S. et al. (eds.) (2000). *Compensation in Organisations: Current Research and Practice*, San Francisco, CA: Jossey-Bass.

Wright, A. (2004). *Reward Management in Context*, London: CIPD.

Zingheim, P.K. and Schuster, J.R. (2000). *Pay People Right!: Breakthrough Reward Strategies to Create Great Companies*, San Francisco, CA: Jossey-Bass.

Useful Websites

www.e-reward.co.uk – information and guidance on rewards, especially business-focused reward strategy

www.eoc.org.uk – downloadable reports and guidance on pay equality

www.incomesdata.co.uk – gives an index of topics covered in IDS journals and research

www.ons.gov.uk – downloadable data such as the *Annual Survey of Hours and Earnings*

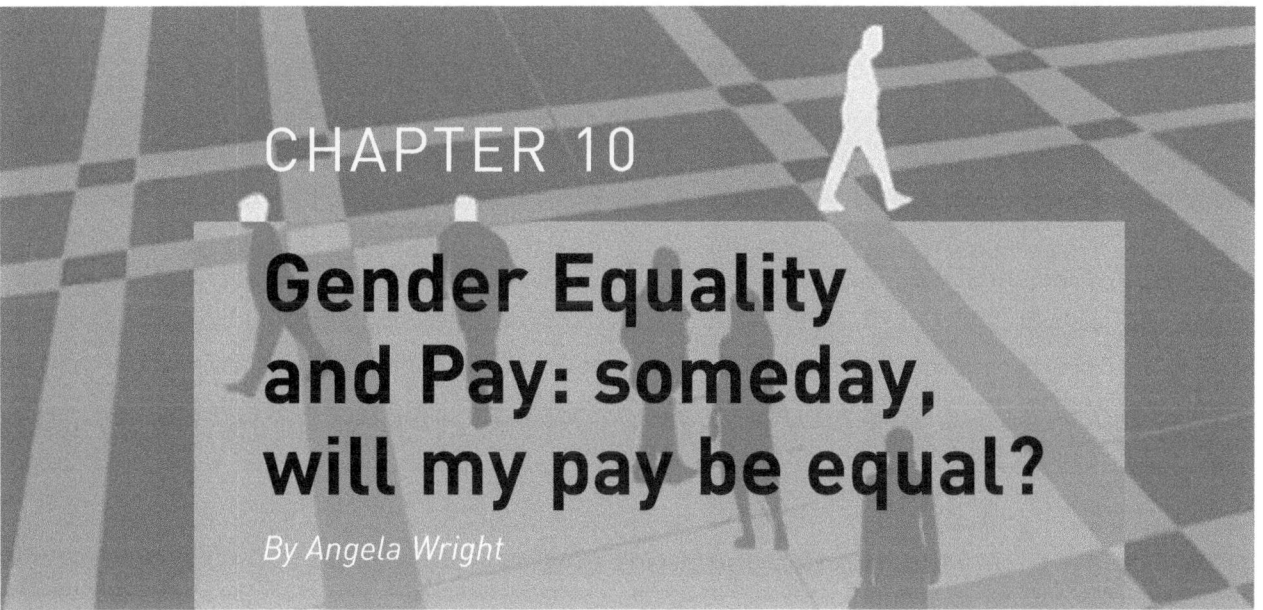

CHAPTER 10

Gender Equality and Pay: someday, will my pay be equal?

By Angela Wright

Chapter outline

This chapter seeks to review the key issues for human resource (HR) specialists of a profound and far-reaching problem. As Chapter 4 shows, diversity and equal opportunities policies may be little more than 'empty shells' – a policy on paper that has little effect in practice. An analysis of pay by gender in an organisation can show just how far, or not, equality initiatives have gone in challenging and changing traditional career and pay relationships. The chapter looks at sources of gender pay inequality and examines the ways in which the gender pay gap may be measured and alleviated. It covers some of the lessons from the legal developments on equal pay, picking up on the kinds of pay systems that are likely to be most unequal, and discusses how such inequality may be rectified.

Learning outcomes

By the end of this chapter, you should be able to:

◆ Identify the main causes of gender pay inequality;

◆ Describe some of the trends in pay and gender in the UK;

◆ Summarise some of the key legal developments;

◆ Explain some aspects of pay systems that lead to inequality;

◆ List some measures that employers can take to reduce pay inequality.

Introduction

In 2006, the latest in a series of government-sponsored studies of the causes of gender pay inequality was published. The Women and Work Commission, like its predecessors, produced a lengthy report with numerous recommendations, but will it lead to any change in a pattern of pay inequality, which seems durable even in the face of increasing legislation? Although many HR practitioners may be fully in tune with the issues of diversity and equal opportunities in employment, equal pay may not be central to the concerns of many managers. The systemic problems of unequal pay in UK pay systems, particularly in the public sector, is a vulnerability which is now forcing its way up the organisational agenda, in part because of some high-profile multi-million pound legal settlements.

Measuring the equal pay gap

The Office for National Statistics (ONS; statistics.gov.uk) compiles and publishes the national level data on pay and gender, principally in the *Annual Survey of Hours and Earnings*, previously the *New Earnings Survey*. The gender pay gap is worked out as the difference between the median earnings of men and women, because the median is less influenced by outlying values in the pay distribution than is the arithmetic average (or mean). The data for 2005 show the gender pay gap between the pay of men and women working full time is 13 per cent measured using *median* hourly pay rates; and 17 per cent measured using *mean* hourly pay rates. The data are based on median hourly earnings, excluding the effects of overtime, since that is the measure that best offers a like-for-like comparison, as a far higher proportion of men than women work paid overtime hours. It should also be noted that the hourly rates used in the calculation are 'effective' hourly rates calculated by ONS – they cover the whole workforce, including the salaried higher paid, and *not* just those people who are paid by the hour.

The *Annual Survey of Hours and Earnings* further shows that men begin to earn more than women soon after they enter the labour market, and the pay gap rises with age. In 2005, the mean gender pay gap for full-time workers aged 18–21 was 3.7 per cent. For those aged 40–49, the age group for whom the gender pay gap is largest, the mean gender pay gap was 21.7 per cent. See Figure 10.1.

A number of studies show that the UK has a poor record on equal pay compared with other European countries. The Women and Work Commission (2006) suggests the key to reducing the pay gap lies in measures to balance work and family and notes that countries such as Sweden and Denmark, that have cultures which promote work-life balance (see also Chapter 21), have lower gender pay gaps than the UK, while having similarly high levels of women's participation in work. However, no country has yet achieved full gender equality in pay and employment.

Sources of pay inequality

Gender pay inequality is a pervasive problem in UK reward. As Joshi and Paci (1998) argue, although higher pay for men is just one of the many ways in which pay levels differ between individuals, it is, in comparison with other factors, a very durable

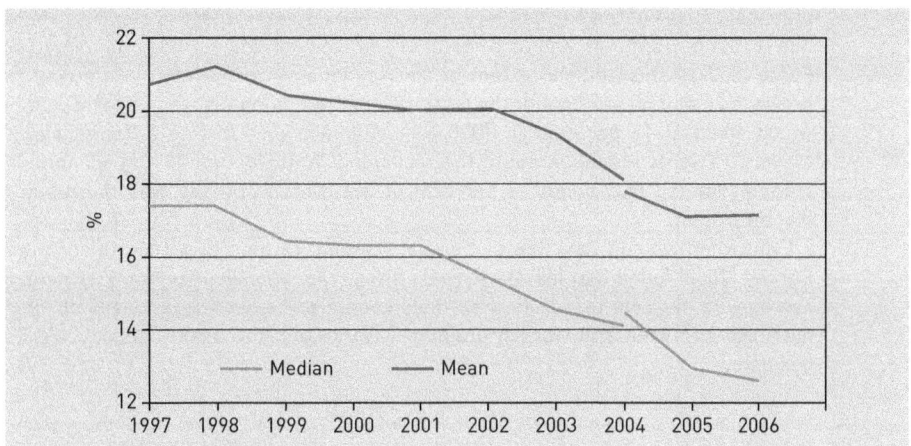

Figure 10.1 Gender pay gap trends, UK 1997–2006
Source: Office of National Statistics

feature. Indeed, Forth and Millward (2000) show the durability of the gender dimension, over a period that saw both significant changes in pay determination arrangements and substantial rises in labour market participation by women. As the Women and Work Commission (2006) points out:

> 'In the 30 years since the Equal Pay Act, major changes in the UK's economy and society have increased the opportunities available to women. It has become more socially acceptable for women to work. In 2005, 70 per cent of women of working age were in employment, compared to 60 per cent in 1975 (Labour Force Survey). Women's education levels have increased and as the traditionally male jobs in the manufacturing sector have disappeared, jobs in the service sector, which are seen as more accessible to women, have expanded. Women are having fewer children and giving birth later in life. Women are more likely to establish a career before having a family and to re-establish themselves at work more easily afterwards. Women are also more likely to work when they have young children than in previous decades; 56 per cent of women whose youngest child was under five were in employment in 2005 compared to 91 per cent of men whose youngest child was under five. The main growth in women's employment rates in the 1990s was among women with very young children (Labour Force Survey). Despite these changes there are still significant barriers to equal pay.'

The concentration of women in lower-paying occupations, known as *occupational segregation*, contributes to the overall gender pay gap. Women tend to be paid less than men within occupations, not climbing the career ladder to the same degree as men. This is known as *vertical segregation* and the barriers to moving up in a profession are also referred to as the *glass ceiling*.

The occupational segregation of women into a narrow range of low-paid jobs or careers, together with the low pay and status of part-time work, are identified as

Financial and Human Resource Management in Organisations, Second Edition

principal causes of the pay gap (see Chapter 14). However, there is also discrimination within pay systems and as a result of some pay practices. The Equal Pay Task Force (2001) estimated the extent of discrimination in pay systems to amount to between 25 and 50 per cent of the total national pay gap between men and women, which stood at 17 per cent in 2005, when factors such as the different pattern of work of women is taken out of the reckoning. Walby et al.'s (2002) econometric study estimated that about 29 per cent of the overall pay gap was the result of discrimination.

Even when women have the same qualifications as men they tend to earn less. Purcell (2002) found that just three years after graduation women were earning, on average, 15 per cent less than their male counterparts, with salary gaps observed even between men and women graduates working in the same occupations. See box below.

Causes of the gender pay gap

◆ Differences between men and women in the jobs they do – *occupational segregation*;

◆ 'Women's jobs' being under-valued;

◆ Length of work experience and the number of interruptions to the work experience of many women;

◆ Part-time employment experience;

◆ Qualifications and skills;

◆ Travel to work issues;

◆ Other factors include discriminatory treatment of women at work and the inaccessibility of training.

(Adapted from Women and Work Commission, 2006)

---

 pause for thought

Think about an organisation known to you.

◆ How much occupational segregation by gender can you observe?

◆ If there are part-time workers in the organisation, are they mainly women?

◆ Do you think there are any pay or benefit consequences of your observations?

◆ Why did you reach this conclusion?

 **exercise**

Do you think there is likely to be occupational segregation at Warbings?

Why did you reach this conclusion?

Some lessons from the legal developments on equal pay

Equal pay for women and men is one of the few areas of pay that is regulated. The law in this area dates back to the Equal Pay Act, which was introduced in 1970, and also within European law which contains the founding principles of the European Union (EU). Many of the high-profile legal cases which have taken place over the past three or four decades have been taken under European law, which is directly applied in the UK legal system (see also Chapter 13). Under both European and domestic law, employers are obliged to pay *equal pay for work of equal value* to women and men. The direct applicability of EU law as part of domestic law in England, Wales and Scotland stems from the European Communities Act 1972, when Britain joined the then Common Market. The effect of this is that UK tribunals and courts must, wherever possible, interpret domestic law in accordance with EU law. In circumstances when EU law has direct effect, it takes precedence over domestic law.

On equal pay, the key element of European law is Article 141 (previously Article 119) of the Treaty of Rome, establishing that the European Community stipulates that men and women should receive equal pay for equal work. Any individual can rely on A141 in bringing an equal pay case.

In domestic law, the Equal Pay Act 1970 gives an individual a right to the same contractual pay and benefits as a person of the opposite sex in the same employment, where the man and the woman are doing:

◆ Like work; or

◆ Work rated as equivalent under an analytical job evaluation study; or

◆ Work that is proved to be of equal value.

Because the UK labour market is segregated by gender, women and men tend not to work in the same jobs. Hence equal pay for work of equal value, not 'like work', is of critical importance. However studies by Morrell et al. (2001) and Brett and Milsome (2004) indicate that many employers have a poor understanding of the concept of equal value and its translation into pay practice. With diverse pay arrangements the process of judging comparability may be difficult because jobs/roles may be flexible and the perceived contribution to the organisation variable (Wright, 2004). It may be argued that the concept is fundamentally flawed, since it relies on an acceptance that comparing the value of jobs that are dissimilar is practicable and systematically possible. Various legal judgements and the work of the independent experts give some guidance in this area (see below), but for many aspects of practical pay management and policy there is no hard and fast guidance about what employers must or must not do to satisfy the requirements of the equal pay legislation.

Legal developments since the end of the 1990s have focused on the problems of a cumbersome tribunal process, and the introduction of the Equal Pay Questionnaire under the Employment Act 2002 was designed to make it simpler to unearth unjustified differences between women and men on an individual basis, prior to any legal action.

In the more than 30 years of the operation of the legislation there have been a number of important cases. Below is a summary of some of the key cases, whose judgements have given guidance on practice.

Financial and Human Resource Management in Organisations, Second Edition

In assessing equal pay for work of equal value – whose pay should be compared?

Can people only compare with current employees? In the *Macarthys v Mrs Smith [1980]* case, it was established by the European Court of Justice (ECJ) that a woman can bring an equal pay claim under European equal pay law, comparing herself with a man who had previously held her post. The Court of Appeal had previously held that the Equal Pay Act did not allow a claim to be brought where the comparator was no longer in employment.

One of the early equal pay for work of equal value cases which showed the potential of the new law to compare across previously rigidly 'male' and 'female' demarcation boundaries was *Ms White and Others v Alstons (Colchester) Ltd, 1987*. In this case women sewing machinists were found to be engaged on work of equal value to male upholsterers and awarded equal pay. One of the main difficulties with the equal pay legislation is that the concept of equal value is not formally defined in either EU or domestic legislation. The Equal Pay Act provides that when a claimant claims equal pay on grounds of equal value, a comparison should be made between the claimant's work and that of the named comparator 'under such headings as effort, skill and decision'. This broad definition leaves many areas of doubt.

Equal value claims can be made using comparators paid under different grading systems, collective agreements or job evaluation schemes. The question of whether two jobs are of equal value involves a weighing and balancing between the features of the claimant's and comparator's jobs, thereby allowing comparisons between quite different types of jobs. The EOC (www.eoc-law.org.uk) gives examples of claims between very different jobs, which have been successful at tribunal or settled in favour of the claimant(s), including:

◆ Primary school classroom assistant with a library service driver messenger;

◆ School nursery nurse with a local government architectural technician;

◆ Wholesale news distribution clerical assistant with a warehouse operative;

◆ Cook with a shipboard painter;

◆ Head of speech and language therapy service with the head of a hospital pharmacy service;

◆ Nursing home sewing room assistant with a plumber;

◆ Motor industry sewing machinist with an upholsterer;

◆ Canteen workers and cleaners with surface mineworkers and clerical workers.

Equal value and the use of job evaluation

Job evaluation is a process used in pay setting that puts a value to the organisation of different jobs. It is important for employers wishing to defend themselves against an equal pay claim, since if there is an unbiased scheme used for this purpose and it gives a higher value to a job done by a man than to one done by a woman, the woman will not be able to take a valid claim for equal value to an employment tribunal. However, it is important to recognise that all job evaluation schemes contain implicit values and these may well be biased against the sort of roles or jobs women do. If the organisation has strong job segregation by gender, questions about professed impartiality of the job evaluation method used may be raised. In some legal cases this issue has been considered. In *Bromley v H* and *J Quick Ltd [1988] IRLR 249 CA*, the study commissioned by the employers used the paired comparisons method (that considers jobs on a 'whole job' basis), rather than split into various factors to provide a rank order of benchmark jobs. Jobs not evaluated in this process were then slotted into the rank order on a 'felt-fair' basis in line with the general level of expectation as to the value of the job. The claimants and comparators had not been chosen for the paired comparison exercise but instead had been slotted into order on a 'felt-fair' basis. The Court of Appeal held that the method used for the study was not analytical (that is, the jobs had not been considered under various factors or headings). This aspect is considered important since there may be more tendency for people to think in terms of the person holding the job (and hence their gender) when rating jobs on a whole job basis rather than rating under different factors.

Tribunals can appoint independent experts to help them in assessing the comparative value of the claimant and comparator jobs. The expert may assess the jobs against a simple low–moderate–high scale. In the first equal value claim referred to an independent expert, *Hayward v Cammell Laird [1984] IRLR 463 ET*, the expert used a small number of factors to compare the work of the claimant (a cook) with that of her comparators (a shipboard painter, carpenter and heating technician), as follows:

- Skill and knowledge demands;
- Responsibility demands;
- Planning and decision-making demands;
- Physical demands;
- Environmental demands.

In contrast, in the *Enderby and Others v Frenchay Health Authority and Anor [1993] IRLR 591 ECJ* case, when comparing a large number of speech therapist jobs with clinical psychologists and hospital pharmacists the team of independent experts used a large numbers of factors, as follows:

- Knowledge;
- Knowledge base;
- Development;
- Experience;
- Responsibilities;
- Patients/clients and the provision of a service;
- Managing work of self and others;
- Plant/equipment/resources;
- Teaching/training/mentoring;
- Mental demands;
- Concentration/accuracy;
- Physical demands and environment;
- Physical effort;
- Working conditions;
- Hazards;

◆ Decision making and initiative;

◆ Complexity and analysis;

◆ Freedom to act;

◆ Communications/relationships.

Each factor had five levels and each job was assessed and then scored against a scale as in a job evaluation scheme. However, as Armstrong and Baron's (1995) survey shows, the usual number of factors used in a job evaluation scheme is between three and eight, since a large number of factors increases the chance that certain attributes in different jobs are recognised under more than one factor, thereby potentially double-counting that attribute. Too few factors and there is a risk of missing important attributes. Both too many and too few factors carry potential equality risks.

In *Eaton Ltd v Nuttall [1977] IRLR 71 EAT*, the importance of objectivity in the job evaluation was emphasised. Here, the company job evaluation exercise led to the setting of pay grades, where management decided where in the pay range the individual job was to be placed, using their own judgement as to how much responsibility was involved in each job. This amounted to a subjective, rather than relatively objective judgement.

Evaluating just a few 'benchmark' jobs and then slotting in the other jobs in the organisation into the pay structure on the basis of the benchmarked jobs has been a common practice. In *Bromley v Quick [1998] IRLR 249 CA*, the job evaluation process used by the study employers was flawed not just because it used a whole job method but also because no evaluation of the claimant's and comparator's jobs had taken place in the process. Instead, they had been ranked against the benchmark jobs.

How equal is 'equal'?

A number of cases have considered the question of 'what amounts to equal?'. Whether a claimant must have either a direct equivalent in points scored, or a greater number of points to be considered 'equal', or whether 'equal' should be assessed in broader terms, is problematic. Case law indicates that small differences in score will not necessarily prevent the jobs from being equal. In *Worsfold v Southampton and South West Hampshire HA ET/18296/87* and *Lawson v South Tees HA ET/17931/87*, the independent expert found a small points difference of less than 5 per cent between the claimant and comparator jobs. In the tribunal's view, work is not of equal value where there is 'an overall measurable and significant difference' between the demands of the respective jobs. The tribunal concluded that there was no measurable and significant difference between the jobs, and their conclusion was supported by the evidence of the independent expert, who said it was unlikely in a company setting that the job score difference between them would have led to any difference in grading.

Material factor defence

To explain why a comparator, although doing equal work, is paid more than the applicant the employer may use the 'material factor defence'. To be successful this factor must be significant and depict a relevant reason why there is a difference in pay. To succeed in such a defence the employer needs to show that the material factor accounts for the *whole* of the difference in pay.

Objective justification

In circumstances where a particular pay practice results in an adverse impact on substantially more members of one or other sex, the ECJ has introduced a test of objective justification. This means that the employer must be able to justify the pay practice in question objectively, in terms unrelated to gender.

Burden of proof

Under both domestic and EU law, the burden of proof falls on the claimant to establish that they do work of equal value to their chosen comparator and that they receive less pay. However, if the pay system lacks transparency (as many do), the principle established in *Brunnhofer v Bank der Österreichischen Postsparkasse AG [2001] IRLR 571 ECJ* was that if the claimant gives evidence that the average pay of, for example, women is less than for men undertaking equal work, then the burden of proof switches.

Back-pay for successful claimants

In the case of *Mrs Levez v T H Jennings [1999]*, Mrs Levez had won her equal pay for like work claim but the Equal Pay Act only allowed her to claim back-pay for two years. Following a decision of the ECJ, the Employment Appeal Tribunal decided that the two-year limit was contrary to European law and ruled that the limit for back-dating awards should be extended to six years.

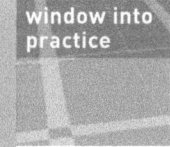

Examples of the effects of successful equal pay claims

window into practice

The public sector, with its large complex organisations and multiplicity of pay systems, has been particularly vulnerable to equal pay claims. In local government, the 1997 national collective single status agreement provided for the establishment of 'single status' terms for manual and white-collar staff, with a new harmonised package of conditions of service, a new minimum wage and provision for local grading reviews based on equal pay for men and women doing equivalent work. Although the agreement stipulated that implementation would take place at local level, it did not schedule a timetable for completion. Councils were faced with negotiating local pay structures in a context of budget constraints, and progress in implementing single status was very slow.

Failure to make progress in implementing local pay and grading left councils exposed to trade unions taking equal pay cases to employment tribunals. Claims have come almost exclusively from women on former manual grades, such as cooks and home helps. These posts are typically held by women, who traditionally had no eligibility for bonuses or overtime payments. However these jobs had been rated as of equal value to mainly male-dominated posts such as gardeners, refuse drivers and road workers, which were eligible for significant bonuses and other basic pay additions. As a consequence of these equal pay claims, many councils are struggling to fund the new job-evaluated local harmonised pay structures, in addition to paying compensation for up to six years' back-pay for employees bringing equal pay claims.

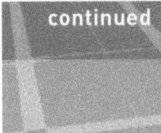 **continued**

Some 12 local authorities in the North East of England have paid compensation totalling more than £100 million to settle equal pay claims, according to the North East Regional Employers' Organisation. For example, around 3,000 women, including cleaners, care assistants and catering workers, employed by Cumbria County Council won claims for equal pay with male colleagues in similarly graded posts. About two-thirds of equal pay cases in local government do not *reach* a tribunal, but are settled by agreement under the auspices of ACAS. To try to protect against claims being taken to employment tribunals, councils may make compromise agreements.

In the NHS a new pay system, Agenda for Change, is being rolled out nationally. This is aimed at delivering equal pay for work of equal value, underpinned as it is by a job evaluation scheme, specifically designed for the NHS with equality to the fore. However, the new system does not provide back-dating. Around 3,000 women staff working for the North Cumbria Acute Hospitals NHS Trust, including nurses, clerical officers, catering assistants, domestics, sewing machine assistants, porters and telephonists, have won an equal pay for equal value case dating back eight years.

(Adapted from Incomes Data Services (2006a) and *Municipal Journal* (2006))

 **pause for thought**

Consider the reasons why unequal access to bonus schemes or overtime payments may be discriminatory. Can you think of any circumstances in which they may be argued to be a *'genuine material factor'*?

What kinds of pay system are most unequal?

Legal judgements have given relatively little guidance about those pay practices most likely to be discriminatory and much of the academic research in this area is inconclusive. Grimshaw and Rubery (2001) argue that the emergence of more flexible pay practices that developed in the UK in the wake of the decline in collective bargaining (Cully et al., 1998) influences the prevalence of gender pay inequality. The emphasis on performance pay during the 1980s and its continuation within UK organisational pay practice in the twenty-first century seems to be a prime contender for perpetuating inequality. However, the evidence on this is very patchy (Wright, 2004), with some studies showing that women can do better out of performance pay than men, because performance pay is used by employers to encourage sustained performance in the current post and women may be promoted less frequently than men, especially when they reach the 'glass ceiling' (Women and Work Commission, 2006). Brett (2006) highlights the view that even pay systems which are not inherently biased but that rely on managers making discretionary judgements can be discriminatory in practice: this can be a surprising finding for employers when they monitor pay decisions that they may firmly believe to be unbiased.

In December 1999, ACAS lost a tribunal case against its own women staff, complaining that its service increment scheme (where pay increased according to length of service) discriminated against women, who on average had shorter service within the organisation than men (Incomes Data Services, 2002). The revised pay system

Table 10.1 Pay structure for ACAS staff, 2002

Grade	Job Examples		Entry £pa	Step 1 £pa	Step 2 £pa	Step 3 £pa	Step 4 £pa	Step 5 £pa	Step 6 £pa
12	Administrative assistant	National	11,220	11,425	11,631	11,837	12,043	–	–
		London	15,122	15,327	15,533	15,739	15,945	–	–
11	Administrative officer	National	13,006	13,370	13,713	14,077	14,441	14,784	15,149
		London	16,908	17,272	17,615	17,979	18,343	18,686	19,051
10	Helpline staff, office supervisor	National	16,361	17,001	17,604	18,245	18,885	19,488	20,129
		London	20,263	20,903	21,506	22,147	22,787	23,390	24,031
9	Conciliator, office manager	National	21,739	22,519	23,254	24,034	24,814	25,549	26,330
		London	25,641	26,421	27,156	27,936	28,716	29,451	30,232
8	Senior advisor/conciliator, conciliation manager, resource manager	National	28,436	29,236	29,990	30,791	31,592	32,346	33,147
		London	32,338	33,138	33,892	34,693	35,494	36,248	37,049
7	Assistant director	National	35,799	37,276	38,666	40,144	41,621	43,011	44,489
		London	39,701	41,178	42,568	44,046	45,523	46,913	48,391
6	Regional director	National	48,048	49,158	50,204	51,213	52,426	53,472	54,583
		London	51,950	53,060	54,106	55,217	56,328	57,374	58,485

Source: *IDS HR Report 852*, March 2002, p. 14

it put in place (see Table 10.1) became something of a model for other public sector organisations to follow when seeking to achieve greater pay equality. At the Welsh Assembly, a new pay structure, that reduced the length of time for people to progress via annual increments through the pay ranges, has contributed to reducing the gender gap from 10 per cent to less than 4 per cent (Simms, 2005). This followed an equal pay review that found the main reason for the pay gap was the slow career progression of staff. Progress up the pay scale was dependent on performance, and women taking time out would return on the same pay point in the pay scale and therefore fail to progress. This system seemed fair but it could take up to 20 years for someone to progress from the minimum in the pay band to the maximum. Negotiations between management and trade unions resulted in the development of new six-point pay bands, allowing staff to progress more rapidly to a target rate of pay for their band. In addition, staff returning to work after career breaks, including maternity leave, return at the pay scale point they would have reached had their service not been interrupted by the break.

The question of the circumstances in which length of service can be considered a genuine material factor is the subject of legal cases. In the case of *Cadman v Health and Safety Executive*, the ECJ ruled (Incomes Data Services, 2006b: 20) that employers will have to objectively justify service-related pay structures which lead to women being paid less than men doing equal work. This is where the disadvantaged worker 'provides evidence raising serious doubts' as to whether recourse to the criterion of length of service is, in the circumstances, appropriate to attain the legitimate objective of rewarding experience which enables the worker to perform his or her duties better.

exercise Summarise the reasons why rewarding length of service can be an equal pay issue. Recommend what should be done by organisations that wish to reward experience but not discriminate against their staff on the basis of gender.

What can be done about the problems of unequal pay?

Wajcman (2000) argues that inequality is entrenched within organisations and Liff and Cameron (1997) further contend that because inequality arises through the totality of patterns of social interaction, it cannot be rectified by conventional HR equality initiatives. Nevertheless, the three committees of enquiry – the Equal Pay Task Force (2001), Kingsmill (2001) and the Women and Work Commission (2006) – set up by the UK government to investigate and report on the gender pay gap, suggest a range of measures that organisations, as well as government, can take to increase equality. The Women and Work Commission, while recognising (2006: IX) that 'the complex and interrelated nature of the causes of the gender pay gap means . . . sustained action (needs) . . . to be taken by a range of players', among other measures asks employers to consider the issues the Commission raises and to take action that will have most impact on women's pay and opportunity. To that end it has recruited some private sector companies to pilot a range of projects and also wants the public sector to be an exemplar of practice. The Commission disappointed some in not recommending that employers must be obliged to undertake an equal pay review or audit (other than in the public sector), while the earlier studies – Equal Pay Task Force (2001) and Kingsmill (2001) – recommend that voluntary audits could be instrumental in revealing the reasons for gender pay differences at organisational level, allowing employers to take remedial action. As the CIPD (2006) found, employers have seemed reluctant to examine gender pay differences in their organisations, some apparently believing there are no problems for them to solve. The window into practice below summarises two major UK companies' experiences of their equal pay auditing processes.

The EOC has produced a *Tool Kit* (eoc.org.uk), a checklist which gives guidance to employers on which variations in pay by gender are considered inequitable, biased by gender or unlawful. This stops short of giving detailed advice on exactly which pay differences are inequitable and which can be treated as merely coincidental in a flexible market-driven pay environment (see also Chapter 9) where no two people can expect to be treated exactly equally.

Equal pay reviews at BT and Nationwide

When **BT** conducted its first equal pay review in 1998, the organisation was already seen as an example of best practice. 'But that review taught us some very basic things and we changed many of our HR practices as a result,' said Caroline Waters, director, people and policy at BT Group.

The company restructured its non-management grading system, and introduced a skills-based system, to reduce traditional differences between, for example, engineering and clerical grades. This encouraged greater movement of men and women across these disciplines.

BT also increased the pay minima for management grades. The company found that by focusing pay expenditure on the lower end of the pay scales, some of the equal pay issues were solved.

Managers responsible for pay reviews were trained in understanding the principles of equal pay. After every pay review BT conducts an audit and, since 2002, has set aside a budget of £4 million to address any equal pay issues that arise. The company works closely with the unions on its equal pay policy.

The company has also addressed barriers to women's career progression by increasing access to flexible working and supporting women on courses to help break down occupational segregation.

BT benefits from being seen to be a fair employer as it is more able to attract the most talented people. In addition, the high (98 per cent) return rate after maternity leave saves about £5 million a year in recruitment costs.

Another major employer, **Nationwide**, undertook its first equal pay review in 2001. This found that basic pay structures were reasonably formalised and unbiased, but the discretionary decisions were problematic from the perspective of equal pay. Nationwide identified a 9 per cent gender pay gap. On delving deeper and looking at the elements of flexibility within pay systems, such as starting salaries, performance review scores, promotions and *ad hoc* pay increases, the company found variances it was largely unaware of because they had developed on a piecemeal basis. Nationwide addressed the problem by putting more controls around *ad hoc* pay, and providing more information, training and support to help managers to make the right decisions. It also trained 'licensed recruiters' within the company and closely monitored performance management scoring. The equitable treatment of part-timers has proved to be a particular challenge, but Nationwide has switched the focus of its assessments from the number of hours an individual works to their productivity and contribution.

'Over time we have seen an improvement, but there is no quick fix,' says Paul Bissell, senior manager of reward at Nationwide.

(Adapted from Simms, 2005)

The Women and Work Commission (2006) looked more broadly at the problem of unequal pay and saw it in the context of a subtle range of inequality of practice more generally in organisations. It recommended that, when managing performance, managers need to focus more on productivity rather than the long hours' culture. However, until society in general moves away from occupations being seen as appropriate for either men or women, progress towards equal pay between the genders may be limited.

Summary

The issues of pay and gender are complex and span a range of issues, from pay to wider employment and social trends. Unpicking the reasons for gender pay differences at organisational level can therefore be a tricky and detailed task. To do so thoroughly involves delving into differences, which superficially may seem unrelated to gender, but at root are indeed gendered.

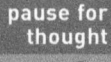

pause for thought Consider the changes that can lead to greater pay equality. What needs to happen to achieve this change?

Review Questions

You may wish to attempt the following as practice examination style questions.

10.1 Consider the causes of gender pay inequality.

10.2 What can employers do to lessen problems of pay discrimination?

10.3 Your Chief Executive is rather reluctant for an equal pay review to be conducted in the organisation. Write a short note to him to persuade him this would be good for the organisation.

10.4 After reading the section on transparency and communication in Chapter 9, as well as this chapter, summarise the business case for greater transparency in pay and identify the barriers to achieving this objective.

· ·

References

Armstrong, M. and Baron, A. (1995). *Job Evaluation Handbook*, London: CIPD.

Brett, S. (2006). *Reward and Diversity – Making Fair Pay Add Up to Business Advantage*, London: CIPD.

Brett, S. and Milsome, S. (2004). *Monitoring Progress on Equal Pay Reviews*, research paper, London: EOC.

CIPD (2006). *Reward Management Survey 2006*, London: CIPD.

Cully, M., O'Reilly, A. and Millward (1998). *The 1998 Workplace Employee Relations Survey: First Findings*, Department of Trade and Industry.

Equal Pay Task (2001). *Just Pay*, Equal Opportunities Commission.

Forth, J. and Millward, N. (2000). *The Determinants of Pay Levels and Fringe Benefit Provision in Britain*, discussion paper No. 171, London: National Institute of Economic and Social Research.

Grimshaw, D. and Rubery, J. (2001). *The Gender Pay Gap: A Research Review*, London: Equal Opportunities Commission.

Incomes Data Services (2002). ACAS: new pay system aims to ensure progression and guarantee equal pay, *IDS Report 852*, March.

Incomes Data Services (2006a). Equal pay claims make waves across the public sector, *IDS Report 950*, April, pp. 12–14.

Incomes Data Services (2006b). Case watch – appeals, *IDS Diversity and Work*, 29, p. 20.

Joshi, H. and Paci, P. (1998). *Unequal Pay for Women and Men: Evidence From the British Birth Cohort Studies*, Cambridge, MA: MIT Press.

Kingsmill (2001). *Review of Women's Pay and Employment*, London: Department of Trade and Industry.

Liff, S. and Cameron, I. (1997). Changing equality cultures to move beyond 'women's problems', *Gender, Work and Organization*, Vol. 4, No. 1, pp. 35–46.

Morell, J. et al. (2001). Gender equality in pay practices, NOP survey for the Equal Opportunities Commission.

Municipal Journal (2006). £50, equal pay bill, 6 April, p. 1.

Purcell, J. (2002). Qualifications and careers: equal opportunities and earnings among graduates, Working Paper Series 1, Equal Opportunities Commission.

Simms, J. (2005). Just out of reach, *People Management*, 10 March, pp. 27–33.

Wajcman, J. (2000). Feminism facing industrial relations in Britain, *British Journal of Industrial Relations*, Vol. 38, No. 2, pp. 13–20.

Walby, S. et al. (2002). Pay and the implications for UK productivity, London: EOC.

Women and Work Commission (2006). Shaping a fairer future, report presented to the Prime Minister.

Wright, A. (2004). *Reward Management in Context*, London: CIPD.

Useful Websites

www.eoc.org.uk – access to Equal Opportunities Commission* reports and guidance on pay equality (e.g. Equal Pay for Equal Value)

* The Commission for Equality and Human Rights from October 2007

www.eoc-law.org.uk – Equal Opportunities Commission website for legal advisors covering, inter alia, equal pay

www.incomesdata.co.uk – access to Income Data Services reports on equal pay

www.ons.gov.uk – access to the Office for National Statistics survey data such as the *Annual Survey of Hours and Earnings*

www.ec.europa.eu/comm/employment_social/gender_equality – European Union website providing details of European Court of Justice cases, including equal pay, pay discrimination, etc.

PART 5

Relations

Part contents

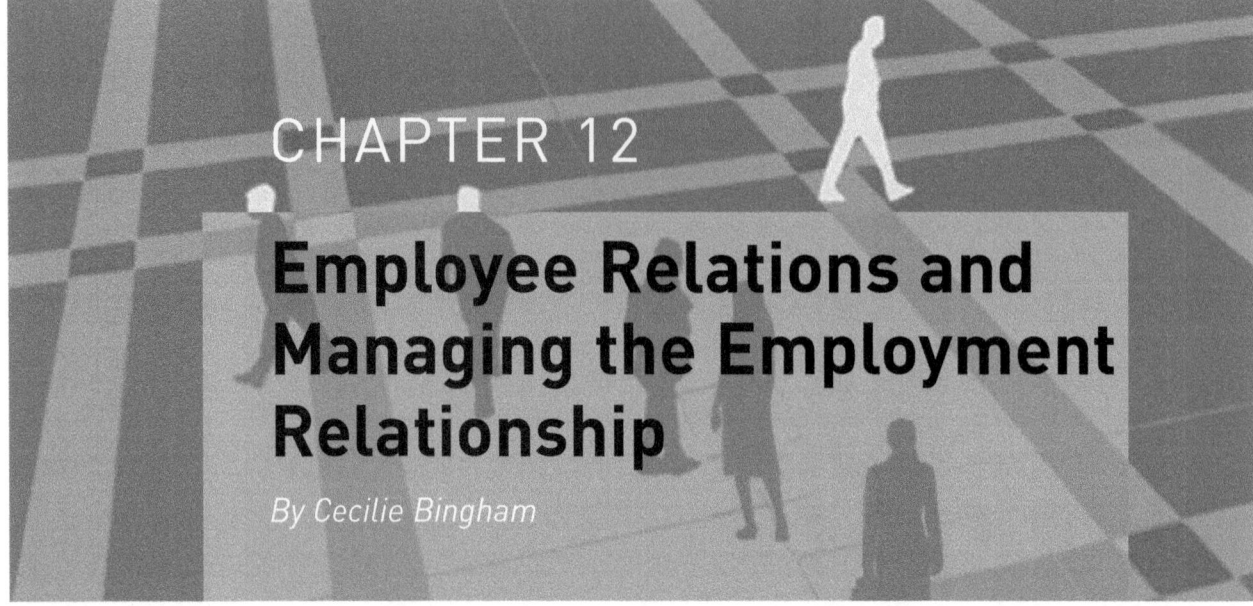

CHAPTER 12

Employee Relations and Managing the Employment Relationship

By Cecilie Bingham

Chapter outline

The way that an organisation chooses to deploy and manage its workforce is central to the human resource (HR) function. This chapter looks at the ways in which employment relationships are managed. In particular, it examines how different managerial styles and frames of reference will have an impact on the sources of power and its distribution within the workplace. The levels of conflict and the ways it is managed are explored; and the mechanisms for employee voice, specifically the impact this has on the psychological contract, are examined.

Learning outcomes

By the end of the chapter, you should be able to:

◆ Describe the different theoretical perspectives which can be applied to employee relations;

◆ Assess the value of different frames of reference for explaining the employment relationship;

◆ Apply appropriate theoretical concepts to the workplace;

◆ Use theoretical concepts to analyse current employee relations situations.

Introduction

Examining the ways people interact at work, both as individuals and in groups, is at the heart of studying the employment relationship. Such interaction is influenced not just by the perceptions of the individuals and their positions within the organisation but by a variety of different factors, such as the economy, the labour market and the strength of external competitors.

The essence of employee relations

Employee relations is the study of workplace relationships and the way in which the parties to such relationships interact with one another. This will involve individual employees (those who work for others), managers (those who organise and control work processes) and employers (those who own the enterprise in question). It may involve groups or organisations that represent or 'talk for' any of these three main groups. Trade unions, for example, may represent some or all of the workforce, the managers may belong to professional bodies such as the CIPD (Chartered Institute of Personnel and Development), while the employers may belong to an employers' organisation, such as the Engineering Employers' Federation or the Institute of Directors. The relationship does not, of course, take place in a vacuum: the economy and the labour market will have an impact on the relationship, as will rules, laws and codes of practice regulating the workplace. These may originate from within the UK or from Europe or indeed from within the workplace itself, sometimes even as a product of the employment relationship. Depending on the type of organisation, there will be a mixture of customers, competitors, creditors and suppliers, all having an impact on the relationship. The size of the organisation, whether it is a small family-run enterprise or a large multinational conglomerate, whether it is based on one site or many, will have an influence on the way in which the employees are managed and on the ways in which they react to that management. On occasions the courts may influence workplace-based behaviour and so too might the media. In addition to all of these factors, the culture of the organisation, the history of the relationships it has with its employees and the values and expectations of the employees themselves will all have an impact on the way in which the employment relationship is managed and perceived.

Employee relations therefore is about the formal and informal relationships at work. It concerns the ways in which people interact both with one another and with the jobs that they undertake; specifically, it concerns individuals who voluntarily subordinate themselves to the demands of the organisation by exchanging their time, effort and possibly experience and knowledge, for monetary and non-monetary rewards within a regulated work environment. The interaction of the parties involved is crucially affected by the balance of power between them. As Lewis et al. (2003: 6) say, the employment relationship is an 'economic, legal, social, psychological and political relationship in which employees devote their time and expertise to the inter-ests of their employer in return for a range of personal, financial and non-financial rewards.'

Each party to the relationship is influenced by a number of different factors or interests and, in order to understand employee relations as a topic, it is necessary to be aware of the different influences that may affect each of the parties.

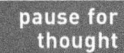
pause for thought

What do you think the main concerns of employees are?

Why did you reach this conclusion?

Individual employees work for a number of reasons. Financial reward is perhaps the most obvious, but social status, friendship, professional interest in an area, a sense of achievement, the ability to 'put something back into society' are all other aspects that induce/motivate people to participate in paid employment. Once participating, such motivators influence the expectations that employees bring to the workplace. So, for example, they expect to be treated with respect, paid for the work they do and that the:

- Amount they receive will be a fair reward for the effort that they have expended – and that it will be fair in relation to any remuneration that others they know receive;
- Work they do will be appreciated;
- The workplace will be safe;
- Work expected from them will be within their capabilities;
- Hours that they are required to work will not be excessive;
- Training will be timely and appropriate;
- Holidays will be adequate.

Common expectations that most employees bring to the workplace are listed above. Can you think of any other expectations?

pause for thought

The employers too will have a set of interests that influence them. These may include:

- Making a profit (if it is part of the private sector) while maintaining, if not enlarging, their market share;
- Providing a good service, whether it is part of the private sector or a not-for-profit organisation;
- Providing value for shareholders and stakeholders;
- Deploying the people within the organisation in the most cost-effective way to maximise their time, effort and knowledge for the good of the organisation;
- Ensuring the survival of the organisation;
- Ensuring their corporate social responsibility;
- Maximising any good publicity while minimising any that is bad;
- Operating within the bounds of the law.

Some employers will want to behave ethically, some will not.

In small organisations the employers may well be the managers and have face-to-face interaction with the employees but, in larger organisations, managers are employed to achieve the objectives of the organisation and attached to this role are the concepts of accountability, responsibility and authority.

The employment relationship and human resource management

HRM is regarded as a strategic, holistic way of dealing with the employment relationship; those employed doing so in the light of business planning and development. With HRM there is a move away from centralised personnel departments towards line management control and consequent responsibility for empowering, motivating and regulating those staff for whom they are responsible (Sisson, 1990). (The last decade or so has seen a wide-ranging debate about the nature of HRM and the differences between this and the more traditional aspects of personnel management. John Storey (1992, 1998) clearly delineates the differences and similarities between the two (see Chapters 1 and 3).

David Guest (1987) has examined the academic approaches to HRM and identified two different approaches: the soft and the hard. The former sees employees as an asset to be nurtured and the latter sees employees as a resource to be utilised for the needs of the business. The two are not mutually exclusive; both may be present at the same time depending on the type of employee in question. What is important is the impact that the 'type' has on the employment relationship. Staff who are valued, rewarded, consulted and feel integrated into an organisation are more likely to feel commitment and loyalty to that organisation than those who are treated merely as a resource. Hence the former are more likely to have an employment relationship that is characterised less by 'command and control' mechanisms and more by the four Cs: **C**ommunicate, **C**onsult and **C**are combined with **C**ontrol.

Power and the employment relationship

Power is the degree to which one party can influence, persuade, encourage or force another to do something that they might not otherwise do. The relationship between an employer and an employee can be said to be based around the realities of power, the employee submitting to the control of the employer. Yet in practice the position is not quite that clear cut. The relationship between an employer and an employee is symbiotic. That is, each is dependent on the other and, despite differences, they work together for the mutual benefit of each because it is in the interests of neither to destroy the other. This does not, however, mean that the relationship is one where each has an equal amount of influence and power over the other. The very nature of the relationship is such that the employer, who has the power to hire and fire, to dictate which work is to be done, to control the ways in which the work is to be done, and specify the time in which it is to be done, has the controlling stake in the relationship. Employees, however, are not without power. Their willingness to work, their labour, skills, expertise, knowledge, and availability mean that the employer cannot function without them. While the condition of the labour market (i.e. the supply of those able to work), the degree to which vital skills are available and the legislation in place at the time all play a part in shaping the power balance within the relationship as do the culture and values permeating the organisation.

Financial and Human Resource Management in Organisations, Second Edition

> **pause for thought**
>
> Do you think the balance of power always lies with the management of an organisation? Why did you reach this conclusion?

> **exercise**
>
> Read the Warbings case study. How would you describe the ways in which power is exercised across the company?

The amount of power that individuals hold can be defined as the degree of influence that one party has over the other in order to achieve their own goals. Individuals may have power because their employer depends on their knowledge, expertise or skills that, on occasion, may be in demand because there are few like them available in the labour market. Sometimes power is achieved by individuals banding together to present a united front to the employer, as when they join a union. In practice the balance of power often means one party subjugating their own desires in order to execute the requirements of the other. Employers share with or delegate power to the managers in the organisation – the amount of power the managers hold will therefore be dependent on their freedom to engage in discretionary behaviour.

Yet there is a balance in the employment relationship. Whoever is in the ascendancy will not want to push the other to such an extreme that the relationship breaks down, leading to the mutual destruction of them both. Indeed on occasions the power of decision making is shared in order to achieve results that are palatable to everyone. Analysis of the power balance can depend on the perspective of those undertaking the analysis; as Gospel and Palmer (1993: 11) say: 'While some people assume that employers always have the real power in industrial relations, others assume that employees, when organised into trade unions, can be as powerful or more so.' Such differing perspectives influence the philosophies behind employment legislation: hence the resulting legislation sometimes promotes collective representation and at other times restricts it. Consequently EU legislation requiring collective representation is sometimes anathema to a UK government and UK employers that prefer to restrict such representation.

Lukes (1974, 1986) and Clegg (1989) develop the notion of power, suggesting that it may be exercised to check, eliminate or enhance certain behaviours, in such a way that the specific values predominate within an organisation, creating cultural norms for each workplace. Such views presuppose that everyone is happy to go along with the dominant values and that individual differences are subsumed in respect of those in power. In many ways it is rather simplistic: individuals, different groups within an organisation, different segments within the same workforce interact with one another and exchange views and information in ways that influence one another's behaviour. The degree of power exercised may change from day to day depending on circumstances, individuals and the market in which they find themselves.

Sources of power (and the ways in which it may be exercised within the workplace) are not homogeneous. French and Raven (1962), in their classic study, delineated five distinct sources of power; two of these sources, expert and referent power, derive from the holder's individual characteristics. The other three, legitimate, reward and coercive power, derive from the holder's position within the organisation.

An individual has **expert power** when they have specific knowledge and expertise that others rely upon, for example an IT specialist in a company of non-specialists. Here the sharing or withholding of specialist knowledge will have a direct impact on the organisation.

Referent power, on the other hand, derives not from expertise, but from the sometimes inspirational, often charismatic, personality of the holder. Such people are liked and respected and others want to do their bidding because they want to please them. In terms of the employment relationship, such people are often able to motivate and persuade their colleagues to undertake difficult tasks, stay late at work and perform duties outside their contract, merely because they are liked and because people don't want to let them down. Arthur Scargill could have been said to exercise referent power when, without a ballot, in 1984–85, he led the miners to strike against pit closures.

Coercive power is in evidence when a compelling argument based on threat is used to encourage obedience: in employee relations terms, this could be displayed by a manager deciding to withhold resources, or perhaps bully colleagues, in order to ensure compliance. The atmosphere created is not one of trust, people often performing to the minimum rather than the maximum standard required because they resent the explicit or implicit threats. Sexual harassment and bullying can be regarded as forms of coercive power. The trade union Unison (2003: 2) says that bullying behaviour in the workplace is an abuse of power that is 'offensive, intimidating, malicious, insulting'. Coercive power in the form of bullying behaviour, even if it is regarded as acceptable in some workplaces, is not acceptable under law. Should cases go to trial they are often settled out of court: in *Kirk v Nacanco*, for example, Kirk eventually received an out of court settlement for £200,000. The company acknowledged that he had been subjected to impossibly escalating production targets coupled with continual criticism both at work and through phone calls at home that contributed to his breakdown.

Reward power is where individuals persuade others to do their bidding in exchange for something that they want. In employment terms, this is epitomised by the pay–work bargain (Farnham 1997: 3), where employees exchange their labour for monetary reward. The reward may not be monetary; it could be promotion, or the opportunity to work on a prestigious project. The strength of the power that a person holds depends on the perception of others that they can actually deliver. Sometimes rewards do not match the expectations of the rewarded and conflict may result.

Legitimate power is where someone's position within the organisation gives them the authority to make decisions and control the activities of others. Line managers therefore have the authority to control the work processes of their subordinates merely because of their position in the organisation. Perceptions, too, are important here. If someone is not perceived as being worthy of the position they hold, their power may be diminished. So, for example, if someone with little experience is brought in to manage an existing sales team the perception of the team may be that the person's inexperience renders them unfit for the job and non-cooperation, conflict and a breakdown in the employment relationship can be the result.

Exercise

Read the scenario below and then answer the following questions:

◆ Who are the parties involved?

◆ What are the issues involved?

◆ How would you describe the balance of power?

> In December 2004, airline pilots in the UK threatened not to co-operate with their employers if changes were made to the ways in which they worked. Specifically, they did not want to work the new hours being discussed by transport ministers from the EU that they believed could result in longer hours at work with fewer rest periods. On 10 December, BALPA (the British Airline Pilots Association, the pilots' trade union) took out a number of advertisements in national newspapers explaining its worries: a particular concern was about pilot fatigue and the risks that this posed for the lives of both passengers and air crews. So worried were they that the advertisements said, 'If this European fudge is adopted and we are asked to fly hours we believe to be unsafe we will not take-off.' In addition the union's general secretary, Jim McAuslan, claimed 'Dangerously fatigued foreign pilots will be flying over and landing in Britain, putting at risk communities living around airports.' The union accused the European politicians of trying to impose regulations that were less safe than the existing ones and certainly less scientific. Mr Gramshaw, the chairman of BALPA, and a pilot at Britannia Airways, commenting on the fact that, for a pilot beginning a night flight in Europe, the limit would exceed 12 hours while the existing one in the UK was 10 hours, used emotive language. He compared the long hours to those of junior doctors: 'They kill the patients one at a time. We tend to kill ours hundreds at a time.'
>
> BALPA called for the UK government to veto the proposals and ensure that independent safety experts scrutinised them.
>
> (Sources: case study compiled with information from the
> TUC *Risks* magazine, *Personnel Today*, *Hansard* and the BBC)

◆ Look at the Warbings case study and list all of the parties you think are involved in the employment relationship.

◆ What types of power are in evidence? Don't forget to give examples to back up your answer.

◆ Is power evenly distributed between the parties?

◆ Why did you reach this conclusion?

exercise

W

The exercise of power is constrained by circumstance and perception. As the unions in the UK have become constrained by legislative restrictions, and weakened by falling membership, they have looked to a number of different ways to maintain a continuing influence within the workplace. (In autumn 2005, 6.68 million people were union members and the rate of union membership (union density) among employees was 29 per cent. It was higher for women and older employees (Grainger, 2006).) Whereas in the past unions may have asserted their power by means of industrial action, in the twenty-first century this is not always possible. Alternative methods of influence have to be found: sometimes this is via partnership arrangements where the emphasis is on consensual problem solving; at other times it is by a reliance on rules and procedures to help create a fairer employment relationship.

Oxenbridge and Brown (2004) point out that contemporary union influence is no longer as reliant on the mechanisms of negotiation, and hence on the explicit exercise of power. In order to influence the employment relationship, the mechanisms of consultation, partnership and a reliance on procedures are utilised to ensure that they continue to have some sway in the ways in which the employment relationship operates. Other researchers (for example, Jenkins in a paper given at the 2006 International Labour Process Conference) have argued that by entering into partnership arrangements with organisations unions often lose a further degree of power. Indeed long before partnership agreements were in vogue, Flanders (1970: 172) pointed out that managements often maintain control by sharing it.

The Transport and General Workers' Union* is determined to buck this trend of partnership working where it leads to ever-diminishing levels of union influence. It deliberately emphasises the difference between its members' interests and those of management; and rather than develop partnership approaches has declared an interest in being adversarial where necessary.

In his 2003 conference address, Tony Woodley, General Secretary of the Transport and General Workers' Union, stated:

> 'Real change must start at the sharp end – in the workplace . . . We live in a society where workers can be sacked by text message. Where unscrupulous employers close down factories here because it is quicker, cheaper and easier to sack British workers than those elsewhere in Europe. Where poverty pay remains rife, and women and black people are second-class citizens at work. [. . .]
>
> And we have to recognise it – a society where the trade union movement has been able to do too little to help those who need us most. [. . .] How many times have I heard workers say, "why isn't the union doing anything for us?" Even, "what is the point in the union?" And if those who are already our members are saying that, we can only imagine what the attitude is among those millions who aren't in unions.
>
> Why? Because we have taken our eye off the ball, because we are sometimes seen as too close to the gaffer [boss], because we are not delivering satisfaction at the sharp end, in the workplace, we have become almost irrelevant to our members.
>
> That is why we must refocus our time, money and effort on the workplace and industrial priorities of the union, on the T&G becoming once more a fighting back union.
>
> Because fighting back makes a difference to our members.
>
> Some people may misinterpret that as a permanent call to arms, or a programme of endless strikes. That is not the case. What I mean is a T&G that:

Never lets an injustice in the workplace go by without challenging it. Encourages, rather than damps down, the aspirations of working people. When a problem arises, always meets the members before we meet the governor. And, if our members decide they need to fight to secure improvements in pay and conditions, equality, or to save their jobs, gets right behind them one hundred and ten per cent and fights to win.

If we fight we may not always win, but if we don't fight we will surely lose. . . . I have said loud and clear that social partnership is not the way forward for working people. Of course, I don't mean that we stop negotiating, that we stop reaching pragmatic agreements with employers, that we don't have constructive engagement, or that we stop respecting companies that respect their own workforce and their unions. But it does mean ending the situation where we look at a company's business plan and demands before we look at our own members' needs and demands.

We want workplace improvements. Concession bargaining must end, our members want real improvements in the workplace.'

* The TGWU merged with Amicus in May 2007 to become Unite

Identify Tony Woodley's view of power within the employment relationship. Give your reasoning behind reaching this conclusion.

pause for thought

Managerial styles

The ways that management behaves within a workplace will depend on the type of power that is exercised, which in turn is affected by the culture and values of the organisation. The ways that employees are treated relate not just to power and perceptions of power but also to managerial styles.

In order to analyse and evaluate current workplace behaviours with their complicated set of interrelated activities, there are a number of ways of categorising and sorting the activities associated with managing the employment relationship. Such analysis can be used to predict what is likely to happen in the future if particular managerial styles are adopted.

Allan Fox (1966) organised the ways in which employers and hence managers operated into two main categories. He said that those whose managerial approach was one where management was regarded as a single source of authority without any interference from others, whose management was characterised by a common organisational purpose that was expressed as management's prerogative to manage, displayed a **unitarist** 'frame of reference'. The managerial perspective in such organisations emphasises loyalty, unity and harmony and assumes that the goals, values and aims of those within the organisation exhibit a high level of congruence – such affinity of ideology legitimises management behaviour. Within this framework conflict is therefore regarded as pathological; should it materialise it is perceived as being due to poor communication or to 'maverick' nonconformist employees. On

Category	Characteristics
Traditionalists	Unitarist Strong managerial prerogative, i.e. management has a *right* to manage Exploitative attitude to the workforce Hostile towards third parties
Sophisticated paternalists	Unitarist Strong commitment to employee well-being Training and development encouraged Third parties discouraged because conditions of work, encouraging loyalty and commitment, are so good that unions are deemed unnecessary
Standard moderns	Pragmatic pluralists Much managerial authority devolved to line managers Unions recognised but employee relations issues are dealt with on a fire-fighting rather than on a strategic basis

Sophisticated moderns	Pluralist
	Consulters
	  Unions recognised and consulted with, although there is a strong emphasis on direct communication with employees
	Constitutionalists
	  Unions recognised, well developed bargaining machinery and procedures

Figure 12.1 Characteristics of managerial styles

the other hand, Fox (1974) categorised the thinking behind those employers and managers willing to share power, and accept that a uniformity of ideology and values throughout the organisation was not necessarily the case, indeed that there might be more than a single 'right' viewpoint in the organisation, as **pluralist**. The distinction however needed refinement and a number of academics have developed the model (Fox, 1974; Purcell and Sisson, 1983). See Figure 12.1 for a summary of these.

Within these frameworks employees may be dealt with in a calculative HRM hard way, or by means of the softer developmental approach. As noted earlier, hard and soft approaches are not always mutually exclusive. Organisations pick and mix the strategies and processes that they think will work best; sometimes this process can be rather *ad hoc*. There is not always a clear line of sight between what an organisation opts to do and ideological purity. Parts of HRM may be adopted, hard and soft strategies may be pursued simultaneously and unions may be recognised in organisations that utilise a number of HRM practices. Arguably, the style chosen will influence whether or not employee relationships are part of the strategic planning within an organisation (Gunnigle et al., 1998).

In general it could be argued that pluralist organisations are associated with a **collective** way of managing, which in many ways is reactive, and not strategic; while unitarist organisations, employing soft HRM, are linked to an **individualistic** way of management and have a tendency to incorporate managing the employment relationship with organisational strategy (Purcell and Grey, 1986; Purcell, 1987).

Traditional indications of collectivism

These include:

- 'The recognition by management of the collective interests of groups of employees in the decision making process' (Purcell and Gray, 1986: 213);
- One or more trade unions recognised for consultation and/or negotiation as well as for representation;
- High density of trade union membership within the organisation;
- Unions have an impact on the employment relationship;
- Formalisation of union arrangements, e.g. time off for trade union duties;
- Agreements between the union and the organisation;
- Communication through representation;
- Possibility of an employer's organisation bargaining for/representing the employer;
- Collective agreements regulating pay and conditions;
- May be adversarial or consensual, as with partnership agreements.

Indications of individualism

These include:

- Individuals are valued and developed for what they bring to the organisation;
- Direct communication with individual employees;
- Performance management and monitoring;
- Individual remuneration packages – such as performance-related pay and/or bonuses;
- Non-standard work packages – such as flexibility around hours or place of work;
- Individuals are assumed to put their own interests first, rather than subordinate their particular needs for the good of others.

Are employees less powerful as individuals than when they act as a group?

Why did you reach this conclusion?

Can you think of any exceptions?

pause for thought

The psychological contract and employee relations

The psychological contract, first discussed by Argyris (1962), describes the implicit, rather than explicit, exchange relationship between employers and those whom they employ. It is concerned with unwritten, unrecorded expectations and perceptions. In the past, for example, job security in exchange for high-quality work could have been perceived as part of the contract. Now, when *beliefs* about job security are sometimes more uncertain, it is not unusual for employees to expect employers to provide them with opportunities for development (Martin et al., 1998). Taylor (2002: 12) talks about a 'growing and widespread lack of satisfaction at work and little advance in any sense of organisational commitment by workers', but points out that the permanent job remains 'very much the overwhelming norm and this is true across every occupational category'.

Each contract will be unique to the individual concerned and will consist of an unwritten 'deal' that indicates the individual's expectations about what they will bring to the relationship and, importantly, of what the employer will give in exchange. As Rousseau said: 'A psychological contract emerges when one party believes that a promise of future returns has been made, a contribution has been given and thus an obligation has been created to provide future benefits' (1989: 123). This can be problematic: if the contract is a matter of perception and unspoken, there is a good deal of room for misunderstanding and the potential for unwitting damage to the employment relationship.

Individuals expect a fair balance in the exchange of services and when this is apparent they honour their part of the contract with commitment and loyalty towards the organisation. If, however, they perceive their expectations as being thwarted, or frustrated in any way, the contract becomes damaged and the employee demotivated.

Managerial styles and frames of reference affect the ways in which employees perceive their psychological contracts. HRM, with the prominence it gives to direct communication, coupled with its emphasis on the individual, taps into the emotional needs of employees and should help promote healthy psychological contracts: high commitment policies leading to positive psychological contracts and hence improved business performance (Guest, 1998; Guest and Conway, 2002a, 2002b, 2002c). Hard management practices treating individuals as resources may lead to damaged contracts depending on the expectations of the participants. Breaches of the contract can lead to drops in productivity, increases in turnover, higher levels of grievances and on occasions an increased commitment to trade unions (Turnley et al., 2004). Aggrieved employees with damaged psychological contracts are more likely to join unions.

exercise

Describe the impact that the increasing surveillance at Warbings has had on the psychological contract of the employees.

Is this a positive change?

Why did you reach this conclusion?

Conflict

The fact that employers and their employees have different requirements from the work process and different perceptions about their needs and requirements sometimes leads to conflict in the workplace.

pause for thought

Think about employer and employee expectations.

How might the apparent differences in expectations lead to conflict?

While, much of the time, co-operation is the norm in the majority of workplaces it should not be forgotten that employers need to maximise the efforts made by employees to ensure that their employment is worth while and that the balance of power, and the ways in which power is exercised, will have an impact on the perceptions of the parties to the employment relationship. Edwards (1995) says this relationship is characterised by structured antagonism – explaining that employees need to be supervised and controlled, and yet need a degree of autonomy in order to perform well. Depending on the managerial style, conflict may be seen as an unusual aberration or a normal expression of differing values and views. In 2004, 904,900 working days were lost in the UK as a result of labour disputes (Monger, 2005). Yet in total there were just 130 stoppages of work – the lowest annual total on record: the high number of days lost was due to the large number of employees involved in just a few disputes. Most of the disagreements were about pay: not just strikes endeavouring to persuade employers to pay more but disputes endeavouring to persuade employers *not to pay less*.

There are a number of mechanisms used by employers to contain, diffuse, prevent and solve conflict. They can include direct and indirect communication (see Chapter 4) and may range from comprehensive procedural arrangements to negotiating with individuals, bargaining with representatives and perhaps introducing partnership arrangements.

The type of management style adopted will have an impact on the ways that conflict is perceived and dealt with. For a traditional unitarist, the possibility of conflict occurring is considered to be unlikely, and so there will be fewer mechanisms in place to diffuse and resolve disputed incidents and disgruntled employees are more likely to show their displeasure by taking time off, changing their employer and/or resorting to the courts. Legally, UK organisations have to provide employees with a means of airing their grievances (with a fair grievance procedure) and a three-stage disciplinary process that complies with the principles of natural justice, but even these are seen by some as unnecessary interference with management prerogative. (The Box on page 229 gives the principles of Natural Justice.)

Those employing HRM practices are likely to use a number of strategies that contribute to making employees feel committed to the organisation and less likely to question the way in which they are treated. Such practices include comprehensive induction programmes to socialise new employees into the culture of the organisation, ensuring they understand their roles, as well as direct communication and teamwork as a means to engage employees and get their buy-in to organisational requirements, together with professional development to encourage loyalty (Marchington and Wilkinson, 2005: 277).

The pluralist framework is more accommodating, acknowledging that a variety of different stakeholders within the organisation will have different views and these are not always likely to show high levels of congruence. Procedures, rules, consultation and negotiation are some of the mechanisms used to resolve differences. According to ACAS, conflict potentially inherent in the employment relationship can be managed successfully (ACAS, 2004/5: 4). Procedures, providing they are perceived as being fair, help to do this. They achieve a number of things, from providing a consistent way of dealing with issues to helping defuse problems by providing a process by which they are managed. Negotiation, too, is often the means by which conflicts of interest are resolved.

Managerial style	**Conflict minimising mechanisms**							Company examples Can you think of any others?
	Providing information	Involving employees	Open channels of communication	Partnership working	Negotiation and bargaining	Procedures	Clear contracts of employment	
Collective	✓	✓	✓	✓	✓	✓	✓	Ford
Individual	✓	✓	✓		✓ with some individuals	✓	✓	Marks and Spencer
Traditionalist					✓ sometimes – often linked to dismissal of difficult employees	✓ sometimes		Amazon
Sophisticated paternalists	✓	✓	✓	✓ sometimes		✓	✓	Gillette UK Ltd Listawood
Standard moderns	✓ sometimes	✓	✓ sometimes		✓ reluctant fire-fighting	✓	✓	Gate Gourmet London Underground
Sophisticated moderns	✓	✓	✓	✓	✓	✓	✓	Monarch Aircraft Engineering Tesco

Figure 12.2 Managerial styles and methods of dealing with and minimising conflict

Source: © Bingham 2006

The ways of coping with conflict promoted by the Labour Government at the end of the twentieth century and the beginning of the twenty-first have centred around the concepts of fairness, employee voice and alternative dispute resolution, such as workplace-based mediation. Figure 12.2 summarises some of the ways that organisations choose to operate in order to minimise the number of potential disagreements within the employment relationship before things escalate to full-blown disputes or either party resorts to legal remedies.

Procedures

Employers have always used reward as a means of gaining employee compliance but procedures too have played an important part in regulating the relationship, minimising disruption and standardising behaviours. Procedures are sets of organisation-specific rules that provide a framework of processes for handling issues. Such regulations may result from unilateral management decisions, negotiations and/or statutory requirements. In effect, they are a means of restraining behaviour (limiting power) and promoting consistent and fair treatment between the managed and those managing. They clarify relationships and make explicit the processes that the organisation requires its employees to follow; on occasions providing a safety valve and mechanism for the resolution of differences that is fair to all parties yet showing consideration for the employee's point of view and inhibiting bias against him or her. Procedures therefore enable natural and procedural justice; enhancing the psychological contract because they provide a backdrop of fairness around the way that an organisation operates. They institutionalise conflict management and the process of working through a procedure often defuses difficult situations and enables speedier, less emotionally charged resolutions. Procedures may add to the bureaucracy of the workplace and inhibit flexible approaches to individual problems – but with the plethora of legislative requirements impacting upon employment relationships they do promote consistency of treatment, accurate recordkeeping and provide a standardised means of problem solving.

Principles of Natural Justice

That employees know the expected standards of behaviour.

That, should there be allegations against someone, they have the right to:

♦ Be informed of the complaint,

♦ Have the opportunity of stating their case before a decision is reached,

♦ Be accompanied to any hearing,

♦ Be given the outcome in writing,

♦ Be provided with – and informed of – their legal right of appeal.

In many ways these principles are integral to the HRM practices of the four Cs, (**C**ommunicate, **C**onsult, **C**are and **C**ontrol.) Making certain that managers abide by these principles helps ensure healthy psychological contracts. Such principles should be inherent in the ways that employees are dealt with, particularly if their performance is not all that it might be. Employers control employee behaviour by using a number of techniques such as: performance management, training, coaching, mentoring and disciplining. When disciplinary action is considered it is essential that the principles of natural justice be adhered to. Employers abiding by the ACAS code of practice, requiring that normally employees be given an oral warning, a written warning and a final written warning prior to dismissal (most cases, never progress past the first informal warning, if that) will find, provided they tell their employees what is wrong and allow them to answer any accusations, that the principles will have been adhered to. The legislation reinforces this.

Schedule 2 of the Employment Act 2002 lays down the following steps that employers must stick to when taking disciplinary action:

---

1. Put the events in writing and write to the employee telling them about the alleged misdemeanour and invite them to attend a meeting – there must be enough time for the employee to consider the situation prior to the meeting.

2. Undertake an exploratory meeting where the incidents are discussed and the employee has a chance to put their side of the story: the employer must then take time to consider this evidence: the employee is told of the decision and informed of the right to appeal if disciplinary action is taken.

3. If the employee chooses to appeal they must inform the employer who invites them to a meeting. The employee has to take all reasonable attempts to attend this. If possible the appeal meeting must be held by a more senior manager: the final decision must then be communicated to the employee.

If the offence is classed as a gross misdemeanour, e.g. setting fire to company property, the process may be reduced to two steps – the decision to dismiss communicated to the employee in writing together with details of the alleged misconduct and notifying the employee of their right to appeal. The last stage remains the same.

Sections 10–15 of the Employment Relations Act 1999 also promotes a fair process by giving workers the right to be accompanied by a fellow worker, or trade union rep, when faced with the prospect of formal disciplinary action.

Employee voice

This is based on the principle that employees can enhance the workplace by contributing not just their labour but also their views. (This has echoes of the Farnham dictum that to share power is to regain control.) The recent emphasis on 'high commitment workplaces' (Applebaum, 2002; Applebaum et al., 2000; DTI, 2002) has encouraged organisations to adopt the mechanisms of employee voice by promoting the integration of employees into the processes of decision making and problem solving. The philosophy underpinning the emphasis on employee voice is that hermetically sealed managements who fail to engage with their staff are stifling goodwill, productivity, knowledge sharing and commitment, thereby damaging the psychological contract and failing to meet employee interests within the employment relationship. The mechanisms for voice, on the other hand, are designed to promote all of these. The direct and indirect methods used (see Chapter 4) will depend on the managerial style adopted; for the pluralists, collective representation, informing, consulting and negotiating with unions, staff associations and workplace representatives is the means by which this is achieved. For those with a more unitarist perspective, direct communication in the form of team meetings, appraisals, problem-solving forums and employee surveys is often the way used to engage staff and circumvent discontent.

Legislation plays a part, too, so even traditional unitarist management approaches on occasions adopt more pluralist methods, from listening to an employee grievance or request for flexible working, where the employee is accompanied by a colleague, to health and safety committees making workplace recommendations and representatives consulting about redundancy or business transfers. Similarly, where managements have to recognise trade unions following a ruling from the Central Arbitration Committee they may become reluctant pluralists. Those that pre-empt legislative compulsion and set up their own systems of staff representation discover a mismatch between their unitarist principles and the reality of having to listen to their workforce. Such unitarists on the cusp of pluralism find their management styles changing in order to accommodate or avoid legislative requirements. Information and Consultation Regulations broaden the areas where managements are obliged to inform and consult employees about the business. European Works Councils are required by law (for those businesses with at least 1,000 employees and with 150 employees in no less than two different member states) to consult about European matters affecting the business. Under the Information and Consultation of Employees (ICE) Regulations (2002), an employer must ensure that the timing, method content and level of any consultations are appropriate. It is not acceptable, for example, to consult on something after a decision has been made.

exercise

A recent ACAS policy discussion paper by Grell and Sisson (2005: 1) stated:

'. . . there are particular problems with consultation, stemming from our employment relations history. Like Cinderella, consultation is very much the poor relation – for management it compares unfavourably to communications, while trade unions much prefer collective bargaining.'

What do you think is meant by this?

For pluralists, one of the ways of managing the inevitable conflict that arises within the workplace is to enter into a partnership agreement with trade union representatives. This joint problem-solving approach to management gives employees a say, through their representatives, about the running of the business, and is particularly important in times of change. It does not, however, eradicate conflict and sometimes it results in quite strong disagreements between the representatives and those they represent.

Partnership, when linked to the employment relationship, has no precise theoretical definition or evidence-based practical connotations. The imprecision of the term is a weakness, leading to confusion about what it is meant to imply. It is therefore difficult to disagree with – consequently for many employers and employees the idea of partnership may seem vague and difficult to put into practice. Guest and Peccei (1998) say that organisations operating in a partnership way may well exhibit the following:

◆ Direct participation by employees in decisions about their own work and about personal employment issues;

◆ Participation by employee representatives in decisions about employment issues and about broader organisational policy issues;

◆ Flexible job design, with a focus on quality;

◆ Performance management;

◆ Employee share ownership;

◆ Communication;

◆ Harmonisation;

◆ Employment security.

232   CHAPTER 12 EMPLOYEE RELATIONS AND MANAGING EMPLOYMENT RELATIONSHIP

However all of these categories may well be present in organisations that, rather than practise partnership, exhibit adversarial employee relations such as those associated with parts of the rail industry.

exercise

Look at the case study on Warbings.

What methods of employee voice do you think would be most appropriate for this organisation?

What mechanisms promoting employee voice would you recommend the management to adopt?

Information sharing: informing, consulting, negotiating

Where employee representatives are present, employee voice occurs indirectly for individual employees through the processes of joint consultation or collective bargaining. Where there is no system of representation, these processes may occur directly – often even where there are indirect mechanisms, an employer may additionally use direct methods. Negotiation is 'a process of interaction by which two or more parties who consider they need to be jointly involved in an outcome but who initially have different objectives, seek, by the use of argument and persuasion, to resolve their differences in order to achieve a mutually acceptable solution' (Fowler, 1996: 3).

The outcomes of such discussions can please everyone (win-win), no one (lose-lose) or just one party (win-lose). Negotiations about how to divide up resources are known as distributive bargaining, while those concerned with reaching agreement about the ways to solve problems are interest-based bargaining. Before negotiations begin, the parties will have some idea of why they want things to change – see Figure 12.3.

Negotiations occur within the employment relationship at individual and collective levels. They are individual when an employee discusses pay, workload and workflow with the line manager. They are collective, and therefore indirect, when representatives act on behalf of others and negotiate for them. Negotiations typically follow a pattern whereby the participants:

♦ Prepare their own case (including anticipating the position and arguments to be presented by the other side);

♦ Exchange views establishing and confirming what each party wants;

♦ Explore the issues and examine potential outcomes;

♦ Negotiate around such issues and outcomes;

♦ Secure agreement;

♦ Implement the agreement.

There are a number of issues about which negotiations frequently occur; the most recently available statistics are from the Workplace Employee Relations Survey 2004 (see Table 12.1), which show that issues such as pay hours and holidays are

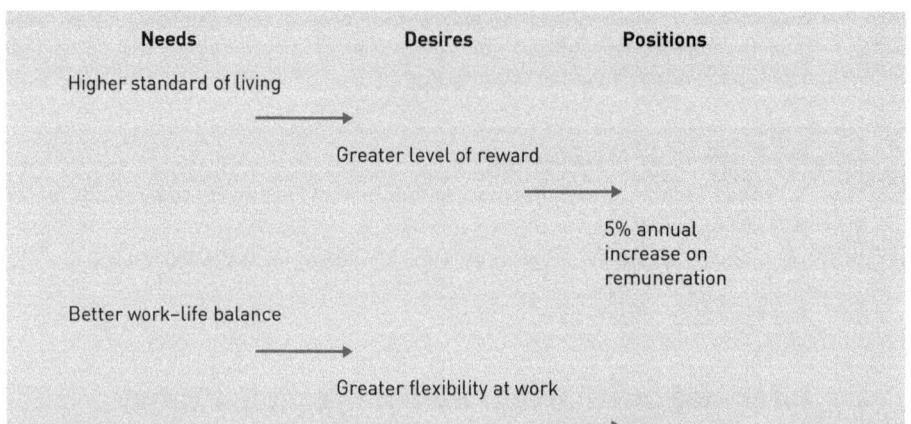

Figure 12.3 Examples showing the pre-negotiation movement from needs to positions
Source: © Bingham 2006

Table 12.1 Joint regulation of terms and conditions[a,b]

Issue	% of workplaces			
	Nothing	Inform	Consult	Negotiate
Pay	70 (16)	6 (10)	5 (13)	18 (61)
Hours	71 (18)	5 (10)	8 (20)	16 (53)
Holidays	71 (19)	9 (17)	5 (13)	15 (52)
Pensions	73 (22)	11 (25)	6 (16)	10 (36)
Staff selection	78 (42)	10 (26)	9 (23)	3 (9)
Training	75 (36)	10 (24)	13 (31)	3 (9)
Grievance procedure	69 (15)	9 (20)	14 (36)	9 (28)
Disciplinary procedure	69 (15)	9 (21)	13 (35)	8 (29)
Staffing plans	75 (33)	11 (26)	12 (34)	3 (7)
Equal opportunities	72 (22)	10 (23)	14 (40)	5 (15)
Health and safety	69 (17)	9 (19)	17 (49)	5 (15)
Performance appraisal	75 (33)	9 (20)	12 (33)	4 (14)

Base: All workplaces with ten or more employees.
Figures are weighted and based on responses from at least 2,007 managers.

Notes:
[a] Managerial respondent was asked 'whether management normally negotiates, consults, informs or does not involve unions' on 12 items. Also asked with respect to non-union employee representatives.
[b] Figures in parentheses relate to workplaces with recognised trade unions and are based on responses from at least 1,004 managers.

Source: Kersley et al. (2005)

more often than not decided unilaterally but where there is a trade union presence these are the issues about which negotiations are most likely to take place. While, in terms of consultation, it is issues surrounding health and safety where – if there is union representation – the union is most likely to be consulted. Unsurprisingly managerial prerogative is at its most pervasive around issues of staffing, particularly those of staff selection.

Summary

It is apparent that different employment relationships are dependent on not just the personalities of those involved or on the type of business in which they are conducted, but also on the prevailing legislation and managerial frames of reference adopted by the organisation. Different frameworks will lead to different mechanisms for managing and engaging staff: where there is a mismatch between the frame of reference used and the processes of managing the workforce, there is a potential for conflict and damage to the psychological contracts of individual employees. By ensuring that systems are perceived as fair, and by endeavouring to give employees an opportunity to 'voice' their opinions, there is the potential for managing conflict within the workplace and creating high levels of commitment and productivity.

Review Questions

You may wish to attempt the following as practice examination style questions.

12.1   Explain the differences between a unitarist and a pluralist frame of reference, giving examples of how each impacts on managerial styles.

12.2   Give details of a sophisticated modern organisation and say why it belongs in this category. How does it differ from a sophisticated paternalist organisation that you are familiar with?

12.3   How do different sorts of power affect the employment relationship? Give examples to illustrate your answer.

12.4   What is the psychological contract? Why is it important in the employment relationship?

12.5   'Natural justice is just an outdated concept, not relevant to twenty-first century employment relationships.' Critically evaluate this point of view.

12.6   Describe five different mechanisms for containing conflict in the workplace and evaluate their efficacy.

12.7   Is partnership partnership? What were the reasons behind your answer?

12.8   Enumerate the stages negotiators usually go through.

References

ACAS (2004/5). Managing conflict at work – lessons from ACAS, *Employment Relations Matters*, Issue 2.

Applebaum, E. (2002). The impact of new forms of work organisation on workers, in G. Murry, J. Bélanger, A. Giles and P.-A. Lapointe (eds.) *Work and Employment Relations in the High Performance Workplace*, London: Continuum.

Applebaum, E., Bailey, T., Berg, P. and Kalleberg, A.L. (2000). *Manufacturing Advantage: Why High Performance Work Systems Pay Off*, Ithaca: NY: Cornell University Press.

Argyris, C. (1962). *Understanding Organisational Behavior*, Homewood, IL: Dorsey Press.

Clegg, S.R. (1989). *Frameworks of Power*, London: Sage.

DTI (2002). *High Performance Workplaces: The Role of Employee Involvement in a Modern Economy*, London: Department of Trade and Industry.

Edwards, P. (1995). *Industrial Relations: Theory and Practice in Britain*, Oxford: Blackwell.

Farnham, D. (1997). *Employee Relations in Context*, p. 3, London: IPD.

Flanders, A. (1970). *Management and Unions: The Theory and Reform of Industrial Relations*, London: Faber.

Fox, A. (1974). *Beyond Contract: Work, Power and Trust Relations*, London: Faber.

Fox, A. (1966). Managerial ideology and labour relations, *British Journal of Industrial Relations*, Vol. IV, pp. 366–387.

Fowler, A. (1996). *Negotiation Skills and Strategies*, 2nd edition, London: IPD.

French, J.R.P. and Raven, B. (1962). The bases of social power, in D. Cartwright (ed.) *Group Dynamics; Research and Theory*, Evanston, pp. 607–623, IL: Row Peterson.

Gospel, H.F. and Palmer, G. (1993). *British Industrial Relations*, 2nd edition, London: Routledge.

Grainger, H. (2006). *Trade Union Membership 2005*, London: DTI.

Grell, M. and Sisson, K. (2005). *Has Consultation's Time Come*, ACAS Policy Discussion Papers No. 2, at: www.acas.org.uk/media/pdf/8/8/AcasPolicyPaper2_1.pdf.

Guest, D. (1987). Human resource management and industrial relations, *Journal of Management Studies*, Vol. 24, No. 5, pp. 503–521.

Guest, D. (1998). Is the psychological contract worth taking seriously?, *Journal of Organisational Behaviour*, Vol. 19, pp. 649–664.

Guest, D. and Conway, N. (2002a). Communicating the psychological contract: an employer perspective, *Human Resource Management Journal*, Vol. 12, No. 2, pp. 22–38.

Guest, D. and Conway, N. (2002b). Pressure of work and the psychological contract, CIPD Survey Report, London: CIPD.

Guest, D. and Conway, N. (2002c). Organisational change and the psychological contract, CIPD Survey Report, London: CIPD.

Guest, D. and Peccei, R. (1998). *The Partnership Company: Benchmarks for the Future*, London: IPA.

Gunnigle, P., Turner, T. and Morley, M. (1998). Strategic integration and employee relations: the impact of managerial styles, *Employee Relations*, Vol. 20, No. 2, pp. 115–131.

Kersley, B., Alpin, C., Forth, J., Bryson, A., Bewley, H., Dix, G. and Oxenbridge, S. (2005). *Inside the Workplace: First Findings from the 2004 Workplace Employment Relations Survey*, at: www.dti.gov.uk/er/insideWP_finalweb_jan_2006.pdf.

Lewis, et al. (2003). *Employee Relations; Understanding the Employment Relationship*, London: FT/Prentice Hall.

Lukes, S. (1974). *Power: A Radical View*, London: Macmillan.

Lukes, S. (ed.) (1986). *Power*, Oxford: Basil Blackwell.

Marchington, M. and Wilkinson, A. (2005). *Human Resource Management at Work*, 3rd edition, London: CIPD.

Martin, G., Stains, H. and Pate, J. (1998). Linking job security and career development in a new psychological contract, *Human Resource Management Journal*, Vol. 8, No. 3, pp. 20–40.

Monger, J. (2005). Labour disputes in 2004, *Labour Market Trends*, Vol. 113, No. 06, pp. 239–252.

Oxenbridge, S. and Brown, W. (2004). Achieving a new equilibrium? The stability of cooperative employer–union relationships, *Industrial Relations Journal*, Vol. 35, No. 5, pp. 388–402.

Purcell, J. (1987). Mapping management styles in employee relations, *Journal of Management Studies*, Vol. 24, No. 5, pp. 533–548.

Purcell, J. and Grey, A. (1986). Corporate personnel departments and the management of industrial relations, *Journal of Management Studies*, Vol. 23, No. 2, pp. 205–223.

Purcell, J. and Sisson, K. (1983). Strategics and practice in the management of industrial relations, in G. Bain (ed.) *Industrial Relations in Britain*, Oxford: Blackwell.

Rousseau D.M. (1989). Psychological and implied contracts in organisations, *Employee Rights and Responsibilities Journal*, Vol. 2, pp. 121–139.

Sisson, K. (1990). Introducing the *Human Resource Management Journal*, Vol. 1, No. 1, pp. 1–11.

Storey, J. (1992). *Developments in the Management of Human Resources*, Oxford: Blackwell.

Storey, J. (1998). Is HRM catching on?, *International Journal of Manpower*, Vol. 16, No. 4, pp. 3–10.

Taylor, R. (2002). *Britain's World of Work – Myths and Realities*, London: ESRC.

Turnley, W.H., Bolino, M.C., Lester, S.W. and Bloodgood, J.M. (2004). The effects of psychological contract breach on union commitment, *Journal of Occupational and Organisational Psychology*, Vol. 3, No. 77, pp. 421–428.

Unison (2003). *Bullying at work*, at: www.unison.org.uk/acrobat/13375.pdf.

Further Reading

ACAS (2004–06). *Employment Relations matters*. All issues of this quarterly publication are useful and can be accessed from www.acas.org.uk/index.aspx?articleid=402.

Hollinshead, G. et al. (2003). *Employee Relations*, 2nd edition, FT/Prentice Hall.

Murry, G., Bélanger, J., Giles, A. and Lapointe P.-A. (eds.) (2002). *Work and Employment Relations in the High Performance Workplace*, London: Continuum.

Healy, G. et al. (eds.) (2004). *The Future of Workplace Representation*, London: Palgrave Macmillan.

Useful Websites

www.acas.org.uk – for ACAS (Advisory, Conciliation and Arbitration Service)

www.acas.org.uk/index.aspx?articleid=402 – for the quarterly issues of *Employment Relations Matters*; currently issues 1–7 can be accessed individually:

Issue 7 – Winter 2006 [399kb]
Issue 6 – Spring 2006 [411kb]
Issue 5 – Winter 2005 [329kb]
Issue 4 – Summer 2005 [254kb]
Issue 3 – Spring 2005 [257kb]
Issue 2 – Winter 2004/5 [380kb]
Issue 1 – Autumn 2004 [310kb]

Note: Adobe Acrobat needed for downloading

www.cipd.co.uk – for general information about employee relations

www.dti.gov.uk – for general information about employee relations, case studies and updates on employment legislation from the Department of Trade and Industry website

www.incomesdata.co.uk – for general information about employee relations, case studies and updates on employment legislation; is useful for legislative updates and information about pay

www.irseclipse.co.uk – for general information about employee relations, case studies and updates on employment legislation in Industrial Relations Services reviews

www.tuc.org.uk – for general information about employee relations, case studies and updates on employment legislation from the Trade Union Congress website focused on protecting workers' rights

www.worksmart.org.uk – for general information about employee relations – TUC newsboard

www.ons.gov.uk – for statistical information relating to employment and the labour market from Office of National Statistics, with focus on economic and population statistics

www.unison.org.uk/resources/docs_list.asp – for general information about employee relations, case studies and updates on employment legislation, focus on news, guidance tips (e.g. how to calculate your pension benefits) from the largest public sector trade union

PART 6

Development

Part contents

CHAPTER 15

Training and Learning

By David Simmonds

Chapter outline

This chapter examines the organisational structure, strategies and work processes that have implications for the ways that organisational and individual training and learning occur. It examines specific training initiatives in wider organisational contexts and looks at how training and learning can aid planned change in an organisation's internal and external environments.

Learning outcomes

By the end of this chapter, you should be able to:
- Explain the practical implications of organisational goals on training and learning;
- Explain current and future performance problems and their training implications;
- Understand the responsibility of the training and learning function in addressing skills imbalances;
- Evaluate models and roles of training and learning.

Introduction

The area of learning and training at work is both vast and fast-changing. In this chapter, we can only explore some of the more fundamental issues. It is also important to remember that – as a learner – you need to take responsibility for your own learning! Further reading and links to websites will help you to explore this fascinating area.

The chapter has been structured to help you gain an insight into the immense area of learning at work. It begins by exploring the important relationship between training and change. It then looks at some of the organisational characteristics that pertain to training. Models of strategic human resource development (SHRD) are analysed. Finally, the future of training and learning is investigated.

Change: managing it or making it happen?

Change is here to stay! The only thing we can know for sure is that tomorrow is likely to be different from yesterday. This is true for our families, our friends and ourselves. It is certain that there will be changes in our workgroups, our departments and our organisations. There has always been change, since the beginning of time.

What alarms many of us is the phenomenal **rate** of such change. It often seems that we are rushing out of control, as if somebody else has got their foot on the accelerator. There probably has been more change in your lifetime than all the other changes in the history of civilisation put together. We are all in a constant state of change. Literature on the subject seems to suggest that there are two basic forms of change – incremental change and transformational change:

- **Incremental change** often happens slowly or in small stages. Little steps lead eventually to big changes. Let's take an example from the retail sector in the last five years. A shop I know had always sold music cassette tapes. Gradually, they started selling CDs and videos as well. Now, they are introducing DVDs, and since they sell so few audiocassettes these days, these are being withdrawn. Soon, no doubt, they will stop selling videos as well.

- **Transformational change**, on the other hand, usually happens fairly quickly. The build-up to it can – and should – take quite a while, and the subsequent implementation can take place over an extended period. But the change itself is so radical that it is introduced relatively quickly. One example happened at a university. The new vice chancellor wanted to streamline the administrative systems and arrangements. He commissioned some outside consultants to advise the senior management team. Within a very short period of time, through a process known as 'rewiring', the administrative staff were moved from the familiar teams that were previously formed under programme leaders and associated with particular academic programmes. These professional administrators were summarily – and compulsorily – 'reallocated' into new departmental and cross-functional groupings on either an undergraduate or postgraduate basis. The administrators, academics and students alike found the new systems very difficult to operate.

So, what are some of the essential components of change processes, and what are the links to training and learning?

Learning may occur through:

- teaching
- studying
- discussing
- observing
- experiencing
- practising
- committing to memory . . . or not!

Training, on the other hand, facilitates learning directed towards job *performance* and can modify knowledge, skills and attitudes. Training focuses upon *implementation*

– doing things. to the required standard; *improvement* – doing things to a new standard; and *innovation* – doing new things.

If training and learning are to do with performance at work, then **performance standards** should identify: the task; the performance criteria; range indicators; and evidence. **Competency** statements outline the ability to perform the activities, within an occupational area, to the levels of performance expected in employment. For example, below are the competencies of an HR practitioner in the area of resourcing and recruitment:

◆ Design, deliver and evaluate changes to organisational structure;

◆ Contribute to the design, delivery and evaluation of work procedures;

◆ Design, deliver and evaluate recruitment procedures;

◆ Design, deliver and evaluate selection procedures;

◆ Design, deliver and evaluate employee reward and benefits procedures;

◆ Design, deliver and evaluate employee support procedures;

◆ Design, deliver and evaluate the delivery of personnel procedures in international contexts (www.i-l-m.com/qualifications/specialist0/level0.ilm).

HR managers clearly have a responsibility for training, but why should individuals and their employers undertake training and development? Here are some reasons for training:

◆ Achieving full job performance;

◆ Development of employee potential;

◆ Improved morale;

◆ Improved quality;

◆ Greater customer satisfaction;

◆ Less waste of resources;

◆ Better utilisation of resources;

◆ Reduced cost and increased productivity;

◆ Reduced need for supervision.

How can we ensure that training is successful?
  To succeed, training must:

◆ Be the appropriate solution to the problem;

◆ Have the support of management and the individual;

◆ Meet correctly identified needs;

◆ Be carried out in an environment favourable to learning.

Organisations wishing to carry out an audit on their training systems should consider a number of questions to ensure that they are relating training with business results:

◆ Is your training linked to your strategic decisions and business goals?

◆ Is it supported by strong leadership?

♦ Does it reflect the needs and values of your customers?

♦ Does it communicate your organisation's values?

♦ Does it help you address customer retention, acquisition, lower costs, less waste, higher speed and greater innovation?

♦ Does it build on the core principles of learning?

♦ Is it immediately relevant to your organisation?

♦ Can you clearly map an individual's path toward human resource development and human resource managements mastery?

♦ Does the environment empower employees to use what they learn?

♦ Does it lead to measurable results?

Once these questions are answered to the satisfaction of all major stakeholders, then not only will learning take place but both the organisation and the individual will benefit from it.

Systematic training

What is the best way to get started with training and learning? This is the systematic approach to training:

♦ **Examine** – identify training needs at the organisational, team and individual levels;

♦ **Plan** – plan and design training to meet these needs;

♦ **Do** – implement the training plan effectively;

♦ **Review** – assess the results of the training.

See Figure 15.1.

This widely reported model is unfortunately not widely implemented. Many organisations often merely repeat previously designed programmes with little or no thought to their relevance, applicability or value.

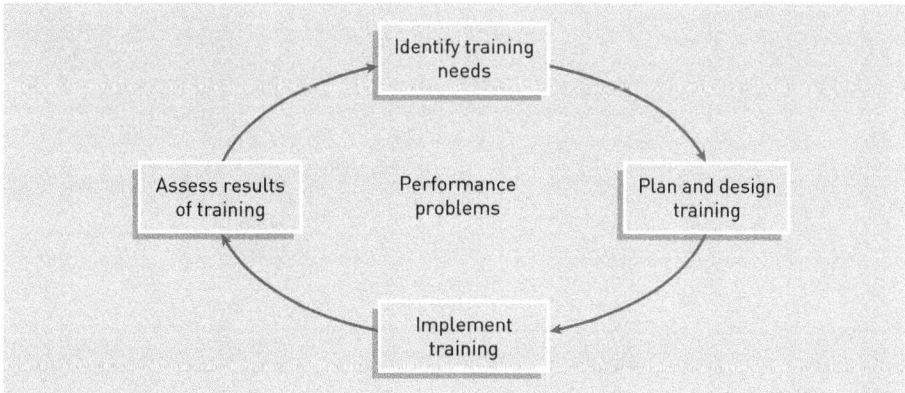

Figure 15.1 Systematic training

Human resource development and human resource management

There has been much discussion (Stewart and McGoldrick, 1996; Simmonds, 2003) concerning the relationship between HRM and HRD. The management of people at work must necessarily include their development. Figure 15.2 is an illustration of the links between HRM and HRD. It shows the various roles and responsibilities of the HRM manager, including the activities normally associated with HRD.

There is no one universally accepted model of the relationship between HRM and HRD. Figure 15.2 illustrates one view of this. McLagan's model (1989) acknowledges the existence of both HRM and HRD. The developmental aspects of the human resource

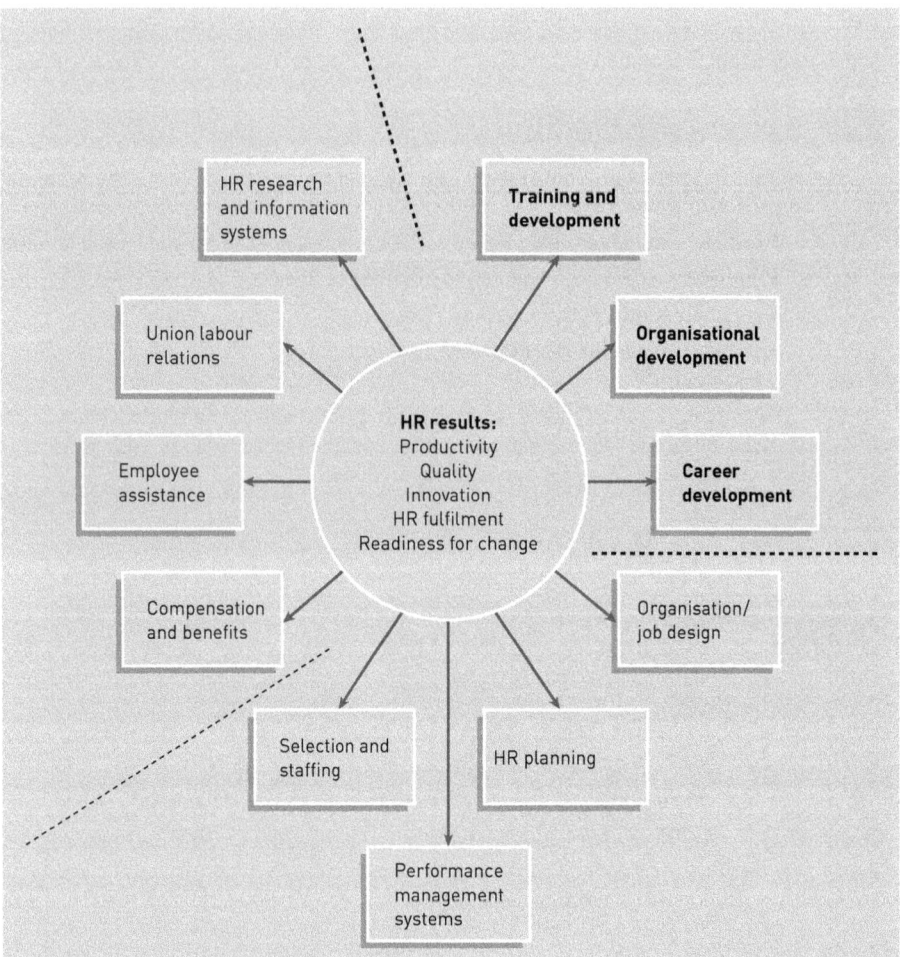

Figure 15.2 A representation of the HR wheel
Source: McLagan (1989)

(HR) function are clearly highlighted in bold, and their links with other aspects of the role of the HR practitioner, and the HR outcomes which should result can be discerned. McLagan has pointed out (1989) that, 'HRD must be the strategic partner with the business in all of the eleven areas of the HR wheel'. If the organisation is going to achieve its strategic objectives, HRD implications of any change need to be given serious consideration at an early stage. The alternative point of view, discussed in Chapter 3, would be that HR is the business partner, of which HRD is a subsidiary function.

◆ **Think about an organisation known to you. How would you describe the relationship between HRM and HRD?**

◆ **What is the relationship between HRD and organisational objectives?**

The organisational environment for training

Garavan (1991) cites the work of Johnson and Scholes (1993) in advocating the use of three categories of evaluation criteria, namely: suitability, feasibility and acceptability. Suitability will determine the fit with the organisation's goals; feasibility can assess the practicality of HRD plans and policies; and acceptability requires an analysis of the overall organisational mindset and cultural web.

So let's have a look at an organisation's cultural web (Figure 15.3). Each of the elements of the cultural web can be analysed further in order to obtain a fuller understanding of an organisation's culture:

◆ **Rituals and routines** – these are the formal and informal ways in which things take place within an organisation and the processes by which the different parts of the organisation interact. These aspects can be encapsulated in the phrase 'the

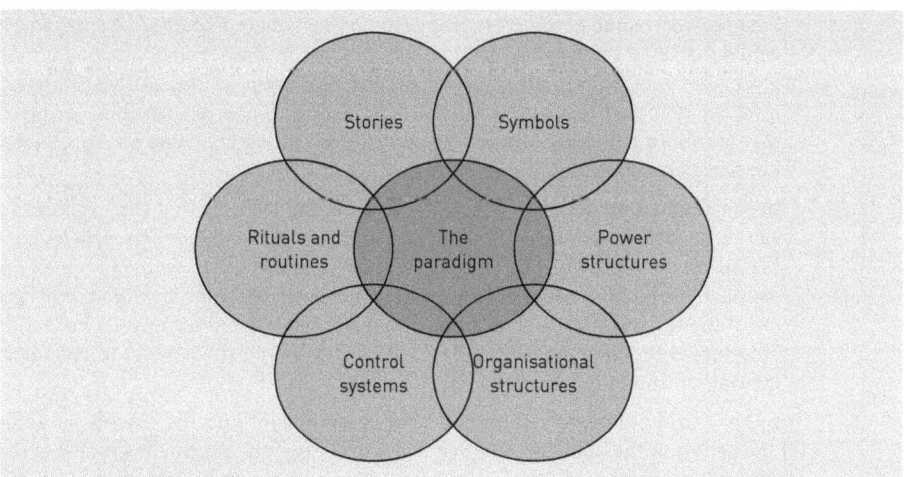

Figure 15.3 The cultural web
Source: Johnson and Scholes (1993: 61)

way we do things around here'. For example, in an organisation like a local authority, much emphasis is placed upon formal committees and their minutes, as well as rituals such as ceremonies and elections.

- ◆ **Stories** – these are told about the major events and personalities, past and present, and become embedded in organisational 'folklore'. Through constant repetition, stories reflect those aspects of an organisation that people within it see as being particularly important. For example, in a local football club, the stories of heroes passed from one generation to another may be of the great players who typified a style of game where entertainment was seen as more important than results.

- ◆ **Symbols** – these can indicate who and what is seen to be important within the organisation. Things like the design of offices, the award of company cars and the use of titles can all point to the way in which the organisation views itself. For example, in one hierarchical multinational oil company, a newly appointed manager was given an office with two doors, though his position warranted only one. It took the carpenters less than 24 hours to block off the 'surplus' door!

- ◆ **Control systems** – the measurement and reward systems are likely to reflect aspects of organisational activity that it is important to monitor or encourage, even if strategy documents, or the chairperson's statements, may stress other issues. The extent of these systems can also indicate how much management within the organisation is centralised or devolved. For example, within most UK universities, academics are expected to engage in teaching, administration and research, but as promotion is largely based on the quantity of an individual's research publications, many feel the 'real' priority lies in this one area.

- ◆ **Power structures** – indicate which individuals comprise the most important groups within the organisation, the people who take the decisions. The importance of these groups and individuals might not be immediately apparent from the formal organisational structure, so there needs to be an awareness of informal networks. Such power might come from seniority or particular expertise. For example, within the UK electricity generation industry, engineers traditionally had a more prominent role than in other organisations and the priorities of the companies involved reflected this emphasis on engineering. Since privatisation, priorities that are more commercial seem to be reflected in the changing backgrounds of key decision makers.

- ◆ **Organisational structure** – this is likely to reflect the way that the organisation works, as well as its power structures and important relationships. The levels of hierarchy, the decision-making bodies and what is discussed within them, as well as the information flowing within the structure, will all point towards the priorities of the organisation. For example, an advertising agency may well have a flat structure with teams formed to deal with specific projects in order to encourage innovation, and to focus on the client's needs.

Together these elements reflect and provide an insight into the overall paradigm (at the centre of the Johnson and Scholes' (1993) model) that drives the day-to-day actions of organisational life. Furthermore, the cultural web highlights the way in which the corporate culture is reflected in the formal and informal elements of the organisation. Lying as it does at the centre, the paradigm also tends to preserve and reinforce the key of the cultural web, and this has important implications for managing strategic elements.

It is important therefore to use the web to analyse an organisation's culture so that the implications for training and learning can be ascertained. It is particularly helpful when identifying and analysing training needs. Moreover, it is useful to apply the cultural web to an organisation before, during and after a major organisational change in order to map the ways that the change is affecting different aspects of the organisation. This can offer pointers to the learning that has taken place – and that still needs to take place.

pause for thought

Think of an organisation that you know well. How have the stories that you know about the organisation influenced the ways that you think about it?

In order to be able to identify the importance of training and learning to the success of an organisation, let's look at this example from Marks & Spencer.

Mini case study: Change and learning at Marks & Spencer

The major UK retailer Marks & Spencer has, over time, developed an unusual relationship with its clothing suppliers. It has a huge market share, accounting for about a third of all sales in its sector and has accomplished an enviable reputation for its sophisticated supply chain activities. Courtaulds is one of the top four suppliers to Marks & Spencer. There are a number of key stages in the contracting process:

1. A pre-production contract to the supplier authorising the purchase of raw materials.

2. The full contract, including cost prices.

3. A series of 'alterations to order' with colour and ratio requirements.

This contract management system was integrated with the product development process. However, requests for stock to be distributed to stores was managed separately. This caused problems for both parties. The supplier took most of the risk and bore the cost of maintaining stock in the warehouses and for discounting, or disposing of stock, that did not sell. Moreover, Marks & Spencer would suddenly cancel orders on a range of items in the middle of production. It caused significant problems and involved considerable cost.

Clearly, by 1991 change was needed. After much discussion at Courtaulds, people agreed that the abrupt changes in demand was not because of the fluctuations in the market place, but because the merchandisers in Marks & Spencer were unable to forecast the demand. Courtaulds proposed that, in exchange for a continual feed of sales and stock information from Marks & Spencer, the supplier would adjust their production schedules in line with sales and would assume responsibility for replenishment.

This led to innovations in the supply chain relationship that worked well in the early 1990s. However, by 1997, there were signs that the solutions were no longer effective. A number of factors led to another major crisis: a complete internal reorganisation at the clothing giant;

Financial and Human Resource Management in Organisations, Second Edition

the launch of 'collections'; offshoring production by the supplier; and an extra six weeks lead time. By 2001, sales volumes were halved and profits reduced.

Eventually, Marks & Spencer started its own investigation. Because the initiative came from within the organisation, it had the advantage of top-level sponsorship. Despite this, even these innovations have so far only experienced partial take-up. Many buying departments are still sceptical of their value. The newly created system is rather less advanced than the one abandoned a couple of years previously. It is a web-based service, rather than feeding the data directly to the supplier as previously. However, Marks & Spencer is now relearning the importance of co-operating with its suppliers. Partnership had been largely abandoned from the late 1990s until 2002. It is now very much a part of the current strategy. The streaming of strategic sourcing is now a joint decision.

Many of the Marks & Spencer merchandisers had become complacent, and accustomed to buying from salespeople without having to consider supply issues. Short-term 'macho-style' recruits to these positions seemed to approach the role with overconfidence and aggression. Managers within the company had also become insular. They were recruited at a young age and stayed within the organisation. Company routines and procedures were deeply entrenched. Staff found it very difficult to accept that change was necessary – or to see what different approaches might look like. There was a very strong devotion to traditional methods that had previously brought great success.

(Adapted from Storey et al., 2005)

---

exercise

The Marks & Spencer case reveals considerable resistance to learning. How many examples can you find?

Strategic HRD (SHRD)

Commentators have examined the theoretical issues surrounding the role of HRD in organisational strategic planning. Torraco and Swanson (1995) point out that HRD not only plays a strategic role by assuring the competency of employees to meet the performance demands of the organisation, but also serves the additional function of helping to shape business strategy. They suggest that HRD has been a key enabling force in strategies based on product innovation, quality and cost leadership, customised service, or global relocation based on workforce skills. They also argue for the strategy-supporting and strategy-shaping roles of HRD, considering the use of HRD to support business objectives. They examine the relationship between HRD, expertise and strategy, and HRD as a shaper of strategy. In addition, they look at the need for the adoption of a SHRD perspective. Torraco and Swanson highlight the distinctive features of the strategic roles of HRD, which are evident in the business practices of successful organisations, and illustrate these roles with examples from some of today's most innovative companies.

Various organisations value training and development differently. In many organisations, training is implemented, at best, on only an *ad hoc* basis, whereas at the other extreme some organisations fully embrace the learning and development function at a strategic level (McCracken and Wallace, 2000: 434). Figure 15.4 illustrates the various ways that training and development may be viewed and valued in an organisation. On the left, training is only seen in an *ad hoc* or supporting role. The middle model shows HRD as having a mainly reactive supporting role. And finally, on the right, SHRD is valued as having a strong proactive, shaping role. From these different viewpoints, you can contrast the three different kinds of focus; the relative maturity of the organisation; nine diverse aspects of the extent to which training is integrated within the organisation; and the relative strength of the learning culture.

As we can see from Figure 15.4, it is possible to distinguish not only the marked differences between training, HRD and SHRD, but also the paradigms that reflect different types of focus, levels of HRD maturity and strength of learning culture. For SHRD to become a reality, the organisation needs to empower the HRD function to adopt a proactive approach in relation to corporate strategy (Walton, 1999).

To contrast with the model by McCracken and Wallace, Figure 15.5 is that of Stewart and McGoldrick (1996). There are a number of differences between these two models. By critically utilising a number of separate parameters, we can now proceed to formulate an assessment of these two different models of SHRD.

Analysing models of SHRD

Deliberate or emergent?

There is some debate as to whether strategy is deliberate or emergent. Stewart and McGoldrick's model (Figure 15.5) suggests that strategy is deliberate and is the result of analysis, which leads to the development of organisational plans in a linear fashion. McCracken and Wallace, on the other hand, argue that strategy emerges from, at times, unrelated and *ad hoc* decisions as a result of compromise and competing interests. Resource-based strategy (as discussed in Chapter 3), on the other hand, focuses on internal competencies in order to gain competitive advantage. In this approach, HRD becomes a more prominent feature of all HRM activities.

Burgoyne's typology (Stewart 1999) of organisational maturity

In Stewart and McGoldrick's model (1999), HRD is driven by the corporate strategy. It is reactive and can be placed at Level 4 of Burgoyne's (1992) typology of the learning organisation:

- **Level 1** – no systematic HRD development;
- **Level 2** – isolated tactical HRD;
- **Level 3** – integrated and co-ordinated structural HRD;
- **Level 4** – an HRD strategy to implement corporate policy;
- **Level 5** – HRD strategy input to corporate policy formulation;
- **Level 6** – strategic development of the management of corporate policy;
- **Level 7** – strategic leverage of learning and development processes to enhance the core competences of the organisation.

However, in McCracken and Wallace's model, HRD also informs and shapes corporate strategy, and can therefore be placed at the highest point of sophistication and maturity – Level 7 of the typology.

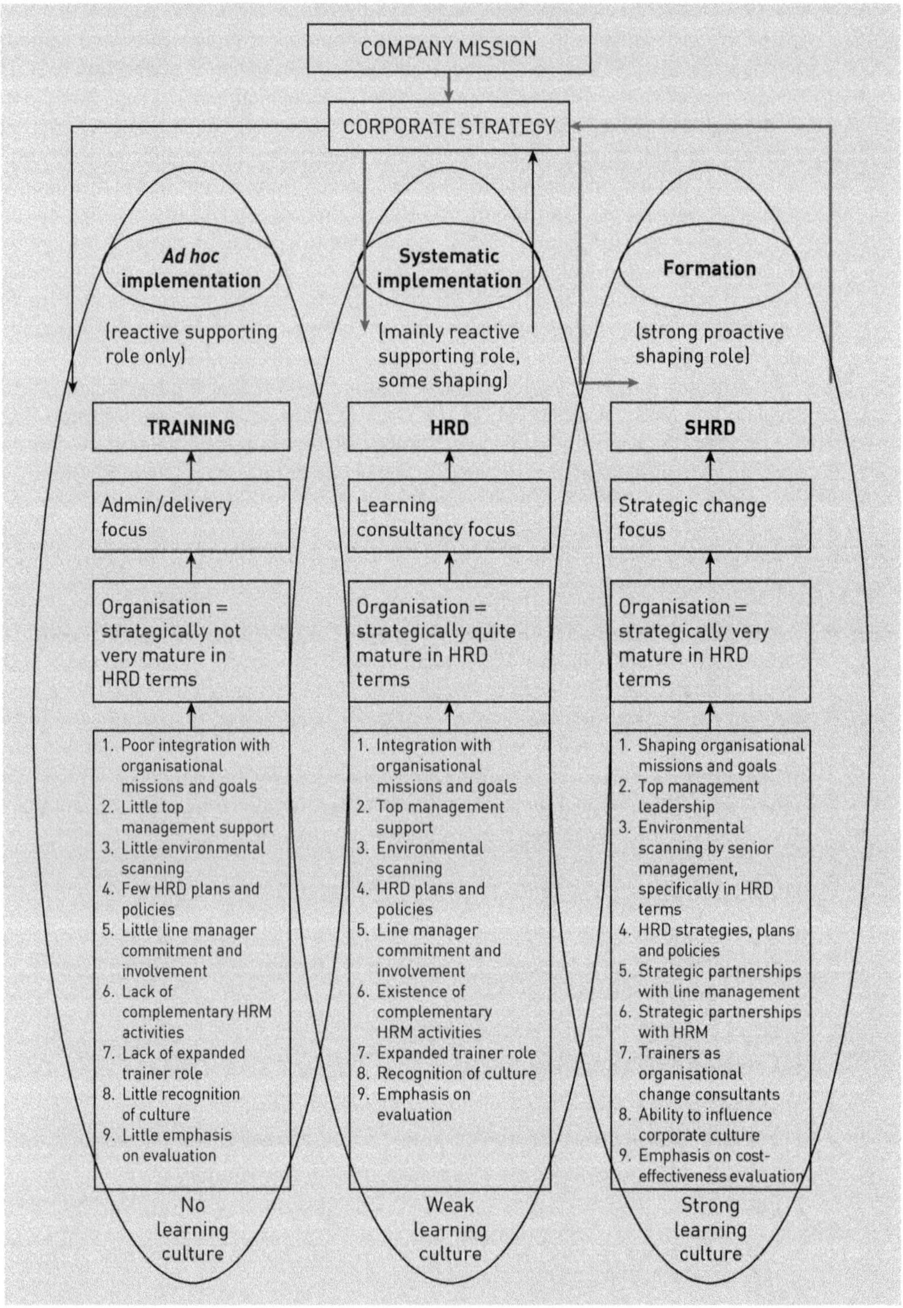

Figure 15.4 Three separate views of the ways in which learning can be aligned with organisational strategy

Source: McCraken and Wallace (2000: 434)

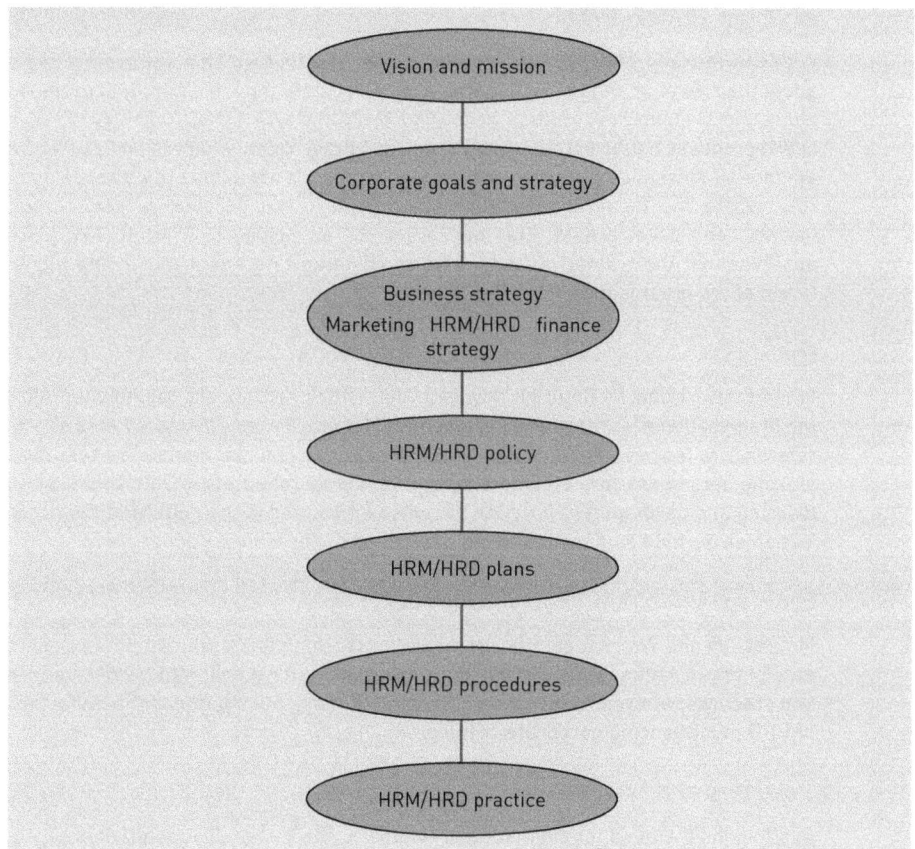

Figure 15.5 HRD model
Source: Stewart and McGoldrick (1996)

External focus for strategy (Johnson and Scholes, 1993)

Stewart and McGoldrick's model makes no reference to the external environment, indicating that HRD might be slow to respond to outside transformational imperatives. McCracken and Wallace conversely make specific reference to environmental scanning. Such a model appears to be more dynamic in relation to change.

Vertical and horizontal integration (Guest, 2002)

Both Stewart and McGoldrick's and McCracken and Wallace's models make explicit the vertical integration with wider organisational goals and strategies, but only McCracken and Wallace's model takes the further step towards horizontal integration with other HRM initiatives. Nevertheless, both Storey (2001) and Harrison (2005) question whether horizontal integration can in fact exist in practice.

Pettigrew's (1982) typology of trainer roles

With Stewart and McGoldrick's model, it can be assumed that the trainer would adopt the role of 'manager' – planning and co-ordinating the training processes and allocating training resources – according to Pettigrew's (1982) typology. Garavan (1991) proposes Pettigrew's 'innovator' or 'consultant' roles, whereas McCracken and Wallace's model goes further in advocating that the trainer adopts the 'change agent' role, where the focus is squarely upon organisational problem solving through learning and development. This appears to be supported by Walton (1999), who observes that the trainer must be able to communicate effectively at the highest levels of the organisation.

Ownership

While Stewart and McGoldrick advocate that HRD practitioners take ownership of the organisation's learning and development, McCracken and Wallace make specific reference to the need for a strategic partnership with line managers. As a result, key stakeholders share in the ownership and implementation of HRD. In this way, the learning and development function becomes embedded in the culture of the organisation as a whole rather than being possessed by the training department.

Lewin's (1951) model of organisational change

McCracken and Wallace clearly see a role for learning and development in the process of organisational change in order to prevent cultural drift into former patterns and practices, whereas Stewart and McGoldrick make no mention of the importance of HRD in influencing corporate culture.

Evaluation and feedback

Overlooking the need for evaluation or feedback, Stewart and McGoldrick imply that training and development is seen as a cost or a luxury rather than as an investment in the long-term prospects of the organisation. McCracken and Wallace, though, refer explicitly to the need for an evaluation of cost-effectiveness. This should focus not only on pay-back investment to achieve short-term tangible results, but also on pay-forward investment to accomplish longer-term intangible results, as proposed by Lee (1996). The rational, linear nature of Stewart and McGoldrick's model allows no feedback into corporate strategy. The forming and shaping function of HRD, as illustrated by McCracken and Wallace, provides the necessary opportunities for continuous improvement and development. They argue against Garavan (1991), who posits a reactive or responsive view of HRD, in so far as it contributes to organisational objectives and is aware of the organisational mission. Their analysis is nearer that of Torraco and Swanson (1995), in that they see HRD as having a role that is pivotal, proactive and strategic.

Unitary or pluralistic approach

Both Stewart and McGoldrick's and McCracken and Wallace's models assume a unilateral approach to organisational mission and vision, and that everyone in the organisation is working towards its achievement. Both models appear to ignore the reality that all organisations comprise a range of individuals working towards a variety of goals, that may be tangential to those of their employer.

Generic or specific considerations

Stewart and McGoldrick present a generic model that could easily be applied to any one of a number of organisational functions, such as marketing, finance or purchasing, while McCracken and Wallace's representation is exclusively HRD orientated.

Summary

It may appear that in effect Stewart and McGoldrick's model is not actually strategic but more operational in approach. Their primary characteristics are, in reality, difficult to achieve. These models lack detail in terms of practical implementation or application. I would therefore recommend instead Walton's (1999) model, where there is an explicit commitment to learning in the organisation's mission and core values. It is supported by corresponding systems, policies, resources, partners, sponsors and stewards. Such collective and collaborative learning produces innovation, creativity, strategic awareness and enhanced job performance. Inevitably, this leads to improved customer satisfaction. Walton insists that learning and development must form a foundational, and holistic, business process rather than being an accidental or tangential postscript.

All these approaches demonstrate the need for the training and development of employees to be undertaken not just on an organisation-wide basis, but also for SHRD to be central to the organisation's accomplishment of its strategic plan. As it addresses its plans in a cycle of continuous improvement, so SHRD will also change and adapt.

pause for thought   To what extent do you think training needs to be undertaken on an organisation-wide basis?

So what has all of this to say to us about the way we work, and about the places where we are employed? Well, there is a fundamental connection between work, learning and change. So, let's examine the nature of change in the workplace.

The future of learning at work

Stewart and Tansley (2002: 32) propose a future role for trainers with almost evangelistic zeal:

> 'A key role of the training function in the future will be in the support of knowledge management initiatives and social capital construction. Training specialists need to be involved in disseminating the message throughout the organisation that attempts to manage organisational knowledge must be founded on an understanding of how people learn, how they implement what they learn, and how they share their knowledge.'

They continue:

> 'The building of social capital, a widening client base and the support of know-ledge management all imply a shift from the role of training provider to one of learning facilitator. This in turn suggests the need for the adoption of new teaching methodologies in fulfilling the new role of the training function. [. . .] In other words, how training and development are delivered becomes more important than what is delivered. [. . .] Training processes rather than content, then, are more significant in developing the ability to learn, and should there-fore be the primary focus.'

So, what are some of the important functions of effective training? Lynton and Pareek (2000) outline three such functions that are less well recognised than that of conducting training sessions: providing guidance and support through, for example, mentoring; helping to design and implement organisational change strategies, through, say, coaching in the workplace; and the leadership, managerial and admin-istrative aspects of preparing an entire training programme.

In a more restricted sense, Burack et al. (1997) look at how the role of manage-ment development (MD) is also changing as organisations increasingly merge their strategic goals with HR planning goals, in order to involve staffing and development. They assert that this new pattern of MD focuses on enhancing an organisation's effectiveness while maintaining competitive advantage. They consider the influence that MD has on performance improvement, examining the features of MD approaches adopted by the more successful organisations. Burack et al. (ibid.) propose the application of core competencies and the relationship between these and strategic MD. These writers introduce a general core competency model that reflects the integration of business strategy and HR practices through the progressive building of competencies and their alignment to specific jobs. For a fuller discussion of these issues, refer to Chapter 16.

Such an approach has been developed still further by Noel and Dennehy (1991), who present us with six steps for the introduction of HRD in an organisation:

1. The development of a focused strategic approach.

2. Involvement of top management.

3. The 'refocusing' of course content.

4. The development of 'impactful' learning methods (e.g. action learning).

5. Focused participation of the employees who can provide significant difference.

6. The provision of a learning atmosphere.

They believe that adherence to these steps will help the HRD professional become a significant force for transforming the organisation. This could be very important for most organisations, including those in the public and voluntary sectors.

Sawdon (1999) traces three broad development paths for trainers in the future:

◆ From training to consulting;

◆ From training to learning;

◆ From individual change to organisational change.

Sawdon then arrives at four approaches to training and consultancy:

1. Trainer.
2. Training consultant.
3. Learning consultant.
4. Organisational change consultant.

pause for thought

How do you see the future roles for trainers and developers?

How do trainers themselves describe their roles? Darling and her colleagues (1999) find that, in practice, people describe the roles they carry out in training in one of three broad categories. Table 15.1 summarises their views.

Training roles, and their description, have changed over time. Summarising much of the literature on trainer roles over the past three decades, Walton (1999: 165) provides a most helpful synopsis of the scope and development of trainer roles in this country and the US since the 1970s. In Table 15.2 he offers a useful comparison of traditional and emergent functions.

One of the roles in which trainers can have a major impact is in helping employers to begin the journey towards becoming a learning organisation. Hoffman and Withers (1995: 472) tabulate their comparison (Table 15.3) of traditional training with the learning organisation.

Table 15.1 Trainer roles

Philosophical	Strategic	Operational
◆ Moderniser	◆ Facilitator at organisational level	◆ Facilitator at personal and team level
◆ Stabiliser of chaos	◆ Integrator	◆ Direct trainer
◆ Creator/supporter of an innovative culture	◆ Internal advisor – organisational development	◆ Internal advisor – personal development
◆ Leader/supporter of the vision/champion	◆ Organisational 'confidant(e)'	◆ Coach/mentor
◆ Surfacer of myths and assumptions	◆ Interpreter of people implications of changes in the business	◆ Modeller
◆ Banner carrier (in conjunction with HR)	◆ Change agent (learning is by definition change)	◆ Manager of learning
◆ Gateway to learning – supporter of lifelong learning – illuminator	◆ Influencer	◆ Operational manager, team leader
◆ Prophet	◆ Manager of expectations	

Table 15.2 Traditional and emergent development functions

Old		Emergent	
Functional roles	**Interpretive roles**	**Functional roles**	**Interpretive roles**
♦ Direct trainer	♦ Passive provider	♦ Learning and development manager	♦ Co-learner
♦ Training administrator	♦ Provider	♦ Contract/partnership manager	♦ Change facilitator
♦ Technical instructor	♦ Caretaker	♦ Facilitator at corporate university	♦ Learning architect
♦ Needs analyst	♦ Evangelist	♦ Internal consultant	♦ Orchestrator of learning processes
♦ Programme designer	♦ Innovator	♦ Performance consultant	♦ Intrapreneur
♦ Transfer agent	♦ Educator	♦ Organisation development consultant	♦ Facilitator of strategic processes
	♦ Change agent	♦ Knowledge manager/intellectual asset controller	

Table 15.3 Traditional training versus the learning organisation

Traditional training	Learning organisation
Teaching content	Learning processes
Classroom-focused	Workplace-focused
Teacher-centred	Learner-centred
'Belongs to' training department	'Belongs to' each person
Activity-centred	Outcomes-based
Training specialist	Learning consultants

Applying such an analysis will enable many organisations to embrace organisational learning strategies, rather than having to rely on traditional approaches to training and development. As we focus more on the impact and consequences of their roles in organisations, so we shall see the importance of adopting a contingency approach. Situations and contexts call for adaptability and flexibility. Training professionals need to take the lead here.

The training programme for employees at English Nature epitomises the ways in which individual learning meshes with strategic goals. Walton's (1999) exploration of this process is shown in Table 15.4.

So, we can see from Table 15.4 the links between learning, strategy and change, together with the developing roles for HRD in effecting continuous cycles of performance improvement throughout an organisation.

Table 15.4 An assessment of English Nature as a learning organisation	
Feature	**Progress so far**
Learning approach to strategy	Strategy is reviewed and refined but it is not always seen as easy to change direction.
Participative policy making	Everyone has an opportunity to influence policy; there are tensions between bottom-up and top-down management.
Open information systems	Information is not always readily accessible: a project aims to improve information flow and use.
Formative accounting and control	Government accounting procedures require some control, although the finance team does help other teams to control their own resources.
Internal exchange	Variable. The internal customer ethos is still not fully accepted. Some teams have made considerable progress. Networking is crude.
Flexibility of rewards	Government rules restrict options. Performance-related pay, small special bonuses and flexible working are possible.
Enabling structures	Individuals do move and flexibility is encouraged, but boundaries are seen as fixed in the short to medium term.
Boundary workers act as environmental scanners	Local teams and national partner teams have access to considerable information but to date have not always taken opportunities to influence their environmental scanners.
Inter-company learning	Although there is a liaison with nature conservation groups, in both the UK and abroad, meetings with organisations not involved in nature issues are rare.
Learning climate	There is a history of knowledge-based learning and expectations are high. Process reviews for continual improvement are less common.
Self-development opportunities for all	There are many opportunities to learn and develop, but time and money often limit such activity to key areas of the job.

Using the chart below to help you, assess Warbings in terms of the progress it has made towards becoming a learning organisation. What additional steps do you think the company needs to take to become a learning organisation? Compare notes with a friend; have you reached the same conclusions?

Feature	Progress so far
Learning approach to strategy	
Participative policy making	
Open information systems	
Formative accounting and control	
Internal exchange	
Flexibility of rewards	
Enabling structures	
Boundary workers act as environmental scanners	
Inter-company learning	
Learning climate	
Self-development opportunities for all	

298   CHAPTER 15 TRAINING AND LEARNING

Summary

We have seen how change can be viewed as learning and individual development. The amount and rate of change in work and life roles will continue to have a profound effect on the nature and function of adult development. Training – and trainers – will have a pivotal and foundational role to play in those organisations that seek to embrace an agenda of innovation and creativity. This chapter has explored the organisational context of structure, strategies and work processes that have implications for the ways that organisational and individual training and learning occur. It examined specific training initiatives in wider organisational contexts and looked at how training and learning can aid planned change in an organisation's internal and external environments.

Review Questions

You may wish to attempt the following as practice examination style questions.

15.1   What are the links between learning, development and corporate strategy?

15.2   How can training and development affect national skills shortages?

15.3   Critically evaluate two models of strategic human resource development.

References

Burack, E., Hochwater, H., Mathys, W. and Nicholas, J. (1997). The new management development paradigm, *Human Resources Planning*, Vol. 20, No. 1.

Burgoyne, J. (1992). *Creating a Learning Organisation*, London: Royal Society of Arts.

Darling, J. et al. (1999). *The Changing Role of the Trainer*, London: CIPD.

Garavan, T. (1991). Strategic human resource development, *Journal of European Industrial Training*, Vol. 15, No. 1, pp. 17–31.

Guest, D. (2002). *Managing Excellence and High Performance*, Milton Keynes: Open University Press.

Harrison, R. (2005). *Learning and Development*, London: CIPD.

Hoffman, F. and Withers, B. (1995). Shared values: nutrients for learning, in S. Chawla and J. Renesch (eds.) *Learning Organisations*, Portland, MA: Productivity Press.

Johnson, G. and Scholes, K. (1993). *Exploring Corporate Strategy*, London: Prentice Hall.

Lee, R. (1996). The 'pay-forward' view of training, *People Management*, Vol. 2, No. 3, pp. 30–32.

Lewin, K. (1951). *Field Theory in Social Science*, London: Tavistock.

Lynton, R. and Pareek, U. (2000). *Training for Organisational Transformation*: Volume 2, New Delhi: Sage.

McCracken, M. and Wallace, M. (2000). Towards a redefinition of strategic HRD, *Journal of European Industrial Training*, Vol. 24, No. 5, pp. 281–290.

McLagan, P. (1989). *Models for HR Practice*, Alexandria, VA: American Society for Training and Development.

Noel, J. and Dennehy, R. (1991). Making HRD a force in strategic organisational change, *Industrial and Commercial Training*, Vol. 23, No. 2, pp. 17–19.

Pettigrew, A. (1982). *Training and Development Roles in their Organisational Setting*, Sheffield: MSC.

Sawdon, D. (1999). Making the most of consultancy: perspectives on partnership, in J. Wilson (ed.) *Human Resource Development*, London: Kogan Page.

Simmonds, D. (2003). *Designing and Delivering Training*, London: CIPD.

Stewart, J. (1999). *Employee Development Practice*, London: Pitman.

Stewart, J. and McGoldrick, J. (eds.) (1996). *Human Resource Development: Perspectives, Strategies and Practice*, London: Pearson.

Stewart, J. and Tansley, C. (2002). *Training in the Knowledge Economy*, London: CIPD.

Storey, J. (2001). *New Perspectives on Human Resource Management*, London: Routledge.

Storey, J. et al. (2005). The barriers to customer responsive supply chain management, *International Journal of Operations and Production Management*, Vol. 25, No. 3, pp. 242–260.

Torraco, R. and Swanson, R. (1995). The strategic roles of human resource development, *Human Resource Planning*, Vol. 18, No. 4, pp.

Walton, J. (1999). *Strategic Human Resource Development*, London: Pitman.

Useful Websites

www.trainingzone.co.uk – training professionals network with news reports, research advice and guidance on professional development for trainers from Training Zone.co.uk

www.b.shuttle.de/wifo/ehrd-rev/=index.htm – gateway to research on education in Europe

www.nwlink.com/~donclark/hrd/hrdlink.html – Donald Clark website with news and reports on learning, performance and knowledge links

www.trainersnetwork.org – wide range of items (e.g. online meetings, working from home) from the Trainers Network

www.managementhelp.org – access to the free Management Library, covering a wide range of learning, performance and knowledge issues

www.squarewheels.com – Dr Scott Simmerman's performance management

company offering trainer products and services (e.g. team-building games)

www.tip.psychology.org – psychology organisation coverage of learning theory, research on adult learning, articles and course information

www.thiagi.com – the Thiagi Group's source for training games and interactive strategies, including online newsletter and courses

www.trainingmag.com/training/index/jsp – Nielsen's business media information on training publications and courses

www.ibstpi.org – the website of the International Board of Standards for Training, Performance and Instruction, offering research reports, articles and guidance

www.clomedia.com/content/templates/clo_home.asp?articleid=714&zoneid=145 – training media information and guidance

Chapter 1
Accounting and decision making in business

 Learning **objectives**

After studying Chapter 1, you should be able to:
1 Describe what managers do and why they need accounting information
2 Appreciate the key characteristics of management accounting information
3 Review the impact on business of organizational and technological change, managing for value, the sustainability agenda and corporate governance
4 Appreciate that management accounting principles can be useful irrespective of who applies them or where they are located in an organization

Concepts **in Context**

We will see in this chapter how management accounting practices have had to respond to changes in the business environment. For example, airlines such as easyJet have developed a business model enabled by new technology and deregulation in the airline industry. According to the company website, easyJet keeps costs low by eliminating the unnecessary costs and 'frills' which characterize 'traditional' airlines. This is done in a number of ways: 1. Use of the internet to reduce distribution costs; 2. Maximizing the utilization of the substantial assets thus reducing unit cost;

© Paul Trendell

3. Ticketless travel which helps to reduce significantly the cost of issuing, distributing, processing and reconciling millions of tickets each year; 4. No free lunch – eliminating free catering on-board reduces cost and unnecessary bureaucracy and management; 5. Efficient use of airports – easyJet flies to main destination airports throughout Europe, but gains efficiencies through rapid turnaround times, and progressive landing charge agreements with the airports; 6. Paperless operations – the management and administration of the company is undertaken entirely on IT systems which can be accessed through secure servers from anywhere in the world enabling huge flexibility in the running of the airline.[1]

What is management accounting?

Planning

In simple terms, **management accounting** provides information that may be used to plan, direct, motivate and control an organization. Although it is predominantly used by managers in an organization, management accounting information might also be the basis of a business plan that can be presented to outside interested parties such as banks or potential private investors. Among other data, potential investors look at the *sales volumes*, *profit margins* and *costs*. They will also consider the *cash* needs of the business. Going forward, the plan should indicate not just long-term projections of profit but suggest a way of co-ordinating and controlling the business so that it is 'kept on track'.

The plans of management are often expressed formally in **budgets**, and the term budgeting is applied generally to describe this part of the planning process. Typically, budgets are prepared annually and represent management's plans in specific, quantitative terms. These data will be collected, analysed and summarized for management use in the form of budgets. Although they may be prepared annually, ever cheaper and more powerful computer packages now mean that actual outturns can be checked against the planned budget with great frequency and with a high level of detail, with data that can be 'sliced and diced'.

Directing and motivating

In addition to planning for the future, managers must oversee day-to-day activities and keep the organization functioning smoothly. This requires the ability to motivate and effectively direct people. Managers assign tasks to employees, arbitrate disputes, answer questions, solve on-the-spot problems, and make many small decisions that affect customers and employees. In effect, directing is that part of the managers' work that deals with the routine and the here and now. Management accounting data, such as daily sales reports, are often used in this type of day-to-day decision making.

Controlling

In carrying out the **control** function, managers seek to ensure that the plan is being followed. **Feedback**, which signals whether operations are on track, is the key to effective control. In sophisticated organizations this feedback is provided by detailed reports of various types. One of these reports, which compares budgeted to actual results, is called a **performance report**. Performance reports suggest where operations are

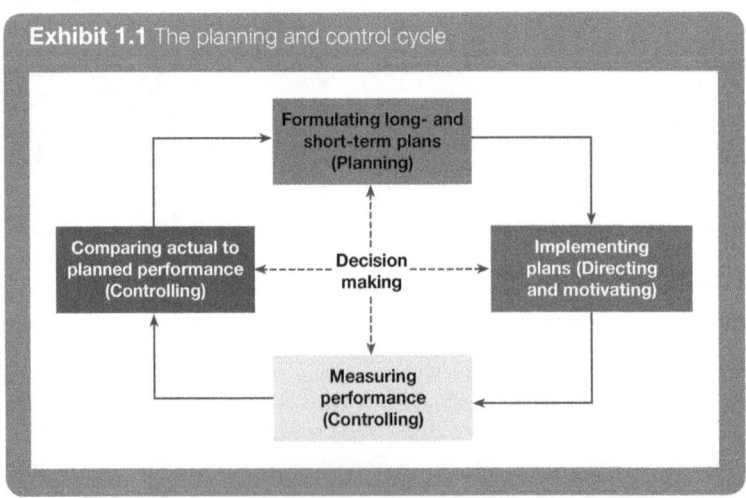

Exhibit 1.1 The planning and control cycle

Focus on Business Practice

Business planning: Eco-hotel

© Sashi Ono

James has a proposal to build an 'Eco-hotel' on an island in the Red Sea. The project involves renovating a historic site using local labour and materials and the latest 'green' sustainable technologies. In order to attract investors, James has produced a prospectus which includes detailed forecasts of revenues, costs and profits for the next ten years. In the prospectus, he has also explained what assumptions he has made about likely visitor numbers and possible competitors for the main recreational activity in the area, which is scuba diving in the warm and spectacular waters of the Red Sea.

James has produced a business *plan* but this plan can also form the basis of a *control model*. Once the project is under way, James can check whether his plans are being realized – are the costs over-running? Are the visitor numbers coming through? Are there any actions that need to be taken to keep the project on track? Or maybe the plans have to be modified?

Exercise: Refer to Exhibit 1.1 and see how the hotel project matches up to the planning and control features of the model in the exhibit.

---

not proceeding as planned and where some parts of the organization may require additional attention. As we shall see in following chapters, providing this kind of feedback to managers is one of the central purposes of management accounting.

The planning and control cycle

The work of management can be summarized in a model such as the one shown in Exhibit 1.1. The model, which depicts the **planning and control cycle**, illustrates the smooth flow of management activities from planning through directing and motivating, controlling, and then back to planning again. All of these activities involve *decision making*, so it is depicted as the hub around which the other activities revolve.

An overview of management accounting principles

LO 2

Financial accounting is mandatory; that is, it must be done. Various outside parties such as the Stock Exchange regulators and the tax authorities require periodic financial statements. Management accounting, on the other hand, is not mandatory. A company is completely free to do as much or as little as it wishes. Since management accounting is completely optional, the important question is always, 'Is the information useful?' rather than, 'Is the information required?' With these criteria in mind, management accounting is characterized by:

- **An emphasis on the future.** Since planning is such an important part of the manager's job, management accounting has a strong future orientation. In contrast, financial accounting primarily provides

summaries of past financial transactions. Changes are constantly taking place in economic conditions, customer needs and desires, competitive conditions and so on.

- **Relevance and flexibility of data.** Managers want information that is relevant even if it is not completely objective or verifiable. By relevant, we mean appropriate for the problem at hand. The management accounting information system should be flexible enough to provide whatever data are relevant for a particular decision.

- **Emphasis on timeliness rather than precision.** Timeliness is often more important than precision to managers. If a decision must be made, a manager would much rather have a good estimate now than wait a week for a more precise answer. A decision involving tens of millions of pounds does not have to be based on estimates that are precise down to the penny, or even to the pound. Management accounting increasingly places considerable weight on non-monetary data. For example, information about customer satisfaction is of tremendous importance even though it would be difficult to express such data in a monetary form. If customers are dissatisfied then the future revenues and profits of the organization might be at risk.

- **Focus on the segments of an organization.** Financial accounting is primarily concerned with reporting for the company as a whole. By contrast, management accounting focuses much more on the parts, or segments, of a company. These segments may be product lines, sales territories, divisions, departments, or any other categorization of the company's activities that management finds useful.

Focus on Business Practice

Accounting in human resources

© Andresr

Human resources (HR) professionals often say 'people are our greatest asset', but might not understand what an asset is, or forget to look at the profit and loss account to see what payroll and related costs are. According to a recent article in *People Management*, not many HR professionals have sufficient basic accounting knowledge to understand basic accounting principles. They need to be familiar with the basic financial statements – the profit and loss account (income statement), balance sheet and cash flow statement – as well as understand costs. The article suggests accounting is a communication medium, a language indeed, that not everyone understands. While HR professionals may not think they require fluency in accounting, they do need to make business decisions which are underpinned by sound financial information, for example hiring someone, or approving redundancy packages. Having an understanding of accounting information (rather than just accepting it from accountants) would benefit HR managers and staff. Certainly, management accountants within an organization could provide some help by training HR staff in the basics of accounting and costs.[2]

Exercise: Can you think of how other sections of an organization (like product design, for example) might use accounting information?

Management accounting: responding to challenges in the business environment

LO 3

New business processes and technologies

The last three decades have been a period of tremendous ferment and change in the business environment. Competition in many industries has become worldwide in scope, and the pace of innovation in products and services has accelerated. This has been good news for consumers, since intensified competition has generally led to lower prices, higher quality and more choices. However, the last two decades have been a period of wrenching change for many businesses and their employees. Many managers have learned that cherished ways of doing business do not work any more and that major changes must be made in how organizations are managed and in how work gets done.

Another significant influence on management accounting is new and ever-changing technology, especially in computers and telecommunications. These technologies have not just resulted in the automation of existing manual management accounting systems but have enabled the restructuring of whole industries and economies. Even if some of the hype surrounding the internet has died down a little since the heady days of the late 1990s, the internet has, and is, changing the way business is done. Production philosophies pioneered in manufacturing such as lean production are now applied in service as well as manufacturing activities.

Enterprise resource planning systems

Some technological changes have not just affected the environment of management accounting but have had a direct impact on the collection and dissemination of management information.[3] The increasing use of sophisticated real time information systems known as enterprise resource planning (ERP) provided by companies such as SAP, Oracle, J.D. Edwards and Baan, has changed the nature of management accounting work and the role of the finance function.[4] One of the emerging implications for the management accountant is that there is more emphasis on business support rather than routine information gathering. Furthermore, not only is there a greater dispersion of finance personnel into process areas, but accounting information itself has become more dispersed throughout the organization as it becomes more accessible to non-accounting personnel.

More emphasis on business ethics

If ethical standards in business were not generally adhered to, there would be undesirable consequences for everyone. Essentially, abandoning ethical standards would lead to a lower standard of living with lower-quality goods and services, less to choose from, and higher prices. In short, following ethical rules is not just a matter of being 'nice'; it is absolutely essential for the smooth functioning of an advanced market economy. The single-minded emphasis placed on short-term profits in some companies may make it seem as if the only way to get ahead is to act unethically. When top managers say, in effect, that they will only be satisfied with bottom-line results and will accept no excuses, they are asking for trouble, as recent collapses in the banking sector illustrate.

The increased importance of service sector management

Management accounting has expanded its influence from its traditional base in manufacturing to service sectors, which themselves have become increasing sources of employment and income in many economies. Many traditional management accounting approaches to issues such as costing were developed with manufacturing industry in mind. In comparison with traditional manufacturing where the product is easy to see

and touch, products in service industries are less tangible. A bank may offer a number of different 'products' such as types of account or loans which are defined by dimensions such as accessibility or repayment terms, secured or unsecured and so on. Services cannot be stored in inventory so that managers in banks and other service industries may be less interested in *product* cost but, rather, which *customers* are profitable and which customers are not. Service industries provide new challenges and opportunities for management accounting information, particularly as competitive success is especially dependent on intangible assets such as employee expertise and customer relations.

Not only are service activities becoming more important relative to manufacturing but they are increasingly subject to reorganization in both public and private sectors.[5] In particular, we have seen the emergence of shared service centres where the support services of an entire corporation are concentrated in a single geographical location. Other companies have gone a stage further by sub-contracting them to independent companies in a practice known as outsourcing.[6]

Management accounting's spread into the public sector is driven by government demands for new measures of performance and new delivery systems. Although its precise form and motivation varies in different countries, this phenomenon, often referred to as the 'New Public Management',[7] may be seen as a global movement.[8] These developments are not without controversy, especially where there is an attempt to apply, in the not-for-profit, public sector organizations, the same management philosophies and techniques that were originally developed for private, profit-making organizations.

Managing for value

Traditionally, accountants were portrayed as 'bean-counters' or 'corporate policemen' with an emphasis on past performance and organizational control. While these functions are still part of an accountant's role, the trend recently has been to emphasize the creation and management of value. Pressures from corporate raiders and new sources of capital, such as private equity, mean that managers have to be increasingly aware of shareholder value. There are challenges both to *measure* shareholder value and to discover how to *create* it through the adoption and implementation of corporate strategies. Managers are also aware of the importance of *customer value* and its relationship to shareholder value. Managing for value has to balance the possible

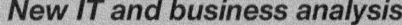

Focus on Business Practice

New IT and business analysis

© Greg Nicholas

Rachel has trained as a management accountant and is now director of divisional finance in a large restaurant and public house chain. The company has an advanced accounting system in which transactions recording and reporting has been automated. Freed up from routine data gathering, Rachel liaises between the regional operational managers and the company's board as she and her team of analysts monitor and manage the financial performance of the many restaurant and pub brands that make up the business.

Exercise: Note how advances in IT have automated the 'score-keeping' aspects of accounting and enabled managers not only to have more up-to-the-minute business intelligence but also freeing up their time for value creation.

gains to short-run profitability arising from cost-cutting exercises to possible long-run damage to shareholder value as costs may be cut at the expense of customer satisfaction. For the management accountant the challenge is not just to devise appropriate financial and non-financial metrics to measure value but to try and understand cause-and-effect relationships.[9]

Managing for environmental sustainability

While concern about the environment has been around for some decades, the threat of rapid man-induced climate change has raised the profile of a whole range of environmental sustainability issues. Even managers focusing on shareholder value may be concerned about the environment for three main reasons. First, there is a compliance motive – companies may find that they are forced through regulation and green taxes to manage environmental resources more carefully. Second, eco-efficiency not only may save the planet but reduce business costs. Finally, there may be strategic reasons – companies may have customers who demand green business policies and who are increasingly suspicious of 'environmental window dressing' through environmental reporting. **Environmental management accounting** is not just about reporting but collecting and analysing *physical* information on flows of energy, water and other materials as well as *monetary* information on environmental costs and benefits in order to make environmentally sensitive decisions.[10]

The practice of management accounting   LO 4

Management accounting principles may be useful for non-specialists as well as specialists

Although management accounting has traditionally been practised by professionals in a specialized finance function, one of the results of the changes discussed above in technology and organizational processes, has meant that it is not just finance workers but other-finance specialists (such as engineers, doctors and many other professionals) who have become more 'finance literate' and aware of the importance of management accounting data. The spread of management accounting practices to non-accounting managers has been influenced by the changes such as privatization. New information technology has also played a part by 'de-centring' accounting knowledge. Some academics have coined the term 'hybrid accountants' to describe individuals who 'may be accountants (but are) ... more likely people from other functions who are financially literate'.[11] The result is that management accounting practices are not simply located in a specialist finance function but are dispersed throughout all levels in many functional areas of the organization.[12]

The sources of business knowledge

The practice and principles of management accounting have been developed over many decades, even centuries. In the early days the main source of practice was practitioners such as early industrialists at Josiah Wedgewood's potteries or at Alfred Sloan's General Motors. More recently other inputs have come from business schools, management consultants and even management gurus.[13] In the particular case of accounting other contributors to managerial knowledge production include professional bodies. Managerial and business knowledge may be visualized as being produced via a circulation of ideas and practices as shown in Exhibit 1.2.

Yet the processes that impact on the production and circulation of managerial knowledge should not be seen as infallible. Academic theories may be rejected by practitioners on the grounds of 'irrelevance' and practices may develop that weaken rather than enhance long-run business performance.[14] The latest practices may not really be 'best practice' but rather introduced because of managerial fashions and fads. One of the aims of this book is to enable the reader to develop a *critical* understanding of the principles behind management accounting so that faulty practices may be recognized even if they cannot always be changed in a particular organizational setting.

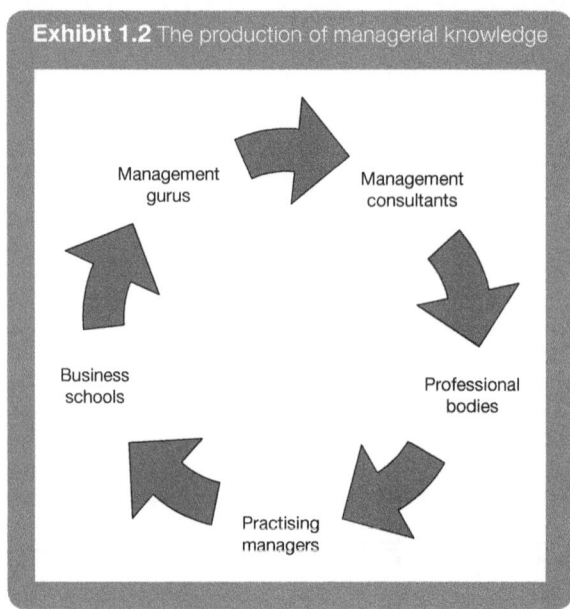

Exhibit 1.2 The production of managerial knowledge

Summary

- Management accounting assists managers in carrying out their responsibilities, which include planning, directing and motivating, and controlling.

- Since management accounting is geared to the needs of the manager rather than to the needs of outsiders, it differs substantially from financial accounting. Management accounting is oriented more towards the future, places less emphasis on precision, emphasizes segments of an organization (rather than the organization as a whole), is not governed by generally accepted accounting principles, and is not mandatory.

- Most organizations are decentralized to some degree. Accountants perform a staff function – they support and provide assistance to others inside the organization.

- The business environment in recent years has been characterized by increasing competition and a relentless drive for continuous improvement. Organizations have also restructured with outsourcing and relocation of company activities. Reformed public sectors are increasingly applying management accounting techniques.

- Management accounting principles and practices may be useful for non-finance specialists and may be useful in many parts of the organization outside the finance function.

Key terms

At the end of each chapter, a list of key terms for review is given, along with the definition of each term. (These terms are highlighted in colour.) Carefully study each term to be sure you understand its meaning, since these terms are used repeatedly in the chapters that follow. The list for Chapter 1 follows.

Budget A detailed plan for the future, usually expressed in formal quantitative terms (p. 4).

Control The process of instituting procedures and then obtaining feedback to ensure that all parts of the organization are functioning effectively and moving towards overall company goals (p. 4).

Environmental management accounting is the collection and analysis of physical and monetary information on environmental costs and benefits in order to make environmentally sensitive decisions (p. 9).

Feedback Accounting and other reports that help managers monitor performance and focus on problems and/or opportunities that might otherwise go unnoticed (p. 4).

Management accounting The phase of accounting concerned with providing information to managers for use in planning and controlling operations and in decision making (p. 4).

Performance report A detailed report comparing budgeted data to actual data (p. 4).

Planning and control cycle The flow of management activities through planning, directing and motivating, and controlling, and then back to planning again (p. 5).

Endnotes

1 Adapted from the easyJet company website, 24 March 2005.

2 *People Management*, July 2009.

3 See Scapens, Ezzamel, Burns and Baldvinsdottir (2003).

4 See May (2002).

5 See, e.g., Bain and Taylor (2000).

6 Hayward (2002), CIMA Technical Briefing (2001a).

7 Hood (1995).

8 Olson, Guthrie and Humphrey (1998).

9 For a historical view on value based management see Ittner and Larcker (2001). For a very recent attempt to analyse the cost of customer satisfaction see Cugini, Caru and Zerbini (2007).

10 See IFAC (2005).

11 Burns and Scapens (2000).

12 May (2002).

13 Thrift (2005).

14 Johnson and Kaplan (1987) and Seal (2010).

When you have read this chapter, log on to the Online Learning Centre for *Management Accounting for Business Decisions* at **www.mcgraw-hill.co.uk/ textbooks/seal**, where you'll find multiple choice questions, practice exams and extra study tools for management accounting.

Assessment

Questions   [Instructors note: these are non-technical exercises that might be used for either individual or group work]

connect™

1-1 Preparing a business plan

Imagine that you are a newly qualified chef and that you want to set up your own restaurant. You need to raise some funds from the bank. Draw up a list of the financial and non-financial information that you would need in order to present a credible business case to the bank.

1-2 Ethics on the job

Ethical standards are very important in business, but they are not always followed. If you have ever held a job – even a summer job – describe the ethical climate in the organization where you worked. Did employees work a full day or did they arrive late and leave early? Did employees honestly report the hours they worked? Did employees use their employer's resources for their own purposes? Did managers set a good example? Did the organization have a code of ethics and were employees made aware of its existence? If the ethical climate in the organization you worked for was poor, what problems, if any, did it create?

1-3 Relevance of management accounting principles

Imagine that you are:
1   A medical doctor
2   An engineer
3   A lawyer
4   An accountant in professional practice
5   A head teacher
6   A local government manager
7   A manager in a job centre
8   A film producer

In each case suggest when and why management accounting concepts and practices may impact on some aspects of your work.

Chapter 2
Cost terms and concepts

LO Learning **objectives**

After studying Chapter 2, you should be able to:
1   Understand the need for costing for external financial reporting
2   Identify each of the three basic cost elements involved in the manufacture of a product
3   Distinguish between product costs and period costs and give examples of each
4   Understand the basics of cost behaviour
5   Identify and give examples of variable costs and fixed costs
6   Define cost classifications used in making decisions: differential costs, opportunity costs and sunk costs

Concepts **in Context**

This chapter introduces issues concerned with the classification of costs. These issues may be controversial. For example, the British Broadcasting Corporation (BBC) has been accused of concealing the true costs of its individual channels by reporting the cost of items such as news gathering, marketing and publicity under separate headings instead of allocating them as overheads to each channel. It was alleged that the corporation wished to reduce the apparent costs both of expanding into digital broadcasting and the budget of BBC1, the channel that competes with the main commercial broadcasters. The BBC responded by claiming that the new format reflected the corporation's internal reporting system and that the new format was 'more transparent'.[1]

© Anthony Baggett

In introductory financial accounting, you learn that firms prepare periodic financial reports for creditors, shareholders and others to show the financial condition of the firm and the firm's earnings performance over some specified interval. Since firms are generally legally obliged to produce financial statements, many organizations may only produce cost data for such *financial reporting* purposes. The financial accounting concepts of cost classification will concern us in the first part of the chapter.

Later in this chapter, we will also consider other ways of looking at costs. For example, how do costs *behave* especially with changes in the level of activity? Which costs are fixed and which are variable and over what range of activity level?

Finally, we will explore different concepts of costs classified according to the principle of 'decision-relevance'. The decision-relevance approach may suggest that the costs collected for finance reporting purposes may not be either appropriate or sufficient for decision-making purposes.[2]

LO 1 Costing for financial reporting purposes: an example from manufacturing

Manufacturing costs

Costs are associated with all types of organizations – business, non-business, manufacturing, retail and service. Generally, the kinds of costs incurred and the way in which these costs are classified depends on the type of organization involved. Management accounting is as applicable to one type of organization as to another. The focus in this chapter is on manufacturing companies, since their basic activities include most of the activities found in other types of business organizations. Manufacturing companies are involved in acquiring raw materials, producing finished goods, marketing, distributing, billing and almost every other business activity. Therefore, an understanding of costs in a manufacturing company can be very helpful in understanding costs in other types of organizations. Most manufacturing companies divide manufacturing costs into three broad categories: **direct materials**, **direct labour**, and **manufacturing overhead**. A discussion of each of these categories follows.

LO 2 Direct materials

The materials that go into the final product are called **raw materials**. This term is somewhat misleading, since it seems to imply unprocessed natural resources like wood pulp or iron ore. Actually, raw materials refer to any materials that are used in the final product; and the finished product of one company can become the raw materials of another company. Direct materials are those materials that become an integral part of the finished product and that can be physically and conveniently traced to it. Sometimes it isn't worth the effort to trace the costs of relatively insignificant materials to the end products. Such minor items would include the solder used to make electrical connections in a TV. Materials such as solder and glue are called **indirect materials** and are included as part of manufacturing overhead, which is discussed later in this section.

Direct labour

The term direct labour is reserved for those labour costs that can easily (i.e., physically and conveniently) be traced to individual units of product. Direct labour is sometimes called *touch labour*, since direct labour workers typically touch the product while it is being made. The labour costs of assembly-line workers, for example, would be direct labour costs, as would the labour costs of carpenters, bricklayers and machine operators.

Labour costs that cannot be physically traced to the creation of products, or that can be traced only at great cost and inconvenience, are termed **indirect labour** and treated as part of manufacturing overhead, along with indirect materials. Indirect labour includes the labour costs of caretakers, supervisors, materials handlers and night security guards. Although the efforts of these workers are essential to production, it would either be impractical or impossible accurately to trace their costs to specific units of product. Hence, such labour costs are treated as indirect labour.

Manufacturing overhead

Manufacturing overhead, the third element of manufacturing cost, includes all costs of manufacturing except direct materials and direct labour. Manufacturing overhead includes items such as indirect materials; indirect labour; maintenance and repairs on production equipment; and heat and light, property taxes, depreciation and insurance on manufacturing facilities. A company also incurs costs for heat and light, property taxes, insurance, depreciation and so forth, associated with its selling and administrative functions, but these costs are not included as part of manufacturing overhead. Only those costs associated with *operating the factory* are included in the manufacturing overhead category.

Various names are used for manufacturing overhead, such as *indirect manufacturing cost, factory overhead,* and *factory burden*. All of these terms are synonymous with *manufacturing overhead*.

Manufacturing overhead combined with direct labour is called **conversion cost**. This term stems from the fact that direct labour costs and overhead costs are incurred in the conversion of materials into finished products. Direct labour combined with direct materials is called **prime cost**.

Non-manufacturing costs

Generally, non-manufacturing costs are subclassified into two categories:

1 Marketing or selling costs
2 Administrative costs

Marketing or selling costs include all costs necessary to secure customer orders and get the finished product or service into the hands of the customer. These costs are often called *order-getting* and *order-filling costs*. Examples of marketing costs include advertising, shipping, sales travel, sales commissions, sales salaries and costs of finished goods warehouses.

Administrative costs include all executive, organizational and clerical costs associated with the *general management* of an organization rather than with manufacturing, marketing or selling. Examples of administrative costs include executive compensation, general accounting, secretarial, public relations and similar costs involved in the overall general administration of the organization *as a whole*.

Product costs versus period costs

LO 3

In addition to the distinction between manufacturing and non-manufacturing costs, there are other ways to look at costs. For instance, they can also be classified as either **product costs** or **period costs**. To understand the difference between product costs and period costs, we must first refresh our understanding of the matching principle from financial accounting.

Generally, costs are recognized as expenses on the *profit and loss account* (sometimes alternatively known as the *income statement*)[3] in the period that benefits from the cost. For example, if a company pays for liability insurance in advance for two years, the entire amount is not considered an expense of the year in which the payment is made. Instead, half of the cost would be recognized as an expense each year. This is because both years – not just the first – benefit from the insurance payment. The unexpensed portion of the insurance payment is carried on the balance sheet as an asset called prepaid insurance. You should be familiar with this type of *accrual* from your financial accounting course.

The *matching principle* is based on the accrual concept and states that *costs incurred to generate a particular revenue should be recognized as expenses in the same period that the revenue is recognized*. This means that if a cost is incurred to acquire or make something that will eventually be sold, then the cost should be recognized as an expense only when the sale takes place – that is, when the benefit occurs. Such costs are called *product costs*.

Product costs

For financial accounting purposes, product costs include all the costs that are involved in acquiring or making a product. In the case of manufactured goods, these costs consist of direct materials, direct labour and manufacturing overhead. Product costs are viewed as 'attaching' to units of product as the goods are

purchased or manufactured, and they remain attached as the goods go into stock awaiting sale. So, initially, product costs are assigned to a stock account on the balance sheet. When the goods are sold, the costs are released from stock as expenses (typically called cost of goods sold) and matched against sales revenue. Since product costs are initially assigned to stocks, they are also known as *stock-related costs*.

We want to emphasize that product costs are not necessarily treated as expenses in the period in which they are incurred. Rather, as explained above, they are treated as expenses in the period in which the related products *are sold*. This means that a product cost such as direct materials or direct labour might be incurred during one period but not treated as an expense until a following period when the completed product is sold.

Period costs

Period costs are all the costs that are not included in product costs. These costs are expensed on the profit and loss account in the period in which they are incurred, using the usual rules of accrual accounting you have already learned in financial accounting. Period costs are not included as part of the cost of either purchased or manufactured goods. Sales commissions and office rent are good examples of the kind of costs we are talking about. Neither commissions nor office rent are included as part of the cost of purchased or manufactured goods. Rather, both items are treated as expenses on the profit and loss account in the period in which they are incurred. Thus, they are said to be period costs.

As suggested above, *all selling and administrative expenses are considered to be period costs*. Therefore, advertising, executive salaries, sales commissions, public relations, and other non-manufacturing costs discussed

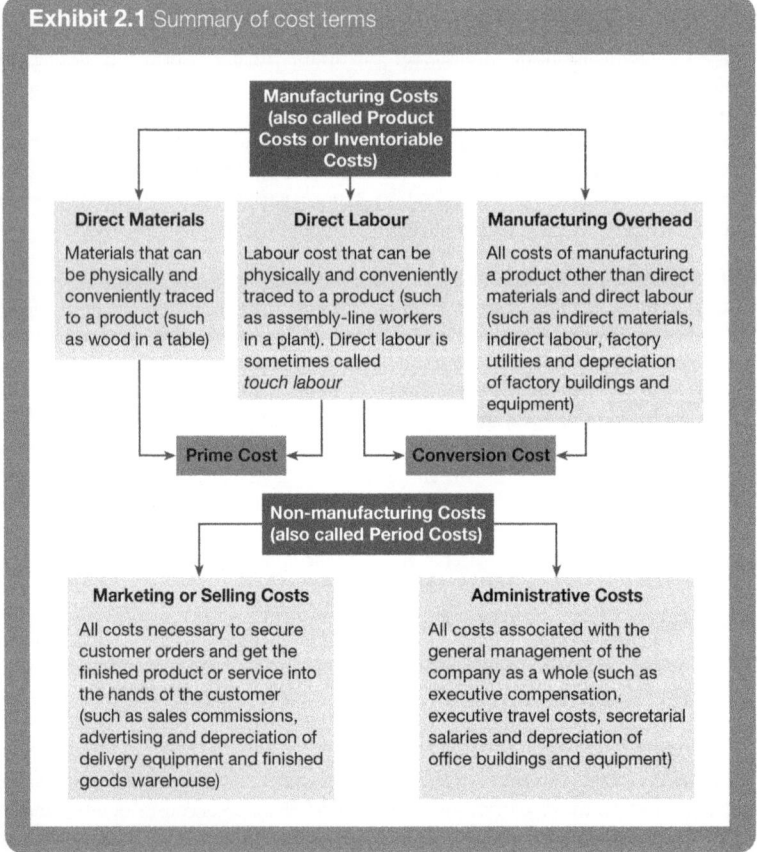

Exhibit 2.1 Summary of cost terms

earlier would all be period costs. They will appear on the profit and loss account as expenses in the period in which they are incurred.

Exhibit 2.1 contains a summary of the cost terms that we have introduced so far.

Product costs – a closer look

To understand product costs more fully, it will be helpful at this point to look briefly at the flow of costs in a manufacturing company. By doing so, we will be able to see how product costs move through the various accounts and affect the balance sheet and the profit and loss account in the course of producing and selling products.

Exhibit 2.2 illustrates the flow of costs in a manufacturing company. Raw materials purchases are recorded in the Raw Materials inventory account. When raw materials are used in production, their costs are transferred to the Work in Progress inventory account as direct materials. Notice that direct labour cost and manufacturing overhead cost are added directly to Work in Progress. Work in Progress can be viewed most simply as an assembly line where workers are stationed and where products slowly take shape as they move from one end of the assembly line to the other. The direct materials, direct labour and manufacturing overhead costs added to Work in Progress in Exhibit 2.2 are the costs needed to complete these products as they move along this assembly line.

Notice from the exhibit that as goods are completed, their cost is transferred from Work in Progress into Finished Goods. Here the goods await sale to a customer. As goods are sold, their cost is then transferred from Finished Goods into Cost of Goods Sold. It is at this point that the various material, labour and overhead costs that are required to make the product are finally treated as expenses.

Stock/inventory-related costs

As stated earlier, product costs are often called stock-related (or inventoriable[4]) costs. The reason is that these costs go directly into inventory accounts as they are incurred (first into Work in Progress and then into Finished Goods), rather than going into expense accounts. Thus, they are termed **stock-related costs**. *This is a key concept in management accounting, since such costs can end up on the balance sheet as assets if goods are only*

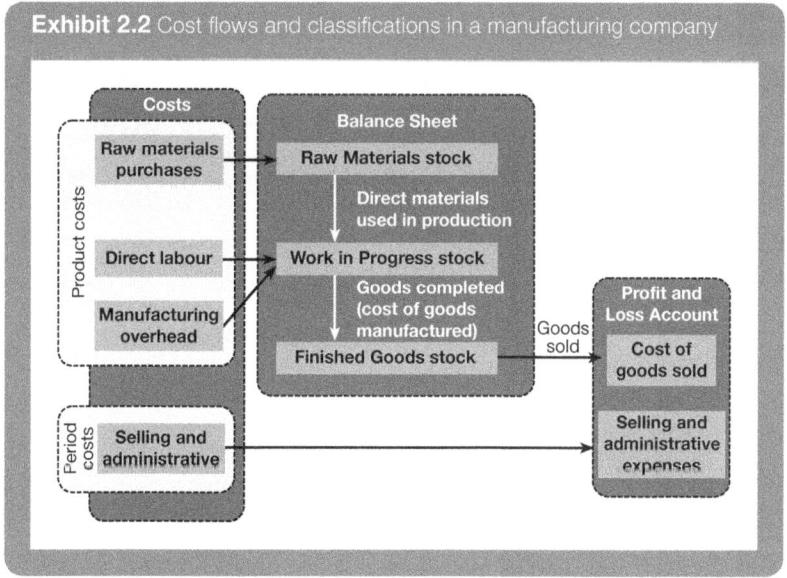

Exhibit 2.2 Cost flows and classifications in a manufacturing company

partially completed or are unsold at the end of a period. At the end of the period, the materials, labour and overhead costs that are associated with the units in the Work in Progress and Finished Goods stock accounts will appear on the balance sheet as part of the company's assets. As explained earlier, these costs will not become expenses until later when the goods are completed and sold.

Focus on Business Practice
The full cost of the 2010 Gulf of Mexico oil spill

© M

When management accountants talk about the full costs of a product or service this usually means that all costs – materials, labour and a portion of overhead – are included in the cost of the product/service. In more basic terms, this means that whatever the cost object is, accountants ensure that the cost calculated includes as many costs as possible (if not all). Consider for a moment an event like the oil spill from a BP-owned well in the Gulf of Mexico in 2010. How could an accountant begin to work out the full cost of this environmental disaster? The first thing to do would be to try to think of all the costs which might arise. Prior to this oil spill, the Exxon Valdez tanker leak off Alaska in 1989 was the biggest oil spill in the US. The full cost of the clean up then was $4 billion, more than 600 times what the oil lost was worth at the time. In the Gulf of Mexico case, which at the time of writing is still ongoing, a picture of the full costs of the disaster is beginning to emerge. The first cost is the cost of the 3 million or so litres of oil per day being lost. The clean-up and containment costs are in the order of $5–10 million per day. As of early June 2010, BP themselves had incurred costs of $1.43 billion in clean-up, claims and other costs. Lawsuits to the tune of $25 billion have been filed against BP and related companies. Lost tourism and fishing in and around the Gulf area accounts for $8–12 billion in cost. In addition to the mentioned costs, the costs of extra personnel and administrative staff involved might also be included. While this example does not portray a product or service, it does highlight the difficulties faced by management accountants in calculating any full cost. This does not mean they abandon efforts, however, as in most cases a reasonably accurate full cost figure can be determined.[5]

Exercise: Look up other examples of cases where large-scale damage has been caused by an industrial or environmental type accident/disaster. Try to find out the full costs to the company and/or the community/environment.

As shown in Exhibit 2.2, selling and administrative expenses are not involved in the manufacture of a product. For this reason, they are not treated as product costs but rather as period costs that go directly into expense accounts as they are incurred.

Thus far, we have been mainly concerned with classifications of manufacturing costs for the purpose of determining inventory valuations on the balance sheet and cost of goods sold on the profit and loss account of external financial reports. There are, however, many other purposes for which costs are used, and each

---

Exhibit 2.3 Summary of cost classifications

Purpose of cost classification	Cost classifications
Preparing external financial statements	• Product costs (inventoriable) • Direct materials • Direct labour • Manufacturing overheads • Period costs (expensed) • Non-manufacturing costs • Marketing or selling costs • Administrative costs
Predicting cost behaviour in response to changes in activity	• Variable cost (proportional to activity) • Fixed cost (constant in total)
Assigning costs to cost objects such as departments or products	• Direct cost (can easily be traced) • Indirect cost (cannot easily be traced; must be allocated)
Making decisions	• Differential cost (differs between alternatives) • Sunk cost (past cost not affected by a decision) • Opportunity cost (forgone benefit)

---

purpose requires a different classification of costs. We will consider several different purposes for cost classifications in the remaining sections of this chapter. These purposes and the corresponding cost classifications are summarized in Exhibit 2.3. To maintain focus, we suggest that you refer back to this exhibit frequently as you progress through the rest of this chapter.

Cost classifications for predicting cost behaviour

LO 4

Quite frequently, it is necessary to predict how a certain cost will behave in response to a change in activity. **Cost behaviour** means how a cost will react or respond to changes in the level of business activity. As the activity level rises and falls, a particular cost may rise and fall as well – or it may remain constant. For planning purposes, a manager must be able to anticipate which of these will happen; and if a cost can be expected to change, the manager must know by how much it will change. To help make such distinctions, costs are often categorized as variable or fixed.

Variable cost

LO 5

A **variable cost** is a cost that varies, in total, in direct proportion to changes in the level of activity. The activity can be expressed in many ways, such as units produced, units sold, miles driven, beds occupied, lines of print, hours worked, and so forth. A good example of a variable cost is direct materials. The cost of direct materials used during a period will vary, in total, in direct proportion to the number of units that are produced. To illustrate this idea, consider the example of a car factory. Each car requires one battery. As the output of cars increases and decreases, the number of batteries used will increase and decrease proportionately. If car production goes up 10%, then the number of batteries used will also go up 10%. The concept of a variable cost is shown in graphic form in Exhibit 2.4.

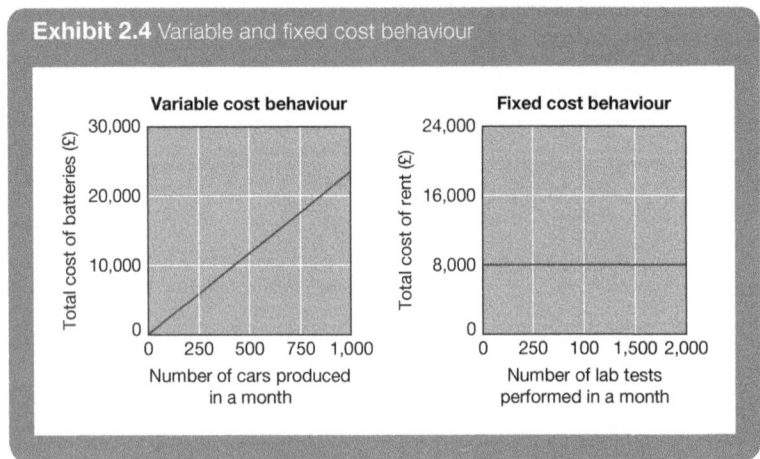

Exhibit 2.4 Variable and fixed cost behaviour

It is important to note that when we speak of a cost as being variable, we mean the *total* cost rises and falls as the activity level rises and falls. This idea is presented below, assuming that a battery costs £24:

Number of cars produced	Cost per battery	Total variable cost-batteries
1	£24	£24
500	24	12,000
1,000	24	24,000

One interesting aspect of variable cost behaviour is that a variable cost is constant if expressed on a *per unit* basis. Observe from the tabulation above that the per unit cost of batteries remains constant at £24 even though the total amount of cost involved increases and decreases with activity.

There are many examples of costs that are variable with respect to the products and services provided by a company. In a manufacturing company, variable costs include items such as direct materials and some elements of manufacturing overhead such as lubricants, shipping costs and sales commissions. For the present we will also assume that direct labour is a variable cost, although as we shall see later, direct labour may act more like a fixed cost in many situations. In a merchandising company, variable costs include items such as cost of goods sold, commissions to salespersons and billing costs. In a hospital, the variable costs of providing healthcare services to patients would include the costs of the supplies, drugs, meals and, perhaps, nursing services.

The activity causing changes in a variable cost need not be how much output is produced or sold. For example, the wages paid to employees at a video outlet will depend on the number of hours the shop is open and not strictly on the number of videos rented. In this case, we would say that wage costs are variable with respect to the hours of operation. Nevertheless, when we say that a cost is variable, we ordinarily mean it is variable with respect to the volume of revenue-generating output – in other words, how many units are produced and sold, how many videos are rented, how many patients are treated and so on.

Fixed cost

A **fixed cost** is a cost that remains constant, in total, regardless of changes in the level of activity. Unlike variable costs, fixed costs are not affected by changes in activity. Consequently, as the activity level rises and falls, the fixed costs remain constant in total amount unless influenced by some outside force, such as price changes. Rent is a good example of a fixed cost. Suppose a hospital rents a machine for £8,000 per month that tests blood samples for the presence of leukaemia cells. The £8,000 monthly rental cost will be sustained regardless of the number of tests that may be performed during the month. The concept of a fixed cost is shown in graphic form in Exhibit 2.4.

Very few costs are completely fixed. Most will change if there is a large enough change in activity. For example, suppose that the capacity of the leukaemia diagnostic machine at the hospital is 2,000 tests per month. If the clinic wishes to perform more than 2,000 tests in a month, it would be necessary to rent an additional machine, which would cause a jump in the fixed costs. When we say a cost is fixed, we mean it is fixed within some *relevant range*. The **relevant range** is the range of activity within which the assumptions about variable and fixed costs are valid. For example, the assumption that the rent for diagnostic machines is £8,000 per month is valid within the relevant range of 0 to 2,000 tests per month.

Fixed costs can create difficulties if it becomes necessary to express the costs on a per unit basis. This is because if fixed costs are expressed on a per unit basis, they will react inversely with changes in activity. In the hospital, for example, the average cost per test will fall as the number of tests performed increases. This is because the £8,000 rental cost will be spread over more tests. Conversely, as the number of tests performed in the clinic declines, the average cost per test will rise as the £8,000 rental cost is spread over fewer tests. This concept is illustrated in the table below:

Monthly rental cost	Number of tests performed	Average cost per test
£8,000	10	£800
8,000	500	16
8,000	2,000	4

Note that if the hospital performs only ten tests each month, the rental cost of the equipment will average £800 per test. But if 2,000 tests are performed each month, the average cost will drop to only £4 per test. More will be said later about the problems created for both the accountant and the manager by this variation in unit costs.

Examples of fixed costs include straight-line depreciation, insurance, property taxes, rent, supervisory salaries, administrative salaries and advertising.

A summary of both variable and fixed cost behaviour is presented in Exhibit 2.5.

Exhibit 2.5 Summary of variable and fixed cost behaviour

	Behaviour of the cost (within the relevant range)	
Cost	In total	Per unit
Variable cost	Total variable cost increases and decreases in proportion to changes in the activity level.	Variable costs remain constant per unit.
Fixed cost	Total fixed cost is not affected by changes in the activity level within the relevant range.	Fixed costs decrease per unit as the activity level rises and increases per unit as the activity level falls.

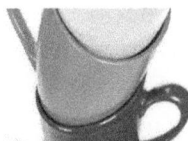

Focus on Business Practice

The cost of phone calls

© Neustockimages

Because of national and European regulation of the tele-communications industry, considerable research has been published on calculating the cost of providing tele-communications such as phone, text and other forms of communication. In a recent report, the UK regulator discussed the way that these costs have been calculated using many of the terms used in this and subsequent chapters (direct cost, variable cost, common cost allocation, overheads, avoidable costs, and so on...). As Exhibit 2.6 shows, they have estimated cost behaviour for different types of calls and networks. The exhibit shows how the cost structure varies between different types of traffic and networks. Much of the debate between the regulators and providers concerns the *allocation* of 'common costs' rather than direct costs which may be estimated using economic cost models.

Exercise: Note how the discussions of fair phone tariffs combine the *technological character* of telecommunications, which helps to explain cost behaviour, with *commercial* decisions based on marketing and accounting issues.

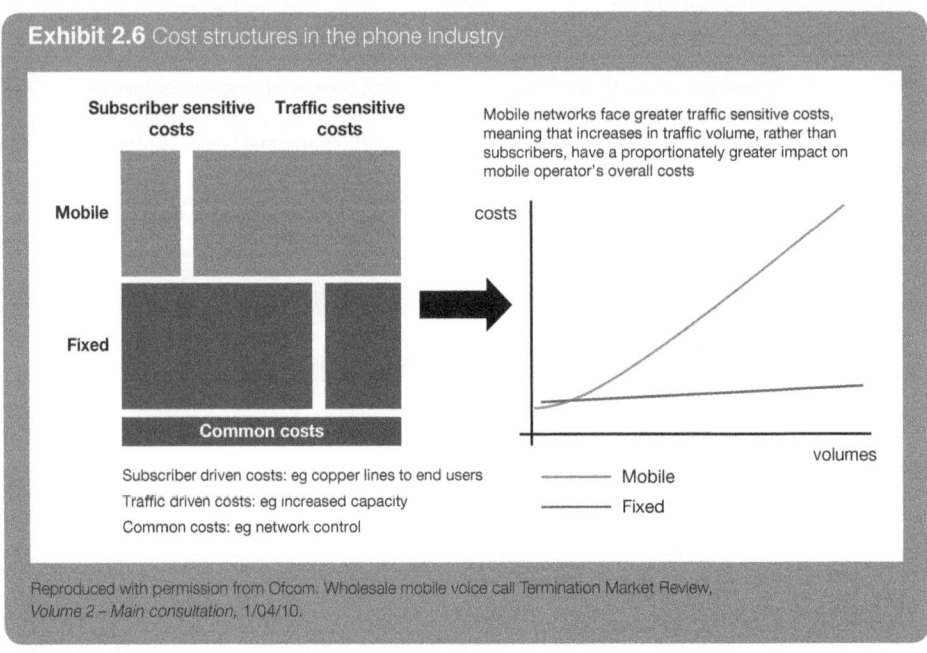

Exhibit 2.6 Cost structures in the phone industry

Mobile networks face greater traffic sensitive costs, meaning that increases in traffic volume, rather than subscribers, have a proportionately greater impact on mobile operator's overall costs

Subscriber driven costs: eg copper lines to end users
Traffic driven costs: eg increased capacity
Common costs: eg network control

Reproduced with permission from Ofcom. Wholesale mobile voice call Termination Market Review, *Volume 2 – Main consultation*, 1/04/10.

The contribution format

Once the manager has separated costs into fixed and variable elements, what is done with the data? We have already answered this question somewhat by showing how a cost formula can be used to predict costs. To answer this question more fully would require most of the remainder of this text, since much of what the manager does rests in some way on an understanding of cost behaviour. One immediate and very significant application of the ideas we have developed, however, is found in a new profit statement format known as the **contribution approach**. The unique thing about the contribution approach is that it provides the manager with a profit statement geared directly to cost behaviour.

Why a new profit and loss statement format?

The *traditional approach* to the profit and loss statement is not organized in terms of cost behaviour. Rather, it is organized in a 'functional' format – emphasizing the functions of production, administration and sales in the classification and presentation of cost data. No attempt is made to distinguish between the behaviour of costs included under each functional heading. Under the heading 'Administrative expense', for example, one can expect to find both variable and fixed costs lumped together.

Although a profit and loss statement prepared in the functional format may be useful for external reporting purposes, it has serious limitations when used for internal purposes. Internally, the manager needs cost data organized in a format that will facilitate planning, control and decision making. These tasks are much easier when cost data are available in a fixed and variable format. The contribution approach to the profit and loss statement has been developed in response to this need.

The contribution approach

Exhibit 2.7 illustrates the contribution approach to the profit and loss statement with a simple example, along with the traditional approach discussed above.

Notice that the contribution approach separates costs into fixed and variable categories, first deducting variable expenses from sales to obtain what is known as the *contribution margin*. The **contribution margin** is

Exhibit 2.7 Comparison of the contribution profit statement with the traditional profit statement

Traditional approach (costs organized by function)			Contribution approach (costs organized by behaviour)		
Sales		£12,000	Sales		£12,000
Less cost of goods sold		6,000*	Less variable expenses:		
Gross margin		6,000	Variable production	£2,000	
Less operating expenses:			Variable selling	600	
Selling	£3,100*		Variable administrative	400	3,000
Administrative	1,900*	5,000	Contribution margin		9,000
Net profit		£1,000	Less fixed expenses:		
			Fixed production	4,000	
			Fixed selling	2,500	
			Fixed administrative	1,500	8,000
			Net profit		£1,000

*Contains both variable and fixed expenses. This is the profit statement for a manufacturing company; thus, when the profit statement is placed in the contribution format, the 'cost of goods sold' figure is divided between variable production costs and fixed production costs. If this were the profit statement for a *merchandising* company (which simply purchases completed goods from a supplier), then the cost of goods sold would *all* be variable.

the amount remaining from sales revenues after variable expenses have been deducted. This amount *contributes* towards covering fixed expenses and then towards profits for the period.

The contribution approach to the profit and loss statement is used as an internal planning and decision-making tool. Its emphasis on costs by behaviour facilitates cost–volume–profit analysis, which we will tackle in Chapter 3. The approach is also very useful in appraising management performance, in segmented reporting of profit data, and in budgeting. Moreover, the contribution approach helps managers organize data pertinent to all kinds of special decisions such as product-line analysis, pricing, use of scarce resources, and make or buy analysis. All of these topics are covered in later chapters.

Managers use costs organized by behaviour as a basis for many decisions. To facilitate this use, the profit statement can be prepared in a contribution format. The contribution format classifies costs on the profit and loss statement by cost behaviour (i.e., variable versus fixed) rather than by the functions of production, administration, and sales.

LO 6 Cost classifications for decision-relevance

Costs are an important feature of many business decisions. In making decisions, it is essential to have a firm grasp of the concepts *differential cost, opportunity cost* and *sunk cost*.

Differential cost and revenue

Decisions involve choosing between alternatives. In business decisions, each alternative will have certain costs and benefits that must be compared to the costs and benefits of the other available alternatives. A difference in costs between any two alternatives is known as a **differential cost**. A difference in revenues between any two alternatives is known as **differential revenue**.

A differential cost is also known as an **incremental cost**, although technically an incremental cost should refer only to an increase in cost from one alternative to another; decreases in cost should be referred to as *decremental costs*. Differential cost is a broader term, encompassing both cost increases (incremental costs) and cost decreases (decremental costs) between alternatives.

The accountant's differential cost concept can be compared to the economist's marginal cost concept. In speaking of changes in cost and revenue, the economist employs the terms *marginal cost* and *marginal revenue*. The revenue that can be obtained from selling one more unit of product is called marginal revenue, and the cost involved in producing one more unit of product is called marginal cost. The economist's marginal concept is basically the same as the accountant's differential concept applied to a single unit of output.

Differential costs can be either fixed or variable. To illustrate, assume that Nature Way Cosmetics is thinking about changing its marketing method from distribution through retailers to distribution by door-to-door direct sale. Present costs and revenues are compared to projected costs and revenues in the following table:

	Retailer distribution (present)	Direct sale distribution (proposed)	Differential costs and revenues
Revenues (V)	£700,000	£800,000	£100,000
Cost of goods sold (V)	350,000	400,000	50,000
Advertising (F)	80,000	45,000	(35,000)
Commissions (V)	0	40,000	40,000
Warehouse depreciation (F)	50,000	80,000	30,000
Other expenses (F)	60,000	60,000	0
Total	540,000	625,000	85,000
Profit	£160,000	£175,000	£15,000

V = Variable; F = Fixed

According to the above analysis, the differential revenue is £100,000 and the differential costs total £85,000, leaving a positive differential profit of £15,000 under the proposed marketing plan.

The decision of whether Nature Way Cosmetics should stay with the present retail distribution or switch to door-to-door direct selling could be made on the basis of the profits of the two alternatives. As we see in the above analysis, the profit under the present distribution method is £160,000, whereas the profit under door-to-door direct selling is estimated to be £175,000. Therefore, the door-to-door direct distribution method is preferred, since it would result in £15,000 higher profit. Note that we would have arrived at exactly the same conclusion by simply focusing on the differential revenues, differential costs and differential profit, which also show a £15,000 advantage for the direct selling method.

In general, only the differences between alternatives are relevant in decisions. Those items that are the same under all alternatives and that are not affected by the decision can be ignored. For example, in the Nature Way Cosmetics example above, the 'Other expenses' category, which is £60,000 under both alternatives, can be ignored, since it has no effect on the decision. If it were removed from the calculations, the door-to-door direct selling method would still be preferred by £15,000.

Opportunity cost

Opportunity cost is the potential benefit that is given up when one alternative is selected over another. To illustrate this important concept, consider the following examples:

Example 1

Vicki has a part-time job that pays her £100 per week while attending college. She would like to spend a week at the beach during spring break, and her employer has agreed to give her the time off, but without pay. The £100 in lost wages would be an opportunity cost of taking the week off to be at the beach.

Example 2

Suppose that Tesco is considering investing a large sum of money in land that may be a site for a future shop. Rather than invest the funds in land, the company could invest the funds in high-grade securities. If the land is acquired, the opportunity cost will be the investment income that could have been realized if the securities had been purchased instead.

Example 3

Steve is employed with a company that pays him a salary of £20,000 per year. He is thinking about leaving the company and going to university. Since going to university would require that he give up his £20,000 salary, the forgone salary would be an opportunity cost of seeking further education.

Opportunity cost is not usually entered in the accounting records of an organization, but it is a cost that must be explicitly considered in every decision a manager makes. Virtually every alternative has some opportunity cost attached to it. In Example 3 above, for instance, if Steve decides to stay at his job, there still is an opportunity cost involved: it is the greater income that could be realized in future years as a result of returning to university.

Sunk cost

A **sunk cost** is a cost *that has already been incurred* and that cannot be changed by any decision made now or in the future. Since sunk costs cannot be changed by any decision, they are not differential costs. Therefore, they can and should be ignored when making a decision.

To illustrate a sunk cost, assume that a company paid £50,000 several years ago for a special-purpose machine. The machine was used to make a product that is now obsolete and is no longer being sold. Even though in hindsight the purchase of the machine may have been unwise, no amount of regret can undo that decision. And it would be folly to continue making the obsolete product in a misguided attempt to 'recover' the original cost of the machine. In short, the £50,000 originally paid for the machine has already been incurred and cannot be a differential cost in any future decisions. For this reason, such costs are said to be sunk and should be ignored in decisions.

We will explore some applications of relevant cost principles further in Chapter 4 when making a number of important business decisions such as replacing equipment, make-or-buy, special orders and dealing with capacity constraints.

Focus on Business Practice

Cost considerations at a retail florist

© Catherine Yeulet

Terri, the owner of a retail florist shop, has been trying to decide for some time whether she should continue to use a local courier service to deliver flowers to customers or buy a delivery van and use one of her employees to make the deliveries. At a recent family dinner, she brought up the subject of the delivery van with her brother-in-law, who fancies himself as an expert on all management subjects. He grabbed this opportunity to impress on Terri his understanding of costs.

In rapid-fire succession, Terri's brother-in-law told her that the fees paid to the courier to deliver flowers are a variable cost and a period cost, but the costs of the flowers are product costs rather than period costs, even though the flower costs are also variable costs. On the other hand, the depreciation of the delivery van would be a fixed cost and a period cost. And while the fuel for the truck would be a variable cost and a differential cost, the wages of the person making the deliveries would be a fixed cost, not a differential cost, and would involve an opportunity cost. At this point, Terri excused herself, pleading that she had to help in the kitchen. Terri felt that her brother-in-law's comments were more confusing than helpful, but she knew that she could no longer put off the decision about the delivery van.

Exercise: Referring to Exhibit 2.3, which costs *should* be considered in this decision?

Focus on Business Practice

Hotel accounting and costs

© Elena Elisseeva

In a recent project, an author was undertaking research into management accounting in the hospitality industry. He noted that many hotels saw room costs in terms of servicing the room and the ongoing expense of maintaining the fixtures and fittings. They did not have an operational measure of the biggest fixed cost of all – the cost of the land and buildings. In the short run, this approach seemed logical as the managers could reduce some of the costs of servicing the rooms through better labour scheduling but they could not (in the short-term) *avoid* the fixed costs of the building itself.

Exercise: In what sense are room servicing costs *variable* in that they vary with activity levels? What other room-related costs are also variable?

Summary

- In this chapter, we have looked at some of the ways in which managers classify costs. How the costs will be used – for preparing external reports, predicting cost behaviour, assigning costs to cost objects, or decision making – will dictate how the costs will be classified.

- For purposes of valuing stocks and determining expenses for the balance sheet and profit and loss account, costs are classified as either product costs or period costs. Product costs are assigned to stocks and are considered assets until the products are sold. At the point of sale, product costs become costs of goods sold on the profit and loss account. In contrast, following the usual accrual practices, period costs are taken directly to the profit and loss account as expenses in the period in which they are incurred.

- For purposes of predicting cost behaviour – how costs will react to changes in activity – managers commonly classify costs into two categories – variable and fixed. Variable costs, in total, are strictly proportional to activity. Thus, the variable cost per unit is constant. Fixed costs, in total, remain at the same level for changes in activity that occur within the relevant range. Thus, the average fixed cost per unit decreases as the number of units increases.

- For purposes of assigning costs to cost objects such as products or departments, costs are classified as direct or indirect. Direct costs can conveniently be traced to the cost objects. Indirect costs cannot conveniently be traced to cost objects.

- For purposes of making decisions, the concepts of differential costs and revenue, opportunity cost and sunk cost are of vital importance. Differential cost and revenue are the cost and revenue items that differ between alternatives. Opportunity cost is the benefit that is forgone when one alternative is selected over another. Sunk cost is a cost that occurred in the past and cannot be altered. Differential cost and opportunity cost should be considered carefully in decisions. Sunk cost is always irrelevant in decisions and should be ignored.

- These various cost classifications are *different* ways of looking at costs. A particular cost, such as the cost of cheese in a cheese burger, could be a manufacturing cost, a product cost, a variable cost, a direct cost, and a differential cost – all at the same time.

Key terms

Administrative costs All executive, organizational and clerical costs associated with the general management of an organization rather than with manufacturing, marketing or selling (p. 17).

Contribution approach A profit statement format that is geared to cost behaviour in that costs are separated into variable and fixed categories rather than being separated according to the functions of production, sales and administration (p. 25).

Contribution margin The amount remaining from sales revenue after all variable expenses have been deducted (p. 25).

Conversion cost Direct labour cost plus manufacturing overhead cost (p. 17).

Cost behaviour The way in which a cost reacts or responds to changes in the level of business activity (p. 22).

Differential cost Any cost that differs between alternatives in a decision-making situation. In managerial accounting, this term is synonymous with avoidable cost and relevant cost. Also see Incremental cost (p. 26).

Differential revenue The difference in revenue between any two alternatives (p. 26).

Direct labour Those factory labour costs that can easily be traced to individual units of product. Also called touch labour (p. 16).

Direct materials Those materials that become an integral part of a finished product and can conveniently be traced into it (p. 16).

Fixed cost A cost that remains constant, in total, regardless of changes in the level of activity within the relevant range. If a fixed cost is expressed on a per unit basis, it varies inversely with the level of activity (p. 23).

Incremental cost An increase in cost between two alternatives. Also see Differential cost (p. 26).

Indirect labour The labour costs of caretakers, supervisors, materials handlers, and other factory workers that cannot conveniently be traced directly to particular products (p. 16).

Indirect materials Small items of material such as glue and nails. These items may become an integral part of a finished product but are traceable to the product only at great cost or inconvenience (p. 16).

Manufacturing overhead All costs associated with manufacturing except direct materials and direct labour (p. 16).

Marketing or selling costs All costs necessary to secure customer orders and get the finished product or service into the hands of the customer (p. 17).

Opportunity cost The potential benefit that is given up when one alternative is selected over another (p. 27).

Period costs Those costs that are taken directly to the profit and loss account as expenses in the period in which they are incurred or accrued; such costs consist of selling (marketing) and administrative expenses (p. 17).

Prime cost Direct materials cost plus direct labour cost (p. 17).

Product costs All costs that are involved in the purchase or manufacture of goods. In the case of manufactured goods, these costs consist of direct materials, direct labour, and manufacturing overhead. Also see Stock-related costs (p. 17).

Raw materials Any materials that go into the final product (p. 16).

Relevant range The range of activity within which assumptions about variable and fixed cost behaviour are valid (p. 23).

Stock-related costs (also known as inventoriable costs) Synonym for product costs (p. 19).

Sunk cost Any cost that has already been incurred and that cannot be changed by any decision made now or in the future (p. 27).

Variable cost A cost that varies, in total, in direct proportion to changes in the level of activity. A variable cost is constant per unit (p. 21).

Endnotes

1 *Financial Management*, September 2003, p. 4.

2 These issues are discussed thoroughly in Johnson and Kaplan (1987).

3 See note 4.

4 In many countries, such as the US, 'stock' is known as 'inventory'. With globalization of capital markets and accounting, terms such as *stock* and *inventory* are increasingly used interchangeably. Other examples of interchangeable terms are *profit* (UK) = *net*

income (US), *debtors* (UK) = *accounts receivable* (US) and *creditors* (UK) = *accounts payable* (US), *work in progress* (UK) = *work in process* (US).

5 http://moneymorning.com/2010/05/10/gulf-oil-spill-2/; http://news.bbc.co.uk/2/hi/americas/8666276.stm; http://www.rte.ie/business/2010/0610/bp.html

When you have read this chapter, log on to the Online Learning Centre for *Management Accounting for Business Decisions* at **www.mcgraw-hill.co.uk/textbooks/seal**, where you'll find multiple choice questions, practice exams and extra study tools for management accounting.

Assessment

Questions
connect

2–1 What are the three major elements of product costs in a manufacturing company?

2–2 Distinguish between the following: (a) direct materials, (b) indirect materials, (c) direct labour, (d) indirect labour, and (e) manufacturing overhead.

2–3 Explain the difference between a product cost and a period cost.

2–4 Why are product costs sometimes called stock-related costs? Describe the flow of such costs in a manufacturing company from the point of incurrence until they finally become expenses on the profit and loss account.

2–5 What is meant by the term *cost behaviour*?

2–6 'A variable cost is a cost that varies per unit of product, whereas a fixed cost is constant per unit of product.' Do you agree? Explain.

2–7 How do fixed costs create difficulties in costing units of product?

2–8 Why is manufacturing overhead considered an indirect cost of a unit of product?

2–9 Define the following terms: differential cost, opportunity cost, and sunk cost.

2–10 Only variable costs can be differential costs. Do you agree? Explain.

Exercises
connect

E2–1 ⏱ **Time allowed:** 15 minutes

The following are a number of cost terms introduced in the chapter:

Variable cost	Product cost
Fixed cost	Sunk cost
Prime cost	Conversion cost
Opportunity cost	Period cost

Choose the term or terms above that most appropriately describe the cost identified in each of the following situations. A cost term can be used more than once.

1 Lake Company produces a bag that is very popular with college students. The cloth going into the manufacture of the bag would be called direct materials and classified as a _____ cost. In terms of cost behaviour, the cloth could also be described as a _____ cost.

2 The direct labour cost required to produce the bags, combined with the manufacturing overhead cost involved, would be known as _____ cost.

3 The company could have taken the funds that it has invested in production equipment and invested them in interest-bearing securities instead. The interest forgone on the securities would be called _____ cost.

4 Taken together, the direct materials cost and the direct labour cost required to produce bags would be called _____ cost.

5 The company used to produce a smaller bag that was not very popular. Some three hundred of these smaller bags are stored in one of the company's warehouses. The amount invested in these bags would be called a _____ cost.

6 The bags are sold through agents who are paid a commission on each bag sold. These commissions would be classified by Lake Company as a _____ cost. In terms of cost behaviour, commissions would be classified as a _____ cost.

7 Depreciation on the equipment used to produce the bags would be classified by Lake Company as a _____ cost. However, depreciation on any equipment used by the company in selling and administrative activities would be classified as _____ cost. In terms of cost behaviour, depreciation would probably be classified as a _____ cost.

8 A _____ cost is also known as a stock-related cost, since such costs go into the Work in Progress stock account and then into the Finished Goods stock account before appearing on the profit and loss account as part of cost of goods sold.

9 The salary of Lake Company's managing director would be classified as a _____ cost, since the salary will appear on the profit and loss account as an expense in the time period in which it is incurred.

10 Costs can often be classified in several ways. For example, Lake Company pays £5,000 rent each month on its factory building. The rent would be part of manufacturing overhead. In terms of cost behaviour, it would be classified as a _____ cost. The rent can also be classified as a _____ cost and as part of _____ cost.

E2–2 Time allowed: 10 minutes

A product cost is also known as a stock-related cost. Classify the following costs as either product (stock-related) costs or period (non-stock-related) costs in a manufacturing company:

1 Depreciation on salespersons' cars
2 Rent on equipment used in the factory
3 Lubricants used for maintenance of machines
4 Salaries of finished goods warehouse personnel
5 Soap and paper towels used by factory workers at the end of a shift
6 Factory supervisors' salaries
7 Heat, water and power consumed in the factory
8 Materials used in boxing units of finished product for shipment overseas (units are not normally boxed)
9 Advertising outlays
10 Workers' compensation insurance on factory employees
11 Depreciation on chairs and tables in the factory lunchroom
12 The salary of the switchboard operator for the company
13 Depreciation on a Lear Jet used by the company's executives
14 Rent on rooms at a West Country resort for holding of the annual sales conference
15 Attractively designed box for packaging breakfast cereal.

E2–3 Time allowed: 10 minutes
Below are a number of costs that are incurred in a variety of organizations:

1 X-ray film used in the radiology lab at Queens Medical Centre in Nottingham
2 The costs of advertising a Madonna rock concert in London
3 Depreciation on the Planet Hollywood restaurant building in Hong Kong
4 The electrical costs of running a roller-coaster at Blackpool
5 Property taxes on a local cinema
6 Commissions paid to salespersons at McGraw-Hill
7 Property insurance on a Coca-Cola bottling plant
8 The costs of synthetic materials used to make Nike running shoes
9 The costs of shipping Panasonic televisions to retail shops
10 The cost of leasing an ultra-scan diagnostic machine at St Thomas's hospital in London.

Required

Classify each cost as being variable or fixed with respect to the number of units of product or services sold by the organization. Set out your answers as below.

	Cost behaviour	
Cost Item	Variable	Fixed

Place an X in the appropriate column for each cost to indicate whether the cost involved would be variable or fixed with respect to the number of units of products or services sold by the organization.

E2–4 Time allowed: 20 minutes
The following cost and stock data are taken from the accounting records of Mason Company for the year just completed:

Costs incurred:		
Direct labour cost		£70,000
Purchases of raw materials		118,000
Indirect labour		30,000
Maintenance, factory equipment		6,000
Advertising expense		90,000
Insurance, factory equipment		800
Sales salaries		50,000
Rent, factory facilities		20,000
Supplies		4,200
Depreciation, office equipment		3,000
Depreciation, factory equipment		19,000
	Beginning of the Year	**End of the Year**
Stocks:		
Raw materials	£7,000	£15,000
Work in progress	10,000	5,000
Finished goods	20,000	35,000

Required

1 Prepare a schedule of cost of goods manufactured in good form
2 Prepare the cost of goods sold section of Mason Company's profit and loss account for the year

E2–5 ⏱ Time allowed: 15 minutes

Below are listed various costs that are found in organizations:

1 Hamburger buns in a McDonald's outlet
2 Advertising by a dental office
3 Apples processed and canned by Del Monte Corporation
4 Shipping canned apples from a Del Monte plant to customers
5 Insurance on a Bausch & Lomb factory producing contact lenses
6 Insurance on IBM's corporate headquarters
7 Salary of a supervisor overseeing production of circuit boards at Hewlett-Packard
8 Commissions paid to *Encyclopaedia Britannica* salespersons
9 Depreciation of factory lunchroom facilities at an ICI plant
10 Steering wheels installed in BMWs.

Required

Classify each cost as being either variable or fixed with respect to the number of units sold. Also classify each cost as either a selling and administrative cost or a product cost. Prepare your answer sheet as shown below.

Cost item	Cost behaviour		Selling and administrative cost	Product cost
	Variable	Fixed cost		

Place an X in the appropriate columns to show the proper classification of each cost.

P2–6 Cost identification

Problems

connect

⏱ Time allowed: 30 minutes

Wollongong Group Ltd of New South Wales, Australia, acquired its factory building about ten years ago. For several years the company has rented out a small annex attached to the rear of the building. The company has received a rental income of £30,000 per year on this space. The renter's lease will expire soon and, rather than renewing the lease, the company has decided to use the space itself to manufacture a new product.

Direct materials cost for the new product will total £80 per unit. To have a place to sell finished units of product, the company will rent a small warehouse nearby. The rental cost will be £500 per month. In addition, the company must rent equipment for use in producing the new product; the rental cost will be £4,000 per month. Workers will be hired to manufacture the new product, with direct labour cost amounting to £60 per unit. The space in the annex will continue to be depreciated on a straight-line basis, as in prior years. This depreciation is £8,000 per year.

Advertising costs for the new product will total £50,000 per year. A supervisor will be hired to oversee production; her salary will be £1,500 per month. Electricity for operating machines will be £1.20 per unit. Costs of shipping the new product to customers will be £9 per unit.

To provide funds to purchase materials, meet payrolls and so forth, the company will have to liquidate some temporary investments. These investments are presently yielding a return of about £3,000 per year.

Required

Prepare an answer sheet with the following column headings:

Name of the cost	Variable cost	Fixed cost	Product cost			Period (selling and administrative) cost	Opportunity cost	Sunk cost
			Direct materials	Direct labour	Manufacturing overhead			

List the different costs associated with the new product decision down the extreme left column (under Name of the cost). Then place an X under each heading that helps to describe the type of cost involved. There may be Xs under several column headings for a single cost (for example, a cost may be a fixed cost, a period cost and a sunk cost; you would place an X under each of these column headings opposite the cost).

P2–7 Supply missing production and cost data

⏱ Time allowed: 30 minutes

Supply the missing data in the following cases. Each case is independent of the others.

	Case			
	1	2	3	4
Direct materials	£4,500	£6,000	£5,000	£3,000
Direct labour	?	3,000	7,000	4,000
Manufacturing overhead	5,000	4,000	?	9,000
Total manufacturing costs	18,500	?	£20,000	?
Beginning work in progress stock	2,500	?	3,000	?
Ending work in progress stock	?	1,000	4,000	3,000
Cost of goods manufactured	£18,000	£14,000	£?	£?
Sales	£30,000	£21,000	£36,000	£40,000
Beginning finished goods stock	1,000	2,500	?	2,000
Cost of goods manufactured	?	?	?	17,500
Goods available for sale	?	?	?	?

(continued)

Ending finished goods stock	?	1,500	4,000	3,500
Cost of goods sold	17,000	?	18,500	?
Gross margin	13,000	?	17,500	?
Operating expenses	?	3,500	?	?
Profit	£4,000	£ ?	£5,000	£9,000

P2–8 Cost classification

⏱ Time allowed: 20 minutes

Various costs associated with the operation of a factory are given below:

1 Electricity used in operating machines
2 Rent on a factory building
3 Cloth used in drapery production
4 Production superintendent's salary
5 Cost of labourers assembling a product
6 Depreciation of air purification equipment used in furniture production
7 Caretaker salaries
8 Peaches used in canning fruit
9 Lubricants needed for machines
10 Sugar used in soft-drink production
11 Property taxes on the factory
12 Cost of workers painting a product
13 Depreciation on cafeteria equipment
14 Insurance on a building used in producing TV sets
15 Picture tubes used in TV sets.

Required

Classify each cost as being either variable or fixed with respect to the number of units produced and sold. Also indicate whether each cost would typically be treated as a direct cost or an indirect cost with respect to units of product. Prepare your answer sheet as shown below:

Cost Item	Cost behaviour		To units of product	
	Variable	Fixed	Direct	Indirect
Example: Factory insurance		X		X

P2–9 Cost identification

⏱ Time allowed: 40 minutes

The Dorilane Company specializes in producing a set of wooden patio furniture consisting of a table and four chairs. The set enjoys great popularity, and the

company has ample orders to keep production going at its full capacity of 2,000 sets per year. Annual cost data at full capacity follow:

To units of product	Product cost
Factory labour, direct	£118,000
Advertising	50,000
Factory supervision	40,000
Property taxes, factory building	3,500
Sales commissions	80,000
Insurance, factory	2,500
Depreciation, office equipment	4,000
Lease cost, factory equipment	12,000
Indirect materials, factory	6,000
Depreciation, factory building	10,000
General office supplies (billing)	3,000
General office salaries	60,000
Direct materials used (wood, bolts, etc.)	94,000
Utilities, factory	20,000

Required

1 Prepare an answer sheet with the column headings shown below. Enter each cost item on your answer sheet, placing the pound amount under the appropriate headings. As examples, this has been done already for the first two items in the list above. Note that each cost item is classified in two ways: first, as variable or fixed, with respect to the number of units produced and sold; and second, as a selling and administrative cost or a product cost. (If the item is a product cost, it should be classified as being either direct or indirect as shown.)

2 Total the pound amounts in each of the columns in 1 above. Compute the cost to produce one patio set.

3 Assume that production drops to only 1,000 sets annually. Would you expect the cost per set to increase, decrease, or remain unchanged? Explain. No computations are necessary.

4 Refer to the original data. The managing director's brother-in-law has considered making himself a patio set and has priced the necessary materials at a building supply shop. The brother-in-law has asked the managing director if he could purchase a patio set from the Dorilane Company 'at cost', and the managing director agreed to let him do so.

   (a) Would you expect any disagreement between the two men over the price the brother-in-law should pay? Explain. What price does the managing director probably have in mind? The brother-in-law?

   (b) Since the company is operating at full capacity, what cost term used in the chapter might be justification for the managing director to charge the full, regular price to the brother-in-law and still be selling 'at cost'?

Cost item	Cost behaviour		Selling or administrative cost	Product cost	
	Variable	Fixed		Direct	Indirect*
Factory labour, direct	£118,000			£118,000	
Advertising		£50,000	£50,000		

*To units of product.

P2–10 Cost classification

Time allowed: 25 minutes

Listed below are a number of costs typically found in organizations:
1 Property taxes, factory
2 Boxes used for packaging detergent
3 Salespersons' commissions
4 Supervisor's salary, factory
5 Depreciation, executive cars
6 Workers assembling computers
7 Packing supplies for shipments
8 Insurance, finished goods warehouses
9 Lubricants for machines
10 Advertising costs
11 'Chips' used in producing calculators
12 Shipping costs on merchandise sold
13 Magazine subscriptions, factory lunchroom
14 Thread in a garment factory
15 Billing costs
16 Executive life insurance
17 Ink used in textbook production
18 Fringe benefits, assembly-line workers
19 Yarn used in sweater production
20 Receptionist, executive offices.

Required

Prepare an answer sheet with column headings as shown below. For each cost item, indicate whether it would be variable or fixed with respect to the number of units produced and sold; and then whether it would be a selling cost, an administrative cost, or a manufacturing cost. If it is a manufacturing cost, indicate whether it would typically be treated as a direct cost or an indirect cost with respect to units of product. Three sample answers are provided for illustration.

Cost Item	Variable or fixed	Selling cost	Administrative cost	Manufacturing (product) cost Direct	Indirect
Direct labour	V			X	
Executive salaries	F		X		
Factory rent	F				X

P2–11 Cost identification

🕐 Time allowed: 20 minutes

Tracy Beckham began dabbling in pottery several years ago as a hobby. Her work is quite creative, and it has been so popular with friends and others that she has decided to quit her job with an aerospace firm and manufacture pottery full time. The salary from Tracy's aerospace job is £2,500 per month.

Tracy will rent a small building near her home to use as a place for manufacturing the pottery. The rent will be £500 per month. She estimates that the cost of clay and glaze will be £2 for each finished piece of pottery. She will hire workers to produce the pottery at a labour rate of £8 per pot. To sell her pots, Tracy feels that she must advertise heavily in the local area. An advertising agency states that it will handle all advertising for a fee of £600 per month. Tracy's brother will sell the pots; he will be paid a commission of £4 for each pot sold. Equipment needed to manufacture the pots will be rented at a cost of £300 per month.

Tracy has already paid some start-up fees associated with her business. These fees amounted to £500. A small room has been located in a tourist area that Tracy will use as a sales office. The rent will be £250 per month. A phone installed in the room for taking orders will cost £40 per month. In addition, a recording device will be attached to the phone for taking after-hours messages.

Tracy has some money in savings that is earning interest of £1,200 per year. These savings will be withdrawn and used to get the business going. For the time being, Tracy does not intend to draw any salary from the new company.

Required

1 Prepare an answer sheet with the following column headings:

Name of the cost	Variable cost	Fixed cost	Product cost Direct materials	Direct labour	Manufacturing overhead	Period (selling and administrative) cost	Opportunity cost	Sunk cost

List the different costs associated with the new company down the extreme left column (under Name of cost). Then place an X under each heading that helps to describe the type of cost involved. There may be Xs under several column headings for a single cost. (That is, a cost may be a fixed cost, a period cost, and a sunk cost; you would place an X under each of these column headings opposite the cost.)

Under the Variable cost column, list only those costs that would be variable with respect to the number of units of pottery that are produced and sold.

2 All the costs you have listed above, except one, would be differential costs between the alternatives of Tracy producing pottery or staying with the aerospace firm. Which cost is not differential? Explain.

P2–12 Cost behaviour; manufacturing statement; unit costs

⏱ Time allowed: 40 minutes

Visic Company, a manufacturing firm, produces a single product. The following information has been taken from the company's production, sales, and cost records for the just completed year.

Production in units	29,000
Sales in units	?
Ending finished goods stock in units	?
Sales in pounds	£1,300,000
Costs:	
Advertising	105,000
Entertainment and travel	40,000
Direct labour	90,000
Indirect labour	85,000
Raw materials purchased	480,000
Building rent (production uses 80% of the space administrative and sales offices use the rest)	40,000
Utilities, factory	108,000
Royalty paid for use of production patent, £1.50 per unit produced	?
Maintenance, factory	9,000
Rent for special production equipment, per year plus £0.30 per unit produced	£7,000
	?
Selling and administrative salaries	210,000
Other factory overhead costs	6,800
Other selling and administrative expenses	17,000

	Beginning of year	End of year
Stocks:		
Raw materials	£20,000	£30,000
Work in progress	50,000	40,000
Finished goods	0	?

The finished goods stock is being carried at the average unit production cost for the year. The selling price of the product is £50 per unit.

Required

1 Prepare a schedule of goods manufactured for the year.
2 Compute the following:
   (a) The number of units in the finished goods stock at the end of the year
   (b) The cost of the units in the finished goods stock at the end of the year.
3 Prepare a profit and loss account for the year.

Chapter 7
Pricing, target costing and transfer pricing

 Learning **objectives**

After studying Chapter 7, you should be able to:

1 Compute the profit-maximizing price using the price elasticity of demand and variable cost
2 Understand the basics of revenue management in capacity constrained businesses
3 Compute the selling price of a product using the absorption costing approach
4 Compute the mark-up percentage under the absorption costing approach
5 Compute the target cost for a new product or service
6 Understand the basics of transfer pricing

Concepts **in Context**

Airlines and hotels are industries with very high fixed costs and 'perishable products'. Since an unfilled seat or empty bedroom is a lost contribution, these industries make use of revenue-maximizing models whereby the price of an airline ticket or a room is altered according to the time of booking relative to departure time or hotel stay. These sectors have learnt the importance of altering prices in order to operate at much higher capacities than they would if prices remained fixed.[1]

© Sieto Verver

Some businesses have no pricing calculation problems. They make a product that is in competition with other, identical products for which a market price already exists. Customers will not pay more than this price, and there is no reason for any company to charge less. Under these circumstances, the company simply charges the prevailing market price. Markets for basic raw materials such as farm products and minerals follow this pattern.

In this chapter, we are concerned with the more common situation in which a company is faced with the problem of setting its own prices. Clearly, the pricing decision can be critical. If the price is set too high, customers will avoid purchasing the company's products. If the price is set too low, the company's costs may not be covered.

The usual approach in pricing is to *mark up* cost. A product's **mark-up** is the difference between its selling price and its cost. The mark-up is usually expressed as a percentage of cost. This approach is called **cost-plus pricing** because the predetermined mark-up percentage is applied to the cost base to determine a target selling price.

$$\text{Selling price} = \text{Cost} + (\text{Mark-up percentage} \times \text{Cost})$$

For example, if a company uses a mark-up of 50%, it adds 50% to the costs of its products to determine the selling price. If a product costs £10, then it would charge £15 for the product.

There are two key issues when the cost-plus approach to pricing is used. First, what cost should be used? Second, how should the mark-up be determined? Several alternative approaches are considered in this chapter, starting with the approach generally favoured by economists.

LO 1 The economists' approach to pricing

If a company raises the price of a product, unit sales ordinarily fall. Because of this, pricing is a delicate balancing act in which the benefits of higher revenues per unit are traded off against the lower volume that results from charging higher prices. The sensitivity of unit sales to changes in price is called the *price elasticity of demand*.

Elasticity of demand

A product's price elasticity should be a key element in setting its price. The **price elasticity of demand** measures the degree to which the volume of unit sales for a product or service is affected by a change in price. Demand for a product is said to be *inelastic* if a change in price has little effect on the number of units sold. The demand for designer perfumes sold by trained personnel at cosmetic counters in department stores is relatively inelastic. Lowering prices on these luxury goods has little effect on sales volume; factors other than price are more important in generating sales. On the other hand, demand for a product is said to be *elastic* if a change in price has a substantial effect on the volume of units sold. An example of a product whose demand is elastic is petrol. If a petrol station raises its price for petrol, there will usually be a substantial drop in volume as customers seek lower prices elsewhere.

Price elasticity is very important in determining prices. Managers should set higher mark-ups over cost when customers are relatively insensitive to price (i.e., demand is inelastic) and lower mark-ups when customers are relatively sensitive to price (i.e., demand is elastic). This principle is followed in department stores. Merchandise sold in the bargain basement has a much lower mark-up than merchandise sold elsewhere in the store because customers who shop in the bargain basement are much more sensitive to price (i.e. demand is elastic).

The price elasticity of demand for a product or service, ε_d, can be estimated using the following formula.[2]

$$\varepsilon_d = \frac{\ln\left(1 + \% \text{ change in quantity sold}\right)}{\ln\left(1 + \% \text{ change in price}\right)}$$

For example, suppose that the managers of Nature's Garden believe that every 10% increase in the selling price of their apple-almond shampoo would result in a 15% decrease in the number of bottles of shampoo sold.[3] The price elasticity of demand for this product would be computed as follows:

$$\varepsilon_d = \frac{\ln\ (1 + (-0.15))}{\ln\ (1 + (0.10))} = \frac{\ln\ (0.85)}{\ln\ (1.10)} = -1.71$$

For comparison purposes, the managers of Nature's Garden believe that another product, strawberry glycerine soap, would experience a 20% drop in unit sales if its price were increased by 10%. (Purchasers of this product are more sensitive to price than the purchasers of the apple-almond shampoo.) The price elasticity of demand for the strawberry glycerine soap is:

$$\varepsilon_d = \frac{\ln\ (1 + (-0.20))}{\ln\ (1 + (0.10))} = \frac{\ln\ (0.80)}{\ln\ (1.10)} = -2.34$$

Both of these products, like other products, have a price elasticity that is less than −1. Note also that the price elasticity of demand for the strawberry glycerine soap is larger (in absolute value) than the price elasticity of demand for the apple-almond shampoo. The more sensitive customers are to price, the larger (in absolute value) is the price elasticity of demand. In other words, a larger (in absolute value) price elasticity of demand indicates a product whose demand is more elastic.

In the next subsection, the price elasticity of demand will be used to compute the selling price that maximizes the profits of the company.

The profit-maximizing price

Under certain conditions, it can be shown that the *profit-maximizing price* can be determined by marking up *variable cost* using the following formula:[4]

$$\text{Profit-maximizing mark-up on variable cost} = \left(\frac{\varepsilon_d}{1 + \varepsilon_d}\right) - 1 \text{ Variable cost per unit}$$

Using the above mark-up is equivalent to setting the selling price using this formula:

$$\text{Profit-maximizing mark-up on variable cost} = \left(\frac{\varepsilon_d}{1 + \varepsilon_d}\right) \text{ Variable cost per unit}$$

The profit-maximizing prices for the two Nature's Garden products are computed below using these formulas:

	Apple-almond Shampoo	Strawberry glycerine soap
Price elasticity of demand (ε_d)	−1.71	−2.34
Profit-maximizing mark-up on variable cost (a)	$\left(\frac{-1.71}{-1.71+1}\right) - 1$	$\left(\frac{-2.34}{-2.34+1}\right) - 1$
	$-2.41 - 1 = 1.41$	$= 1.75 - 1 = 0.75$
	or 141%	or 75%
Variable cost per unit – given (b)	£2.00	£0.40
Mark-up, (a) × (b)	2.82	0.30
Profit-maximizing price	£4.82	£0.70

Note that the 75% mark-up for the strawberry glycerine soap is lower than the 141% mark-up for the apple-almond shampoo. The reason for this is that purchasers of strawberry glycerine soap are more sensitive to price than the purchasers of apple-almond shampoo. This could be because strawberry glycerine soap is a relatively common product with close substitutes available in nearly every grocery store.

Exhibit 7.1 shows how the profit-maximizing mark-up is affected by how sensitive unit sales are to price. For example, if a 10% increase in price leads to a 20% decrease in unit sales, then the optimal mark-up on variable cost according to the exhibit is 75% – the figure computed above for the strawberry glycerine soap. Note that the optimal mark-up drops as unit sales become more sensitive to price.

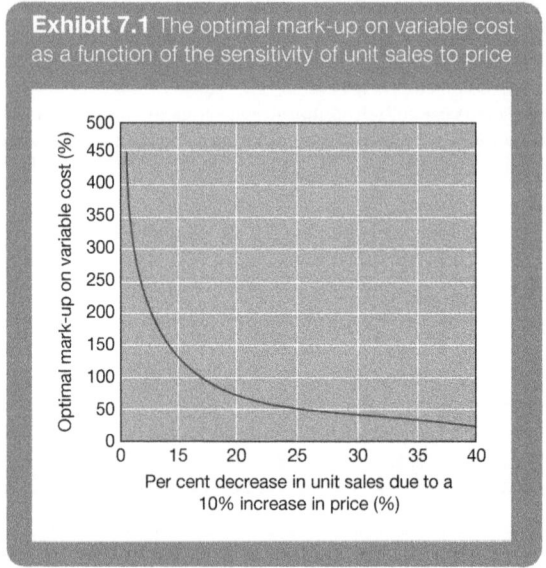

Exhibit 7.1 The optimal mark-up on variable cost as a function of the sensitivity of unit sales to price

(Graph: vertical axis "Optimal mark-up on variable cost (%)" ranging 0 to 500; horizontal axis "Per cent decrease in unit sales due to a 10% increase in price (%)" ranging 0 to 40)

Caution is advised when using these formulas to establish a selling price. The assumptions underlying the formulas are probably not completely true, and the estimate of the percentage change in unit sales that would result from a given percentage change in price is likely to be inexact. Nevertheless, the formulas can provide valuable clues regarding whether prices should be increased or decreased. Suppose, for example, that the strawberry glycerine soap is currently being sold for £0.60 per bar. The formula indicates that the profit-maximizing price is £0.70 per bar. Rather than increasing the price by £0.10, it would be prudent to increase the price by a more modest amount to observe what happens to unit sales and to profits.

The formula for the profit-maximizing price also conveys a very important lesson. The optimal selling price should depend on two factors – the variable cost per unit and how sensitive unit sales are to changes in price. In particular, fixed costs play no role in setting the optimal price. If the total fixed costs are the same whether the company charges £0.60 or £0.70, they cannot be relevant in the decision of which price to charge for the soap. Fixed costs are relevant when deciding whether to offer a product but are not relevant when deciding how much to charge for the product.

Incidentally, we can directly verify that an increase in selling price for the strawberry glycerine soap from the current price of £0.60 per bar is warranted, based just on the forecast that a 10% increase in selling price would lead to a 20% decrease in unit sales. Suppose, for example, that Nature's Garden is currently selling 200,000 bars of the soap per year at the price of £0.60 a bar. If the change in price has no effect on the company's fixed costs or on other products, the effect on profits of increasing the price by 10% can be computed as follows:

	Present price	Higher price
Selling price	£0.60	£0.60 + (0.10 × £0.60) = £0.66
Unit sales	200,000	200,000 − (0.20 × 200,000) = 160,000
Sales	£120,000	£105,600
Variable cost	80,000	64,000
Contribution margin	£40,000	£41,600

Despite the apparent optimality of prices based on marking up variable costs according to the price elasticity of demand, surveys consistently reveal that most managers approach the pricing problem from a completely different perspective. They prefer to mark up some version of full, not variable, costs, and the mark-up is based on desired profits rather than on factors related to demand.

Revenue and yield management

LO 2

Some industries such as hotels and airlines are characterized by high fixed costs and perishability. The capacity of a plane or a hotel is fixed in the short run. Furthermore, an empty bedroom at night or an empty seat in a plane that has taken off represent a sale that is lost forever. Ideally, hotel managers would like to sell all rooms at the highest (rack) rate but they know that a trade-off develops between high occupancy and high room rates. The problem becomes one of determining how much to sell, at what price and to which market segment, so as to maximize revenue. The resolution lies in control over rates (being price restrictive if demand is high and more flexible if it is low) and restrictions to occupancy (blocking of rooms in advance) in order to maximize overall Gross revenue per period of time. These are the principles behind the technique of *yield management*. **Yield management (YM)** is the practice of achieving high capacity utilization through varying prices according to market segments and time of booking.[5]

To use YM, a hotel must know its market segments and why guests need to stay and develop appropriate marketing strategies for each market segment. To ensure the optimization of the total revenues from the room stock of a group of hotels, for example, and to allow access to its demand history, a centralized reservations system is needed. There should be some return from linking YM systems to marketing expenditure plans. For example, predicted periods of low demand from YM team meetings can trigger the need to advertise short-break packages. The overall effectiveness of a YM system is dependent upon the implementation of the following market-focused principles: identification of a customer base using a detailed segmentation strategy; developing an awareness of customers' changing needs and expectations; estimating the price elasticity of demand per market segment; responsiveness of management to cope with changing market conditions; accurate historical demand analysis, combined with a reliable forecasting method. The key performance metric in this model is the *yield percentage*:

$$\text{Yield percentage} = \frac{\text{Actual revenue}}{\text{Maximum potential revenue}}$$

The **yield percentage** will depend on the average price multiplied by the number of units sold (hotel rooms, airline seats). The maximum potential revenue is a full hotel or plane charging the maximum price.[6] With a dynamic pricing strategy, the nearer to the time that the customer who books a flight or a room actually wants to fly or stay, the higher the price. Although it may seem that the price is rising, in actuality, it is rather that the number of lower rates are restricted in advance and later bookers have only the higher priced seats or rooms left.

The absorption costing approach to cost-plus pricing

LO 3

The absorption costing approach to cost-plus pricing differs from the economists' approach both in what costs are marked up and in how the mark-up is determined. Under the absorption approach to cost-plus pricing, the cost base is the absorption costing unit product cost as defined in Chapter 5 rather than variable cost.

Setting a target selling price using the absorption costing approach

To illustrate, let us assume that the management of Ritter Company wants to set the selling price on a product that has just undergone some design modifications. The Accounting Department has provided cost estimates for the redesigned product as shown below:

	Per unit	Total
Direct materials	£6	
Direct labour	4	
Variable manufacturing overhead	3	
Fixed manufacturing overhead	–	£70,000
Variable selling, general and administrative expenses	2	
Fixed selling, general and administrative expenses	–	60,000

The first step in the absorption costing approach to cost-plus pricing is to compute the unit product cost. For Ritter Company, this amounts to £20 per unit at a volume of 10,000 units, as computed below:

Direct materials	£6
Direct labour	4
Variable manufacturing overhead	3
Fixed manufacturing overhead (£70,000 ÷10,000 units)	7
Unit product cost	£20

Ritter Company has a general policy of marking up unit product costs by 50%. A price quotation sheet for the company prepared using the absorption approach is presented in Exhibit 7.2. Note that selling, general and administrative (SG&A) costs are not included in the cost base. Instead, the mark-up is supposed to cover these expenses. Let us see how some companies compute these mark-up percentages.

LO 4 Determining the mark-up percentage

How did Ritter Company arrive at its mark-up percentage of 50%? This figure could be a widely used rule of thumb in the industry or just a company tradition that seems to work. The mark-up percentage may also be the result of an explicit computation.

As we have discussed, the mark-up over cost ideally should be largely determined by market conditions. However, a popular approach is to at least start with a mark-up based on cost and desired profit. The reasoning goes like this. The mark-up must be large enough to cover SG&A expenses and provide an adequate return on investment (ROI). Given the forecasted unit sales, the mark-up can be computed as follows:

$$\text{Mark-up percentage on absorption cost} = \frac{(\text{Required ROI} \times \text{Investment}) + \text{SG\&A expenses}}{\text{Unit sales} \times \text{Unit product cost}}$$

Exhibit 7.2 Price quotation sheet – absorption basis (10,000 units)

Direct materials	£6
Direct labour	4
Variable manufacturing overhead	3
Fixed manufacturing overhead (£70,000 ÷ 10,000 units)	7
Unit product cost	20
Mark-up to cover selling, general and administrative expenses and desired profit – 50% of unit manufacturing costs	10
Target selling price	£30

To show how the formula above is applied, assume Ritter Company must invest £100,000 to produce and market 10,000 units of the product each year. The £100,000 investment covers purchase of equipment and funds needed to carry stocks and debtors. If Ritter Company requires a 20% ROI, then the mark-up for the product would be determined as follows:

$$\text{Mark-up percentage on absorption cost} = \frac{(20\% \times 100{,}000) + (£2 \times 10{,}000 + £60{,}000)}{10{,}000 \times £20}$$

$$\text{Mark-up percentage on absorption cost} = \frac{(£20{,}000) + (£80{,}000)}{£200{,}000} = 50\%$$

As shown earlier, this mark-up of 50% leads to a target selling price of £30 for Ritter Company. As shown in Exhibit 7.3, *if the company actually sells 10,000 units* of the product at this price, the company's ROI on this product will indeed be 20%. If it turns out that more than 10,000 units are sold at this price, the ROI will be greater than 20%. If less than 10,000 units are sold, the ROI will be less than 20%. *The required ROI will be attained only if the forecasted unit sales volume is attained.*

Problems with the absorption costing approach

Using the absorption costing approach, the pricing problem looks deceptively simple. All you have to do is compute your unit product cost, decide how much profit you want, and then set your price. It appears that you can ignore demand and arrive at a price that will safely yield whatever profit you want. However, as noted above, the absorption costing approach relies on a forecast of unit sales. Neither the mark-up nor the unit product cost can be computed without such a forecast.

The absorption costing approach essentially assumes that customers *need* the forecasted unit sales and will pay whatever price the company decides to charge. However, customers have a choice. If the price is too high, they can buy from a competitor or they may choose not to buy at all. Suppose, for example, that when Ritter Company sets its price at £30, it sells only 7,000 units rather than the 10,000 units forecasted. As shown in Exhibit 7.4, the company would then have a loss of £25,000 on the product instead of a profit of £20,000. Some managers believe that the absorption costing approach to pricing is safe. This is an illusion. The absorption costing approach is safe only as long as customers choose to buy at least as many units as managers forecasted they would buy.

Exhibit 7.3 Profit statement and ROI analysis – Ritter Company actual unit sales = 10,000 units; selling price = £30

Direct materials	£6
Direct labour	4
Variable manufacturing overhead	3
Fixed manufacturing overhead (£70,000 ÷ 10,000 units)	7
Unit product cost	£20

Ritter Company Absorption costing profit statement

Sales (£30 × 10,000 units)	£300,000
Less cost of goods sold (£20 × 10,000 units)	200,000
Gross margin	100,000
Less selling, general and administration expenses (£2 × 10,000 units £60,000)	80,000
Net operating profit	£20,000

ROI

$$\text{ROI} = \frac{\text{Net operating profit}}{\text{Average operating assets}}$$

$$= \frac{£20{,}000}{£100{,}000}$$

$$= 20\%$$

Exhibit 7.4 Profit statement and ROI analysis – Ritter Company actual unit sales = 7,000 units; selling price = £30

Direct materials	£6
Direct labour	4
Variable manufacturing overhead	3
Fixed manufacturing overhead (£70,000 ÷ 10,000 units)	10
Unit product cost	£23

Ritter Company Absorption costing profit statement	
Sales (£30 × 7,000 units)	£210,000
Less cost of goods sold (£23 × 7,000 units)	161,000
Gross margin	49,000
Less selling, general and administration expenses (£2 × 7,000 units + £60,000)	74,000
Net operating profit	£(25,000)

ROI

$$ROI = \frac{\text{Net operating profit}}{\text{Average operating assets}}$$

$$= \frac{£(25,000)}{£100,000}$$

$$= -25\%$$

Focus on Business Practice

Pricing methods for hotel services

© Manuela Weschke

Fáilte Ireland (Irish Tourist Board) provides useful business tools and guides on its website which can be used by Irish hotelier and guest house owners. One of the guides provided is on pricing. Two basic pricing methods are proposed as useful: (1) cost-plus pricing and (2) margin pricing. *Cost-plus pricing* is frequently used for food and beverages in restaurants. A typical mark-up on food costs used by chefs is cited as 200%, with 150% mark-up on beverage cost. The second approach, *margin pricing*, starts with a desired selling price of food (e.g. a menu) and deducts a required gross margin to derive the maximum costs of food ingredients. Two other pricing methods are also mentioned. *Value pricing* focuses on setting a price according to the value perceived by customers (e.g. location, premium brand). In other words, value pricing can be used when a service (e.g. WiFi, Spa treatments) differentiates from competitors. The final method is *going rate pricing*, which means services are priced the same as competitors' offerings. The guide advises this method should not be used without reference to underlying costs.[7]

Exercise: In the UK, hotel chains like Travelodge and Premier Inn frequently offer rooms for as low as £19 per night. How do you think they can justify this price? Surely such a price is not profitable?

Target costing

LO 5

Our discussion thus far has presumed that a product has already been developed, has been costed, and is ready to be marketed as soon as a price is set. In many cases, the sequence of events is just the reverse. That is, the company will already *know* what price should be charged, and the problem will be to *develop* a product that can be marketed profitably at the desired price. Even in this situation, where the normal sequence of events is reversed, cost is still a crucial factor. The company's approach will be to employ *target costing*. **Target costing** is the process of determining the maximum allowable cost for a new product and then developing a prototype that can be profitably made for that maximum target cost figure.

The target costing approach was developed in recognition that many companies have less control over price than they would like to think. The market (i.e., supply and demand) really determines prices, and a company that attempts to ignore this does so at its peril. Therefore, the anticipated market price is taken as a given in target costing. Second, target costing is more than just an approach to pricing – it takes a *strategic approach to cost management* by linking a whole series of organizational functions such as marketing, design, production and procurement.

The target cost for a product is computed by starting with the product's anticipated selling price and then deducting the desired profit, as follows:

Target cost = Anticipated selling price − Desired profit

The product development team is given the responsibility of designing the product so that it can be made for no more than the target cost.

An example of target costing

To provide a simple numerical example of target costing, assume the following situation: Handy Appliance Company feels that there is a market niche for a hand mixer with certain new features. Surveying the features and prices of hand mixers already on the market, the Marketing Department believes that a price of £30 would be about right for the new mixer. At that price, Marketing estimates that 40,000 of the new mixers could be sold annually. To design, develop, and produce these new mixers, an investment of £2,000,000 would be required. The company desires a 15% ROI. Given these data, the target cost to manufacture, sell, distribute, and service one mixer is £22.50 as shown below.

Projected sales (50,000 mixers × £30)	£1,200,000
Less desired profit (15% × £2,000,000)	300,000
Target cost for 40,000 mixers	£900,000
Target cost per mixer (£900,000/40,000 mixers)	£22.50

This £22.50 target cost would be broken down into target costs for the various functions: manufacturing, marketing, distribution, after-sales service, and so on. Each functional area would be responsible for keeping its actual costs within target.

Life-cycle costing

Traditional costing sometimes seems to focus too much on costs as they are *incurred* because incurred costs are more visible as they are 'booked' through routine cost accumulation systems. Life-cycle costing draws extensively on the techniques of target costing. Target costing is more than just a pricing technique as it *manages costs* rather than just passively measures them. The aim of target costing is to choose product and process technologies that give an acceptable profit at a planned level of output. Once a product has been designed and has gone into production, not much can be done to significantly reduce its cost. Most of the opportunities to reduce cost come from designing the product so that it is simple to make, uses inexpensive parts, and is robust and reliable. If the company has little control over market price and little control over cost once the product has gone into production, then it follows that the major opportunities for affecting profit come in the design stage where valuable features that customers are willing to pay for can be added and where most of

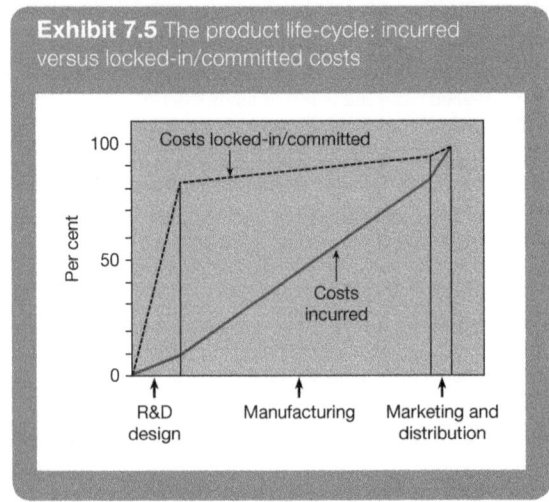

Exhibit 7.5 The product life-cycle: incurred versus locked-in/committed costs

the costs are really determined. So that is where the effort is concentrated – in designing and developing the product. The difference between target costing and other approaches to product development is profound. Instead of designing the product and then finding out how much it costs, the target cost is set first and then the product is designed so that the target cost is attained.

As up to 90% of cost[8] may be committed or locked in at pre-production stages, management accountants have become more aware of the design and planning phases of the product life-cycle. The distinction between and differential timing of incurred and locked-in costs are illustrated in Exhibit 7.5. The biggest gap is at the research and development stage, where although this function may generate a relatively low proportion of a product's total cost, decisions made here lock in the costs incurred in the manufacturing and marketing phases. In recognition of the importance of the planning phase, *life-cycle* costing tries to estimate a product's costs over its lifetime.

As well as recognizing the importance of the design phase, life-cycle costing also anticipates cost improvements during the manufacturing cycle. This aspect is sometimes known as **kaizen costing** as it is part of the wider philosophy of continuous improvement. Some of the cost improvements will occur through a process of 'learning-by-doing' as workers get more adept at their tasks. Managers may routinize cost reduction through an approach known as **kaizen budgeting**. Rather than devise budgets on standard costs that are based on *past* performance, kaizen budgeting plans for *incremental* improvements in efficiency and reductions in costs.

Some problems with target and life-cycle costing

One problem with target costing is that it may reveal an unpalatable view of a company's internal operations, exposing uncompetitive practices and processes that were hidden by more traditional costing techniques. Another problem is that it may be too time-consuming. Thus, while it may be appropriate in the car industry, which is based on relatively mature technologies and lengthy product life-cycles, it is less appropriate in industries such as electronics, where the rate of innovation is extremely rapid and time-to-market must be minimized. The other feature of life-cycle costing is that it implicitly assumes a relatively orderly value chain with a dominant customer who can plan the design and delivery of the product. In an industry such as personal computers (PCs), some of the major players are the companies that supply the software (Microsoft) and the microprocessors (Intel). Leading-edge technical innovation is in the hands of these companies rather than the PC assemblers.

Focus on Business Practice

Producing the £1,300 car

© Getty Images

Target costing is widely used in the car industry. For example, at Tata Motors, engineers had to design a car that could be sold for 100,000 rupees (about £1,375)! The target cost for a new model is decomposed into target costs for each of the elements of the car – down to a target cost for each of the individual parts. The designers draft a trial blueprint, and a check is made to see if the estimated cost of the car is within reasonable distance of the target cost. If not, design changes are made, and a new trial blueprint is drawn up. This process continues until there is sufficient confidence in the design to make a prototype car according to the trial blueprint. If there is still a gap between the target cost and estimated cost, the design of the car will be further modified.

After repeating this process a number of times, the final blueprint is drawn up and turned over to the production department. In the first several months of production, the target costs will ordinarily not be achieved due to problems in getting a new model into production. However, after that initial period, target costs are compared to actual costs and discrepancies between the two are investigated with the aim of eliminating the discrepancies and achieving target costs.[9]

Exercise: Consider the possibility of target costing in other industries such as food retailing (see, e.g. Jack and Jones) (2007).

Transfer pricing

LO 6

A **transfer price** is the price charged when one segment of a company provides goods or services to another segment of the company. There are special problems in evaluating pricing goods or services transferred from one division/segment of a company to another. The problems revolve around the question of what transfer price to charge between the segments. Managers are intensely interested in how transfer prices are set, since they can have a dramatic effect on the apparent profitability of a division. Three common approaches are used to set transfer prices:

1. Allow the managers involved in the transfer to negotiate their own transfer price.
2. Set transfer prices at cost using:
   (a) Variable cost.
   (b) Full (absorption) cost.
3. Set transfer prices at the market price.

We will consider each of these transfer pricing methods in turn, beginning with negotiated transfer prices. Throughout the discussion we should keep in mind that *the fundamental objective in setting transfer prices is to motivate the managers to act in the best interests of the overall company*. In contrast, **sub-optimization** occurs when managers do not act in the best interests of the overall company or even in the best interests of their own segment.

Negotiated transfer prices

A **negotiated transfer price** is a transfer price that is agreed on between the selling and purchasing divisions. Negotiated transfer prices have several important advantages. First, this approach preserves the autonomy of the divisions and is consistent with the spirit of decentralization. Second, the managers of the divisions are

likely to have much better information about the potential costs and benefits of the transfer than others in the company.

When negotiated transfer prices are used, the managers who are involved in a proposed transfer within the company meet to discuss the terms and conditions of the transfer. They may decide not to go through with the transfer, but if they do, they must agree to a transfer price. Generally speaking, we cannot predict the exact transfer price they will agree to. However, we can confidently predict two things: (1) the selling division will agree to the transfer only if the profits of the selling division increase as a result of the transfer, and (2) the purchasing division will agree to the transfer only if the profits of the purchasing division also increase as a result of the transfer. This may seem obvious, but it is an important point.

Clearly, if the transfer price is below the selling division's cost, a loss will occur on the transaction and the selling division will refuse to agree to the transfer. Likewise, if the transfer price is set too high, it will be impossible for the purchasing division to make any profit on the transferred item. For any given proposed transfer, the transfer price has both a lower limit (determined by the situation of the selling division) and an upper limit (determined by the situation of the purchasing division). The actual transfer price agreed to by the two division managers can fall anywhere between those two limits. These limits determine the **range of acceptable transfer prices** – the range of transfer prices within which the profits of both divisions participating in a transfer would increase.

An example will help us to understand negotiated transfer prices. Harris & Louder Ltd owns fast-food restaurants and snack food and beverage manufacturers in the United Kingdom. One of the restaurants, Pizza Maven, serves a variety of beverages along with pizzas. One of the beverages is ginger beer, which is served on tap. Harris & Louder has just purchased a new division, Imperial Beverages, that produces ginger beer. The managing director of Imperial Beverages has approached the managing director of Pizza Maven about purchasing Imperial Beverages' ginger beer for sale at Pizza Maven restaurants rather than its usual brand of ginger beer. Managers at Pizza Maven agree that the quality of Imperial Beverages' ginger beer is comparable to the quality of their regular brand. It is just a question of price. The basic facts are listed below:

Imperial Beverages:	
Ginger beer production capacity per month	10,000 barrels
Variable cost per barrel of ginger beer	£8 per barrel
Fixed costs per month	£70,000
Selling price of Imperial Beverages' ginger	
Pizza Maven:	
Purchase price of regular brand of ginger beer	£18 per barrel
Monthly consumption of ginger beer	2,000 barrels

The selling division's lowest acceptable transfer price

The selling division, Imperial Beverages, will be interested in a proposed transfer only if its profit increases. Clearly, the transfer price must not fall below the variable cost per barrel of £8. In addition, if Imperial Beverages has insufficient capacity to fill the Pizza Maven order, then it would have to give up some of its regular sales. Imperial Beverages would expect to be compensated for the contribution margin on these lost sales. In sum, if the transfer has no effect on fixed costs, then from the selling division's standpoint, the transfer price must cover both the variable costs of producing the transferred units and any opportunity costs from lost sales.

Seller's perspective:

$$\text{Transfer price} \geq \text{Variable cost per unit} + \frac{\text{Total contribution margin on lost sales}}{\text{Number of units transferred}}$$

The purchasing division's highest acceptable transfer price

The purchasing division, Pizza Maven, will be interested in the proposal only if its profit increases. In cases like this where a purchasing division has an outside supplier, the purchasing division's decision is simple. Buy from the inside supplier if the price is less than the price offered by the outside supplier.

Purchaser's perspective:

Transfer price ≤ Cost of buying from outside supplier

We will consider several different hypothetical situations and see what the range of acceptable transfer prices would be in each situation.

Selling division with idle capacity

Suppose that Imperial Beverages has sufficient idle capacity to satisfy the demand for ginger beer from Pizza Maven without cutting into sales of ginger beer to its regular customers. To be specific, let's suppose that Imperial Beverages is selling only 7,000 barrels of ginger beer a month on the outside market. That leaves unused capacity of 3,000 barrels a month – more than enough to satisfy Pizza Maven's requirement of 2,000 barrels a month. What range of transfer prices, if any, would make both divisions better off with the transfer of 2,000 barrels a month?

1   The selling division, Imperial Beverages, will be interested in the proposal only if:

$$\text{Transfer price} \geq \text{Variable cost per unit} + \frac{\text{Total contribution margin on lost sales}}{\text{Number of units transferred}}$$

Since Imperial Beverages has ample idle capacity, there are no lost outside sales. And since the variable cost per unit is £8, the lowest acceptable transfer price as far as the selling division is concerned is also £8.

$$\text{Transfer price} \geq £8 + \frac{£0}{2,000} = £8$$

2   The purchasing division, Pizza Maven, can buy similar ginger beer from an outside vendor for £18. Therefore, Pizza Maven would be unwilling to pay more than £18 per barrel for Imperial Beverages' ginger beer.

Transfer price ≥ Cost of buying from outside supplier = £18

3   Combining the requirements of both the selling division and the purchasing division, the acceptable range of transfer prices in this situation is:

£8 ≤ Transfer price ≤ £18

Assuming that the managers understand their own businesses and that they are co-operative, they should be able to agree on a transfer price within this range.

Selling division with no idle capacity

Suppose that Imperial Beverages has no idle capacity; it is selling 10,000 barrels of ginger beer a month on the outside market at £20 per barrel. To fill the order from Pizza Maven, Imperial Beverages would have to divert 2,000 barrels from its regular customers. What range of transfer prices, if any, would make both divisions better off transferring the 2,000 barrels within the company?

1   The selling division, Imperial Beverage, will be interested in the proposal only if:

$$\text{Transfer price} \geq \text{Variable cost per unit} + \frac{\text{Total contribution margin on lost sales}}{\text{Number of units transferred}}$$

Since Imperial Beverage has no idle capacity, there *are* lost outside sales. The contribution margin per barrel on these outside sales is £12 (£20 − £8).

$$\text{Transfer price} \geq £8 + \frac{(20 - £8) \times 2{,}000}{2{,}000} = £8 + (£20 - £8) = £20$$

Thus, as far as the selling division is concerned, the transfer price must at least cover the revenue on the lost sales, which is £20 per barrel. This makes sense since the cost of producing the 2,000 barrels is the same whether they are sold on the inside market or on the outside. The only difference is that the selling division loses the revenue of £20 per barrel if it transfers the barrels to Pizza Maven.

2   As before, the purchasing division, Pizza Maven, would be unwilling to pay more than the £18 per barrel it is already paying for similar ginger beer from its regular supplier.

Transfer price ≤ Cost of buying from outside supplier = £18

3   Therefore, the selling division would insist on a transfer price of at least £20. But the purchasing division would refuse any transfer price above £18. It is impossible to satisfy both division managers simultaneously; there can be no agreement on a transfer price and no transfer will take place. Is this good? The answer is yes. From the standpoint of the entire company, the transfer doesn't make sense. Why give up sales of £20 to save £18?

Basically, the transfer price is a mechanism for dividing between the two divisions any profit the entire company earns as a result of the transfer. If the company loses money on the transfer, there will be no profit to divide up, and it will be impossible for the two divisions to come to an agreement. On the other hand, if the company makes money on the transfer, there will be a potential profit to share, and it will always be possible for the two divisions to find a mutually agreeable transfer price that increases the profits of both divisions. If the pie is bigger, it is always possible to divide it up in such a way that everyone has a bigger piece.

Selling division has some idle capacity

Suppose now that Imperial Beverages is selling 9,000 barrels of ginger beer a month on the outside market. Pizza Maven can only sell one kind of ginger beer on tap. They cannot buy 1,000 barrels from Imperial Beverages and 1,000 barrels from their regular supplier; they must buy all their ginger beer from one source.

To fill the entire 2,000-barrel a month order from Pizza Maven, Imperial Beverages would have to divert 1,000 barrels from its regular customers who are paying £20 per barrel. The other 1,000 barrels can be made using idle capacity. What range of transfer prices, if any, would make both divisions better off transferring the 2,000 barrels within the company?

1   As before, the selling division, Imperial Beverage, will insist on a transfer price that at least covers their variable cost and opportunity cost:

$$\text{Transfer price} \geq \text{Variable cost per unit} + \frac{\text{Total contribution margin on lost sales}}{\text{Number of units transferred}}$$

Since Imperial Beverage does not have enough idle capacity to fill the entire order for 2,000 barrels, there *are* lost outside sales. The contribution margin per barrel on the 1,000 barrels of lost outside sales is £12 (£20 − £8).

$$\text{Transfer price} \geq £8 + \frac{(£20 - £8) \times 1{,}000}{2{,}000} = £8 + £6 = £14$$

Thus, as far as the selling division is concerned, the transfer price must cover the variable cost of £8 plus the average opportunity cost of lost sales of £6.

2   As before, the purchasing division, Pizza Maven, would be unwilling to pay more than the £18 per barrel it pays its regular supplier.

Transfer price ≤ Cost of buying from outside suppliers = £18

3 Combining the requirements for both the selling and purchasing divisions, the range of acceptable transfer prices is:

£14 ≤ Transfer price ≤ £18

Again, assuming that the managers understand their own businesses and that they are co-operative, they should be able to agree on a transfer price within this range.

No outside supplier

If Pizza Maven has no outside supplier for the ginger beer, the highest price the purchasing division would be willing to pay depends on how much the purchasing division expects to make on the transferred units – excluding the transfer price. If, for example, Pizza Maven expects to earn £30 per barrel of ginger beer after paying its own expenses, then it should be willing to pay up to £30 per barrel to Imperial Beverages. Remember, however, that this assumes Pizza Maven cannot buy ginger beer from other sources.

Evaluation of negotiated transfer prices

As discussed earlier, if a transfer within the company would result in higher overall profits for the company, there is always a range of transfer prices within which both the selling and purchasing division would also have higher profits if they agree to the transfer. Therefore, if the managers understand their own businesses and are co-operative, then they should always be able to agree on a transfer price if it is in the best interests of the company that they do so.

The difficulty is that not all managers understand their own businesses and not all managers are co-operative. As a result, negotiations often break down even when it would be in the managers' own best interests to come to an agreement. Sometimes that is the fault of the way managers are evaluated. If managers are pitted against each other rather than against their own past performance or reasonable benchmarks, a non-cooperative atmosphere is almost guaranteed. Nevertheless, it must be admitted that even with the best performance evaluation system, some people by nature are not co-operative.

Possibly because of the fruitless and protracted bickering that often accompanies disputes over transfer prices, most companies rely on some other means of setting transfer prices. Unfortunately, as we will see below, all the alternatives to negotiated transfer prices have their own serious drawbacks.

Transfers at the cost to the selling division

Many companies set transfer prices at either the variable cost or full (absorption) cost incurred by the selling division. Although the cost approach to setting transfer prices is relatively simple to apply, it has some major defects.

First, the use of cost – particularly full cost – as a transfer price can lead to bad decisions and thus sub-optimization. Return to the example involving the ginger beer. The full cost of ginger beer can never be less than £15 per barrel (£8 per barrel variable cost + £7 per barrel fixed cost at capacity). What if the cost of buying the ginger beer from an outside supplier is less than £15 – for example, £14 per barrel? If the transfer price were bureaucratically set at full cost, then Pizza Maven would never want to buy ginger beer from Imperial Beverages, since it could buy its ginger beer from the outside supplier at less cost. However, from the standpoint of the company as a whole, ginger beer should be transferred from Imperial Beverages to Pizza Maven whenever Imperial Beverages has idle capacity. Why? Because when Imperial Beverage has idle capacity, it only costs the company £8 in variable cost to produce a barrel of ginger beer, but it costs £14 per barrel to buy from outside suppliers.

Secondly, if cost is used as the transfer price, the selling division will never show a profit on any internal transfer. The only division that shows a profit is the division that makes the final sale to an outside party.

A third problem with cost-based prices is that they do not provide incentives to control costs. If the costs of one division are simply passed on to the next, then there is little incentive for anyone to work to reduce costs. This problem can be overcome to some extent by using standard costs rather than actual costs for transfer prices.

Despite these shortcomings, cost-based transfer prices are commonly used in practice. Advocates argue that they are easily understood and convenient to use.

Transfers at market price

Some form of competitive **market price** (i.e., the price charged for an item on the open market) is often regarded as the best approach to the transfer pricing problem – particularly if transfer price negotiations routinely become bogged down.

The market price approach is designed for situations in which there is an *intermediate market* for the transferred product or service. By **intermediate market**, we mean a market in which the product or service is sold in its present form to outside customers. If the selling division has no idle capacity, the market price in the intermediate market is the perfect choice for the transfer price. The reason for this is that if the selling division can sell a transferred item on the outside market instead, then the real cost of the transfer as far as the company is concerned is the opportunity cost of the lost revenue on the outside sale. Whether the item is transferred internally or sold on the outside intermediate market, the production costs are exactly the same. If the market price is used as the transfer price, the selling division manager will not lose anything by making the transfer, and the purchasing division manager will get the correct signal about how much it really costs the company for the transfer to take place.

While the market price works beautifully when there is no idle capacity, difficulties occur when the selling division has idle capacity. Recalling once again the ginger beer example, the outside market price for the ginger beer produced by Imperial Beverages is £20 per barrel. However, Pizza Maven can purchase all of the ginger beer it wants from outside suppliers for £18 per barrel. Why would Pizza Maven ever buy from Imperial Beverages if Pizza Maven is forced to pay Imperial Beverages' market price? In some market price-based transfer pricing schemes, the transfer price would be lowered to £18, the outside vendor's market price, and Pizza Maven would be directed to buy from Imperial Beverages as long as Imperial Beverages is willing to sell. This scheme can work reasonably well, but a drawback is that managers at Pizza Maven will regard the cost of ginger beer as £18 rather than the £8, which is the real cost to the company when the selling division has idle capacity. Consequently, the managers of Pizza Maven will make pricing and other decisions based on an incorrect cost.

Unfortunately, none of the possible solutions to the transfer pricing problem are perfect – not even market-based transfer prices.

Summary

- Pricing involves a delicate balancing act. Higher prices result in more revenue per unit sold but drive down unit sales. Exactly where to set prices to maximize profit is a difficult problem, but, in general, the mark-up over cost should be highest for those products where customers are least sensitive to price. The demand for such products is said to be price inelastic.

- Managers often rely on cost-plus formulas to set target prices. In the absorption costing approach, the cost base is absorption costing unit product cost and the mark-up is computed to cover both non-manufacturing costs and to provide an adequate return on investment. However, costs will not be covered and there will not be an adequate return on investment unless the unit sales forecast used in the cost-plus formula is accurate. If applying the cost-plus formula results in a price that is too high, the unit sales forecast will not be attained.

- Some companies take a different approach to pricing. Instead of starting with costs and then determining prices, they start with prices and then determine allowable costs. Companies that use target costing estimate what a new product's market price is likely to be based on its anticipated features and prices of products already on the market. They subtract desired profit from the estimated market price to arrive at the product's target cost. The design and development team is then given the responsibility of ensuring that the actual cost of the new product does not exceed the target cost.

- A special approach to pricing is required when goods or services are being transferred between segments or divisions of the same company. The theoretically optimal market price may not be appropriate if the company has spare capacity. Overall the aim should be to determine a price that maximizes the profit for the whole company. International transfer prices in multinational companies raise important taxation issues where the interests of the company and national taxation authorities may be in conflict.

Key terms

Cost-plus pricing A pricing method in which a predetermined mark-up is applied to a cost base to determine the target selling price (p. 150).

Intermediate market A market in which a transferred product or service is sold in its present form to outside customers (p. 164).

Kaizen budgeting Rather than base budgets on historical standards, kaizen budgeting plans for incremental improvements in efficiency and reduction in costs (p. 158).

Kaizen costing The reduction of cost during production through continuous gradual improvements that reduce waste and increase efficiency (p. 158).

Market price The price being charged for an item on the open (intermediate) market (p. 164).

Mark-up The difference between the selling price of a product or service and its cost. The mark-up is usually expressed as a percentage of cost (p. 150).

Negotiated transfer price A transfer price agreed on between buying and selling divisions (p. 159).

Price elasticity of demand A measure of the degree to which the volume of unit sales for a product or service is affected by a change in price (p. 150).

Range of acceptable transfer prices The range of transfer prices within which the profits of both the selling division and the purchasing division would increase as a result of a transfer (p. 160).

Sub-optimization An overall level of profitability that is less than a segment or a company is capable of earning (p. 159).

Target costing The process of determining the maximum allowable cost for a new product and then developing a prototype that can be profitably manufactured and distributed for that maximum target cost figure (p. 157).

Transfer price The price charged when one division or segment provides goods or services to another division or segment of an organization (p. 159).

Yield management A practice of achieving high capacity utilization through varying prices according to market segments and time of booking (p. 153).

Yield percentage A performance metric calculated by dividing actual revenue by the maximum potential revenue (p. 153).

Endnotes

1 Mattimoe and Seal (2010).

2 The term 'ln()' is the natural log function. You can compute the natural log of any number using the LN or lnx key on your calculator. For example, ln(0.85) = 20.1625.

  This formula assumes that the price elasticity of demand is constant. This occurs when the relation between the selling price, p, and the unit sales, q, can be expressed in the following form: $\ln(q) = a = \varepsilon_d \ln(p)$. Even if this is not precisely true, the formula provides a useful way to estimate a product's real price elasticity.

3 The estimated change in unit sales should take into account competitors' responses to a price change.

4 The formula assumes that (a) the price elasticity of demand is constant; (b) Total cost = Total fixed cost = Variable cost per unit × q; and (c) the price of the product has no effect on the sales or costs of any other product. The formula can be derived using calculus.

5 Kimes (1989).

6 Harris (1999).

7 Pricing Methods Guide, Fáilte Ireland (Irish Tourist Board), available at http://www.businesstools.failteireland.ie/Accommodation/Hotels/Pricing-Methods.aspx#Cost-plus_pricing

8 Tanaka, Yoshikawa, Innes and Mitchell (1994).

9 Monden and Hamada (1991).

When you have read this chapter, log on to the Online Learning Centre for *Management Accounting for Business Decisions* at **www.mcgraw-hill.co.uk/textbooks/seal**, where you'll find multiple choice questions, practice exams and extra study tools for management accounting.

Assessment

7–1 What is meant by cost-plus pricing?

7–2 What does the price elasticity of demand measure? What is meant by inelastic demand? What is meant by elastic demand?

7–3 According to the economists' approach to setting prices, the profit-maximizing price should depend on which two factors?

7–4 Which product should have a larger mark-up over variable cost, a product whose demand is elastic or a product whose demand is inelastic?

7–5 When the absorption costing approach to cost-plus pricing is used, what is the mark-up supposed to cover?

7–6 What assumption does the absorption costing approach make about how consumers react to prices?

7–7 Discuss the following statement: 'Full cost can be viewed as a floor of protection. If a firm always sets its prices above full cost, it will never have to worry about operating at a loss.'

7–8 What is target costing? How do target costs enter into the pricing decision?

7–9 What are the advantages and disadvantages of cost-based transfer prices?

7–10 If a market price for a product can be determined, why isn't it always the best transfer price?

E7–1 ⏱ Time allowed: 15 minutes

Maria Lorenzi owns an ice cream stand that she operates during the summer months in West Yellowstone, Montana. Her store caters primarily to tourists passing through town on their way to Yellowstone National Park.

Maria is unsure of how she should price her ice cream cones and has experimented with two prices in successive weeks during the busy August season. The number of people who entered the store was roughly the same in the two weeks. During the first week, she priced the cones at $1.89 and 1,500 cones were sold. During the second week, she priced the cones at $1.49 and 2,340 cones were sold. The variable cost of a cone is $0.43 and consists solely of the costs of the ice cream and of the cone itself. The fixed expenses of the ice cream stand are $675 per week.

Required

1 Did Maria make more money selling the cones for $1.89 or for $1.49?

2 Estimate the price elasticity of demand for the ice cream cones.

3 Estimate the profit-maximizing price for ice cream cones.

E7–2 Time allowed: 10 minutes

Martin Company is considering the introduction of a new product. To determine a target selling price, the company has gathered the following information:

Number of units to be produced and sold each year	14,000
Unit product cost	£25
Projected annual selling, general, and administrative expenses	50,000
Estimated investment required by the company	750,000
Desired return on investment (ROI)	12%

Required

The company uses the absorption costing approach to cost-plus pricing.

1   Compute the mark-up the company will have to use to achieve the desired ROI.
2   Compute the target selling price per unit.

E7–3 Time allowed: 5 minutes

Shimada Products Corporation of Japan is anxious to enter the electronic calculator market. Management believes that in order to be competitive in world markets, the electronic calculator that the company is developing cannot be priced at more than £15. Shimada requires a minimum return of 12% on all investments. An investment of £5,000,000 would be required to acquire the equipment needed to produce the 300,000 calculators that management believes can be sold each year at the £15 price.

Required

Compute the target cost of one calculator.

E7–4 Time allowed: 15 minutes

The Reliable TV Repair Shop had budgeted the following costs for next year:

Repair technicians:	
Wages	£120,000
Fringe benefits	30,000
Repairs operation per year	90,000
Materials:	
Costs of ordering, handling, and storing parts	20% of invoice cost

In total, the company expects 10,000 hours of repair time it can bill to customers. According to competitive conditions, the company believes it should aim for a profit of £6 per hour of repair time. The competitive mark-up on materials is 40% of invoice cost. The company uses time and material pricing.

Required

1   Compute the time rate and the material loading charge that would be used to bill jobs.
2   One of the company's repair technicians has just completed a repair job that required 2.5 hours of time and £80 in parts (invoice cost). Compute the amount that would be billed for the job.

E7–5 Ⓙ Time allowed: 30 minutes

Sako Company's Audio Division produces a speaker that is widely used by manufacturers of various audio products. Sales and cost data on the speaker follow:

Selling price per unit on the intermediate market	£60
Variable costs per unit	42
Fixed costs per unit (based on capacity)	8
Capacity in units	25,000

Sako Company has just organized a Hi-Fi Division that could use this speaker in one of its products. The Hi-Fi Division will need 5,000 speakers per year. It has received a quote of £57 per speaker from another manufacturer. Sako Company evaluates divisional managers on the basis of divisional profits.

Required

1   Assume that the Audio Division is now selling only 20,000 speakers per year to outside customers on the intermediate market.
2   (a) From the standpoint of the Audio Division, what is the lowest acceptable transfer price for speakers sold to the Hi-Fi Division?
    (b) From the standpoint of the Hi-Fi Division, what is the highest acceptable transfer price for speakers purchased from the Audio Division?
    (c) If left free to negotiate without interference, would you expect the division managers to voluntarily agree to the transfer of 5,000 speakers from the Audio Division to the Hi-Fi Division? Why or why not?
    (d) From the standpoint of the entire company, should the transfer take place? Why or why not?
3   Assume that the Audio Division is selling all of the speakers it can produce to outside customers on the intermediate market.
4   (a) From the standpoint of the Audio Division, what is the lowest acceptable transfer price for speakers sold to the Hi-Fi Division?
    (b) From the standpoint of the Hi-Fi Division, what is the highest acceptable transfer price for speakers purchased from the Audio Division?

(c) If left free to negotiate without interference, would you expect the division managers to voluntarily agree to the transfer of 5,000 speakers from the Audio Division to the Hi-Fi Division? Why or why not?

(d) From the standpoint of the entire company, should the transfer take place? Why or why not?

E7–6 Time allowed: 20 minutes
In each of the cases below, assume that Division X has a product that can be sold either to outside customers on an intermediate market or to Division Y of the same company for use in its production process. The managers of the divisions are evaluated based on their divisional profits.

	Case	
	A	B
Division X:		
Capacity in units	200,000	200,000
Number of units being sold on the intermediate market	200,000	160,000
Selling price per unit on the intermediate market	£90	£75
Variable costs per unit	70	60
Fixed costs per unit (based on capacity)	13	8
Division Y:		
Number of units needed for production	40,000	40,000
Purchase price per unit now being paid to an outside supplier	£86	£74

Required

1   Refer to the data in case A above. Assume in this case that £3 per unit in variable costs can be avoided on intra-company sales. If the managers are free to negotiate and make decisions on their own, will a transfer take place? If so, within what range will the transfer price fall? Explain.

2   Refer to the data in case B above. In this case there will be no savings in variable costs on intra-company sales. If the managers are free to negotiate and make decisions on their own, will a transfer take place? If so, within what range will the transfer price fall? Explain.

E7–7 Time allowed: 15 minutes
Division A manufactures electronic circuit boards. The boards can be sold either to Division B of the same company or to outside customers. Last year, the following activity occurred in Division A:

Selling price per circuit board	£125
Production cost per circuit board	90
Number of circuit boards:	
Produced during the year	20,000
Sold to outside customers	16,000
Sold to Division B	4,000

Sales to Division B were at the same price as sales to outside customers. The circuit boards purchased by Division B were used in an electronic instrument manufactured by that division (one board per instrument). Division B incurred £100 in additional cost per instrument and then sold the instruments for £300 each.

Required

1 Prepare profit statements for Division A, Division B, and the company as a whole.
2 Assume that Division A's manufacturing capacity is 20,000 circuit boards. Next year, Division B wants to purchase 5,000 circuit boards from Division A rather than 4,000. (Circuit boards of this type are not available from outside sources.) From the standpoint of the company as a whole, should Division A sell the 1,000 additional circuit boards to Division B or continue to sell them to outside customers? Explain.

P7–8 Economists' approach to pricing

Problems

connect™

Time allowed: 30 minutes

The postal service of St Vincent, an island in the West Indies, obtains a significant portion of its revenues from sales of special souvenir sheets to stamp collectors. The souvenir sheets usually contain several high-value St Vincent stamps depicting a common theme, such as the life of Princess Diana. The souvenir sheets are designed and printed for the postal service by Imperial Printing, a stamp agency service company in the United Kingdom. The souvenir sheets cost the postal service $0.80 each. (The currency in St Vincent is the East Caribbean dollar.) St Vincent has been selling these souvenir sheets for $7.00 each and ordinarily sells about 100,000 units. To test the market, the postal service recently priced a new souvenir sheet at $8.00 and sales dropped to 85,000 units.

Required

1 Does the postal service of St Vincent make more money selling souvenir sheets for $7.00 each or $8.00 each?
2 Estimate the price elasticity of demand for the souvenir sheets.
3 Estimate the profit-maximizing price for souvenir sheets.
4 If Imperial Printing increases the price it charges to the St Vincent postal service for souvenir sheets to $1.00 each, how much should the St Vincent postal service charge its customers for the souvenir sheets?

P7–9 Pricing

Time allowed: 30 minutes

A small company is engaged in the production of plastic tools for the garden. Subtotals on the spreadsheet of budgeted overheads for a year reveal:

	Moulding Department	Finishing Department	General factory Overhead
Variable overhead (£000)	1,600	500	1,050
Fixed overhead (£000)	2,500	850	1,750
Budgeted activity			
Machine hours (000)	800	000	
Practical capacity			
Machine hours (000)	1,200	800	

For the purposes of reallocation of general factory overhead it is agreed that the variable overheads accrue in line with the machine hours worked in each department.

General factory fixed overhead is to be reallocated on the basis of the practical machine hour capacity of the two departments.

It has been a long-standing company practice to establish selling prices by applying a mark-up on full manufacturing cost of between 25 and 35%.

A possible price is sought for one new product which is in a final development stage. The total market for this product is estimated at 200,000 units per annum. Market research indicates that the company could expect to obtain and hold about 10% of the market. It is hoped the product will offer some improvement over competitors' products, which are currently marketed at between £90 and £100 each.

The product development department has determined that the direct material content is £9 per unit. Each unit of the product will take two labour hours (four machine hours) in the moulding department and three labour hours (three machine hours) in finishing. Hourly labour rates are £5.00 and £5.50 respectively.

Management estimate that the annual fixed costs which would be specifically incurred in relation to the product are: supervision £20,000, depreciation of a recently acquired machine £120,000 and advertising £27,000. It may be assumed that these costs are included in the budget given above. Given the state of development of this new product, management do not consider it necessary to make revisions to the budgeted activity levels given above, for any possible extra machine hours involved in its manufacture.

Required

1   Briefly explain the role of costs in pricing.   (6 marks)
2   Prepare full cost and marginal cost information which may help with the pricing decision.   (9 marks)
3   Comment on the cost information and suggest a price range which should be considered.   (5 marks)

(Total = 20 marks)

ACCA (adapted)

P7-10 Transfer price; well-defined intermediate market

⏱ Time allowed: 45 minutes

Hrubec Products plc operates a Pulp Division that manufactures wood pulp for use in the production of various paper goods. Revenue and costs associated with a ton of pulp follow:

Selling price		£70
Less expenses:		
Variable	£42	
Fixed (based on a capacity of 50,000 tons per year)	18	60
Net profit		£10

Hrubec Products has just acquired a small company that manufactures paper cartons. This company will be treated as a division of Hrubec with full profit responsibility. The newly formed Carton Division is currently purchasing

5,000 tons of pulp per year from a supplier at a cost of £70 per ton, less a 10% quantity discount. Hrubec's managing director is anxious for the Carton Division to begin purchasing its pulp from the Pulp Division if an acceptable transfer price can be worked out.

Required

For Questions 1 and 2 below, assume that the Pulp Division can sell all its pulp to outside customers at the normal £70 price.

1   Are the managers of the Carton and Pulp Divisions likely to agree to a transfer price for 5,000 tons of pulp next year? Why or why not?
2   If the Pulp Division meets the price that the Carton Division is currently paying to its supplier and sells 5,000 tons of pulp to the Carton Division each year, what will be the effect on the profits of the Pulp Division, the Carton Division, and the company as a whole?

For Questions 3–6 below, assume that the Pulp Division is currently selling only 30,000 tons of pulp each year to outside customers at the stated £70 price.

3   Are the managers of the Carton and Pulp Divisions likely to agree to a transfer price for 5,000 tons of pulp next year? Why or why not?
4   Suppose that the Carton Division's outside supplier drops its price (net of the quantity discount) to only £59 per ton. Should the Pulp Division meet this price? Explain. If the Pulp Division does not meet the £59 price, what will be the effect on the profits of the company as a whole?
5   Refer to Question 4 above. If the Pulp Division refuses to meet the £59 price, should the Carton Division be required to purchase from the Pulp Division at a higher price for the good of the company as a whole?
6   Refer to Question 4 above. Assume that due to inflexible management policies, the Carton Division is required to purchase 5,000 tons of pulp each year from the Pulp Division at £70 per ton. What will be the effect on the profits of the company as a whole?

P7–11 Basic transfer pricing

Time allowed: 60 minutes

Alpha and Beta are divisions within the same company. The managers of both divisions are evaluated based on their own division's return on investment (ROI). Assume the following information relative to the two divisions:

	Case			
	1	2	3	4
Alpha Division:				
Capacity in units	80,000	400,000	150,000	300,000
Number of units now being sold to outside customers				
On the intermediate market	80,000	400,000	100,000	300,000
Selling price per unit on the intermediate market	£30	£90	£75	£50
Variable costs per unit	18	65	40	26
Fixed costs per unit (based on capacity)	6	15	20	9
Beta Division:				
Number of units needed annually	5,000	30,000	20,000	120,000
Purchase price now being paid to an outside supplier	£27	£89	£75*	–

*Before any quantity discount.

Managers are free to decide if they will participate in any internal transfers. All transfer prices are negotiated.

Required

1. Refer to Case 1 above. Alpha Division can avoid £2 per unit in commissions on any sales to Beta Division. Will the managers agree to a transfer and if so, within what range will the transfer price be? Explain.

2. Refer to Case 2 above. A study indicates that Alpha Division can avoid £5 per unit in shipping costs on any sales to Beta Division.

3. (a) Would you expect any disagreement between the two divisional managers over what the transfer price should be? Explain.
   (b) Assume that Alpha Division offers to sell 30,000 units to Beta Division for £88 per unit and that Beta Division refuses this price. What will be the loss in potential profits for the company as a whole?

4. Refer to Case 3 above. Assume that Beta Division is now receiving an 8% quantity discount from the outside supplier.

5. (a) Will the managers agree to a transfer? If so, what is the range within which the transfer price would be?
   (b) Assume that Beta Division offers to purchase 20,000 units from Alpha Division at £60 per unit. If Alpha Division accepts this price, would you expect its ROI to increase, decrease, or remain unchanged? Why?

6. Refer to Case 4 above. Assume that Beta Division wants Alpha Division to provide it with 120,000 units of a different product from the one that Alpha Division is now producing. The new product would require £21 per unit in variable costs and would require that Alpha Division cut back production of its present product by 45,000 units annually. What is the lowest acceptable transfer price from Alpha Division's perspective?

Chapter 8
Profit planning and controlling: budgeting

 Learning **objectives**

After studying Chapter 8, you should be able to:
1   Understand why organizations budget and the processes they use to create budgets
2   Understand the inter-relationships and components that make up a master budget
3   Prepare a budgeted profit and loss statement and a budgeted balance sheet on static and flexible bases
4   Review some criticisms of budgeting and possible responses
5   Review the concept of zero-based budgeting

Concepts **in Context**

After an initial boom, many early dotcom companies have now failed. One reason seems to be that some companies thought that the old business practices such as budgeting were obsolete. The emphasis was on speed, being the first-mover and working out detailed business plans as the business developed. Frequently, many companies squandered their start-up resources before they had established a sustainable business. The collapse of dotcoms and the high tech sector around the turn of the millennium seemed to suggest that the disciplines of planning and control inherent in budgeting should not just be the concern of 'fuddy-duddy', bricks-and-mortar organizations.[1]

© Axaulya

In this chapter, we focus our attention on those steps taken by business organizations to achieve their desired levels of profits – a process that is generally called profit planning. We shall see that profit planning is accomplished through the preparation of a number of budgets, which, when brought together, form an integrated business plan known as the master budget. The master budget is an essential management tool that communicates management's plans throughout the organization, allocates resources and co-ordinates activities.

LO 1   The basic framework of budgeting

Definition of budgeting

A budget is a detailed plan for the acquisition and use of financial and other resources over a specified time period. It represents a plan for the future expressed in formal quantitative terms. The act of preparing a budget is called *budgeting*. The use of budgets to control a firm's activities is known as *budgetary control*.

The *master budget* is a summary of a company's plans that sets specific targets for sales, production, distribution and financing activities. It generally culminates in a *cash budget*, a *budgeted profit and loss account*, and a *budgeted balance sheet*. In short, it represents a comprehensive expression of management's plans for the future and how these plans are to be accomplished.

Personal budgets

Nearly everyone budgets to some extent, even though many of the people who use budgets do not recognize what they are doing as budgeting. For example, most people make estimates of their income and plan expenditures for food, clothing, housing and so on. As a result of this planning, people restrict their spending to some predetermined, allowable amount. While they may not be conscious of the fact, these people clearly go through a budgeting process. Income is estimated, expenditures are planned, and spending is restricted in accordance with the plan. Individuals also use budgets to forecast their future financial condition for purposes such as purchasing a home, financing college education, or setting aside funds for retirement. These budgets may exist only in the mind of the individual, but they are budgets nevertheless.

The budgets of a business firm serve much the same functions as the budgets prepared informally by individuals. Business budgets tend to be more detailed and to involve more work, but they are similar to the budgets prepared by individuals in most other respects. Like personal budgets, they assist in planning and controlling expenditures; they also assist in predicting operating results and financial condition in future periods.

Advantages of budgeting

Managers who have never tried budgeting are usually quick to state that budgeting is a waste of time. These managers may argue that even though budgeting may work well in some situations, it would never work well in their companies because operations are too complex or because there are too many uncertainties. In reality, however, managers who argue this way usually will be deeply involved in planning (albeit on an informal basis). These managers will have clearly defined thoughts about what they want to accomplish and when they want it accomplished. The difficulty is that unless they have some way of communicating their thoughts and plans to others, the only way their companies will ever attain the desired objectives will be through accident. In short, even though companies may attain a certain degree of success without budgets, they never attain the heights that could have been reached with a co-ordinated system of budgets.

Companies realize many benefits from a budgeting programme. Among these benefits are the following:

1   Budgets provide a means of *communicating* management's plans throughout the organization.
2   Budgets force managers to *think about* and plan for the future. In the absence of the necessity to prepare a budget, too many managers would spend all their time dealing with daily emergencies.
3   The budgeting process provides a means of *allocating resources* to those parts of the organization where they can be used most effectively.
4   The budgeting process can uncover potential *bottlenecks* before they occur.

5 Budgets *co-ordinate* the activities of the entire organization by integrating the plans of the various parts. Budgeting helps to ensure that everyone in the organization is pulling in the same direction.

6 Budgets define goals and objectives that can serve as *benchmarks* for evaluating subsequent performance.

The impact of computers on budgeting

In the past, some managers have avoided budgeting because of the time and effort involved in the budgeting process. It can be argued that budgeting is actually 'free' in that the manager's time and effort are more than offset by greater profits. Moreover, with the advent of computer spreadsheets, *any* company – large or small – can implement and maintain a budgeting programme at minimal cost. Budgeting lends itself well to readily available spreadsheet application programs.

Focus on Business Practice

Budgeting in banking firms

© Joshua Hodge Photography

Consider the following situation encountered by one of the authors at a mortgage banking firm. For years, the company operated with virtually no system of budgets whatever. Management contended that budgeting was not well suited to the firm's type of operation. Moreover, management pointed out that the firm was already profitable. Indeed, outwardly the company gave every appearance of being a well-managed, smoothly operating organization. A careful look within, however, disclosed that day-to-day operations were far from smooth, and often approached chaos. The average day was nothing more than an exercise in putting out one brush fire after another. The Cash account was always at crisis levels. At the end of a day, no one ever knew whether enough cash would be available the next day to cover required loan closings. Departments were uncoordinated, and it was not uncommon to find that one department was pursuing a course that conflicted with the course pursued by another department. Employee morale was low, and turnover was high. Employees complained bitterly that when a job was well done, nobody ever knew about it. The company was bought out by a new group who required that an integrated budgeting system be established to control operations. Within one year, significant changes were evident. Brush fires were rare. Careful planning virtually eliminated the problems that had been experienced with cash, and departmental efforts were co-ordinated and directed towards predetermined overall company goals. Although the employees were wary of the new budgeting programme initially, they became 'converted' when they saw the positive effects that it brought about. The more efficient operations caused profits to jump dramatically. Communication increased throughout the organization. When a job was well done everybody knew about it. As one employee stated, 'For the first time, we know what the company expects of us.'

Exercise: One of the key issues that emerged after the recent collapse of the Bradford & Bingley bank was the poor state of the bank's financial controls. How did that contribute to the wider banking problems that became known as the *credit crunch*?[2]

Choosing a budget period

Operating budgets are ordinarily set to cover a one-year period. The one-year period should correspond to the company's fiscal year so that the budget figures can be compared with the actual results. Many companies divide their budget year into four quarters. The first quarter is then subdivided into months, and monthly budget figures are established. These *near-term* figures can often be established with considerable accuracy. The last three quarters are carried in the budget as quarterly totals only. As the year progresses, the figures for the second quarter are broken down into monthly amounts, then the third-quarter figures are broken down, and so forth. This approach has the advantage of requiring periodic review and reappraisal of budget data throughout the year.

Continuous, perpetual or *rolling budgets* are used by a significant number of organizations. A **continuous or perpetual budget** is a 12-month budget that rolls forward one month (or quarter) as the current month (or quarter) is completed. In other words, one month (or quarter) is added to the end of the budget as each month (or quarter) comes to a close. This approach keeps managers focused on the future at least one year ahead. Advocates of continuous budgets argue that with this approach there is less danger that managers will become too focused on short-term results as the year progresses.

The self-imposed or participative budget

The success of a budget programme will be determined in large part by the way in which the budget is developed. The most successful budget programmes involve managers with cost control responsibilities in preparing their own budget estimates – rather than having a budget imposed from above. This approach to preparing budget data is particularly important if the budget is to be used to control and evaluate a manager's activities. If a budget is imposed on a manager from above, it will probably generate resentment and ill will rather than co-operation and increased productivity.

This budgeting approach, in which managers prepare their own budget estimates – called a *self-imposed budget* – is generally considered to be the most effective method of budget preparation. A **self-imposed budget** or **participative budget** is a budget that is prepared with the full co-operation and participation of managers at all levels. Exhibit 8.1 illustrates this approach to budget preparation.

A number of advantages are commonly cited for such self-imposed budgets:

1   Individuals at all levels of the organization are recognized as members of the team whose views and judgements are valued by top management.
2   The person in direct contact with an activity is in the best position to make budget estimates. Therefore, budget estimates prepared by such persons tend to be more accurate and reliable.

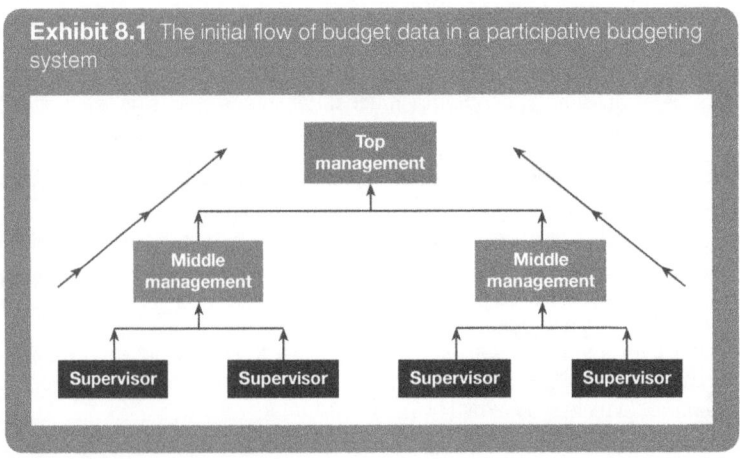

Exhibit 8.1 The initial flow of budget data in a participative budgeting system

3   People are more likely to work at fulfilling a budget that they have participated in setting than they are to work at fulfilling a budget that is imposed from above.
4   A self-imposed budget contains its own unique system of control in that if people are not able to meet budget specifications, they have only themselves to blame. On the other hand, if a budget is imposed from above, they can always say that the budget was unreasonable or unrealistic to start with, and therefore was impossible to meet.

Once self-imposed budgets are prepared, are they subject to any kind of review? The answer is yes. Budget estimates prepared by lower-level managers cannot necessarily be accepted without question by higher levels of management. If no system of checks and balances is present, self-imposed budgets may be too loose and allow too much 'budgetary slack'. The result will be inefficiency and waste. Therefore, before budgets are accepted, they must be carefully reviewed by immediate superiors. If changes from the original budget seem desirable, the items in question are discussed and modified as necessary by mutual consent.

In essence, all levels of an organization should work together to produce the budget. Since top management is generally unfamiliar with detailed, day-to-day operations, it should rely on subordinates to provide detailed budget information. On the other hand, top management has a perspective on the company as a whole that is vital in making broad policy decisions in budget preparation. Each level of responsibility in an organization should contribute in the way that it best can in a *co-operative* effort to develop an integrated budget document.

We have described an ideal budgetary process that involves self-imposed budgets prepared by the managers who are directly responsible for revenues and costs. Most companies deviate from this ideal. Typically, top managers initiate the budget process by issuing broad guidelines in terms of overall target profits or sales. Lower-level managers are directed to prepare budgets that meet those targets. The difficulty is that the targets set by top managers may be unrealistically high or may allow too much slack. If the targets are too high and employees know they are unrealistic, motivation will suffer. If the targets allow too much slack, waste will occur. And, unfortunately, top managers are often not in a position to know whether the targets they have set are appropriate. Admittedly, however, in a pure self-imposed budgeting system, lower-level managers may be tempted to build into their budgets a great deal of budgetary slack and there may be a lack of direction. Nevertheless, because of the motivational advantages of self-imposed budgets, top managers should be cautious about setting inflexible targets or otherwise imposing limits on the budgeting process.

The matter of human relations

Whether or not a budget programme is accepted by lower management personnel will be reflective of (first) the degree to which top management accepts the budget programme as a vital part of the company's activities, and (second) the way in which top management uses budgeted data.

If a budget programme is to be successful, it must have the complete acceptance and support of the persons who occupy key management positions. If lower or middle management personnel sense that top management is lukewarm about budgeting, or if they sense that top management simply tolerates budgeting as a necessary evil, then their own attitudes will reflect a similar lack of enthusiasm. Budgeting is hard work, and if top management is not enthusiastic about and committed to the budget programme, then it is unlikely that anyone else in the organization will be either.

In administering the budget programme, it is particularly important that top management not use the budget as a club to pressure employees or as a way to find someone to blame for a particular problem. This type of negative emphasis will simply breed hostility, tension and mistrust rather than greater co-operation and productivity. Unfortunately, research suggests that the budget is often used as a pressure device and that great emphasis is placed on 'meeting the budget' under all circumstances.[3] Rather than being used as a pressure device, the budget should be used as a positive instrument to assist in establishing goals, in measuring operating results, and in isolating areas that are in need of extra effort or attention. Any misgivings that employees have about a budget programme can be overcome by meaningful involvement at all levels and by proper use of the programme over a period of time. Administration of a budget programme requires a great deal of insight and sensitivity on the part of management. The ultimate object must be to develop the realization that the budget is designed to be a positive aid in achieving both individual and company goals.

Management must keep clearly in mind that the human dimension in budgeting is of key importance. It is easy for the manager to become preoccupied with the technical aspects of the budget programme to the exclusion of the human aspects. Indeed, the use of budget data in a rigid and inflexible manner is the greatest single complaint of persons whose performance is being evaluated through the budget process.[4] Management should remember that the purposes of the budget are to motivate employees and to co-ordinate efforts. Preoccupation with the pounds and pence in the budget, or being rigid and inflexible in budget administration, can only lead to frustration of these purposes.

The budget committee

A standing **budget committee** will usually be responsible for overall policy matters relating to the budget programme and for co-ordinating the preparation of the budget itself. This committee generally consists of the managing director; directors in charge of various functions such as sales, production and purchasing; and the controller. Difficulties and disputes between segments of the organization in matters relating to the budget are resolved by the budget committee. In addition, the budget committee approves the final budget and receives periodic reports on the progress of the company in attaining budgeted goals.

Disputes can (and do) erupt over budget matters. Because budgets allocate resources, the budgeting process, to a large extent, determines which departments get more resources and which get relatively less. Also, the budget sets the benchmarks by which managers and their departments will be at least partially evaluated. Therefore, it should not be surprising that managers take the budgeting process very seriously and invest considerable energy and even emotion in ensuring that their interests, and those of their departments, are protected. Because of this, the budgeting process can easily degenerate into an inter-office brawl in which the ultimate goal of working together towards common goals is forgotten.

Running a successful budgeting programme that avoids inter-office battles requires considerable inter-personal skills in addition to purely technical skills. But even the best inter-personal skills will fail if, as discussed earlier, top management uses the budget process inappropriately as a club or as a way to find blame.

Focus on Business Practice

The game of budgeting

© P_Wei

Budgeting is often an intensely political process in which managers jockey for resources and relaxed goals for the upcoming year. One group of consultants describes the process in this way: Annual budgets 'have a particular urgency in that they provide the standard and most public framework against which managers are assessed and judged. It is, therefore, not surprising that budget-setting is taken seriously...Often budgets are a means for managers getting what they want. A relaxed budget will secure a relatively easy twelve months, a tight one means that their names will constantly be coming up in the monthly management review meeting. Far better to shift the burden of cost control and financial discipline to someone else. Budgeting as an intensely political exercise is conducted with all the sharper managerial skills not taught at business school, such as lobbying and flattering superiors, forced haste, regretted delay, hidden truth, half-truths, and lies.'[5]

Exercise: Why might an organization that has a high level of *trust* between managerial levels achieve a better quality of budgeting than those where mistrust is the rule?

The master budget inter-relationships

LO 2

The **master budget** consists of a number of separate but interdependent budgets. Exhibit 8.2 provides an overview of the various parts of the master budget and how they are related.

The sales budget

A **sales budget** is a detailed schedule showing the expected sales for the budget period; typically, it is expressed in both pounds and units of product. An accurate sales budget is the key to the entire budgeting process. All other parts of the master budget are dependent on the sales budget in some way, as illustrated in Exhibit 8.2. Thus, if the sales budget is sloppily done, then the rest of the budgeting process is largely a waste of time.

The sales budget will help determine how many units will have to be produced. Thus, the *production budget* is prepared after the sales budget. The production budget in turn is used to determine the budgets for manufacturing costs including the *direct materials budget*, the *direct labour budget*, and the *manufacturing overhead budget*. These budgets are then combined with data from the sales budget and the selling and administrative expense budget to determine the cash budget. In essence, the sales budget triggers a chain reaction that leads to the development of the other budgets.

As shown in Exhibit 8.2, the selling and administrative expense budget is both dependent on and a determinant of the sales budget. This reciprocal relationship arises because sales will in part be determined by the funds committed for advertising and sales promotion.

The cash budget

Once the operating budgets (sales, production, and so on) have been established, the cash budget and other financial budgets can be prepared. A **cash budget** is a detailed plan showing how cash resources will be acquired and used over some specified time period. Observe from Exhibit 8.2 that all of the operating budgets have an impact on the cash budget. In the case of the sales budget, the impact comes from the planned cash receipts to be received from sales. In the case of the other budgets, the impact comes from the planned cash expenditures within the budgets themselves.

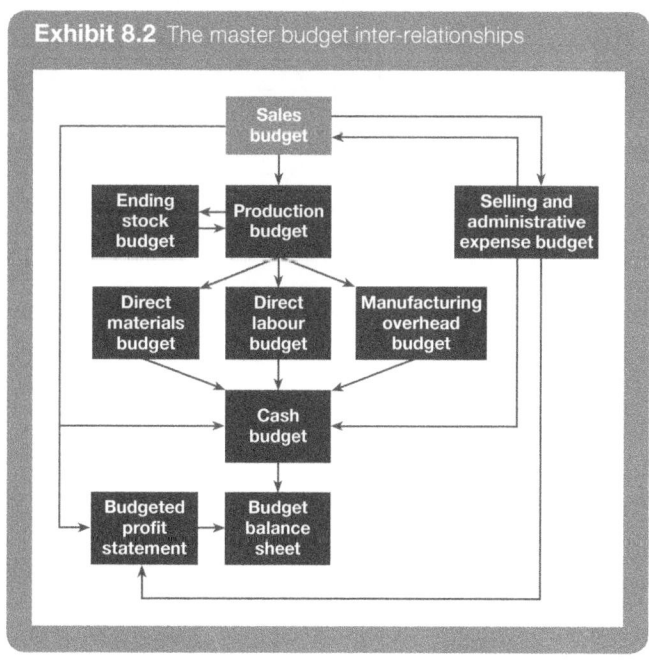

Exhibit 8.2 The master budget inter-relationships

Sales forecasting – a critical step

The sales budget is usually based on the company's *sales forecast*. Sales from prior years are commonly used as a starting point in preparing the sales forecast. In addition, the manager may examine the company's unfilled back orders, the company's pricing policy and marketing plans, trends in the industry and general economic conditions. Sophisticated statistical tools may be used to analyse the data and to build models that are helpful in predicting key factors influencing the company's sales.

Preparing the master budget

The sales budget

The sales budget is the starting point in preparing the master budget. As shown earlier in Exhibit 8.2, all other items in the master budget, including production, purchases, stocks and expenses, depend on it in some way.

The sales budget is constructed by multiplying the budgeted sales in units by the selling price. Schedule 1 contains the sales budget for Hampton Freeze Ltd for the year 2011, by quarters. Notice from the schedule that the company plans to sell 100,000 cases of ice lollies during the year, with sales peaking in the third quarter.

Schedule 1

Hampton Freeze Ltd.
Sales budget
for the year ended 31 December 2011

| | Quarter | | | | |
	1	2	3	4	Year
Budgeted sales in units (cases of lollies)	10,000	30,000	40,000	20,000	100,000
Selling price per unit	× £20	× £20	× £20	× £20	× £20
Total sales	£200,000	£600,000	£800,000	£400,000	£2,000,000

Schedule of expected cash collections

	1	2	3	4	Year
Debtors, beginning balance*	£90,000				£90,000
First-quarter sales (£200,000 × 70%, 30%)†	140,000	60,000			200,000
Second-quarter sales (£600,000 × 70%, 30%)		420,000	180,000		600,000
Third-quarter sales (£800,000 × 70%, 30%)			560,000	240,000	800,000
Fourth-quarter sales (£400,000 × 70%)‡				280,000	280,000
Total cash collections	£230,000	£480,000	£740,000	£520,000	£1,970,000

* Cash collections from last year's fourth-quarter sales. See the beginning-of-year balance sheet on page 190.

†Cash collections from sales are as follows: 70 per cent collected in the quarter of sale, and the remaining 30 per cent collected in the following year.

‡Uncollected fourth-quarter sales appear as debtors on the company's end-of-year balance sheet (see Schedule 10 on page 194).

A schedule of expected *cash collections*, such as the one that appears in Schedule 1 for Hampton Freeze, is prepared after the sales budget. This schedule will be needed later to prepare the cash budget. Cash collections consist of collections on sales made to customers in prior periods plus collections on sales made in the current budget period. At Hampton Freeze, experience has shown that 70% of sales are collected in the quarter in which the sale is made and the remaining 30% are collected in the following quarter. So, for example, 70% of the first quarter sales of £200,000 (or £140,000) is collected during the first quarter and 30% (or £60,000) is collected during the second quarter.

The production budget

The production budget is prepared after the sales budget. The **production budget** lists the number of units that must be produced during each budget period to meet sales needs and to provide for the desired ending stock. Production needs can be determined as follows:

Budgeted sales in units	XXXX
Add desired ending stock	XXXX
Total needs	XXXX
Less beginning stock	XXXX
Required production	XXXX

Schedule 2 contains the production budget for Hampton Freeze.

Note that production requirements for a quarter are influenced by the desired level of the ending stock. Stocks should be carefully planned. Excessive stocks tie up funds and create storage problems. Insufficient stocks can lead to lost sales or crash production efforts in the following period. At Hampton Freeze, management believes that an ending stock equal to 20% of the next quarter's sales strikes the appropriate balance.

Schedule 2

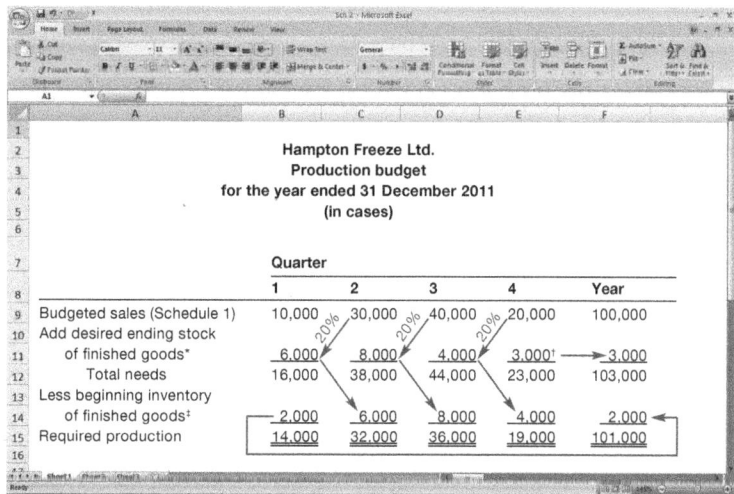

Hampton Freeze Ltd.
Production budget
for the year ended 31 December 2011
(in cases)

	Quarter				
	1	2	3	4	Year
Budgeted sales (Schedule 1)	10,000	30,000	40,000	20,000	100,000
Add desired ending stock of finished goods*	6,000	8,000	4,000	3,000†	3,000
Total needs	16,000	38,000	44,000	23,000	103,000
Less beginning inventory of finished goods‡	2,000	6,000	8,000	4,000	2,000
Required production	14,000	32,000	36,000	19,000	101,000

* 20 per cent of next quarter's sales.
†Estimated.
‡The same as the prior quarter's *ending* stock.

The direct materials budget

Returning to Hampton Freeze's budget data, after the production requirements have been computed, a *direct materials budget* can be prepared. The **direct materials budget** details the raw materials that must be purchased to fulfil the production budget and to provide for adequate stocks. The required purchases of raw materials are computed as follows:

Raw materials needed to meet the production schedule	XXXXX
Add desired ending stock of raw materials	XXXXX
Total raw materials needs	XXXXX
Less beginning stock of raw materials	XXXXX
Raw materials to be purchased	XXXXX

Preparing a budget of this kind is one step in a company's overall **material requirements planning (MRP)**. MRP is an operations management tool that uses a computer to help manage materials and stocks. The objective of MRP is to ensure that the right materials are on hand, in the right quantities, and at the right time to support the production budget. The detailed operation of MRP is covered in most operations management books.

Schedule 3 contains the direct materials budget for Hampton Freeze. The only raw material included in that budget is high fructose sugar, which is the major ingredient in ice lollies other than water. The remaining raw materials are relatively insignificant and are included in variable manufacturing overhead. Notice that materials requirements are first determined in units (kilos, litres, and so on) and then translated into pounds by multiplying by the appropriate unit cost. Also note that the management of Hampton Freeze desires to maintain ending stocks of sugar equal to 10% of the following quarter's production needs.

The direct materials budget is usually accompanied by a schedule of expected cash disbursements for raw materials. This schedule is needed to prepare the overall cash budget. Disbursements for raw materials consist of payments for purchases on account in prior periods plus any payments for purchases in the current budget period. Schedule 3 contains such a schedule of cash disbursements.

The direct labour budget

The **direct labour budget** is also developed from the production budget. Direct labour requirements must be computed so that the company will know whether sufficient labour time is available to meet production needs. By knowing in advance just what will be needed in the way of labour time throughout the budget year, the company can develop plans to adjust the labour force as the situation may require. Firms that neglect to budget run the risk of facing labour shortages, or having to hire and lay off at awkward times. Erratic labour policies lead to insecurity and inefficiency on the part of employees.

To compute direct labour requirements, the number of units of finished product to be produced each period (month, quarter, and so on) is multiplied by the number of direct labour-hours required to produce a single unit. Many different types of labour may be involved. If so, then computations should be by type of labour needed. The direct labour requirements can then be translated into expected direct labour costs. How this is done will depend on the labour policy of the firm. In Schedule 4, the management of Hampton Freeze has assumed that the direct labour force will be adjusted as the work requirements change from quarter to quarter. In that case, the total direct labour cost is computed by simply multiplying the direct labour-hour requirements by the direct labour rate per hour as was done in Schedule 4.

However, many companies have employment policies or contracts that prevent them from laying off and rehiring workers as needed. Suppose, for example, that Hampton Freeze has fifty workers who are classified as direct labour and each of them is guaranteed at least 480 hours of pay each quarter at a rate of £7.50 per hour. In that case, the minimum direct labour cost for a quarter would be as follows:

50 workers × 480 hour × £7.50 = £180,000

Note that in Schedule 4 the direct labour costs for the first and fourth quarters would have to be increased to a £180,000 level if Hampton Freeze's labour policy did not allow it to adjust the workforce at will.

Schedule 3

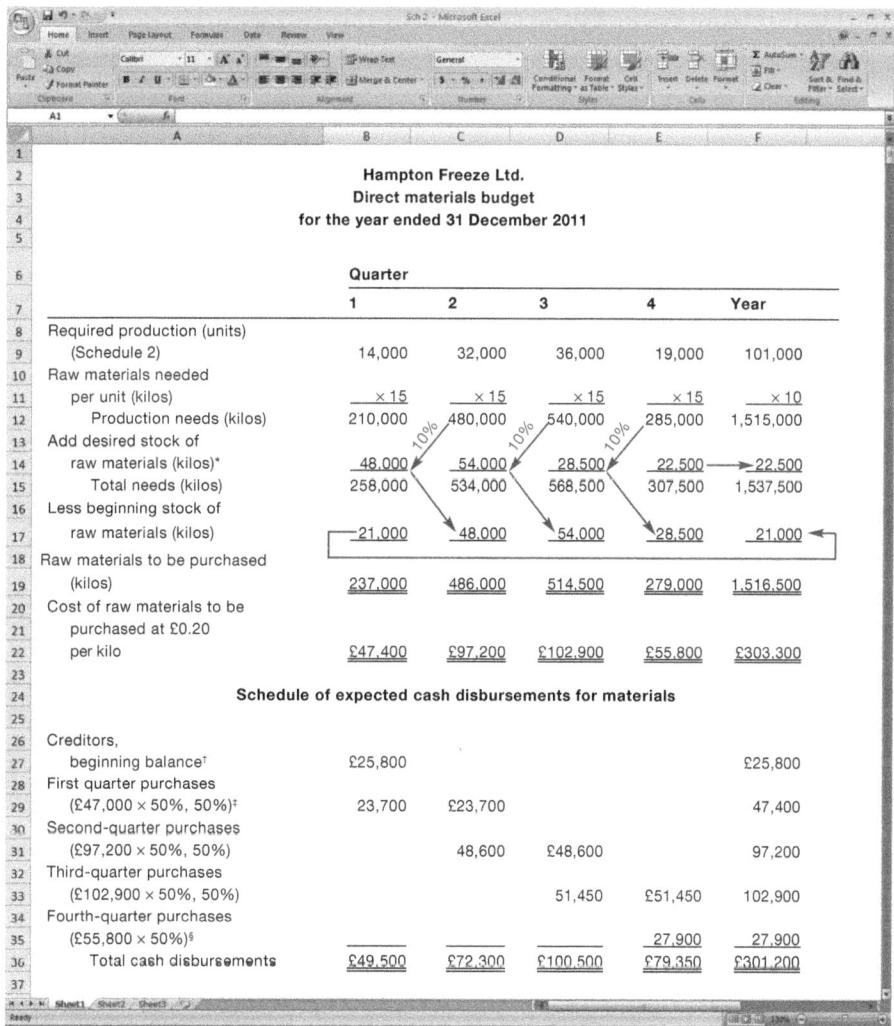

Hampton Freeze Ltd.
Direct materials budget
for the year ended 31 December 2011

	Quarter				
	1	**2**	**3**	**4**	**Year**
Required production (units)					
(Schedule 2)	14,000	32,000	36,000	19,000	101,000
Raw materials needed					
per unit (kilos)	× 15	× 15	× 15	× 15	× 10
Production needs (kilos)	210,000	480,000	540,000	285,000	1,515,000
Add desired stock of					
raw materials (kilos)*	48,000	54,000	28,500	22,500	22,500
Total needs (kilos)	258,000	534,000	568,500	307,500	1,537,500
Less beginning stock of					
raw materials (kilos)	21,000	48,000	54,000	28,500	21,000
Raw materials to be purchased					
(kilos)	237,000	486,000	514,500	279,000	1,516,500
Cost of raw materials to be					
purchased at £0.20					
per kilo	£47,400	£97,200	£102,900	£55,800	£303,300

Schedule of expected cash disbursements for materials

Creditors,					
beginning balance†	£25,800				£25,800
First quarter purchases					
(£47,000 × 50%, 50%)‡	23,700	£23,700			47,400
Second-quarter purchases					
(£97,200 × 50%, 50%)		48,600	£48,600		97,200
Third-quarter purchases					
(£102,900 × 50%, 50%)			51,450	£51,450	102,900
Fourth-quarter purchases					
(£55,800 × 50%)§				27,900	27,900
Total cash disbursements	£49,500	£72,300	£100,500	£79,350	£301,200

*10 per cent of the next quarter's production needs. For example, the second-quarter production needs are 480,000 kilos. Therefore, the desired ending inventory for the first quarter would be 10 per cent × 480,000 kilos – 48,000 kilos. The ending stock of 22,500 kilos for the fourth quarter is estimated.

†Cash payments for last year's fourth-quarter material purchases. See the beginning-of-year balance sheet on page 190.

‡Cash payments for purchases are as follows: 50 per cent paid for in the quarter of purchase, and the remaining 50 per cent paid for in the following quarter.

§Unpaid fourth-quarter purchases appear as creditors on the company's end-of-year balance sheet (see Schedule 10 on page 194).

The manufacturing overhead budget

The **manufacturing overhead budget** provides a schedule of all costs of production other than direct materials and direct labour. Schedule 5 shows the manufacturing overhead budget for Hampton Freeze.

Schedule 4

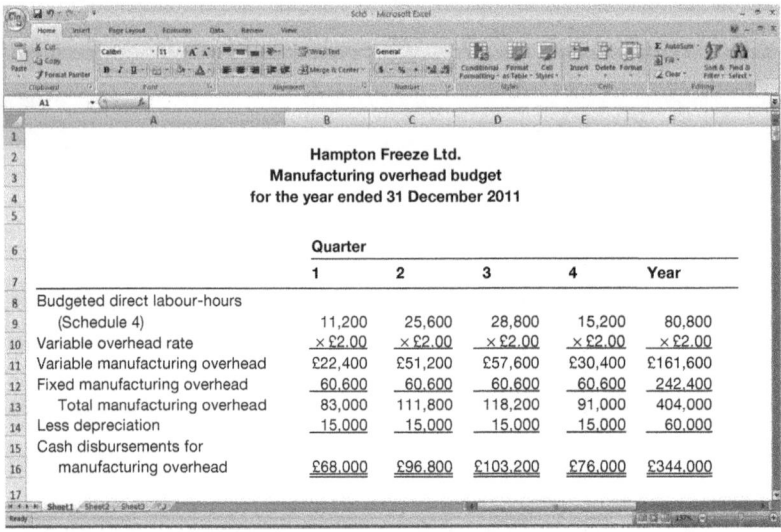

Hampton Freeze Ltd.
Direct labour budget
for the year ended 31 December 2011

	Quarter				
	1	2	3	4	Year
Units (cases) to be produced (Schedule 2)	14,000	32,000	36,000	19,000	101,000
Direct labour time per unit (hours)	× 0.8	× 0.8	× 0.8	× 0.8	× 0.8
Total hours of direct labour time needed	11,200	25,600	28,800	15,200	80,800
Direct labour cost per hour	× £7.50	× £7.50	× £7.50	× £7.50	× £7.50
Total direct labour cost*	£84,000	£192,000	£216,000	£114,000	£606,000

*This schedule assumes that the direct labour workforce will be fully adjusted to the workload (i.e., 'total hours of direct labour time needed') each quarter.

Schedule 5

Hampton Freeze Ltd.
Manufacturing overhead budget
for the year ended 31 December 2011

	Quarter				
	1	2	3	4	Year
Budgeted direct labour-hours (Schedule 4)	11,200	25,600	28,800	15,200	80,800
Variable overhead rate	× £2.00	× £2.00	× £2.00	× £2.00	× £2.00
Variable manufacturing overhead	£22,400	£51,200	£57,600	£30,400	£161,600
Fixed manufacturing overhead	60,600	60,600	60,600	60,600	242,400
Total manufacturing overhead	83,000	111,800	118,200	91,000	404,000
Less depreciation	15,000	15,000	15,000	15,000	60,000
Cash disbursements for manufacturing overhead	£68,000	£96,800	£103,200	£76,000	£344,000

Note how the production costs are separated into variable and fixed components. The variable component is £2 per direct labour-hour. The fixed component is £60,600 per quarter.

The last line of Schedule 5 for Hampton Freeze shows its budgeted cash disbursements for manufacturing overhead. Since some of the overhead costs are not cash outflows, the total budgeted manufacturing overhead costs must be adjusted to determine the cash disbursements for manufacturing overhead. At Hampton Freeze, the only significant non-cash manufacturing overhead cost is depreciation, which is £15,000 per quarter. These non-cash depreciation charges are deducted from the total budgeted manufacturing overhead to determine the expected cash disbursements. Hampton Freeze pays all overhead costs involving cash disbursements in the quarter incurred.

The finished goods stock budget

Schedules 1–5 contain all of the data needed to compute unit product costs. This computation is needed for two reasons: first, to determine cost of goods sold on the budgeted profit and loss account; and second, to know what amount to put on the balance sheet stock account for unsold units. The carrying cost of the unsold units is computed on the **finished goods stock budget**.

The unit product cost computations are shown in Schedule 6. For Hampton Freeze, the absorption costing unit product cost is £13 per case of ice lollies – consisting of £3 of direct materials, £6 of direct labour and £4 of manufacturing overhead. For convenience, the manufacturing overhead is applied to units of product on the basis of direct labour-hours. The budgeted carrying cost of the expected ending stock is £39,000.

The selling and administrative expense budget

The **selling and administrative expense budget** lists the budgeted expenses for areas other than manufacturing. In large organizations, this budget would be a compilation of many smaller, individual budgets submitted by department heads and other persons responsible for selling and administrative expenses. For example, the marketing manager in a large organization would submit a budget detailing the advertising expenses for each budget period.

Schedule 6

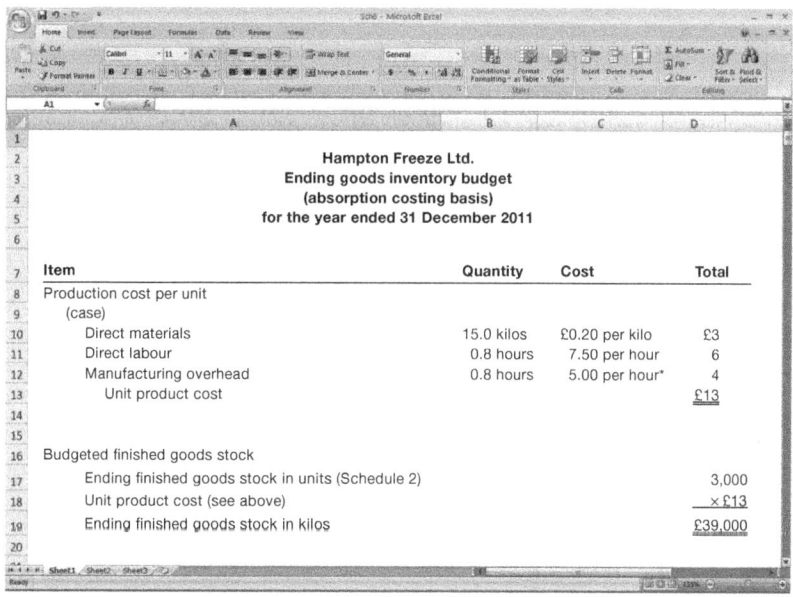

Item	Quantity	Cost	Total
Production cost per unit			
(case)			
Direct materials	15.0 kilos	£0.20 per kilo	£3
Direct labour	0.8 hours	7.50 per hour	6
Manufacturing overhead	0.8 hours	5.00 per hour*	4
Unit product cost			£13
Budgeted finished goods stock			
Ending finished goods stock in units (Schedule 2)			3,000
Unit product cost (see above)			×£13
Ending finished goods stock in kilos			£39,000

*£404,000 + 80,800 hours = £5.

Schedule 7 contains the selling and administrative expense budget for Hampton Freeze.

Schedule 7

Hampton Freeze Ltd.
Selling and administrative expense budget
for the year ended 31 December 2011

| | Quarter | | | | |
	1	2	3	4	Year
Budgeted sales in units (cases)	10,000	30,000	40,000	20,000	100,000
Variable selling and administrative expense per unit*	×£1.80	×£1.80	×£1.80	×£1.80	×£1.80
Variable expense	£18,000	£54,000	£72,000	£36,000	£180,000
Fixed selling and administrative expenses:					
Advertising	20,000	20,000	20,000	20,000	80,000
Executive salaries	55,000	55,000	55,000	55,000	220,000
Insurance		1,900	37,750		39,650
Property taxes				18,150	18,150
Depreciation	10,000	10,000	10,000	10,000	40,000
Total	85,000	86,900	122,750	103,150	397,800
Total selling and administrative expenses	103,000	140,900	194,750	139,150	577,800
Less depreciation	10,000	10,000	10,000	10,000	40,000
Cash disbursements for selling and administrative expenses	£93,000	£130,900	£184,750	£129,150	£537,800

*Commissions, clerical and shipping.

The cash budget

As illustrated in Exhibit 8.2, the cash budget pulls together much of the data developed in the preceding steps. It is a good idea to restudy Exhibit 8.2 to get the big picture firmly in mind before moving on.

The cash budget is composed of four major sections:

1 The receipts section.
2 The disbursements section.
3 The cash excess or deficiency section.
4 The financing section.

The receipts section consists of a listing of all of the cash inflows, except for financing, expected during the budget period. Generally, the major source of receipts will be from sales.

The disbursements section consists of all cash payments that are planned for the budget period. These payments will include raw materials purchases, direct labour payments, manufacturing overhead costs, and so on, as contained in their respective budgets. In addition, other cash disbursements such as equipment purchases, dividends and other cash withdrawals by owners are listed. For instance, we see in Schedule 8 that management plans to spend £130,000 during the budget period on equipment purchases and £32,000 on dividends to the owners. This is additional information that does not appear on any of the earlier schedules.

The cash excess or deficiency section is computed as follows:

Cash balance, beginning	XXXX
Add receipts	XXXX
Total cash available before financing	XXXX
Less disbursements	XXXX
Excess (deficiency) of cash available over disbursements	XXXX

Schedule 8

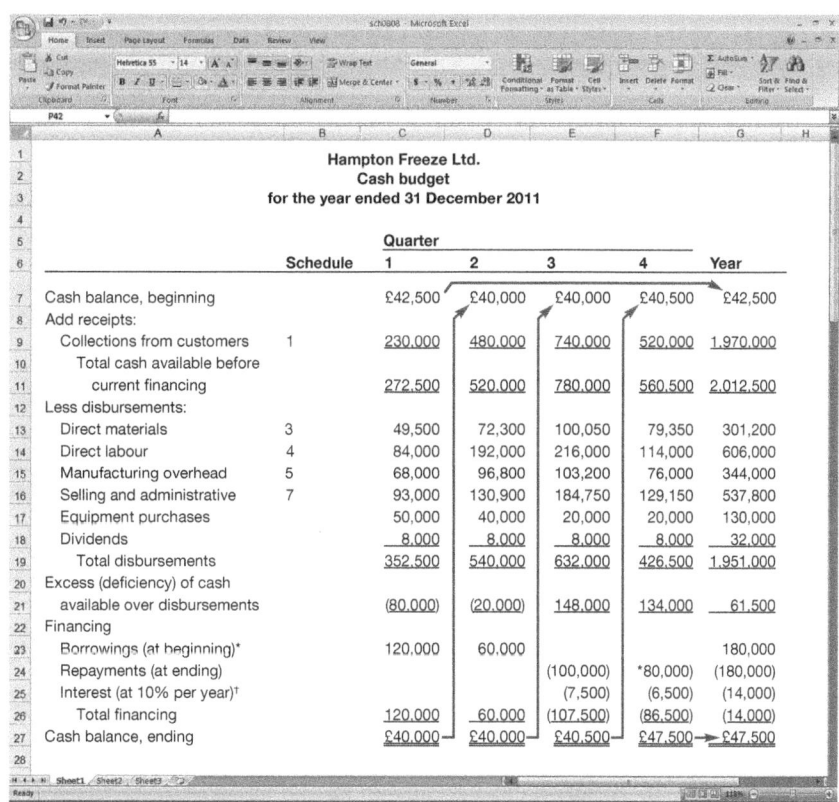

*The company requires a minimum cash balance of £40,000. Therefore, borrowing must be sufficient to cover the cash deficiency of £80,000 in quarter 1 and to provide for the minimum cash balance of £40,000. All borrowings and all repayments of principal are in round £1,000 amounts.

† The interest payments relate only to the principal being repaid at the time it is repaid. For example, the interest in quarter 3 relates only to the interest due on the £100,000 principal being repaid from quarter 1 borrowing: £100,00 × ¾ × 10 per cent – £7,500. The interest paid in quarter 4 is computed as follows:

£20,000 × 10 per cent × 1 year	£2,000
£60,000 × 10 per cent × ¾	4,500
Total interest paid	£6,500

If there is a cash deficiency during any budget period, the company will need to borrow funds. If there is a cash excess during any budget period, funds borrowed in previous periods can be repaid or the idle funds can be placed in short-term or other investments.

The financing section provides a detailed account of the borrowings and repayments projected to take place during the budget period. It also includes a detail of interest payments that will be due on money borrowed. Generally speaking, the cash budget should be broken down into time periods that are as short as feasible. There can be considerable fluctuations in cash balances that would be hidden by looking at a longer time period. While a monthly cash budget is most common, many firms budget cash on a weekly or even daily basis. The quarterly cash budget for Hampton Freeze can be further refined as necessary. This budget appears in Schedule 8; it is assumed that an open line of credit can be arranged with the bank that can be used as needed to bolster the company's cash position. It is also assumed that the interest on any loans taken out with this line of credit would carry an interest rate of 10% per year. For simplicity, it is assumed that all borrowings and repayments are in round £1,000 amounts and that all borrowing occurs at the beginning of a quarter and all repayments are made at the end of a quarter.

In the case of Hampton Freeze, all loans have been repaid by year-end. If all loans are not repaid and a budgeted profit and loss account or balance sheet is being prepared, then interest must be accrued on the unpaid loans. This interest will *not* appear on the cash budget (since it has not yet been paid), but it will appear as part of interest expense on the budgeted profit and loss account and as a liability on the budgeted balance sheet.

LO 3

A budgeted profit and loss account can be prepared from the data developed in Schedules 1–8. The budgeted profit and loss account is one of the key schedules in the budget process. It shows the company's planned profit for the upcoming budget period, and it stands as a benchmark against which subsequent company performance can be measured. Schedule 9 contains the budgeted profit and loss account for Hampton Freeze.

Schedule 9

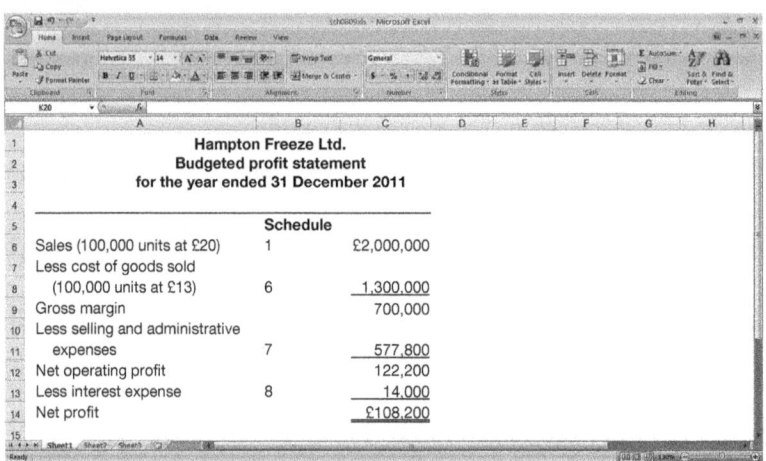

Hampton Freeze Ltd.
Budgeted profit statement
for the year ended 31 December 2011

	Schedule	
Sales (100,000 units at £20)	1	£2,000,000
Less cost of goods sold		
(100,000 units at £13)	6	1,300,000
Gross margin		700,000
Less selling and administrative		
expenses	7	577,800
Net operating profit		122,200
Less interest expense	8	14,000
Net profit		£108,200

The budgeted balance sheet

The budgeted balance sheet is developed by beginning with the current balance sheet and adjusting it for the data contained in the other budgets. Hampton Freeze's budgeted balance sheet is presented in Schedule 10. Some of the data on the budgeted balance sheet has been taken from the company's end of-year balance sheet for 2010 which appears below:

Hampton Freeze Ltd		
Balance sheet		
31 December 2010		
Assets		
Current assets:		
Cash	£42,500	
Debtors	90,000	
Raw materials stock (21,000 kilos)	4,200	
Finished goods stock (2,000 cases)	26,000	
Total current assets		£162,700
Plant and equipment:		
Land	80,000	
Buildings and equipment	700,000	
Accumulated depreciation	(292,000)	
Plant and equipment, net		488,000
Total assets		£650,700
Liabilities and shareholders' equity		
Current liabilities:		
Creditors (raw materials)		£25,800
Shareholders' equity:		
Common stock, no par	£175,000	
Retained earnings	449,900	
Total shareholders' equity		624,900
Total liabilities and shareholders' equity		£650,700

Flexible budgeting: expanding the budgeted profit and loss account

The master budget profit and loss account in Schedule 9 focuses on a single level of activity and has been prepared using absorption costing. Some managers prefer an alternative format that focuses on a *range of activity* and that is prepared using the contribution approach. An example of a master budget profit and loss account using this alternative format is presented in Exhibit 8.3.

A statement such as that in Exhibit 8.3 is flexible, since it is geared to more than one level of activity. If, for example, the company planned to sell 2,000 units during a period but actually sold only 1,900 units, then the budget figures at the 1,900-unit level would be used to compare against actual costs and revenues. Other columns could be added to the budget as needed by simply applying the budget formulas provided. In short, a master budget profit and loss account in this expanded format can be very useful in planning and controlling operations.

Schedule 10

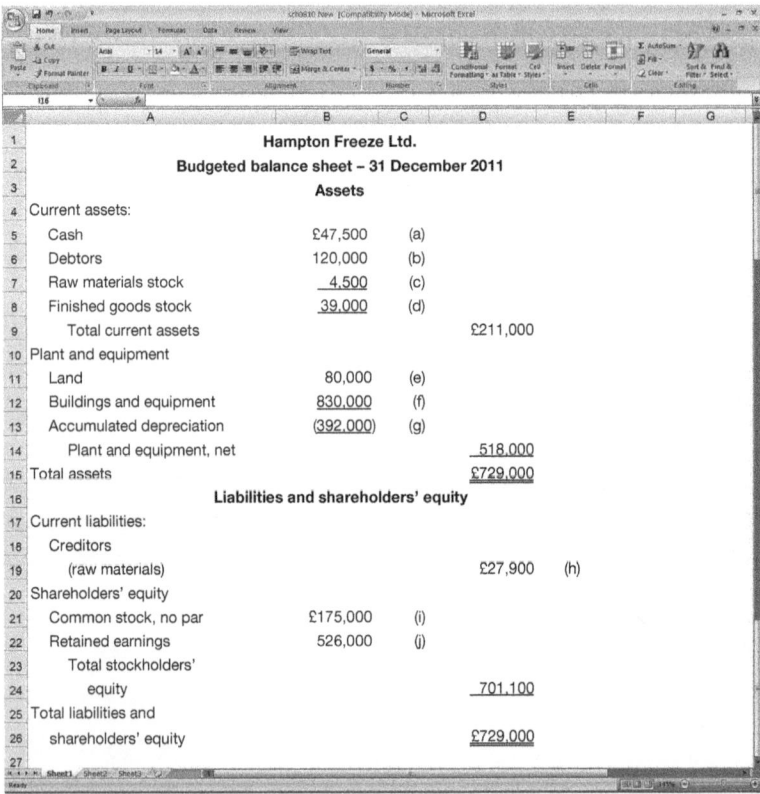

Explanation of 31 December 2011 balance sheet figures:

a   The ending cash balance, as projected by the cash budget in Schedule 8.

b   30% of fourth-quarter sales, from Schedule 1 (£400,000 × 30 per cent = £120,000).

c   From Schedule 3, the ending raw materials stock will be 22,500 kilos. This material costs £0.20 per kilo. Therefore, the ending stock in kilos will be 22,500 kilos × £0.20 = £4,500.

d   From Schedule 6.

e   From the 31 December 2010 balance sheet (no change).

f   The 31 December 2010 balance sheet indicated a balance of £700,000. During 2011, £130,000 additional equipment will be purchased (see Schedule 8), bringing the 31 December 2011 balance to £830,000.

g   The 31 December 2010 balance sheet indicated a balance sheet of £292,000. During 2011, £100,000 of depreciation will be taken (£60,000 on Schedule 5 and £40,000 on Schedule 7), bringing the 31 December 2011 balance to £392,000.

h   One-half of the fourth-quarter raw materials purchases, from Schedule 3.

i   From the 31 December 2010 balance sheet (no change).

j   31 December 2010 balance   £449,000
    Add net profit, from Schedule 9   108,200
                                                    558,100
    Deduct dividends paid, from Schedule 8   32,000
    31 December 2011 balance   £526,100

Exhibit 8.3 Flexible budget profit statement

	Budget formula (per unit)	Sales in units		
		1,900	2,000	2,100
Example company Master budget profit statement				
Sales	£75.00	£142,500	£150,000	£157,500
Less variable expenses:				
Direct materials	12.00	22,800	24,000	25,200
Direct labour	31.00	58,900	62,000	65,100
Variable manufacturing overhead	7.50	14,250	15,000	15,750
Variable selling and administrative	4.00	7,600	8,000	8,400
Total variable expenses	54.50	103,550	109,000	114,450
Contribution margin	£20.50	38,950	41,000	43,050
Less fixed expenses:				
Fixed manufacturing overhead		18,000	18,000	18,000
Fixed selling administrative		9,000	9,000	9,000
Total fixed expenses		27,000	27,000	27,000
Net profit		£11,950	£14,000	£16,050

Some criticisms of budgeting as a performance management system

LO 4

For many, if not most businesses, the budget is a key planning and control mechanism with many desirable characteristics. Yet budgeting has come in for much criticism in recent years. It has been described by Jan Wallander as 'an unnecessary evil' and Jack Welch as the 'bane of corporate America'.[6] Such criticisms of budgeting are easier to appreciate when looked at in the wider context of performance management systems. Furthermore, not only may we consider some organizational problems caused by budgeting but we can see that there are alternative, or at least supplementary, control models suggested by the performance management perspective.

One common criticism is that budgets produce a particular type of **constrained management style**, they concentrate on easy to measure events and they are *too historically based*. The last point is often linked to the view that budgets tend to be *incrementalist*. Particularly in not-for-profit organizations in the public sector, discussions about changes to budgets concentrate on marginal or incremental increases or decreases in particular departmental budgets. The problem with incrementalism is that activities become institutionalized through the budget and there is a reluctance to ask questions about fundamental purposes.

Another criticism is that budgeting makes organizations *inflexible* and *unable to respond to uncertainty*. Budgeting is seen as being *mechanistic* with *rigid, formalized* and *tightly coupled* systems. Budgeting-led

organizations may be slow to recognize changes in the market and also slow to react to changes even when they have been noticed. Other criticisms of budgeting are that it is *too time consuming*, it tends to *focus on cost control* rather than value creation, it tends to be *top down*, it encourages *gaming* and *opportunism*, it reinforces departmental *barriers* and it *hinders knowledge sharing*. Overall it makes *people feel undervalued*.[7]

Much of the criticism of budgeting is driven by a changing business environment, especially the belief that competition in modern markets has increased the importance of *intellectual capital* relative to physical or tangible capital.[8] In order to respond to this new competitive challenge, it is argued that companies need to adopt a *network* rather than a hierarchical, departmental structure. A network model may still use budgets for cash forecasting but not for cost control. The aim is to avoid 'actual versus budget' reports and concentrate on relative performance. These alternative approaches draw on other forms of management control such as benchmarking and the mix of financial and non-financial measures found in approaches such as the balanced scorecard.

Reform or abandon budgeting?

Given the criticisms of budgeting, what is the appropriate response? Currently, there seems to be two main practice-led approaches. One approach is to improving budgeting and the other is to abandon it.[9] If we review the criticisms of budgeting there seems to be two main issues. One issue concerns the question of *predictability*. It could be argued that budgets work well if managers' predictions are reliable because the budget can then represent a viable plan. Conversely, budgets tend to work badly in conditions of great uncertainty and turbulent environments.[10] The other issue concerns *organizational* and *time-frame problems*. It is argued that budgeting fosters a centralizing and stifling atmosphere as well as a possible mismatch between operational strategies and annual reporting cycles. These organizational problems tend to reduce the ability of units and employees to use their initiative as they lack empowerment.

When it is advocated that organizations abandon budgeting, it may mean that budgets are still used for financial purposes but, crucially, not for *performance evaluation*. The aim is to avoid the annual performance trap associated with budgeting by working with what have been called 'relative performance contracts with hindsight'.[11] The significance of the term 'relative' is that performance is benchmarked against *internal* or *external comparators* rather than against historical standards such as last year's results. The term 'with hindsight' means that rather than referring to fixed targets set at the *beginning* of the period, 'targets are adjusted by looking back and incorporating the actual operating and economic circumstances during the period'.[12] Managerial and employee rewards tend to be based on subjective and group criteria with an 'objective to engender a philosophy doing what is best for the firm in the light of current circumstance and to promote teamwork'.[13]

LO 5 Zero-based budgeting

One way to reform budgeting is known as **zero-based budgeting**. Under a zero-based budget, managers are required to justify all budgeted expenditures, not just changes in the budget from the previous year. The baseline is zero rather than last year's budget. A zero-based budget requires considerable documentation. In addition to all the schedules in the usual master budget, the manager must prepare a series of 'decision packages' in which all the activities of the department are ranked according to their relative importance and the cost of each activity is identified. Higher-level managers can then review the decision packages and cut back in those areas that appear to be less critical or whose costs do not appear to be justified.

Under zero-based budgeting, the review is performed every year. Critics of zero-based budgeting charge that properly executed zero-based budgeting is too time consuming and too costly to justify on an annual basis. In addition, it is argued that annual reviews soon become mechanical and that the whole purpose of

Focus on Business Practice

Base budget review

© Mark Evans

Public sector managers have tried to move away from the more traditional incremental approach by introducing priority-led budgeting and base budget review. With priority-led budgeting, budget holders are encouraged to take an investment view, (e.g. spend more now to save later) based on a three year rather than annual perspective. With base budget review, managers do not start with a blank sheet of paper (an extreme view of zero-based budgeting) but are required to take a line-by-line approach and ask 'Do we need that line and do we need that much money?'[14]

Exercise: Consider the impact of employment contracts which seem to make labour costs in the public sector more 'fixed' than in the private sector.

zero-based budgeting is then lost. Whether or not an organization should use an annual review is a matter of judgement. In some situations annual zero-based reviews may be justified; in other situations they may not because of the time and cost involved. However, most managers would at least agree that, on occasion, zero-based reviews can be very helpful.

Summary

- Our purpose has been to present an overview of the budgeting process and to show how the various operating budgets relate to each other.

- We have seen how the sales budget forms the foundation for profit planning. Once the sales budget has been set, the production budget and the selling and administrative budget can be prepared since they depend on how many units are to be sold.

- The production budget determines how many units are to be produced, so after it is prepared, the various manufacturing cost budgets can be prepared. All of these various budgets feed into the cash budget and the budgeted profit and loss account and balance sheet.

- There are many connections between these various parts of the master budget. For example, the schedule of expected cash collections, which is completed in connection with the sales budget, provides data for both the cash budget and the budgeted balance sheet.

- Although budgeting is a very widespread practice, it has come in for some criticism and some suggestions for reform and even calls the abandonment of budgeting as a performance control system.

Key terms

Budget committee A group of key management persons who are responsible for overall policy matters relating to the budget programme and for co-ordinating the preparation of the budget (p. 182).

Cash budget A detailed plan showing how cash resources will be acquired and used over some specific time period (p. 183).

Constrained management style A management approach that concentrates on easy to measure events and lacks flexibility (p. 195).

Continuous or perpetual budget A 12-month budget that rolls forward one month as the current month is completed (p. 180).

Direct labour budget A detailed plan showing labour requirements over some specific time period (p. 186).

Direct materials budget A detailed plan showing the amount of raw materials that must be purchased during a period to meet both production and stock needs (p. 186).

Finished goods stock budget A budget showing the cost expected to appear on the balance sheet for unsold units at the end of a period (p. 189).

Manufacturing overhead budget A detailed plan showing the production costs, other than direct materials and direct labour, that will be incurred over a specified time period (p. 187).

Master budget A summary of a company's plans in which specific targets are set for sales, production, distribution, and financing activities and that generally culminates in a cash budget, budgeted profit and loss account, and budgeted balance sheet (p. 183).

Material requirements planning (MRP) An operations management tool that uses a computer to help manage materials and stocks (p. 186).

Participative budget *See* Self-imposed budget (p. 180).

Production budget A detailed plan showing the number of units that must be produced during a period in order to meet both sales and stock needs (p. 185).

Sales budget A detailed schedule showing the expected sales for coming periods; these sales are typically expressed in both pounds and units (p. 183).

Self-imposed budget A method of preparing budgets in which managers prepare their own budgets. These budgets are then reviewed by the manager's supervisor, and any issues are resolved by mutual agreement (p. 180).

Selling and administrative expense budget A detailed schedule of planned expenses that will be incurred in areas other than manufacturing during a budget period (p. 189).

Zero-based budgeting A method of budgeting in which managers are required to justify all costs as if the programmes involved were being proposed for the first time (p. 196)

Endnotes

1 Bates, Rizvi, Tewari and Vardan (2001).

2 See, e.g., Aldrick (2008).

3 Carruth, McClendon and Ballard (1983).

4 Hope and Hope (1997).

5 Wildavsky (1975).

6 Wildavsky (1975).

7 Neely, Sutcliff and Heyns (2001).

8 Hope and Hope (1997).

9 Hansen, Otley and Van der Stede (2003).

10 Wallander (1999).

11 Hansen *et al.* (2003), p. 101.

12 Hansen *et al.* (2003), p. 101.

13 Hansen *et al.* (2003), p. 102.

14 Seal and Ball (2008).

When you have read this chapter, log on to the Online Learning Centre for *Management Accounting for Business Decisions* at **www.mcgraw-hill.co.uk/ textbooks/seal**, where you'll find multiple choice questions, practice exams and extra study tools for management accounting.

Assessment

Questions

connect™

8–1   What is a budget? What is budgetary control?

8–2   Discuss some of the major benefits to be gained from budgeting.

8–3   What is a master budget? Briefly describe its contents.

8–4   Why is the sales forecast the starting point in budgeting?

8–5   Describe the flow of budget data in an organization. Who are the participants in the budgeting process, and how do they participate?

8–6   What is a self-imposed/participatory budget? What are the major advantages of self-imposed budgets? What caution must be exercised in their use?

8–7   How can budgeting assist a firm in its employment policies?

8–8   'The principal purpose of the cash budget is to see how much cash the company will have in the bank at the end of the year.' Do you agree? Explain.

8–9   How does zero-based budgeting differ from traditional budgeting?

Exercises

connect™

E8–1 ⏱ Time allowed: 20 minutes

Silver Company makes a product that has peak sales in May of each year. These peak sales are shown in the company's sales budget for the second quarter given below:

	April	May	June	Total
Budgeted sales	£300,000	£500,000	£200,000	£1,000,000

From past experience, the company has learned that 20% of a month's sales are collected in the month of sale, that another 70% is collected in the month following sale, and that the remaining 10% is collected in the second month following sale. Bad debts are negligible and can be ignored. February sales totalled £230,000 and March sales totalled £260,000.

Required

1   Prepare a schedule of expected cash collections from sales, by month and in total, for the second quarter.

2   Assume that the company will prepare a budgeted balance sheet as of 30 June. Compute the debtors as of that date.

E8–2 ⏱ Time allowed: 10 minutes

Down Under Products Ltd of Australia has budgeted sales of its popular boomerang for the next four months as follows:

	Sales in units
April	50,000
May	75,000
June	90,000
July	80,000

The company is now in the process of preparing a production budget for the second quarter. Past experience has shown that end-of-month stock levels must equal 10% of the following month's sales. The stock at the end of March was 5,000 units.

Required
Prepare a production budget for the second quarter. In your budget, show the number of units to be produced each month and for the quarter in total.

E8–3   Time allowed: 15 minutes
Three grams of musk oil are required for each bottle of Mink Caress, a very popular perfume made by a small company in western Siberia. The cost of the musk oil is 150 roubles per gram. (Siberia is located in Russia, whose currency is the rouble.) Budgeted production of Mink Caress is given below by quarters for Year 2 and for the first quarter of Year 3.

| | Year 2 quarter | | | | Year 3 quarter |
	First	Second	Third	Fourth	First
Budgeted production, in bottles	60,000	90,000	150,000	100,000	70,000

Musk oil has become so popular as a perfume base that it has become necessary to carry large inventories as a precaution against stock-outs. For this reason, the stock of musk oil at the end of a quarter must be equal to 20% of the following quarter's production needs. Some 36,000 grams of musk oil will be on hand to start the first quarter of Year 2.

Required
Prepare a materials purchases budget for musk oil, by quarter and in total, for Year 2. At the bottom of your budget, show the amount of purchases in roubles for each quarter and for the year in total.

E8–4   Time allowed: 25 minutes
You have been asked to prepare a December cash budget for Ashton Company, a distributor of exercise equipment. The following information is available about the company's operations:
1   The cash balance on 1 December will be £40,000.
2   Actual sales for October and November and expected sales for December are as follows:

	October	November	December
Cash sales	£65,000	£70,000	£83,000
Sales on account	400,000	525,000	600,000

Sales on account are collected over a three-month period in the following ratio: 20% collected in the month of sale, 60% collected in the month following sale, and 18% collected in the second month following sale. The remaining 2% is uncollectable.

3   Purchases of stock will total £280,000 for December and 30% of a month's stock purchases are paid during the month of purchase. The accounts payable remaining from November's stock purchases total £161,000, all of which will be paid in December.
4   Selling and administrative expenses are budgeted at £420,000 for December. Of this amount, £50,000 is for depreciation.
5   A new web server for the Marketing Department costing £76,000 will be purchased for cash during December, and dividends totalling £9,000 will be paid during the month.
6   The company must maintain a minimum cash balance of £20,000. An open line of credit is available from the company's bank to bolster the cash position as needed.

Required
1   Prepare a schedule of expected cash collections for December.
2   Prepare a schedule of expected cash disbursements during December to suppliers for materials for stock purchases.
3   Prepare a cash budget for December. Indicate in the financing section any borrowing that will be needed during the month.

Problems

connect

P8–5 Production and purchases budgets

🕐 Time allowed: 40 minutes

Pearl Products Limited of Shenzhen, China, manufactures and distributes toys throughout South East Asia. Three cubic centimetres (cc) of solvent H300 are required to manufacture each unit of Supermix, one of the company's products. The company is now planning raw materials needs for the third quarter, the quarter in which peak sales of Supermix occur. To keep production and sales moving smoothly, the company has the following stock requirements:

1   The finished goods stock on hand at the end of each month must be equal to 3,000 units of Supermix plus 20% of the next month's sales. The finished goods stock on 30 June is budgeted to be 10,000 units.
2   The raw materials stock on hand at the end of each month must be equal to one-half of the following month's production needs for raw materials. The raw materials stock on 30 June is budgeted to be 54,000 cc of solvent H300.
3   The company maintains no work in progress stocks.

A sales budget for Supermix for the last six months of the year follows.

	Budgeted sales in units
July	35,000
August	40,000
September	50,000
October	30,000
November	20,000
December	10,000

Required

1   Prepare a production budget for Supermix for the months July–October.
2   Examine the production budget that you prepared in Question 1 above. Why will the company produce more units than it sells in July and August, and fewer units than it sells in September and October?
3   Prepare a budget showing the quantity of solvent H300 to be purchased for July, August and September, and for the quarter in total.

P8–6 Evaluating a company's budget procedures

⏱ Time allowed: 30 minutes

Springfield Corporation operates on a calendar-year basis. It begins the annual budgeting process in late August, when the managing director establishes targets for the total pound sales and net income before taxes for the next year.

The sales target is given to the Marketing Department, where the marketing manager formulates a sales budget by product line in both units and pounds. From this budget, sales quotas by product line in units and pounds are established for each of the corporation's sales districts.

The marketing manager also estimates the cost of the marketing activities required to support the target sales volume and prepares a tentative marketing expense budget.

The operations manager uses the sales and profit targets, the sales budget by product line, and the tentative marketing expense budget to determine the pound amounts that can be devoted to manufacturing and corporate office expense. The operations manager prepares the budget for corporate expenses, and then forwards to the Production Department the product-line sales budget in units and the total pound amount that can be devoted to manufacturing.

The production manager meets with the factory managers to develop a manufacturing plan that will produce the required units when needed within the cost constraints set by the operations manager. The budgeting process usually comes to a halt at this point because the Production Department does not consider the financial resources allocated to be adequate.

When this standstill occurs, the director of finance, the operations manager, the marketing manager and the production manager meet to determine the final budgets for each of the areas. This normally results in a modest increase in the total amount available for manufacturing costs, while the marketing expense and corporate office expense budgets are cut. The total sales and profit figures proposed by the managing director are seldom changed. Although the participants are seldom pleased with the compromise, these budgets are final. Each executive then develops a new detailed budget for the operations in his or her area.

None of the areas has achieved its budget in recent years. Sales often run below the target. When budgeted sales are not achieved, each area is expected to cut costs so that the managing director's profit target can still be met. However, the profit target is seldom met because costs are not cut enough. In fact, costs often run above the original budget in all functional areas. The managing director is disturbed that Springfield has not been able to meet the sales and profit targets. He hired a consultant with considerable experience with companies in Springfield's industry. The consultant reviewed the budgets

for the past four years. He concluded that the product-line sales budgets were reasonable and that the cost and expense budgets were adequate for the budgeted sales and production levels.

Required

1 Discuss how the budgeting process as employed by Springfield Corporation contributes to the failure to achieve the managing director's sales and profit targets.
2 Suggest how Springfield Corporation's budgeting process could be revised to correct the problem.
3 Should the functional areas be expected to cut their costs when sales volume falls below budget? Explain your answer.

(CMA, adapted)

Chapter 9
Standard costing and variance analysis

 Learning **objectives**

After studying Chapter 9, you should be able to:
1   Explain how direct materials standards and direct labour standards are set
2   Compute the direct materials price and quantity variances and explain their significance
3   Compute the direct labour rate and efficiency variances and explain their significance
4   Compute the variable manufacturing overhead spending and efficiency variances
5   Understand the advantages of and the potential problems with using standard costs

Concepts **in Context**

Natuzzi SpA, founded and run by Pasquale Natuzzi, produces handmade leather furniture for the world market in Santeramo in Colle in southern Italy. Natuzzi is export-oriented and has, for example, about 7% of the US leather furniture market. The company's furniture is handmade by craftsmen, each of whom has a computer terminal that is linked to a sophisticated computer network. The computer terminal provides precise instructions on how to accomplish a particular task in making a piece of furniture. And the computer keeps track of how quickly the craftsman completes the task. If the craftsman beats the standard time to complete the task, the computer adds a bonus to the craftsman's pay.

Reproduced with permission from Natuzzi SpA

The company's computers know exactly how much thread, screws, foam, leather, labour, and so on, is required for every model. 'Should the price of Argentinian hides or German dyes rise one day, employees in Santeramo enter the new prices into the computer, and the costs for all sofas with that leather and those colours are immediately recalculated. "Everything has to be clear for me," says Natuzzi. "Why this penny? Where is it going?" '

How do managers control the prices that are paid for inputs and the quantities that are used? They could examine every transaction in detail, but this obviously would be an inefficient use of management time. For many companies, the answer to this control problem lies at least partially in standard costs[2] which are part of an approach to management known as management by exception.

A *standard* is a *benchmark* or '*norm*' for measuring performance. Standards are found everywhere. Your doctor evaluates your weight using standards that have been set for individuals of your age, height and gender. The food we eat in restaurants must be prepared under specified standards of cleanliness. The buildings we live in must conform to standards set in building codes. Standards are also used widely in management accounting where they relate to the *quantity* and *cost* of inputs used in manufacturing goods or providing services.

Standard costs – management by exception

Managers – often assisted by engineers and accountants – set quantity and cost standards for each major input such as raw materials and labour time. *Quantity standards* indicate how much of an input should be used in manufacturing a unit of product or in providing a unit of service. *Cost (price) standards* indicate what the cost, or purchase price, of the input should be. Actual quantities and actual costs of inputs are compared to these standards. If either the quantity or the cost of inputs departs significantly from the standards, managers investigate the discrepancy. The purpose is to find the cause of the problem and then eliminate it so that it does not recur. This process is called **management by exception**.

In our daily lives, we operate in a management by exception mode most of the time. Consider what happens when you sit down in the driver's seat of your car. You put the key in the ignition, you turn the key, and your car starts. Your expectation (standard) that the car will start is met; you do not have to open the car bonnet and check the battery, the connecting cables, the fuel lines and so on. If you turn the key and the car does not start, then you have a discrepancy (variance). Your expectations are not met, and you need to investigate why. Note that even if the car starts after a second try, it would be wise to investigate anyway. The fact that the expectation was not met should be viewed as an opportunity to uncover the cause of the problem rather than as simply an annoyance. If the underlying cause is not discovered and corrected, the problem may recur and become much worse.

Who uses standard costs?

Manufacturing, service, food, and not-for-profit organizations all make use of standards to some extent; car service centres, for example, often set specific labour time standards for the completion of certain work tasks, such as installing a carburettor or doing a valve job, and then measure actual performance against these standards. Fastfood outlets such as McDonald's have exacting standards as to the quantity of meat going into a sandwich, as well as standards for the cost of the meat. In short, you are likely to run into standard costs in virtually any line of business that you enter.

Manufacturing companies often have highly developed standard costing systems in which standards relating to materials, labour and overhead are developed in detail for each separate product. These standards are listed on a **standard cost card** that provides the manager with a great deal of information concerning the inputs that are required to produce a unit and their costs. In the following section, we provide a detailed example of the setting of standard costs and the preparation of a standard cost card.

Setting standard costs

Setting price and quantity standards is more an art than a science. It requires the combined expertise of all persons who have responsibility over input prices and over the effective use of inputs. In a manufacturing setting, this might include accountants, purchasing managers, engineers, production supervisors, line managers and production workers. Past records of purchase prices and of input usage can be helpful in setting standards. However, the standards should be designed to encourage efficient *future* operations, not a repetition of past inefficient operations.

Focus on Business Practice
Setting standards for machine running speeds

© James Grimes

Corrugated containers, more commonly known as cardboard boxes, are a relatively standardized product in terms of material content and manufacturing process. The appearance (or print) on boxes varies considerably according to customers' requirements however. The raw materials consist of heavy papers, one or two of which is corrugated (wavy) providing strength. This material, termed corrugated board, is produced in a highly automated process resulting in large flat sheets. These sheets, in turn, are cut to shape and size, and printed on according to customer orders.

A typical corrugated manufacturing plant will have one machine called a corrugator which makes the sheets of corrugated board, and four to six conversion machines which cut and print the board. For costing and production scheduling purposes, each machine is assigned a standard running speed(s). The standard running speeds are input into costing and scheduling software and updated regularly. How are these standards set and updated? When a new machine is installed at a corrugated plant, the manufacturers provide a maximum running speed (the ideal standard) and also an achievable speed (the practical standard) based on their prior installation experience. As the machine operates, data on running speed can be recorded – automatically usually – as most machines provide interfaces to production scheduling software. This actual data can be used to check against the initial standard speeds and updated if required. Some costing and scheduling software gets even smarter (e.g. Kiwiplan, www.kiwiplan.com), by using a rolling-average running speed based on a products manufacturing history. It may also be possible to have multiple standard running speeds on a machine, for example where a particularly complex customer graphic slows down the printing on a box.

Exercise: Having read the piece above, what role do you think machine operators can play in setting standard running speeds and keeping them updated?

Ideal versus practical standards

Should standards be attainable all of the time, should they be attainable only part of the time, or should they be so tight that they become, in effect, 'the impossible dream'? Opinions among managers vary, but standards tend to fall into one of two categories – either ideal or practical.

Ideal standards are those that can be attained only under the best circumstances. They allow for no machine breakdowns or other work interruptions, and they call for a level of effort that can be attained only by the most skilled and efficient employees working at peak effort 100% of the time. Some managers feel that such standards have a motivational value. These managers argue that even though employees know they will

rarely meet the standard, it is a constant reminder of the need for ever-increasing efficiency and effort. Few firms use ideal standards. Most managers feel that ideal standards tend to discourage even the most diligent workers. Moreover, when ideal standards are used, variances from the standards have little meaning. Because of these ideal standards, large variances are normal and it is difficult to 'manage by exception'.

Practical standards are defined as standards that are 'tight but attainable'. They allow for normal machine downtime and employee rest periods, and they can be attained through reasonable, though highly efficient, efforts by the average worker. Variances from such a standard are very useful to management in that they represent deviations that fall outside of normal operating conditions and signal a need for management attention. Furthermore, practical standards can serve multiple purposes. In addition to signalling abnormal conditions, they can also be used in forecasting cash flows and in planning stocks. By contrast, ideal standards cannot be used in forecasting and planning; they do not allow for normal inefficiencies, and therefore they result in unrealistic planning and forecasting figures.

Throughout the remainder of this chapter, we will assume the use of practical rather than ideal standards.

Setting direct materials standards

To illustrate the development of a standard costing system, consider the example of the Colonial Pewter Company that was organized a year ago. The company's only product at present is a reproduction of an eighteenth-century pewter bookend. The bookend is largely made by hand, using traditional metal-working tools. Consequently, the manufacturing process is labour intensive and requires a high level of skill.

The first task was to prepare price and quantity standards for the company's only significant raw material, pewter ingots. The **standard price per unit** for direct materials should reflect the final, delivered cost of the materials, net of any discounts taken. The company prepared the following documentation for the standard price of a kilo of pewter in ingot form:

Purchase price, top-grade pewter ingots, in 40-kilo ingots	£3.60
Freight, by truck, from the suppliers	0.44
Receiving and handling	0.05
Less purchase discount	(0.09)
Standard price per kilo	£4.00

Notice that the *standard price* reflects a particular grade of material (top grade), purchased in particular lot sizes (40-kilo ingots), and delivered by a particular type of carrier (truck). Allowances have also been made for handling and discounts. If everything proceeds according to these expectations, the net standard price of a kilo of pewter should therefore be £4.00.

The **standard quantity per unit** for direct materials should reflect the amount of material going into each unit of finished product, as well as an allowance for unavoidable waste, spoilage and other normal inefficiencies. The company prepared the following documentation for the standard quantity of pewter going into a pair of bookends:

Material requirements as specified in the bill of materials for a pair of bookends, in kilos	2.7
Allowance for waste and spoilage, in kilos	0.2
Allowance for rejects, in kilos	0.1
Standard quantity per pair of bookends, in kilos	3.0

A **bill of materials** is a list that shows the type and quantity of each item of material going into a unit of finished product. It is a handy source for determining the basic material input per unit, but it should be adjusted for waste and other factors, as shown above, when determining the standard quantity per unit of product. 'Waste and spoilage' in the table above refers to materials that are wasted as a normal part of the production process or that spoil before they are used. 'Rejects' refers to the direct material contained in units that are defective and must be scrapped.

Once the price and quantity standards have been set, the standard cost of material per unit of finished product can be computed as follows:

3.0 kilos per unit × £4.00 per kilo = £12 per unit

This £12 cost figure will appear as one item on the standard cost card of the product.

Setting direct labour standards

Direct labour price and quantity standards are usually expressed in terms of a labour rate and labour-hours. The **standard rate per hour** for direct labour would include not only wages earned but also fringe benefits and other labour costs. Using last month's wage records, the company determined the standard rate per hour at the Colonial Pewter Company as follows:

Basic wage rate per hour	£10
Employment taxes at 10% of the basic rate	1
Fringe benefits at 30% of the basic rate	3
Standard rate per direct labour-hour	£14

Many companies prepare a single standard rate for all employees in a department. This standard rate reflects the expected 'mix' of workers, even though the actual wage rates may vary somewhat from individual to individual due to differing skills or seniority. A single standard rate simplifies the use of standard costs and also permits the manager to monitor the use of employees within departments. According to the standard computed above, the direct labour rate for Colonial Pewter should average £14 per hour.

The standard direct labour time required to complete a unit of product (generally called the **standard hours per unit**) is perhaps the single most difficult standard to determine. One approach is to divide each operation performed on the product into elemental body movements (such as reaching, pushing, and turning over). Published tables of standard times for such movements are available. These times can be applied to the movements and then added together to determine the total standard time allowed per operation. Another approach is for an industrial engineer to do a time and motion study, actually clocking the time required for certain tasks. As stated earlier, the standard time should include allowances for coffee breaks, personal needs of employees, cleanup, and machine downtime. After consulting with the production managers, the company prepared the following documentation for the standard hours per unit:

Basic labour time per unit, in hours	1.9
Allowance for breaks and personal needs	0.1
Allowance for cleanup and machine downtime	0.3
Allowance for rejects	0.2
Standard labour-hours per unit of product	2.5

Once the rate and time standards have been set, the standard labour cost per unit of product can be computed as follows:

2.5 hours per unit × £14 per hour = £35 per unit

This £35 cost figure appears along with direct materials as one item on the standard cost card of the product.

Setting variable manufacturing overhead standards

As with direct labour, the price and quantity standards for variable manufacturing overhead are generally expressed in terms of rate and hours. The rate represents *the variable portion of the predetermined overhead rate* discussed in Chapter 5; the hours represent whatever hours base is used to apply overhead to units of product (usually machine-hours or direct labour-hours). At Colonial Pewter, the variable portion of the

Exhibit 9.1 Standard cost card – variable production cost

Input	(1) Standard quantity or hours	(2) Standard price or rate	(3) Standard cost (1) × (2)
Direct materials	3.0 kilos	£4.00	£12.00
Direct labour	2.5 hours	14.00	35.00
Variable manufacturing overhead	2.5 hours	3.00	7.50
Total standard cost per unit			£54.50

predetermined overhead rate is £3 per direct labour-hour. Therefore, the standard variable manufacturing overhead cost per unit is computed as follows:

2.5 hours per unit × £3 per hour = £7.50 per unit

This £7.50 cost figure appears along with direct materials and direct labour as one item on the standard cost card in Exhibit 9.1. Observe that the **standard cost per unit** is computed by multiplying the standard quantity or hours by the standard price or rate.

Are standards the same as budgets?

Standards and *budgets* are very similar. The major distinction between the two terms is that a standard is a *unit* amount, whereas a budget is a *total* amount. The standard cost for materials at Colonial Pewter is £12 per pair of bookends. If 1,000 pairs of bookends are to be manufactured during a budgeting period, then the budgeted cost of materials would be £12,000. In effect, *a standard can be viewed as the budgeted cost for one unit of product.*

Focus on Business Practice

Cost controlling in restaurants

© stockstudioX

VIRBUS is a European Union funded initiative which offers an online learning, help and business management platform to the hospitality sector. One of the items to be found on their website is some useful advice to restaurateurs on controlling costs. One basic piece of advice offered is to use standard recipes as the basis of a menu, which in turn can be used to control costs and set prices. By using standard quantities/recipes for each item on a menu, kitchen staff can monitor usage of ingredients and record wastage. Apart from ingredients, labour is another major cost in restaurants. Here, VIRBUS recommends a median or average (i.e. standard) labour cost can be calculated and used for costing and pricing purposes. This labour cost can be increased to reflect additional payroll items such as overtime or social insurance. The labour cost can be combined with the hours worked by kitchen and waiting staff to determine a total labour cost per week or month if required.[3]

Exercise: Do you think a restaurant owner can ensure that standard recipes and ingredients are *always* used? Try to think of examples when this would not occur and the effects on cost.

A general model for variance analysis

An important reason for separating standards into two categories – price and quantity – is that different managers are usually responsible for buying and for using inputs and these two activities occur at different points in time. In the case of raw materials, for example, the purchasing manager is responsible for the price, and this responsibility is exercised at the time of purchase. In contrast, the production manager is responsible for the amount of the raw material used, and this responsibility is exercised when the materials are used in production, which may be many weeks or months after the purchase date. It is important, therefore, that we cleanly separate discrepancies due to deviations from price standards from those due to deviations from quantity standards. Differences between *standard* prices and *actual* prices and *standard* quantities and *actual* quantities are called **variances**. The act of computing and interpreting variances is called *variance analysis*.

Price and quantity variances

A general model for computing standard cost variances for variable costs is presented in Exhibit 9.2. This model isolates price variances from quantity variances and shows how each of these is computed. We will be using this model throughout the chapter to compute variances in direct materials, direct labour and variable manufacturing overhead.

Three things should be noted from Exhibit 9.2. First, note that a price variance and a quantity variance can be computed for all three variable cost elements – direct materials, direct labour and variable manufacturing overhead – even though the variance is not called by the same name in all cases. For example, a price variance is called a *materials price variance* in the case of direct materials but a *labour rate variance* in the case of direct labour and an *overhead spending variance* in the case of variable manufacturing overhead.

Second, note that even though a price variance may be called by different names, it is computed in exactly the same way regardless of whether one is dealing with direct materials, direct labour or variable manufacturing overhead. The same is true with the quantity variance.

Third, note that *variance analysis* is actually a type of input–output analysis. The inputs represent the actual quantity of direct materials, direct labour and variable manufacturing overhead used; the output represents the good production of the period, expressed in terms of the *standard quantity (or the standard hours) allowed for the actual output* (see column 3 in Exhibit 9.2). By **standard quantity allowed** or

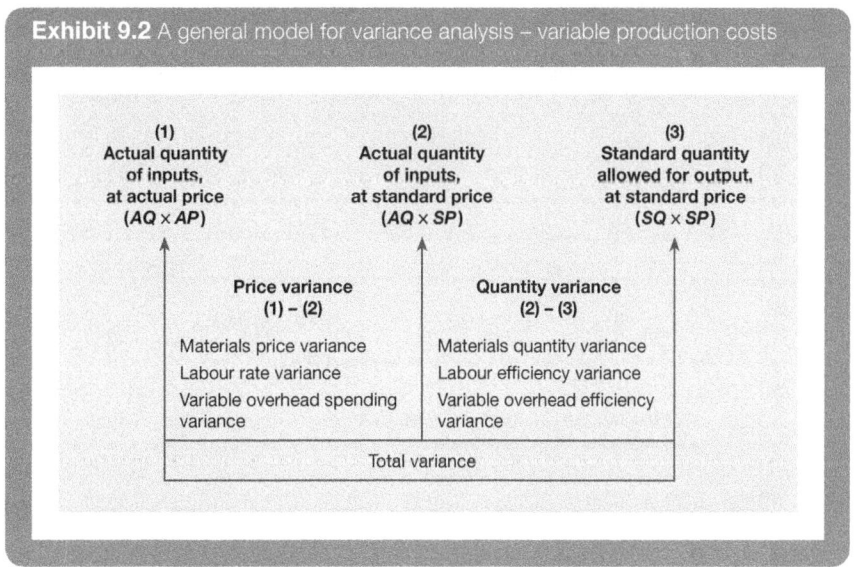

Exhibit 9.2 A general model for variance analysis – variable production costs

standard hours allowed, we mean the amount of direct materials, direct labour or variable manufacturing overhead *that should have been used to* produce the actual output of the period. This could be more or could be less materials, labour or overhead than was *actually* used, depending on the efficiency or inefficiency of operations. The standard quantity allowed is computed by multiplying the actual output in units by the standard input allowed per unit.

With this general model as a foundation, we will now examine the price and quantity variances in more detail.

LO 2 Using standard costs – direct materials variances

After determining standard costs for direct materials, direct labour, and variable manufacturing overhead, Colonial Pewter Company's next step was to compute the company's variances for June, the most recent month. As discussed in the preceding section, variances are computed by comparing standard costs to actual costs. To facilitate this comparison, the company referred to the standard cost data contained in Exhibit 9.1. This exhibit shows that the standard cost of direct materials per unit of product is as follows:

3.0 kilos per unit × £4.00 per kilo = £12 per unit

Colonial Pewter's purchasing records for June showed that 6,500 kilos of pewter were purchased at a cost of £3.80 per kilo. This cost figure included freight and handling and was net of the quantity discount. All of the material purchased was used during June to manufacture 2,000 pairs of pewter bookends. Using these data and the standard costs from Exhibit 9.1, the company computed the price and quantity variances shown in Exhibit 9.3.

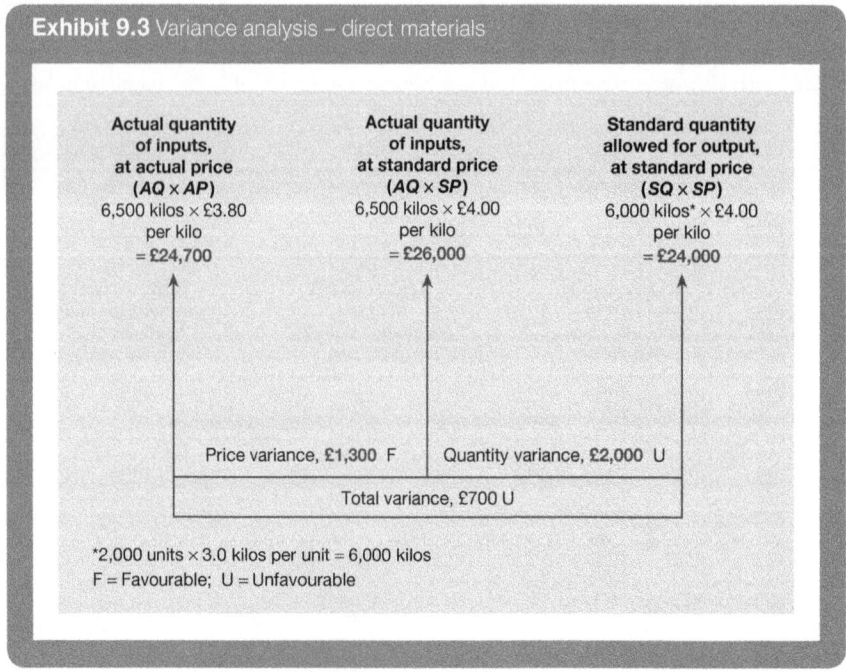

Exhibit 9.3 Variance analysis – direct materials

The three arrows in Exhibit 9.3 point to three different total cost figures. The first, £24,700, refers to the actual total cost of the pewter that was purchased during June. The second, £26,000, refers to what the pewter would have cost if it had been purchased at the standard price of £4.00 a kilo rather than the actual price of £3.80 a kilo. The difference between these two figures, £1,300 (£26,000 − £24,700), is the price variance. It exists because the actual purchase price was £0.20 per kilo less than the standard purchase price. Since 6,500 kilos were purchased, the total amount of the variance is £1,300 (£0.20 per kilo × 6,500 kilos). This variance is labelled favourable (denoted by F), since the actual purchase price was less than the standard purchase price. A price variance is labelled unfavourable (denoted by U) if the actual price exceeds the standard price.

The third arrow in Exhibit 9.3 points to £24,000 – the cost that the pewter would have been had it been purchased at the standard price and only the amount allowed by the standard quantity had been used. The standards call for 3 kilos of pewter per unit. Since 2,000 units were produced, 6,000 kilos of pewter should have been used. This is referred to as the standard quantity allowed for the output. If this 6,000 kilos of pewter had been purchased at the standard price of £4.00 per kilo, the company would have spent £24,000. The difference between this figure, £24,000, and the figure at the end of the middle arrow in Exhibit 9.3, £26,000, is the quantity variance of £2,000.

To understand this quantity variance, note that the actual amount of pewter used in production was 6,500 kilos. However, the standard amount of pewter allowed for the actual output is only 6,000 kilos. Therefore, a total of 500 kilos too much pewter was used to produce the actual output. To express this in monetary terms, the 500 kilos is multiplied by the standard price of £4.00 per kilo to yield the quantity variance of £2,000. Why is the standard price, rather than the actual price, of the pewter used in this calculation? The production manager is ordinarily responsible for the quantity variance. If the actual price were used in the calculation of the quantity variance, the production manager would be held responsible for the efficiency or inefficiency of the purchasing manager. Apart from being unfair, fruitless arguments between the production manager and purchasing manager would occur every time the actual price of an input is above its standard price. To avoid these arguments, the standard price is used when computing the quantity variance.

The quantity variance in Exhibit 9.3 is labelled unfavourable (denoted by U). This is because more pewter was used to produce the actual output than is called for by the standard. A quantity variance is labelled unfavourable if the actual quantity exceeds the standard quantity and is labelled favourable if the actual quantity is less than the standard quantity.

The computations in Exhibit 9.3 reflect the fact that all of the material purchased during June was also used during June. How are the variances computed if a different amount of material is purchased than is used? To illustrate, assume that during June the company purchased 6,500 kilos of materials, as before, but that it used only 5,000 kilos of material during the month and produced only 1,600 units. In this case, the price variance and quantity variance would be as shown in Exhibit 9.4.

Most firms compute the materials price variance, for example, when materials *are purchased* rather than when the materials are placed into production. This permits earlier isolation of the variance, since materials may remain in storage for many months before being used in production. Isolating the price variance when materials are purchased also permits the company to carry its raw materials in the stock accounts at standard cost. This greatly simplifies assigning raw materials costs to work in progress when raw materials are later placed into production.

Note from the exhibit that the price variance is computed on the entire amount of material purchased (6,500 kilos), as before, whereas the quantity variance is computed only on the portion of this material used in production during the month (5,000 kilos). A quantity variance on the 1,500 kilos of material that was purchased during the month but not used in production (6,500 kilos purchased − 5,000 kilos used = 1,500 kilos unused) will be computed in a future period when these materials are drawn out of stocks and used in production. The situation illustrated in Exhibit 9.4 is common for companies that purchase materials well in advance of use and store the materials in warehouses while awaiting the production process.

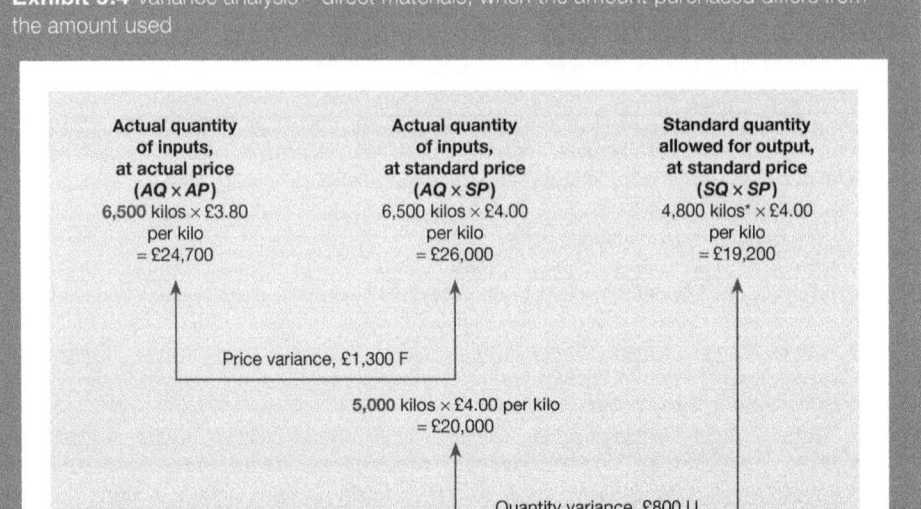

Exhibit 9.4 Variance analysis – direct materials, when the amount purchased differs from the amount used

| Actual quantity of inputs, at actual price ($AQ \times AP$) 6,500 kilos × £3.80 per kilo = £24,700 | Actual quantity of inputs, at standard price ($AQ \times SP$) 6,500 kilos × £4.00 per kilo = £26,000 | Standard quantity allowed for output, at standard price ($SQ \times SP$) 4,800 kilos* × £4.00 per kilo = £19,200 |

Price variance, £1,300 F

5,000 kilos × £4.00 per kilo = £20,000

Quantity variance, £800 U

A total variance cannot be completed in this situation, since the amount of materials purchased (6,500 kilos) differs from the amount used in production (5,000 kilos)

*1,600 units × 3.0 kilos per unit = 4,800 kilos

Materials price variance – a closer look

A **materials price variance** measures the difference between what is paid for a given quantity of materials and what should have been paid according to the standard that has been set. From Exhibit 9.3, this difference can be expressed by the following formula:

$$\text{Materials price variance} = (AQ \times AP) - (AQ \times SP)$$

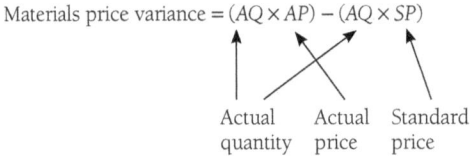

Actual   Actual   Standard
quantity   price   price

The formula can be factored into simpler form as follows:

$$\text{Materials price variance} = AQ(AP - SP)$$

Some managers prefer this simpler formula, since it permits variance computations to be made very quickly. Using the data from Exhibit 9.3 in this formula, we have the following:

$$6,500 \text{ kilos} (£3.80 \text{ per kilo} - £4.00 \text{ per kilo}) = £1,300 \text{ F}$$

Notice that the answer is the same as that yielded in Exhibit 9.3. If the company wanted to put these data into a performance report, the data might appear as follows:

	Colonial Pewter Company					
	Performance report – purchasing department					
Item purchased	(1) Quantity purchased	(2) Actual price	(3) Standard price	(4) Difference in price (2) – (3)	(5) Total price variance (1) × (4)	Explanation
Pewter	6,500 kilos	£3.80	£4.00	£0.20	£1,300 F	Bargained for an especially favourable price

F = Favourable; U = Unfavourable.

Isolation of variances

At what point should variances be isolated and brought to the attention of management? The answer is, the earlier the better. The sooner deviations from standard are brought to the attention of management, the sooner problems can be evaluated and corrected.

Once a performance report has been prepared, what does management do with the price variance data? The most significant variances should be viewed as 'red flags', calling attention to the fact that an exception has occurred that will require some explanation and perhaps follow-up effort. Normally, the performance report itself will contain some explanation of the reason for the variance, as shown above. In the case of Colonial Pewter Company, the purchasing manager said that the favourable price variance resulted from bargaining for an especially favourable price.

Responsibility for the variance

Who is responsible for the materials price variance? Generally speaking, the purchasing manager has control over the price paid for goods and is therefore responsible for any price variances. Many factors influence the prices paid for goods, including how many units are ordered in a lot, how the order is delivered, whether the order is a rush order, and the quality of materials purchased. A deviation in any of these factors from what was assumed when the standards were set can result in a price variance. For example, purchase of second grade materials rather than top-grade materials may result in a favourable price variance, since the lower-grade materials would generally be less costly (but perhaps less suitable for production).

There may be times, however, when someone other than the purchasing manager is responsible for a materials price variance. Production may be scheduled in such a way, for example, that the purchasing manager must request delivery by airfreight, rather than by truck. In these cases, the production manager would bear responsibility for the resulting price variances.

A word of caution is in order. Variance analysis should not be used as an excuse to conduct witch hunts or as a means of beating line managers and workers over the head. The emphasis must be on the control function in the sense of *supporting* the line managers and *assisting* them in meeting the goals that they have participated in setting for the company. In short, the emphasis should be positive rather than negative. Excessive dwelling on what has already happened, particularly in terms of trying to find someone to blame, can be destructive to the functioning of an organization.

Materials quantity variance – a closer look

The **materials quantity variance** measures the difference between the quantity of materials used in production and the quantity that should have been used according to the standard that has been set. Although the

variance is concerned with the physical usage of materials, it is generally stated in monetary terms, as shown in Exhibit 9.3. The formula for the materials quantity variance is as follows:

Materials price variance $= (AQ \times SP) - (SQ \times SP)$

Actual quantity   Standard price   Standard quantity allowed for output

Again, the formula can be factored into simpler terms:

Materials price variance $= SP(AQ - SQ)$

Using the data from Exhibit 9.3 in the formula, we have the following:

£4.00 per kilo (6,500 kilos − 6,000 kilos*) = £2,000 U
*2,000 units × 3.0 kilos per unit = 6,000 kilos.

The answer, of course, is the same as that yielded in Exhibit 9.3. The data might appear as follows if a formal performance report were prepared:

Colonial Pewter Company
Performance report – production department

Type of materials	(1) Standard price	(2) Actual quantity	(3) Standard quantity allowed	(4) Difference in quantity (2) − (3)	(5) Total price variance (1) × (4)	Explanation
Pewter	£4.00	6,500 kilos	6,000 kilos	500 kilos	£2,000 U	Second-grade materials unsuitable for production

F = Favourable; U = Unfavourable.

The materials quantity variance is best isolated at the time that materials are placed into production. Materials are drawn for the number of units to be produced, according to the standard bill of materials for each unit. Any additional materials are usually drawn with an excess materials requisition slip, which is different in colour from the normal requisition slips. This procedure calls attention to the excessive usage of materials *while production is still in process* and provides an opportunity for early control of any developing problem.

Excessive usage of materials can result from many factors, including faulty machines, inferior quality of materials, untrained workers and poor supervision. Generally speaking, it is the responsibility of the production department to see that material usage is kept in line with standards. There may be times, however, when the purchasing department may be responsible for an unfavourable materials quantity variance. If the purchasing department obtains inferior quality materials in an effort to economize on price, the materials may be unsuitable for use and may result in excessive waste. Thus, purchasing rather than production would be responsible for the quantity variance. At Colonial Pewter, the production manager said that second-grade materials were the cause of the unfavourable materials quantity variance for June.

LO 3 Using standard costs – direct labour variances

The next step in determining Colonial Pewter's variances for June was to compute the direct labour variances for the month. Recall from Exhibit 9.1 that the standard direct labour cost per unit of product is £35, computed as follows:

2.5 hours per unit × £14.00 per hour = £35 per unit

Exhibit 9.5 Variance analysis – direct labour

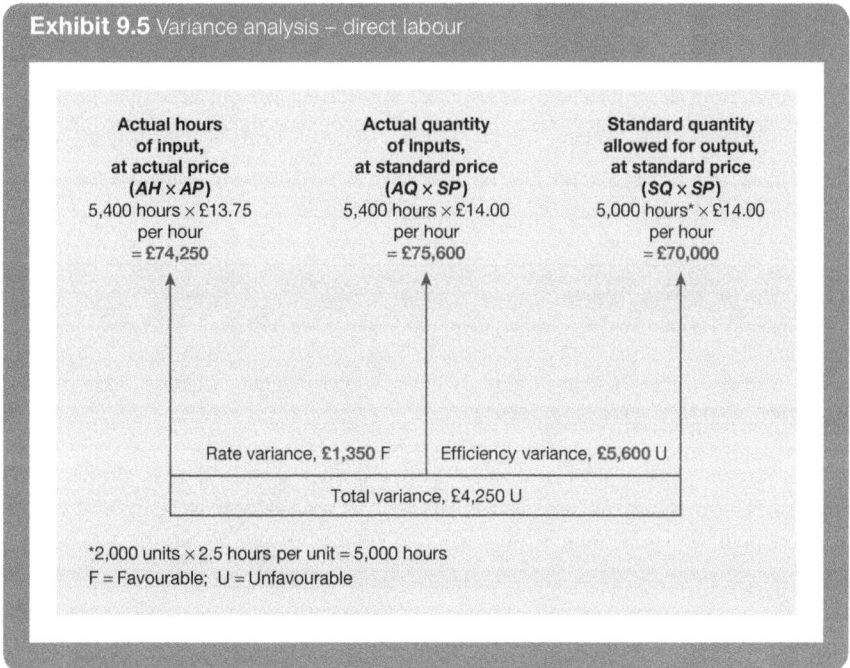

Actual hours of input, at actual price ($AH \times AP$)	Actual quantity of inputs, at standard price ($AQ \times SP$)	Standard quantity allowed for output, at standard price ($SQ \times SP$)
5,400 hours × £13.75 per hour = £74,250	5,400 hours × £14.00 per hour = £75,600	5,000 hours* × £14.00 per hour = £70,000

Rate variance, £1,350 F   Efficiency variance, £5,600 U

Total variance, £4,250 U

*2,000 units × 2.5 hours per unit = 5,000 hours
F = Favourable; U = Unfavourable

During June, the company paid its direct labour workers £74,250, including employment taxes and fringe benefits, for 5,400 hours of work. This was an average of £13.75 per hour. Using these data and the standard costs from Exhibit 9.1, the direct labour rate and efficiency variances are shown in Exhibit 9.5.

Notice that the column headings in Exhibit 9.5 are the same as those used in the prior two exhibits, except that in Exhibit 9.5 the terms *hours* and *rate* are used in place of the terms *quantity* and *price*.

Labour rate variance – a closer look

As explained earlier, the price variance for direct labour is commonly termed a **labour rate variance**. This variance measures any deviation from standard in the average hourly rate paid to direct labour workers. The formula for the labour rate variance is expressed as follows:

$$\text{Labour rate variance} = (AH \times AR) - (AH \times SR)$$

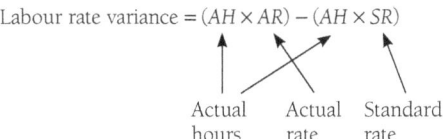

Actual   Actual   Standard
hours   rate   rate

The formula can be factored into simpler form as follows:

$$\text{Labour rate variance} = AH (AR - SR)$$

Using the data from Exhibit 9.5 in the formula, we have the following:

5,400 hours (£13.75 per hour − £14.00 per hour) = £1,350 F

In most firms, the rates paid to workers are quite predictable. Nevertheless, rate variances can arise through the way labour is used. Skilled workers with high hourly rates of pay may be given duties that require little

skill and call for low hourly rates of pay. This will result in unfavourable labour rate variances, since the actual hourly rate of pay will exceed the standard rate specified for the particular task being performed. A reverse situation exists when unskilled or untrained workers are assigned to jobs that require some skill or training. The lower pay scale for these workers will result in favourable rate variances, although the workers may be inefficient. Finally, unfavourable rate variances can arise from overtime work at premium rates if any portion of the overtime premium is added to the direct labour account.

Who is responsible for controlling the labour rate variance? Since rate variances generally arise as a result of how labour is used, supervisors bear responsibility for seeing that labour rate variances are kept under control.

Labour efficiency variance – a closer look

The quantity variance for direct labour, more commonly called the **labour efficiency variance**, measures the productivity of labour time. No variance is more closely watched by management, since it is widely believed that increasing the productivity of direct labour time is vital to reducing costs. The formula for the labour efficiency variance is expressed as follows

$$\text{Variable overhead efficiency variance} = (AH \times SR) - (SH \times SR)$$

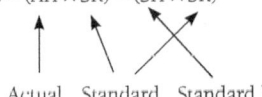

| Actual | Standard | Standard hours allowed |
| hours | rate | for output |

Factored into simpler terms, the formula is:

$$\text{Variable overhead efficiency variance} = SR(AH - SH)$$

Using the data from Exhibit 9.5 in the formula, we have the following:

£14.00 per hour (5,400 hours – 5,000 hours*) = £5,600 U
*2,000 units × hours per unit = 5,000 hours.

Possible causes of an unfavourable labour efficiency variance include poorly trained or motivated workers; poor quality materials, requiring more labour time in processing; faulty equipment, causing breakdowns and work interruptions; poor supervision of workers; and inaccurate standards. The managers in charge of production would generally be responsible for control of the labour efficiency variance. However, the variance might be chargeable to purchasing if the acquisition of poor materials resulted in excessive labour processing time.

When the labour force is essentially fixed in the short term, another important cause of an unfavourable labour efficiency variance is insufficient demand for the output of the factory. In some firms, the actual labour-hours worked is basically fixed – particularly in the short term. Managers in these firms argue that it is difficult, and perhaps even unwise, constantly to adjust the workforce in response to changes in the workload. Therefore, the only way a work centre manager can avoid an unfavourable labour efficiency variance in such firms is by keeping everyone busy all the time. The option of reducing the number of workers on hand is not available.

Thus, if there are insufficient orders from customers to keep the workers busy, the work centre manager has two options – either accept an unfavourable labour efficiency variance or build stocks. A central lesson of just-in-time production is that building stocks with no immediate prospect of sale is a bad idea. Stocks – particularly work in progress stocks – lead to high defect rates, obsolete goods, and generally inefficient operations. As a consequence, when the workforce is basically fixed in the short term, managers must be cautious about how labour efficiency variances are used. Some managers advocate dispensing with labour efficiency variances entirely in such situations – at least for the purposes of motivating and controlling workers on the shop floor.

Using standard costs – variable manufacturing overhead variances

LO 4

The final step in the analysis of Colonial Pewter's variances for June is to compute the variable manufacturing overhead variances. The variable portion of manufacturing overhead can be analysed using the same basic formulas that are used to analyse direct materials and direct labour. Recall from Exhibit 9.1 that the standard variable manufacturing overhead is £7.50 per unit of product, computed as follows:

2.5 hours per unit × £3.00 per hour = £7.50 per unit

Colonial Pewter's cost records showed that the total actual variable manufacturing overhead cost for June was £15,390. Recall from the earlier discussion of the direct labour variances that 5,400 hours of direct labour time were recorded during the month and that the company produced 2,000 pairs of bookends. The analysis of this overhead data appears in Exhibit 9.6.

Notice the similarities between Exhibits 9.5 and 9.6. These similarities arise from the fact that direct labour-hours are being used as a base for allocating overhead cost to units of product; thus, the same hourly figures appear in Exhibit 9.6 for variable manufacturing overhead as in Exhibit 9.5 for direct labour. The main difference between the two exhibits is in the standard hourly rate being used, which in this company is much lower for variable manufacturing overhead.

Manufacturing overhead variances – a closer look

The formula for **variable overhead spending variance** is expressed as follows:

Variable overhead spending variance = $(AH \times AR) - (AH \times SR)$

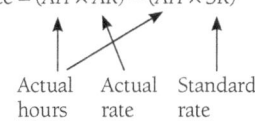

Actual   Actual   Standard
hours   rate   rate

Exhibit 9.6 Variance analysis – variable manufacturing overhead

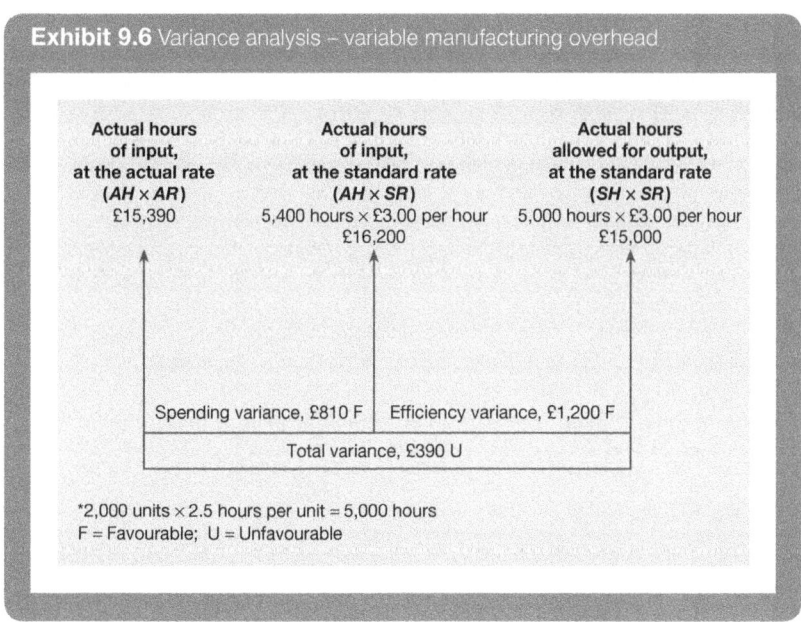

Actual hours of input, at the actual rate ($AH \times AR$)	Actual hours of input, at the standard rate ($AH \times SR$)	Actual hours allowed for output, at the standard rate ($SH \times SR$)
£15,390	5,400 hours × £3.00 per hour £16,200	5,000 hours × £3.00 per hour £15,000

| Spending variance, £810 F | Efficiency variance, £1,200 F |

| Total variance, £390 U |

*2,000 units × 2.5 hours per unit = 5,000 hours
F = Favourable; U = Unfavourable

Or, factored into simpler terms:

Variable overhead spending variance = $AH(AR - SR)$

Using the data from Exhibit 9.6 in the formula, we have the following:

5,400 hours (£2.85 per hour* − £3.00 per hour) = £810 F
*£15,390 ÷ 5,400 hours = £2.85 per hour.

The formula for the **variable overhead efficiency variance** is expressed as follows:

Variable overhead efficiency variance = $(AH \times SR) - (SH \times SR)$

| Actual hours | Standard rate | Standard hours allowed for output |

Or, factored into simpler terms:

Variable overhead efficiency variance = $SR(AH - SH)$

Again using the data from Exhibit 9.6, the computation of the variance would be as follows:

£3.00 per hour (5,400 hours − 5,000 hours*) = £1,200 U
*2,000 units × 2.5 hours per unit = 5,000 hours.

Before proceeding further, we suggest that you pause at this point and go back to review the data contained in Exhibits 9.1 to 9.6. These exhibits and the accompanying text discussion provide a comprehensive, integrated illustration of standard setting and variance analysis.

Structure of performance reports

On preceding pages we have learned that performance reports are used in a standard cost system to communicate variance data to management. Exhibit 9.7 provides an example of how these reports can be integrated in a responsibility reporting system.

Note from the exhibit that the performance reports *start at the bottom and build upwards*, with managers at each level receiving information on their own performance as well as information on the performance of each manager under them in the chain of responsibility. This variance information flows upward from level to level in a pyramid fashion, with the managing director finally receiving a summary of all activities in the organization. If the manager at a particular level (such as the production superintendent) wants to know the reasons behind a variance, he or she can ask for the detailed performance reports prepared by the various operations or departments.

In the following section, we turn our attention to the question of how a manager can determine which variances on these reports are significant enough to warrant further attention.

Variance analysis and management by exception

Variance analysis and performance reports are important elements of *management by exception*. Simply put, management by exception means that the manager's attention should be directed towards those parts of the organization where plans are not working out for one reason or another. Time and effort should not be wasted attending to those parts of the organization where things are going smoothly.

Exhibit 9.7 Upward flow of performance reports

Managing director's report		Budget	Actual	Variance
The managing director's performance report summarizes all company data. The managing director can trace the variances downwards through the company as needed to determine where top management time should be spent.	Responsibility centre:			
	Sales manager	X	X	X
	Production superintendent	£26,000	£29,000	£3,000 U
	Engineering head	X	X	X
	Personnel supervisor	X	X	X
	Controller	X	X	X
		£54,000	£61,000	£7,000 U

Production superintendent		Budget	Actual	Variance
The performance of each department head is summarized for the production superintendent. The totals on the superintendent's performance report are then passed upwards to the next level of responsibility.	Responsibility centre:			
	Cutting department	X	X	X
	Machining department	X	X	X
	Finishing department	£11,000	£12,500	£1,500 U
	Packing department	X	X	X
		£26,000	£29,000	£3,000 U

Finishing department head		Budget	Actual	Variance
The performance report of each supervisor is summarized on the performance report of the department head. The department totals are then passed upwards to the production superintendent	Responsibility centre:			
	Sanding operation	X	X	X
	Wiring operation	£5,000	£5,800	£800 U
	Assembly operation	X	X	X
		£11,000	£12,500	£1,500 U

Wiring operation supervisor		Budget	Actual	Variance
The supervisor of each operation receives a performance report. The totals on these reports are then communicated upwards to the next higher level of responsibility.	Variable costs:			
	Direct materials	X	X	X
	Direct labour	X	X	X
	Manufacturing overhead	X	X	X
		£5,000	£5,890	£800 U

The budgets and standards discussed in this chapter and in the preceding chapter reflect management's plans. If all goes according to plan, there will be little difference between actual results and the results that would be expected according to the budgets and standards. If this happens, managers can concentrate on other issues. However, if actual results do not conform to the budget and to standards, the performance reporting system sends a signal to the manager that an 'exception' has occurred. This signal is in the form of a variance from the budget or standards.

However, are all variances worth investigating? The answer is no. Differences between actual results and what was expected will almost always occur. If every variance were investigated, management would waste a great deal of time tracking down trivial differences. Variances may occur for any of a variety of reasons – only some of which are significant and warrant management attention. For example, hotter than normal weather in the summer may result in higher than expected electrical bills for air conditioning. Or, workers may work slightly faster or slower on a particular day. Because of unpredictable random factors, one can expect that virtually every cost category will produce a variance of some kind.

How should managers decide which variances are worth investigating? One clue is the size of the variance. A variance of £5 is probably not big enough to warrant attention, whereas a variance of £5,000 might

well be worth tracking down. Another clue is the size of the variance relative to the amount of spending involved. A variance that is only 0.1% of spending on an item is likely to be well within the bounds one would normally expect due to random factors. On the other hand, a variance of 10% of spending is much more likely to be a signal that something is basically wrong.

What value of X should be chosen? The bigger the value of X, the wider the band of acceptable variances that would not be investigated. Thus, the bigger the value of X, the less time will be spent tracking down variances, but the more likely it is that a real out-of-control situation would be overlooked. Ordinarily, if X is selected to be 1.0, roughly 30% of all variances will trigger an investigation even when there is no real problem. If X is set at 1.5, the figure drops to about 13%. If X is set at 2.0, the figure drops all the way to about 5%. Don't forget, however, that selecting a big value of X will result not only in fewer investigations but also a higher probability that a real problem will be overlooked.

LO 5 Evaluation of controls based on standard costs

Advantages of standard costs

Standard cost systems have a number of advantages.

1. As stated earlier, the use of standard costs is a key element in a management by exception approach. So long as costs remain within the standards, managers can focus on other issues. When costs fall significantly outside the standards, managers are alerted that there may be problems requiring attention. This approach helps managers focus on important issues.
2. So long as standards are viewed as reasonable by employees, they can promote economy and efficiency. They provide benchmarks that individuals can use to judge their own performance.
3. Standard costs can greatly simplify bookkeeping. Instead of recording actual costs for each job, the standard costs for materials, labour and overhead can be charged to jobs.
4. Standard costs fit naturally in an integrated system of 'responsibility accounting'. The standards establish what costs should be, who should be responsible for them, and whether actual costs are under control.

Potential problems with the use of standard costs

The use of standard costs can present a number of potential problems. Most of these problems result from improper use of standard costs and the management by exception principle or from using standard costs in situations in which they are not appropriate.[4]

1. Standard cost variance reports are usually prepared on a monthly basis and often are released days or even weeks after the end of the month. As a consequence, the information in the reports may be so stale that it is almost useless. Timely, frequent reports that are approximately correct are better than infrequent reports that are very precise but out of date by the time they are released. As mentioned earlier, some companies are now reporting variances and other key operating data daily or even more frequently.
2. If managers are insensitive and use variance reports as a club, morale may suffer. Employees should receive positive reinforcement for work well done. Management by exception, by its nature, tends to focus on the negative. If variances are used as a club, subordinates may be tempted to cover up unfavourable variances or take actions that are not in the best interests of the company to make sure the variances are favourable. For example, workers may put on a crash effort to increase output at the end of the month to avoid an unfavourable labour efficiency variance. In the rush to produce output, quality may suffer.
3. Labour quantity standards and efficiency variances make two important assumptions. First, they assume that the production process is labour-paced; if labour works faster, output will go up. However, output in many companies is no longer determined by how fast labour works; rather, it is determined by the processing speed of machines. Second, the computations assume that labour is a variable cost. However, as discussed in earlier chapters, in many companies, direct labour may

be essentially fixed. If labour is fixed, then an undue emphasis on labour efficiency variances creates pressure to build excess work in progress and finished goods inventories.

4   In some cases, a 'favourable' variance can be as bad or worse than an 'unfavourable' variance. For example, McDonald's has a standard for the amount of hamburger meat that should be in a Big Mac. If there is a 'favourable' variance, it means that less meat was used than the standard specifies. The result is a substandard Big Mac and possibly a dissatisfied customer.

5   There may be a tendency with standard cost reporting systems to emphasize meeting the standards to the exclusion of other important objectives such as maintaining and improving quality, on-time delivery, and customer satisfaction. This tendency can be reduced by using supplemental performance measures that focus on these other objectives.

6   Just meeting standards may not be sufficient; continual improvement may be necessary to survive in the current competitive environment. For this reason, some companies focus on the trends in the standard cost variances – aiming for continual improvement rather than just meeting the standards. In other companies, engineered standards are being replaced either by a rolling average of actual costs, which is expected to decline, or by very challenging target costs. This approach is sometimes known as kaizen costing which involves the reduction of cost during production through continuous gradual improvements that reduce waste and increase efficiency. While continuous improvement can be built into the costing system by setting small percentage reductions in cost, kaizen involves more than just technical changes because the philosophy relies on the development of a motivated and empowered workforce.[5]

In sum, managers should exercise considerable care in their use of a standard cost system. It is particularly important that managers go out of their way to focus on the positive, rather than just on the negative, and to be aware of possible unintended consequences.

Nevertheless, standard costs are still found in the vast majority of manufacturing companies and in many service companies, although their use is changing. For evaluating performance, standard cost variances may be supplanted by the *balanced scorecard* which we will look at in Chapter 11.

Focus on Business Practice

Survey of standard costing in global firms

© Jacob Wackerhausen

In a recent survey of major global companies,[6] it was argued that the limitations of standard costing are not always fully understood 'with users often treating it as a science rather than an art'. Among its recommendations, the report suggested that a selective use of standard costs such as direct costs may lead to better production decisions; that rapid changes in input and output prices should lead to more frequent updates of standards; that care should be taken that performance targets do not 'bake in inefficiency'; and that effective performance management should focus on the controllable elements of performance. One of the most surprising findings was continued and widespread use of spreadsheets rather than more sophisticated computer models such as enterprise resource planning systems.

Exercise: Review the advantages and disadvantages of a globalized company having a single, centralized standard costing system.

Summary

- A standard is a benchmark or 'norm' for measuring performance. In business organizations, standards are set for both the cost and the quantity of inputs needed to manufacture goods or to provide services. Quantity standards indicate how much of a cost element, such as labour time or raw materials, should be used in manufacturing a unit of product or in providing a unit of service. Cost standards indicate what the cost of the time or the materials should be.

- Standards are normally practical in nature, meaning that they can be attained by reasonable, though highly efficient, efforts. Such standards are generally felt to have a favourable motivational impact on employees.

- When standards are compared to actual performance, the difference is referred to as a variance. Variances are computed and reported to management on a regular basis for both the price and the quantity elements of materials, labour and overhead. Price and rate variances for inputs are computed by taking the difference between the actual and standard prices of the inputs and multiplying the result by the amount of input purchased. Quantity and efficiency variances are computed by taking the difference between the actual amount of the input used and the amount of input that is allowed for the actual output, and then multiplying the result by the standard price of the input.

- Not all variances require management time or attention. Only unusual or particularly significant variances should be investigated – otherwise a great deal of time would be spent investigating unimportant matters. Additionally, it should be emphasized that the point of the investigation should not be to find someone to blame. The point of the investigation is to pinpoint the problem so that it can be fixed and operations improved.

- Traditional standard cost variance reports should often be supplemented with other performance measures. Overemphasis on standard cost variances may lead to problems in other critical areas such as product quality, stocks levels, and on-time delivery.

Key terms

Bill of materials A listing of the quantity of each type of material required to manufacture a unit of product (p. 208).

Ideal standards Standards that allow for no machine breakdowns or other work interruptions and that require peak efficiency at all times (p. 207).

Labour efficiency variance A measure of the difference between the actual hours taken to complete a task and the standard hours allowed, multiplied by the standard hourly labour rate (p. 218).

Labour rate variance A measure of the difference between the actual hourly labour rate and the standard rate, multiplied by the number of hours worked during the period (p. 217).

Management by exception A system of management in which standards are set for various operating activities, with actual results then compared to these standards. Any differences that are deemed significant are brought to the attention of management as 'exceptions' (p. 206).

Materials price variance A measure of the difference between the actual unit price paid for an item and the standard price, multiplied by the quantity purchased (p. 214).

Materials quantity variance A measure of the difference between the actual quantity of materials used in production and the standard quantity allowed, multiplied by the standard price per unit of materials (p. 215).

Practical standards Standards that allow for normal machine downtime and other work interruptions and that can be attained through reasonable, though highly efficient, efforts by the average worker (p. 208).

Standard cost card A detailed listing of the standard amounts of materials, labour and overhead that should go into a unit of product, multiplied by the standard price or rate that has been set for each cost element (p. 206).

Standard cost per unit The standard cost of a unit of product as shown on the standard cost card; it is computed by multiplying the standard quantity or hours by the standard price or rate for each cost element (p. 210).

Standard hours allowed The time that should have been taken to complete the period's output as computed by multiplying the actual number of units produced by the standard hours per unit (p. 212).

Standard hours per unit The amount of labour time that should be required to complete a single unit of product, including allowances

for breaks, machine downtime, cleanup, rejects, and other normal inefficiencies (p. 209).

Standard price per unit The price that should be paid for a single unit of materials, including allowances for quality, quantity purchased, shipping, receiving, and other such costs, net of any discounts allowed (p. 208).

Standard quantity allowed The amount of materials that should have been used to complete the period's output as computed by multiplying the actual number of units produced by the standard quantity per unit (p. 211).

Standard quantity per unit The amount of materials that should be required to complete a single unit of product, including allowances for normal waste spoilage, rejects and similar inefficiencies (p. 208).

Standard rate per hour The labour rate that should be incurred per hour of labour time, including employment taxes, fringe benefits and other such labour costs (p. 209).

Variable overhead efficiency variance The difference between the actual activity (direct labour-hours, machine-hours, or some other base) of a period and the standard activity allowed, multiplied by the variable part of the predetermined overhead rate (p. 220).

Variable overhead spending variance The difference between the actual variable overhead cost incurred during a period and the standard cost that should have been incurred based on the actual activity of the period (p. 219).

Variance The difference between standard prices and quantities on the one hand and actual prices and quantities on the other hand (p. 211).

Endnotes

1 Morais (1997).

2 Standard costing has been around for such a long time that recent articles are not that common. See, however, Fleischmann and Tyson (1996).

3 http://www.virbusgame.eu/virbus/mediawiki/index. php/Cost_Controlling_in_Restaurants

4 While the evils of standard cost systems are recounted in many articles and books, two particularly thorough accounts of their drawbacks can be found in Johnson (1990) and Kaplan (1986b).

5 Monden and Hamada (1991).

6 KPMG/CIMA, Standard costing: Insights from leading companies, February 2010.

When you have read this chapter, log on to the Online Learning Centre for *Management Accounting for Business Decisions* at **www.mcgraw-hill.co.uk/ textbooks/seal**, where you'll find multiple choice questions, practice exams and extra study tools for management accounting.

Assessment

Questions

connect

9–1 What is a quantity standard? What is a price standard?
9–2 Distinguish between ideal and practical standards.
9–3 If employees are chronically unable to meet a standard, what effect would you expect this to have on their productivity?
9–4 What is the difference between a standard and a budget?
9–5 What is meant by the term *variance*?
9–6 What is meant by the term *management by exception*?
9–7 Why are variances generally segregated in terms of a price variance and a quantity variance?
9–8 Who is generally responsible for the materials price variance? The materials quantity variance? The labour efficiency variance?
9–9 The materials price variance can be computed at what two different points in time? Which point is better? Why?
9–10 An examination of the cost records of the Chittenden Furniture Company reveals that the materials price variance is favourable but that the materials quantity variance is unfavourable by a substantial amount. What might this indicate?
9–11 What dangers lie in using standards as punitive tools?
9–12 'Our workers are all under labour contracts; therefore, our labour rate variance is bound to be zero.' Discuss.
9–13 What effect, if any, would you expect poor quality materials to have on direct labour variances?
9–14 If variable manufacturing overhead is applied to production on the basis of direct labour-hours and the direct labour efficiency variance is unfavourable, will the variable overhead efficiency variance be favourable or unfavourable, or could it be either? Explain.

Exercises

connect

E9–1 ⏱ Time allowed: 15 minutes
Bandar Industries Berhad of Malaysia manufactures sporting equipment. One of the company's products, a football helmet for the North American market, requires a special plastic. During the quarter ending 30 June, the company manufactured 35,000 helmets, using 22,500 kilograms of plastic in the process. The plastic cost the company RM 171,000. (The currency in Malaysia is the ringgit, which is denoted here by RM.)

According to the standard cost card, each helmet should require 0.6 kilograms of plastic, at a cost of RM 8 per kilogram.

Required

1 What cost for plastic should have been incurred in the manufacture of the 35,000 helmets? How much greater or less is this than the cost that was incurred?
2 Break down the difference computed in Question 1 above in terms of a materials price variance and a materials quantity variance.

E9-2 ⏱ Time allowed: 15 minutes

Huron Company produces a commercial cleaning compound known as Zoom. The direct materials and direct labour standards for one unit of Zoom are given below:

	Standard quantity or hours	Standard price or rate	Standard cost
Direct materials	4.6 kilos	£2.50 per kilo	£11.50
Direct labour	0.2 hours	12.00 per hour	2.40

During the most recent month, the following activity was recorded:
1. Twenty thousand kilos of material were purchased at a cost of £2.35 per kilo.
2. All of the material purchased was used to produce 4,000 units of Zoom.
3. A total of 750 hours of direct labour time was recorded at a total labour cost of £10,425.

Required
1. Compute the direct materials price and quantity variances for the month.
2. Compute the direct labour rate and efficiency variances for the month.

E9-3 ⏱ Time allowed: 10 minutes

Refer to the data in E9-2. Assume that instead of producing 4,000 units during the month, the company produced only 3,000 units, using 14,750 kilos of material in the production process. (The rest of the material purchased remained in stocks.)

Required
Compute the direct materials price and quantity variances for the month.

E9-4 ⏱ Time allowed: 20 minutes

Erie Company manufactures a small cassette player called the Jogging Mate. The company uses standards to control its costs. The labour standards that have been set for one Jogging Mate cassette player are as follows:

Standard hours	Standard rate per hour	Standard cost
18 minutes	£12.00	£3.60

During August, 5,750 hours of direct labour time were recorded in the manufacture of 20,000 units of the Jogging Mate. The direct labour cost totalled £73,600 for the month.

Required
1. What direct labour cost should have been incurred in the manufacture of the 20,000 units of the Jogging Mate? By how much does this differ from the cost that was incurred?
2. Break down the difference in cost from Question 1 above into a labour rate variance and a labour efficiency variance.
3. The budgeted variable manufacturing overhead rate is £4 per direct labour-hour. During August, the company incurred £21,850 in variable

manufacturing overhead cost. Compute the variable overhead spending and efficiency variances for the month.

E9–5 Time allowed: 30 minutes
Dawson Toys Ltd produces a toy called the Maze. The company has recently established a standard cost system to help control costs and has established the following standards for the Maze toy:

Direct materials: 6 microns per toy at £0.50 per micron

Direct labour: 1.3 hours per toy at £8 per hour

During July, the company produced 3,000 Maze toys. Production data for the month on the toy follow:

Direct materials: 25,000 microns were purchased for use in production at a cost of £0.48 per micron. Some 5,000 of these microns were still in stock at the end of the month

Direct labour: 4,000 direct labour-hours were worked at a cost of £36,000

Required
1   Compute the following variances for July:
    (a) Direct materials price and quantity variances.
    (b) Direct labour rate and efficiency variances.
2   Prepare a brief explanation of the significance and possible causes of each variance.

P9–6 Standard costing

Problems

Time allowed: 45 minutes
As a recently appointed assistant management accountant you are attending a monthly performance meeting. You have with you a statement of monthly actual costs, a summary of cost variances and other pieces of information you have managed to collect, as shown below:

	£
Actual cost of direct material purchased and used	62,700
Actual direct wages paid	97,350
Variable overheads incurred	19,500
Fixed overheads incurred	106,500

The variances from standard cost were:

Direct material price variance	5,700 Adv.
Direct material usage variance	3,000 Fav.
Direct labour rate variance	1,650 Fav.
Direct labour efficiency variance	9,000 Fav.
Variable overhead variance	1,500 Adv.
Fixed overhead expenditure variance	1,500 Adv.
Fixed overhead volume variance	15,000 Adv.

The actual wage rate paid for the period was £8.85 per hour. It takes three standard hours to produce one unit of the finished product.

The single direct material used in the period cost 30p per kilogram above the standard price. Five kilograms of raw material input is allowed for as standard for one unit of output.

All figures relate to the single product which is manufactured at the plant. There were no stocks at the beginning or end of the accounting period. Variable and fixed overhead absorption rates are based on standard hours produced.

Managers from various functions have brought to the meeting measures which they have collected for their own areas of responsibility. In order to demonstrate the link between the accounting values and their measures you decide to work from the variances to confirm some of them.

Required

1 The formula for the calculation of the labour cost variance is:

$$(SH \times SR) - (AH \times AR)$$

Provide formulae for the calculation of the labour rate variance and labour efficiency variance using similar notation to that above. Demonstrate how they will sum to the labour cost variance given above.   *(2 marks)*

2 Using variance formulae, such as those above, or otherwise, determine:
   (a) the actual number of direct labour hours worked
   (b) the standard rate of pay per direct labour-hour
   (c) the standard hours of production
   (d) the actual production in units
   (e) the actual quantity of direct material consumed
   (f) the actual price paid for the direct material (per kilogram)
   (g) the standard direct material usage in kilograms for the actual number of units produced.   *(10 marks)*

3 From Question 2 above and any other calculations which may be appropriate, compute the standard cost per unit of finished product. Show separately standard prices and standard quantities for each element of cost.   *(4 marks)*

4 Briefly interpret the overhead variances given in the question.   *(4 marks)*

(Total 20 marks)
ACCA (adapted)

P9–7 Hospital; basic variance analysis

⏱ Time allowed: 45 minutes

John Fleming, chief administrator for Valley View Hospital, is concerned about costs for tests in the hospital's lab. Charges for lab tests are consistently higher at Valley View than at other hospitals and have resulted in many complaints. Also, because of strict regulations on amounts reimbursed for lab tests, payments received from insurance companies and governmental units have not been high enough to provide an acceptable level of profit for the lab.

Mr Fleming has asked you to evaluate costs in the hospital's lab for the past month. The following information is available:

1 Basically, two types of tests are performed in the lab – blood tests and smears. During the past month, 1,800 blood tests and 2,400 smears were performed in the lab.
2 Small glass plates are used in both types of tests. During the past month, the hospital purchased 12,000 plates at a cost of £28,200. This cost is net of a 6% quantity discount. Some 1,500 of these plates were still on hand unused at the end of the month; there were no plates on hand at the beginning of the month.
3 During the past month, 1,150 hours of labour time were recorded in the lab. The cost of this labour time was £13,800.
4 Variable overhead cost last month in the lab for utilities and supplies totalled £7,820.

Valley View Hospital has never used standard costs. By searching industry literature, however, you have determined the following nationwide averages for hospital labs:

Plates:	Two plates are required per lab test. These plates cost £2.50 each and are disposed of after the test is completed.
Labour:	Each blood test should require 0.3 hours to complete, and each smear should require 0.15 hours to complete. The average cost of this lab time is £14 per hour.
Overhead:	Overhead cost is based on direct labour-hours. The average rate for variable overhead is £6 per hour.

Mr Fleming would like a complete analysis of the cost of plates, labour and overhead in the lab for the last month so that he can get to the root of the lab's cost problem.

Required

1 Compute a materials price variance for the plates purchased last month and a materials quantity variance for the plates used last month.
2 For labour cost in the lab:
   (a) Compute a labour rate variance and a labour efficiency variance.
   (b) In most hospitals, one-half of the workers in the lab are senior technicians and one-half are assistants. In an effort to reduce costs, Valley View Hospital employs only one-quarter senior technicians and three-quarters assistants. Would you recommend that this policy be continued? Explain.
3 Compute the variable overhead spending and efficiency variances. Is there any relationship between the variable overhead efficiency variance and the labour efficiency variance? Explain.

P9–8 Straightforward variance analysis

ⓙ Time allowed: 45 minutes

Becton Labs Ltd produces various chemical compounds for industrial use. One compound, called Fludex, is prepared by means of an elaborate distilling

process. The company has developed standard costs for one unit of Fludex, as follows:

	Standard quantity	Standard price or rate	Standard cost
Direct materials	2.5 grams	£20.00 per gram	£50.00
Direct labour	1.4 hours	12.50 per hour	17.50
Variable manufacturing overhead	1.4 hours	3.50 per hour	4.90
			£72.40

During November, the following activity was recorded by the company relative to production of Fludex:

1 Materials purchased, 12,000 grams at a cost of £225,000.
2 There was no beginning stocks of materials on hand to start the month; at the end of the month, 2,500 grams of material remained in the warehouse unused.
3 The company employs 35 lab technicians to work on the production of Fludex. During November, each worked an average of 160 hours at an average rate of £12 per hour.
4 Variable manufacturing overhead is assigned to Fludex on the basis of direct labour-hours. Variable manufacturing overhead costs during November totalled £18,200.
5 During November, 3,750 good units of Fludex were produced. The company's management is anxious to determine the efficiency of the activities surrounding the production of Fludex.

Required

1 For materials used in the production of Fludex:
 (a) Compute the price and quantity variances.
 (b) The materials were purchased from a new supplier who is anxious to enter into a long-term purchase contract. Would you recommend that the company sign the contract? Explain.
2 For direct labour employed in the production of Fludex:
 (a) Compute the rate and efficiency variances.
 (b) In the past, the 35 technicians employed in the production of Fludex consisted of 20 senior technicians and 15 assistants. During November, the company experimented with only 15 senior technicians and 20 assistants in order to save costs. Would you recommend that the new labour mix be continued? Explain.
3 Compute the variable overhead spending and efficiency variances. What relationship can you see between this efficiency variance and the labour efficiency variance?

Chapter 11
Strategic management accounting and the balanced scorecard

 Learning **objectives**

After studying Chapter 11, you should be able to:

1 Define the concepts of strategy and strategic management accounting
2 Understand the impact of corporate strategy on management accounting
3 Understand some basic strategic models and their relationship with management accounting techniques
4 Understand how a balanced scorecard fits together and how it supports a company's strategy

Concepts **in Context**

The term strategic management accounting (SMA) has been used to describe the process of 'provision and analysis of management accounting data about a business and its competitors for use in developing and monitoring business strategy'.[1] We may illustrate the basic ideas of SMA by looking at one of the leading retailers in the United Kingdom, Tesco, which has tailored its key performance indicators to the economics of its business. For example, rather than maximize EVA, Tesco has realized that its main fixed assets are its stores. With this type of asset base, the company aims to reduce the cost of building good quality new stores through strategic partnering with construction companies. In order to check its market positioning, the company is constantly monitoring the prices of its merchandise relative to the prices charged by its main competitors. As well as promoting customer loyalty, it uses its store card as a database for targeting the specific needs of individual customers as revealed through their purchase patterns. It also keeps a close eye on non-financial indicators such as the length of queues at the check-outs.

© Joshua Hodge Photography

In this chapter we will review both short- and long-term financial planning but in the context of *strategic choice*. **Strategic choice** means that companies can *choose* which industries and products they want to compete in but it also means that different companies in the *same* industry may decide to adopt different strategies with quite different implications for management accounting and control. For example, a company's strategy may determine whether management will be concentrating on a tight control of costs, maintaining quality or generating new product ideas.

As more and more reliance is placed on bought-in goods and services, a higher proportion of costs are generated by a firm's suppliers, which suggests that major improvements in cost, quality and innovation are potentially available through the effective management of the firm's supply chain. In *strategic* as opposed to *traditional* management accounting, there is a recognition that managers may have some freedom to choose which industry they operate in, which technology is used and how the organization is structured. Thus, rather than passively adapting to given competitive, technological and organizational circumstances, **strategic management accounting (SMA)** helps managers make choices through information support. Strategic management accounting is also concerned with the *implementation* of strategies by setting up control systems that drive through the chosen strategies. For example, if a company wishes to pursue a low-cost strategy then traditional budgetary control may help implementation. However, few companies compete on price alone so additional performance measures may be non-financial, such as delivery or queuing time.

As described above, Tesco's approach in linking its goals and its management information systems demonstrates many of the principles of SMA. The company has decided how it is going to compete, reviewed its internal and external operations and chosen key performance indicators that enable it to monitor the development of its chosen business model. The search for data is driven by decision needs rather than by what is simply easily available.

Some basic techniques of strategic management accounting

SMA has an orientation towards the firm's environment. The relevant environment may be in its value chain, that is, its 'upstream' relations with suppliers and 'downstream' relations with its customers. The other relevant environment is its competitive position relative to both existing and potential competitors. Its competitive position will not just depend on price but on a **marketing mix**.

Sometimes SMA will use existing information and sometimes new information will be sought. For example, the increased emphasis on marketing may involve the use of techniques such as **attribute costing** that costs product attributes that appeal to customers, using brand value as a basis for managerial decisions and measuring the costs of quality. The competitive position is monitored through competitor cost assessment through estimates of competitors' costs based on an appraisal of facilities, technology, economies of scale, market share, volume, unit costs and return on sales. Strategic management accounting is also concerned with the long run through the use of target and **life-cycle costing** that looks at the costs incurred throughout the life of a product as it goes through various stages such as development and full production.

SMA and the concept of strategic positioning

Both the choice of strategic options and the ongoing search for strategic information may be informed by a variety of corporate strategy models. In short, a further development of SMA integrates the more outward and forward-looking aspects of the strategic intelligence approach with some well-known models of strategic choice.

Some strategic choice models involve deciding on a company's *strategic position*. For example, following Miles and Snow,[2] should the company be a **defender** concentrating on reducing costs and/or improving quality, a **prospector** continually searching for market opportunities or an analyser which combines the defender and prospector positions? Or, following Michael Porter,[3] should the company concentrate on **cost leadership**

(aiming to be the lowest-cost producer in an industry) or **product differentiation** (maintain a price premium based on superior product quality)? Porter argues that: '[T]he worst strategic error is to be *stuck in the middle* or to try simultaneously to pursue all the strategies. This is a recipe for strategic mediocrity and below-average performance, because pursuing all strategies simultaneously means that a firm is not able to achieve any of them because of their inherent contradictions.'

The implications for management accounting of these positional strategies could be that a company that seeks cost leadership may use standard costing with flexible budgets for manufacturing cost control. With product cost being the key input to pricing decisions, it may also analyse costs of competitors in order to review its positioning. If the company is a differentiator then traditional costing may be less important, and more attention is paid to new product development and marketing expenditures.

Porter's generic strategy model may be linked to another of his innovations, the concept of the **value chain**. The value chain,[4] which is illustrated in Exhibit 11.1, consists of the major business functions that add value to a company's products and services. All these functions, from research and development through product design, manufacturing, marketing, distribution and customer service, are required to bring a product or service to the customer and generate revenues.

With value-chain analysis, the aim is to find linkages between value-creating activities, which result in lower costs and/or enhanced differentiation. John Shank's *strategic cost management*[5] approach shows how Porter's ideas on strategic positioning and gaining competitive advantage can have an impact on management accounting. Shank advocates a cost-driver analysis, which suggests that costs are driven by *structural* and *executional* factors. **Structural drivers** consider factors such as scale, scope, experience, technology and complexity, while **executional drivers** include factors such as work force involvement, quality management capacity utilization, plant lay-out efficiency, product configuration effectiveness, and exploitation of linkages.

Strategic investment appraisal: investment appraisal with strategic 'bolt-ons'?

In Chapter 10, we considered the various techniques of investment appraisal such as net present value (NPV) and internal rate of return. In principle, many strategic decisions, such as acquisitions or major marketing initiatives, could be analysed using these techniques by estimating and discounting future net cash flows and choosing the option that seems to give the highest return or largest NPV. Yet some advocates of more strategic approaches have argued that the conventional investment appraisal approach may set up business problems in a misleading way with an overemphasis on financial calculation leaving strategic issues either neglected or treated in an *ad hoc*, 'bolt-on' manner. John Shank argues that the NPV model follows four steps:

Step 1	Identifying spending proposals
Step 2	Quantitative analysis of incremental cash flows
Step 3	Qualitative issues that cannot be fitted into NPV are then treated in an *ad hoc* manner
Step 4	Decision – *Yes/No*

According to Shank, in conventional capital budgeting/investment appraisals, *Step 1* is hardly analysed since the investment proposals just appear out of thin air. *Step 2*, in contrast, gets a great deal of attention with

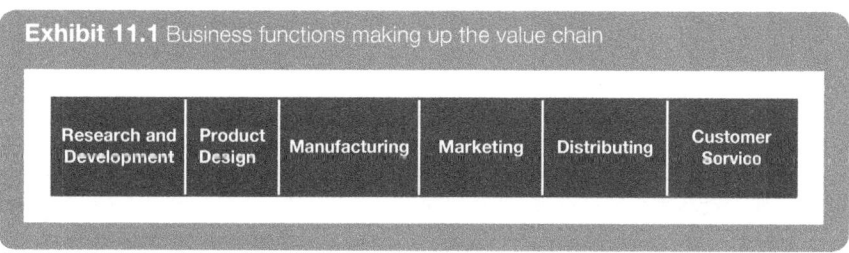

Exhibit 11.1 Business functions making up the value chain

Research and Development	Product Design	Manufacturing	Marketing	Distributing	Customer Service

elaborate considerations of relevant cash flows and sophisticated treatments of risk. *Step 3* is a 'step-child' concerned with 'soft-issues' that cannot be handled in *Step 2*. *Step 4*, the decision, *then generally flows out of Step 2*.

Shank[6] argues that the finance framework sets up strategic problems in a misleading way and argues that pure NPV analysis misses the richness of real business problems and is often merely set up to rationalize a prior decision. He illustrates the point with a case study, *Mavis Machines*.

The Mavis Machines case

Mavis Machines is a small metal working company producing drill bits for oil exploration. At present, the shop has four large manual lathes each operated by a skilled worker. The question facing the Managing Director of Mavis Machines is whether the company should install a numerically controlled lathe to replace all manual lathes. The numerical lathe would require only one operator but with different skills in computerized automation.

The decision can be set up using an NPV model and produces a very high rate of internal rate of return, as shown in Exhibit 11.2.

Exhibit 11.2 Summary of the quantitative analysis of the automation project in Mavis Machines

Net Investment

Purchase price		$680,000
Less:		
Trade-in value of old machines		(240,000)
Tax saving from trade-in (46%)		(108,000)
Book value	476,000	
Selling price	240,000	
Loss on resale	236,000	
Investment tax credit (10%)		(68,000)
Net		**($263,400)**

Annual cash savings

Labour – six operators (3/shift × 2 shifts) × $20,800 each		($124,800)
Factory space savings (no difference in cash flows)		0
Other cash savings (supplies, maintenance and power)		20,000
Total, pre-tax		$144,800
Less additional taxes (46%)		(60,600)
Cash saved – pre-tax	144,800	
Additional depreciation	(13,000)*	
Additional taxable income	131,800	
Annual after tax cash savings		**$84,200**
(ignoring inflation in savings in future years)		

*Old depreciation = $590 − $20/15 = $38,000
New depreciation = $680 − $68/12 = $51,000
Difference = $13,000

Summary of cash flows*
Period 0 (263,400) 12 year IRR = 32 + %, real
Periods 1–12 $84,200

*Ignoring the minor impact from the lost salvage values in year 12.

Reprinted from Management Accounting Research, 7/2, Shank, J., 'Analyzing technology investments – from NPV to Strategic Cost Management', 185–97. Copyright (1996), with permission from Elsevier.

The main cash savings stem from the need for fewer workers. However, other significant savings can be made in the net cost of the initial investment because of the healthy trade-in value of the relatively modern manual lathes. Indeed, 60% of the attractiveness of the project comes from the scrap value of the old machines, which suggests that the previous replacement decision might have been faulty. In an NPV approach other factors such as *flexibility, marketing* and *corporate image* are treated in rather an *ad hoc* manner.

An alternative strategic approach suggests a different perspective on the choice. Indeed when explicit strategic models are used to explore the issues the emphasis on a positive NPV in the financial analysis is eclipsed by other factors. *Competitive analysis* suggests that as a small machine shop, Mavis is best positioned as a *niche* player rather than a cost leader. The manual lathes and the skilled operators give it more product flexibility and greater security than one numerical lathe. Its strength lies in its flexibility to vary its products and sources of raw material. *Value chain analysis* suggested that it would lose both buyer and seller power because it would be more dependent only on those suppliers that could meet stringent quality requirements and would be more dependent on a single customer. There were also questions concerning the ease of maintenance of the new machine and the likely impact that firing eight workers out of a small workforce would have on morale and the firm's local reputation.

Strategic investment appraisal: an iterative model

Does the criticism of NPV by Shank and others mean that the material in Chapter 10 is of limited relevance for strategic decisions? Not according to Tomkins and Carr,[7] who suggest that strategic investment decisions may be modelled to include both financial and strategic analysis as shown in Exhibit 11.3. They suggest that a three-stage is followed:

1   The firm decides which markets to be in, by assessing both customer requirements and the relative ability of rivals to meet them. The firm will generate a number of investment possibilities based on product attributes related to volume of sales.
2   Analysis of the value chain assesses the means by which the attributes of the product can be delivered. This analysis will review possible suppliers and distributors as part of an iterative process to check on performance throughout the whole product life cycle.
3   The first two steps may then be modelled in terms of a cost and attribute driver analysis to see if the attributes can be delivered at an acceptable profit. The process is iterative in that a first assessment may suggest unacceptable low levels of profitability. The next assessment may then consider whether the profitability can be improved through piecemeal cost savings or whether existing delivery systems must be changed more radically through process re-engineering. Tomkins and Carr call this search for improvement, a process of 'probing' that uses discounted cash flow analysis but which also draws on an array of market, technological and other data.[8]

Modelling and monitoring strategy: the balanced scorecard and other non-financial measures

LO 4

So far in this chapter although we have discussed strategic choice, our focus on *financial metrics* of various sorts is arguably inappropriate for strategic decision making. We will now consider a very influential model, the *balanced scorecard*, which may be used by organizations to develop, implement and control strategy through a balanced use of financial and *non-financial* indicators. Rather than focus on an individual strategic investment, the balanced scorecard is concerned with the maintenance of an outward and forward-looking stance on a continuous and routine basis through a systematic process of monitoring and reporting on a variety of different performance dimensions.

A **balanced scorecard (BSC)** consists of an integrated set of performance measures that are derived from the company's strategy and that support the company's strategy throughout the organization.[9] A strategy is

Exhibit 11.3 A systematic formal analysis for strategic investment decisions

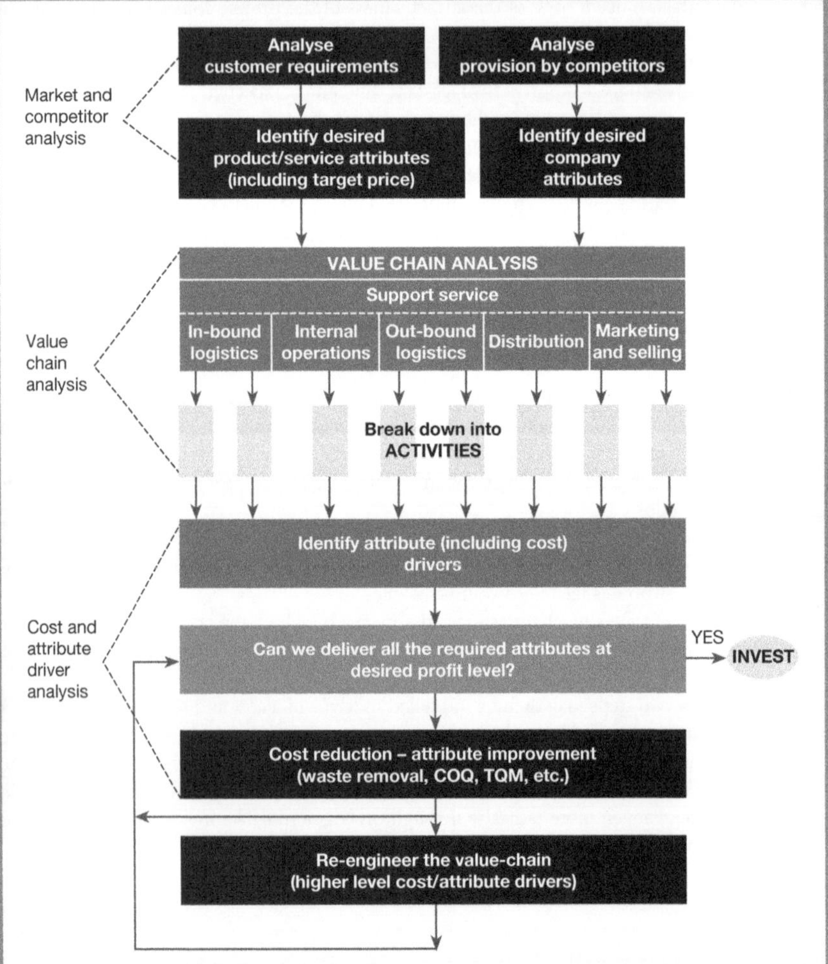

Market and competitor analysis

- Analyse customer requirements
- Analyse provision by competitors
- Identify desired product/service attributes (including target price)
- Identify desired company attributes

VALUE CHAIN ANALYSIS

Support service

Value chain analysis

| In-bound logistics | Internal operations | Out-bound logistics | Distribution | Marketing and selling |

Break down into ACTIVITIES

Identify attribute (including cost) drivers

Cost and attribute driver analysis

Can we deliver all the required attributes at desired profit level? — YES → **INVEST**

Cost reduction – attribute improvement (waste removal, COQ, TQM, etc.)

Re-engineer the value-chain (higher level cost/attribute drivers)

essentially a theory about how to achieve the organization's goals. For example, low-cost European carriers such as easyJet and Ryanair have copied Southwestern Airlines' strategy of offering passengers low prices and fun on short-haul jet service. The low prices result from the absence of costly frills such as meals and assigned seating. The fun is provided by flight attendants who go out of their way to entertain passengers with their antics. This is an interesting strategy. Southwestern Airlines consciously hires people who have a sense of humour and who enjoy their work. Hiring and retaining such employees probably costs no more – and may cost less – than retaining grumpy flight attendants who view their jobs as a chore. Southwestern Airlines' strategy is to build loyal customers through a combination of 'fun' – which does not cost anything to provide – and low prices that are possible because of the lack of costly frills offered by competing airlines. The theory is that low prices and fun[10] will lead to loyal customers, which, in combination with low costs, will lead to high profits. So far, this theory has worked.

Under the balanced scorecard approach, top management translates its strategy into performance measures that employees can understand and can do something about. For example, the amount of time passengers have to wait in line to have their baggage checked might be a performance measure for a supervisor in charge of the check-in counter at an airport. This performance measure is easily understood by the supervisor, and can be improved by the supervisor's actions.

Common characteristics of balanced scorecards

Performance measures used in the balanced scorecard approach tend to fall into the four groups illustrated in Exhibit 11.4: financial, customer, internal business processes, and learning and growth. Internal business processes are what the company does in an attempt to satisfy customers. For example, in a manufacturing company, assembling a product is an internal business process. In an airline, handling baggage is an internal business process. The basic idea is that learning is necessary to improve internal business processes; improving business processes is necessary to improve customer satisfaction; and improving customer satisfaction is necessary to improve financial results.

Note that the emphasis in Exhibit 11.4 is on *improvement* – not on just attaining some specific objective such as profits of £10 million. In the balanced scorecard approach, continual improvement is encouraged. In many industries, this is a matter of survival. If an organization does not continually improve, it will eventually lose out to competitors that do.

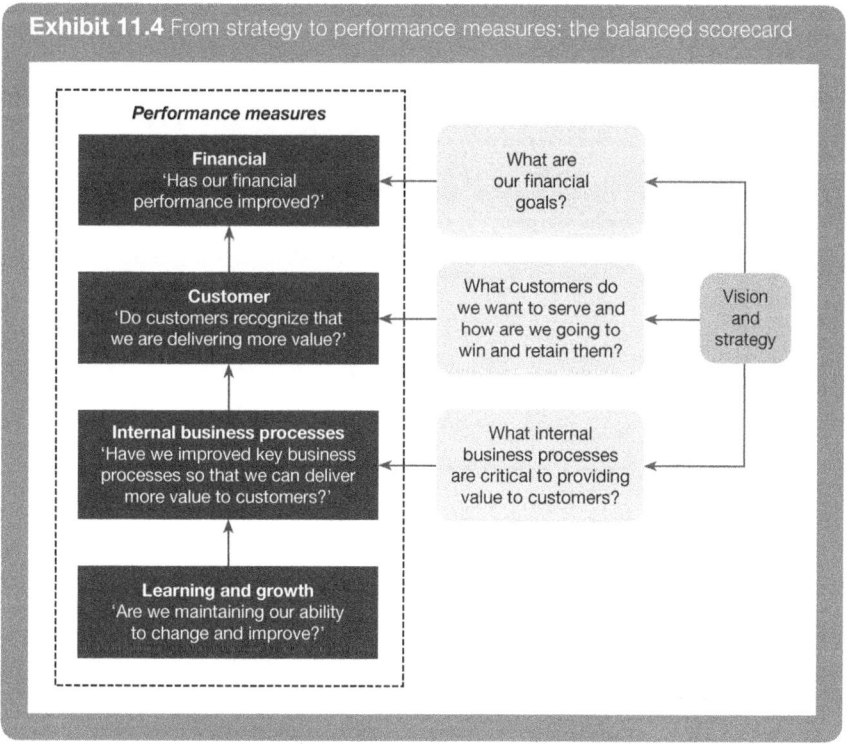

Exhibit 11.4 From strategy to performance measures: the balanced scorecard

Financial performance measures appear at the top of Exhibit 11.4. Ultimately, most companies exist to provide financial rewards to owners. There are exceptions. Some companies may have loftier goals, such as providing environmentally friendly products to consumers. However, even non-profit organizations must generate enough financial resources to stay in operation.

Ordinarily, top managers are responsible for the financial performance measures – not lower level managers. The supervisor in charge of checking in passengers can be held responsible for how long passengers have to queue. However, this supervisor cannot reasonably be held responsible for the entire company's profit. That is the responsibility of the airline's top managers.

Exhibit 11.5 lists some examples of performance measures that can be found on the balanced scorecards of companies. However, few companies, if any, would use all of these performance measures, and almost all companies would add other performance measures. Managers should carefully select the performance measures for their company's balanced scorecard, keeping the following points in mind. First and foremost, the performance measures should be consistent with, and follow from, the company's strategy. If the

---

Exhibit 11.5 Examples of performance measures for balanced scorecards

Customer perspective performance measure	Desired change
Customer satisfaction as measured by survey results	+
Number of customer complaints	−
Market share	+
Product returns as a percentage of sales	−
Percentage of customers retained from last period	+
Number of new customers	+

Internal business processes perspective performance measure	Desired change
Percentage of sales from new products	+
Time to introduce new products to market	−
Percentage of customer calls answered within 20 seconds	+
On-time deliveries as a percentage of all deliveries	+
Work in progress inventory as a percentage of sales	−
Unfavourable standard cost variances	−
Defect-free units as a percentage of completed units	+
Delivery cycle time*	−
Throughput time*	−
Manufacturing cycle efficiency*	+
Quality costs	−
Set-up time	−
Time from call by customer to repair of product	−
Percentage of customer complaints settled on first contact	+
Time to settle a customer claim	−

Learning and growth perspective performance measure	Desired change
Suggestions per employee	+
Value-added employee†	+
Employee turnover	−
Hours of in-house training per employee	+

*Explained later in this chapter.
†Value-added is revenue less externally purchased materials, supplies and services.

performance measures are not consistent with the company's strategy, people will find themselves working at cross-purposes. Second, the scorecard should not have too many performance measures. This can lead to a lack of focus and confusion.

While the entire organization will have an overall balanced scorecard, each responsible individual will have his or her own personal scorecard as well. This scorecard should consist of items the individual can personally influence that relate directly to the performance measures on the overall balanced scorecard. The performance measures on this personal scorecard should not be overly influenced by actions taken by others in the company or by events that are outside of the individual's control.

With those broad principles in mind, we will now take a look at how a company's strategy affects its balanced scorecard.

A company's strategy and the balanced scorecard

Returning to the performance measures in Exhibit 11.5, each company must decide which customers to target and what internal business processes are crucial to attracting and retaining those customers. Different companies, having different strategies, will target different customers with different kinds of products and services. Take the car industry as an example. BMW stresses engineering and handling; Volvo, safety; Jaguar, luxury detailing; and Toyota,[11] reliability. Because of these differences in emphases, a one-size-fits-all approach to performance measurement will not work even within this one industry. Performance measures must be tailored to the specific strategy of each company.

Suppose, for example, that Jaguar's strategy is to offer distinctive, richly finished luxury automobiles to wealthy individuals who prize handcrafted, individualized products. Part of Jaguar's strategy might be to create such a large number of options for details, such as leather seats, interior and exterior colour combinations, and wooden dashboards, that each car becomes virtually one of a kind. For example, instead of just offering tan or blue leather seats in standard cowhide, the company may offer customers the choice of an almost infinite palate of colours in any of a number of different exotic leathers. For such a system to work effectively, Jaguar would have to be able to deliver a completely customized car within a reasonable amount of time – and without incurring more cost for this customization than the customer is willing to pay. Exhibit 11.6 suggests how Jaguar might reflect this strategy in its balanced scorecard.

If the balanced scorecard is correctly constructed, the performance measures should be linked together on a cause-and-effect basis. Each link can then be read as a hypothesis in the form 'If we improve this performance measure, then this other performance measure should also improve.' Starting from the bottom of Exhibit 11.6, we can read the links between performance measures as follows. If employees acquire the skills to install new options more effectively, then the company can offer more options and the options can be installed in less time. If more options are available and they are installed in less time, then customer surveys should show greater satisfaction with the range of options available. If customer satisfaction improves, then the number of cars sold should increase. In addition, if customer satisfaction improves, the company should be able to maintain or increase its selling prices, and if the time to install options decreases, the costs of installing the options should decrease. Together, this should result in an increase in the contribution margin per car. If the contribution margin per car increases and more cars are sold, the result should be an increase in profits.

In essence, the balanced scorecard articulates a theory of how the company can attain its desired outcomes (financial, in this case) by taking concrete actions. While the strategy laid out in Exhibit 11.6 seems plausible, it should be regarded as only a theory that should be discarded if it proves to be invalid. For example, if the company succeeds in increasing the number of options available and in decreasing the time required to install options and yet there is no increase in customer satisfaction, the number of cars sold, the contribution margin per car, or profits, the strategy would have to be reconsidered. One of the advantages of the balanced scorecard is that it continually tests the theories underlying management's strategy. If a strategy is not working, it should become evident when some of the predicted effects (i.e. more car sales) do not occur. Without this feedback, management may drift on indefinitely with an ineffective strategy based on faulty assumptions.

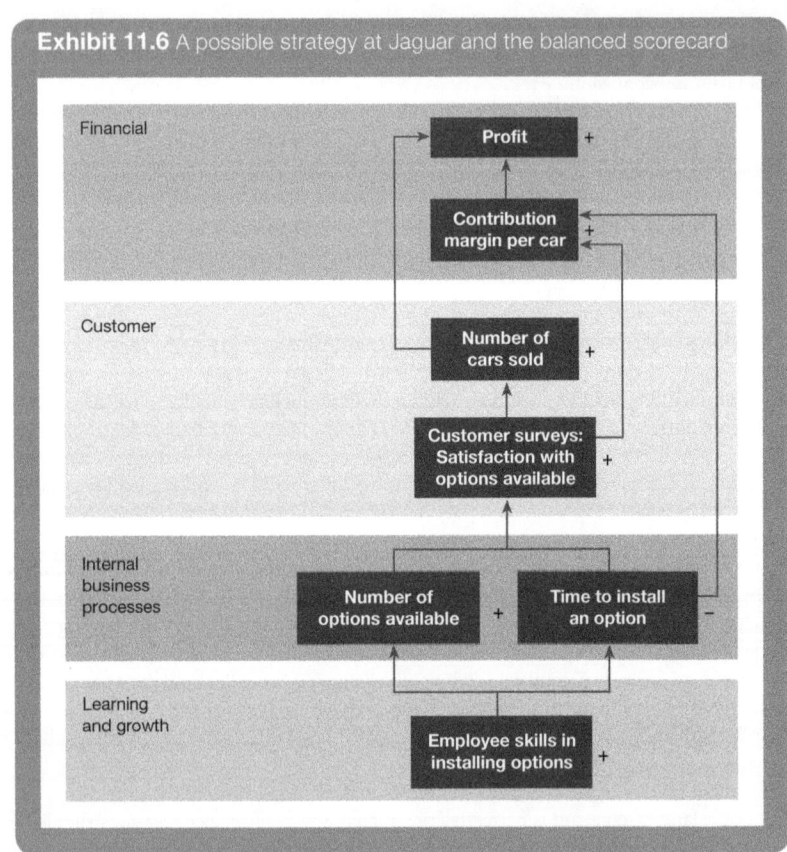

Exhibit 11.6 A possible strategy at Jaguar and the balanced scorecard

Advantages of timely feedback

Whatever performance measures are used, they should be reported on a frequent and timely basis. For example, data about defects should be reported to the responsible managers at least once a day so that action can quickly be taken if an unusual number of defects occurs. In the most advanced companies, any defect is reported *immediately*, and its cause is tracked down before any more defects can occur. Another common characteristic of the performance measures under the balanced scorecard approach is that managers focus on trends in the performance measures over time. The emphasis is on progress and *improvement* rather than on meeting any specific standard.

Some measures of internal business process performance

Most of the performance measures listed in Exhibit 11.5 are self-explanatory. However, three are not – *delivery cycle time, throughput time* and *manufacturing cycle efficiency* (MCE). These three important performance measures are discussed next.

Delivery cycle time

The amount of time between when an order is received from a customer to when the completed order is shipped is called the **delivery cycle time**. This time is clearly a key concern to many customers, who would like the delivery cycle time to be as short as possible. Cutting the delivery cycle time may give a company

Focus on Business Practice

A health service scorecard

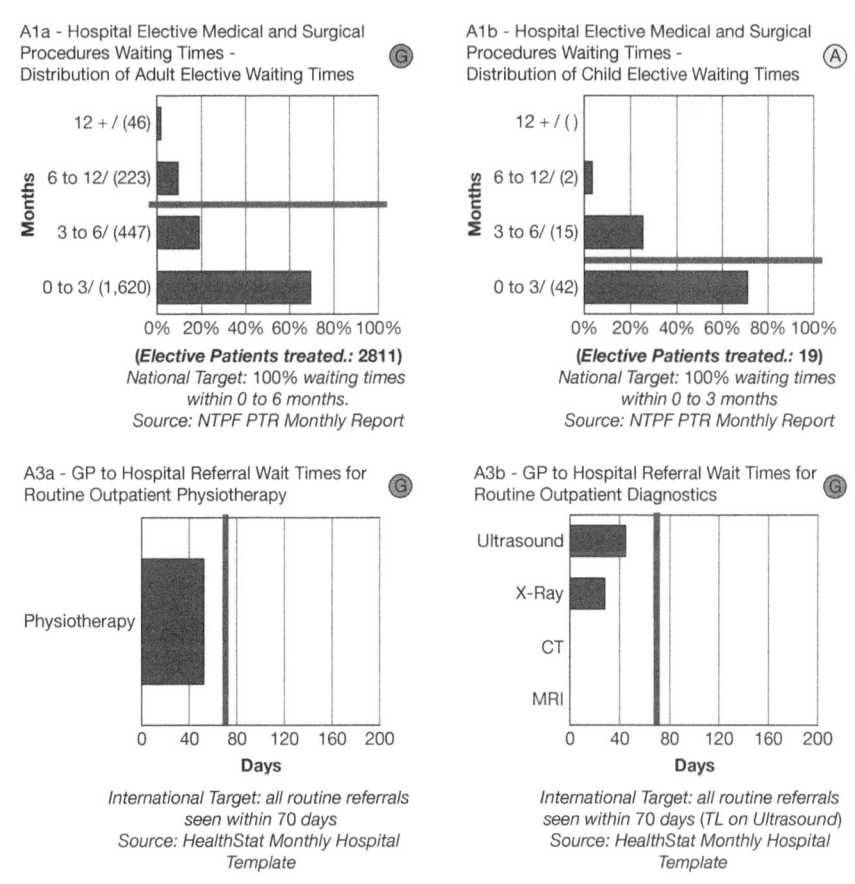

Many businesses and services use a balanced scorecard type system to report on key operating statistics and performance indicators. The Health Service Executive (HSE) is the state agency responsible for the running of the public health service in Ireland. It has over 100,000 employees and an annual budget of approximately €15 billion. The HSE uses a reporting system called HealthStat to monitor its performance in delivering health and care services.

HealthStat is described by the HSE as 'a comprehensive databank of performance information for Irish public health services'. To provide a comprehensive view of how services are delivered, HealthStat groups performance indicators under three headings: (1) Access – measuring waiting time for services; (2) Integration – checks that patients receive the correct services, in the right location and are informed about their treatment; and (3) Resources – whether a hospital or care facility is making best use of its financial and human resources. In total, 18 performance

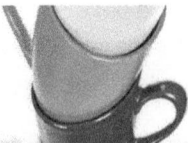

metrics across these three headings are reported on a monthly basis. Each metric is compared to a national target – these targets have been set against best international practice and are regularly reviewed. Each month, a traffic-light type dashboard (green = better than target, amber = below target, but improving, red = well below target) is compiled and reported to clinical managers, hospitals and the HSE's board. The data are also released to the public via the HSE's website – see example above. According to the HSE, HealthStat, being the first unified reporting systems used by the HSE, provides all staff and managers with a platform to monitor and improve service delivery.[12]

Exercise: Looking at the example given, do you think these performance metrics take into account factors like quality of care received, willingness of medical professionals to communicate to patients and so on? Should such things be included in performance measurements?

a key competitive advantage – and may be necessary for survival – and therefore many companies would include this performance measure on their balanced scorecard.

Throughput (manufacturing cycle) time

The amount of time required to turn raw materials into completed products is called **throughput time**, or manufacturing cycle time. The relationship between the delivery cycle time and the throughput (manufacturing cycle) time is illustrated in Exhibit 11.7.

Note that, as shown in Exhibit 11.7, the throughput time, or manufacturing cycle time, is made up of process time, inspection time, move time and queue time. Process time is the amount of time in which work is actually done on the product. Inspection time is the amount of time spent ensuring that the product is not defective. Move time is the time required to move materials or partially completed products from workstation to workstation. Queue time is the amount of time a product spends waiting to be worked on, to be moved, to be inspected, or in storage waiting to be shipped.

As shown at the bottom of Exhibit 11.7, the only one of these four activities that adds value to the product is process time. The other three activities – inspecting, moving and queueing – add no value and should be eliminated as much as possible.

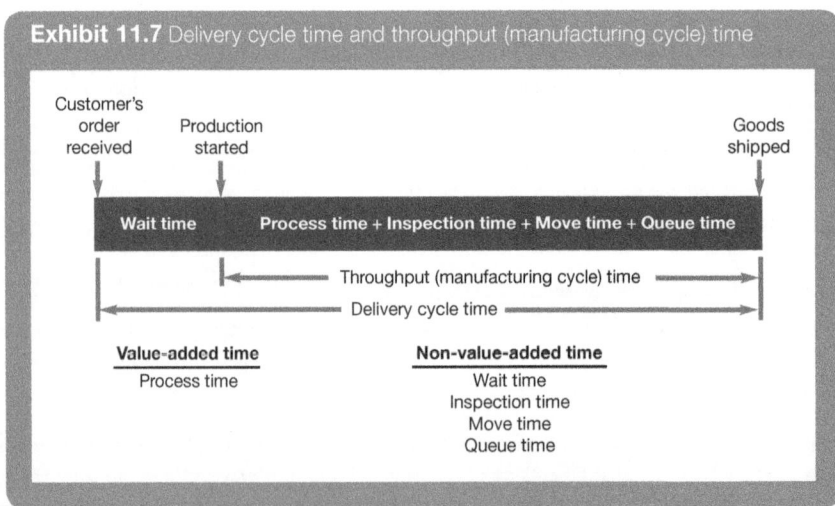

Exhibit 11.7 Delivery cycle time and throughput (manufacturing cycle) time

Manufacturing cycle efficiency (MCE)

Through concerted efforts to eliminate the non-value-added activities of inspecting, moving and queueing, some companies have reduced their throughput time to only a fraction of previous levels. In turn, this has helped to reduce the delivery cycle time from months to only weeks or hours. The throughput time, which is considered to be a key measure in delivery performance, can be put into better perspective by computing the **manufacturing cycle efficiency (MCE)**. The MCE is computed by relating the value-added time to the throughput time. The formula is as follows:

$$MCE = \frac{\text{Value-added time}}{\text{Throughput (manufacturing cycle) time}}$$

If the MCE is less than 1, then non-value-added time is present in the production process. An MCE of 0.5, for example, would mean that half of the total production time consisted of inspection, moving and similar non-value-added activities. In many manufacturing companies, the MCE is less than 0.1 (10%), which means that 90% of the time a unit is in process is spent on activities that do not add value to the product. By monitoring the MCE, companies are able to reduce non-value-added activities and thus get products into the hands of customers more quickly and at a lower cost.

We would like to emphasize a few points concerning the balanced scorecard. First, the balanced scorecard should be tailored to the company's strategy; each company's balanced scorecard should be unique. The examples given in this chapter are just that – examples. They should not be interpreted as general templates to be fitted to each company. Second, the balanced scorecard reflects a particular strategy, or theory, about how a company can further its objectives by taking specific actions. The theory should be viewed as tentative and subject to change if the actions do not in fact lead to attaining the company's financial and other goals. If the theory (i.e. strategy) changes, then the performance measures on the balanced scorecard should also change. The balanced scorecard should be viewed as a dynamic system that evolves as the company's strategy evolves.[13,14]

The balanced scorecard should not be seen just as 'a four bucket' model[15] with four boxes that must be filled. Organizations may choose to have five main dimensions. For example, banks may wish to have an extra box labelled risk management. As we have seen recently with the world-wide 'credit crunch', banks that have failed to manage risk have suffered financially or even gone out of business completely.

Focus on Business Practice

Risk and the balanced scorecard

© slobo

The author was recently involved in a research project looking at the implementation of the balanced scorecard in a major European bank. The bank had 'customized' the scorecard by including 'risk' as a major objective. Relative to some of its competitors, this bank did seem to be better prepared for the credit crunch with a much less risky approach to lending. Another interesting feature of the bank was the way that each employee had a personal scorecard which was aligned to the local business unit through to corporate objectives. The scorecard implementation had a board level corporate champion and was 'owned' by both human resource and finance functions.[16]

Exercise: Not all performance indicators in the balanced scorecard are positively related. Consider in this example the potential trade-off between risk and financial return.

Summary

- Profit and shareholder value metrics may be used for business planning but they may not provide sufficient information for developing and implementing strategies.

- Strategic management accounting has evolved from the collection of competitor information to attempts to match management accounting systems with an organization's strategic position.

- A balanced scorecard consists of an integrated system of performance measures that are derived from and support the company's strategy. Different companies will have different balanced scorecards because they have different strategies. A well-constructed balanced scorecard provides a means for guiding the company and also provides feedback concerning the effectiveness of the company's strategy.

Key terms

Attribute costing Costing the product attributes that appeal to customers (p. 260).

Balanced scorecard (BSC) An integrated set of performance measures that is derived from and supports the organization's strategy (p. 263).

Cost leadership Aiming to be the lowest cost producer in an industry (p. 260).

Defender A company which concentrates on reducing costs and/or improving quality in existing markets/products (p. 260).

Delivery cycle time The amount of time required from receipt of an order from a customer to shipment of the completed goods (p. 268).

Executional drivers Cost factors such as work force involvement, quality management capacity utilization, plant lay-out efficiency, product configuration effectiveness, and exploitation of linkages (p. 261).

Life-cycle costing Analyses costs incurred throughout the life of a product from development through to full production (p. 260).

Manufacturing cycle efficiency (MCE) Process (value-added) time as a percentage of throughput time (p. 271).

Marketing mix Price is one element in product competitiveness together with product, promotion and place (p. 260).

Product differentiation Aims to maintain a price premium based on superior product quality (p. 261).

Prospector A company that is continually searching for market opportunities (p. 260).

Strategic choice Choosing not only which industries and products to compete in but also how a company plans to compete (p. 260).

Strategic management accounting The use of management accounting information to help managers choose where and how to compete (p. 260).

Structural drivers Factors such as scale, scope, experience, technology and complexity (p. 261).

Throughput time The amount of time required to turn raw materials into completed products (p. 270).

Value chain The major business functions that add value to a company's products and services (p. 261).

Endnotes

1 Simmonds (1981).

2 Miles and Snow (1978).

3 Porter (1980).

4 Porter (1985).

5 Shank (1996).

6 Shank (1996).

7 Tomkins and Carr (1996).

8 For a discussion of strategic investment appraisal see also Northcott and Alkaraan (2007).

9 The balanced scorecard concept was developed by Robert Kaplan and David Norton. For further details, see their articles Kaplan and Norton (1992) (1996a) (1996b), (1997) and (2004). In the 1960s, the French developed a concept similar to the balanced scorecard called Tableau de Bord or 'dashboard'. For details, see Lebas (1994).

10 Some low cost airlines have only copied the 'no-frills' and seem less concerned with 'fun'. There is also an emerging trend to encourage online check-in.

11 Of course, Toyota, *as a company*, is associated with the development of lean production, which, as we have seen is based on trying to achieve both low cost, reliability, and high quality specifications. It may not try to achieve all these characteristics *in a particular model*.

12 http://www.hse.ie/eng/staff/Healthstat/about/

13 Kaplan and Norton (1996b).

14 For a critical evaluation of the BSC see Norreklit (2000).

15 Ittner and Larcker (2003).

16 Ye and Seal (2009).

When you have read this chapter, log on to the Online Learning Centre for *Management Accounting for Business Decisions* at **www.mcgraw-hill.co.uk/textbooks/seal**, where you'll find multiple choice questions, practice exams and extra study tools for management accounting.

Assessment

Questions

connect

11–1   Why is market share an important indicator to monitor?
11–2   What aspects of a competitor's costs should be analysed in a strategic assessment?
11–3   What sources are useful for strategic intelligence gathering?
11–4   What is the difference between a prospector and a defender company?
11–5   What is the difference between a cost leader and a product differentiator?
11–6   What are the three steps/dimensions that combine financial and strategic analysis as proposed by Tomkins and Carr?
11–7   What are the implications of the 'strategy as collision' model?
11–8   Why does the balanced scorecard include financial performance measures as well as measures of how well internal business processes are doing?
11–9   What is the difference between the delivery cycle time and the throughput time? What four elements make up the throughput time? Into what two classes can these four elements be placed?
11–10 Why does the balanced scorecard differ from company to company?

Exercises

connect

E11–1   ⏱ Time allowed: 20 minutes

Management of Mittel Rhein AG of Köln, Germany, would like to reduce the amount of time between when a customer places an order and when the order is shipped. For the first quarter of operations during the current year the following data were reported:

	Days
Inspection time	0.3
Wait time (from order to start of production)	14.0
Process time	2.7
Move time	1.0
Queue time	5.0

Required

1   Compute the throughput time, or velocity of production.
2   Compute the manufacturing cycle efficiency (MCE) for the quarter.
3   What percentage of the throughput time was spent in non-value-added activities?
4   Compute the delivery cycle time.

Problems

connect

P11–2 Perverse effects of some performance measures

⏱ Time allowed: 30 minutes

There is often more than one way to improve a performance measure. Unfortunately, some of the actions taken by managers to make their performance look better may actually harm the organization. For example, suppose the marketing department is held responsible only for increasing the performance measure 'total revenues'. Increases in total revenues may be achieved by working harder and smarter, but they can also usually be achieved by simply cutting prices. The increase in volume from cutting prices almost always results in greater total revenues; however, it does not always lead to greater total profits. Those who design performance measurement systems need to keep in mind that managers who are under pressure to perform may take actions to improve performance measures that have negative consequences elsewhere.

Required

For each of the following situations, describe actions that managers might take to show improvement in the performance measure but which do not actually lead to improvement in the organization's overall performance.

1 Concerned with the slow rate at which new products are brought to market, top management of a consumer electronics company introduces a new performance measure – speed-to-market. The research and development department is given responsibility for this performance measure, which measures the average amount of time a product is in development before it is released to the market for sale.

2 The Chief Executive of a telephone company has been under public pressure from city officials to fix the large number of public pay phones that do not work. The company's repair people complain that the problem is vandalism and damage caused by theft of coins from coin boxes – particularly in high crime areas in the city. The Chief Executive says she wants the problem solved and has pledged to city officials that there will be substantial improvement by the end of the year. To ensure that this is done, she makes the managers in charge of installing and maintaining pay phones responsible for increasing the percentage of public pay phones that are fully functional.

3 A manufacturing company has been plagued by the chronic failure to ship orders to customers by the promised date. To solve this problem, the production manager has been given the responsibility of increasing the percentage of orders shipped on time. When a customer calls in an order, the production manager and the customer agree to a delivery date. If the order is not completed by that date, it is counted as a late shipment.

4 Concerned with the productivity of employees, the board of directors of a large multinational corporation has dictated that the manager of each subsidiary will be held responsible for increasing the revenue per employee of his or her subsidiary.

P11–3 Strategic analysis

🕐 Time allowed: 45 minutes

M-HK provides a passenger ferry service between two large cities separated by the mouth of a major river. The ferries are frequent, well-supported by passengers and cover the distance between the cities in one hour. M-HK also transports passengers and goods by water ferry to other cities located on the

river mouth. There are other ferry operators providing services between each of these locations besides M-HK.

Required

1   Explain what strategic information is required by M-HK's management in respect of customer demand, competition, competitiveness, and finance in order to plan its future ferry services.   *(10 marks)*

2   Using the information in your answer to Question 1, discuss how M-HK's Chartered Management Accountant should provide reports to M-HK's senior management for operational and strategic planning purposes.   *(15 marks)*

(Total = 25 marks)

CIMA Management Accounting – Business Strategy, May 2001

P11–4   Strategic analysis

⏱ **Time allowed:** 45 minutes

R is a large high-class hotel situated in a thriving city. It is part of a worldwide hotel group owned by a large number of shareholders. The majority of the shares are held by individuals, each holding a small number; the rest are owned by financial institutions.

The hotel provides full amenities, including a heated swimming pool, as well as the normal facilities of bars, restaurants and good-quality accommodation. There are many other hotels in the city which all compete with R. The city in which R is situated is old and attracts many foreign visitors, particularly in its summer season.

Required

1   State the main stakeholders with whom relationships need to be established and maintained by the management of R. Explain why it is important that relationships are developed and maintained with each of these stakeholders.   *(10 marks)*

2   Explain how the management of R should carry out a benchmarking exercise on its services, and recommend ways in which the outcomes should be evaluated.   *(15 marks)*

Note: Do NOT describe different methods of benchmarking in answering this question.   *(Total = 25 marks)*

CIMA Management Accounting – Business Strategy, May 2001

P11-5 Balanced scorecard

⏱ **Time allowed:** 45 minutes

The Royal Hotel Ltd is privately owned and situated in Keswick, an inland resort in the English Lake District. It is a medium-sized hotel with 50 bedrooms. Whilst high standards of building maintenance exist, the hotel has been conservatively managed by William Wordsworth, who owns 100% of its share capital. The hotel currently offers accommodation and restaurant facilities only, and has experienced little innovation in services offered during recent years.

William Wordsworth intends to retire in five years' time, so he has invited Pam Ayres to join him in partnership, with a view to her taking a controlling interest in the hotel on his retirement. She has recently qualified with a Master's Degree from the University of Birmingham, and has some knowledge of the latest approaches to the measurement of business performance. She has conducted a preliminary investigation of the hotel's performance over the past two years, to form a basis for taking a decision on joining William in partnership. The data she has gathered, based on the balanced scorecard approach to performance measurement, is presented in Appendix 1 and Appendix 2.

Appendix 1: Financial data

	Current year	Previous year
Estimated market value of the business	£2,000,000	£2,000,000
Turnover	£1,000,000	£950,000
Net profit	£200,000	£188,000
Current assets (cash, stock and credit card debtors)	£30,000	£25,000
Current liabilities (trade creditors)	£7,000	£10,000

Appendix 2: Non-financial data

Customer perspective

	Current year	Previous year
Room occupancy (during the 300 days the hotel is open each year)	55%	65%
Market share of overnight hotel accommodation in Keswick	4.33%	3.67%
Customer satisfaction rating (score maximum 100%)	55%	65%
Customers indicating they would return to the Royal Hotel if visiting Keswick again	25%	45%

Internal business processes

	Current year	Previous year
Audited percentage of procedures done according to job specification	75%	85%
Year on year employee retention rate	30%	50%
Customer rating of staff responsiveness (score maximum 100%)	60%	85%
Customer rating of staff competence (score maximum 100%)	50%	90%
Customer rating of staff courtesy (score maximum 100%)	60%	78%

Learning and growth perspective

	Current year	Previous year
Royal Hotel percentage of revenue from accommodation and restaurant	100%	100%
Keswick hotels industry average percentage of revenue from accommodation and restaurants	65%	75%
Average percentage of staff with hotel and restaurant qualifications	55%	65%

Required

1 Assess the financial performance of the Royal Hotel based only on the information provided in Appendix 1.
2 Explain why the information in Appendix 2 is likely to give a better indication of future success than the information in Appendix 1.
3 Using all the information at your disposal, assess the future prospects of the Royal Hotel, and advise Pam Ayres on the desirability of becoming a partner in the business

(Thanks to Alan Coad, University of Birmingham)

Chapter 12
Performance measurement and management control in segmented organizations

Learning **objectives**

After studying Chapter 12, you should be able to:
1   Differentiate between performance measurement in cost centres, profit centres and investment centres
2   Compute the return on investment (ROI)
3   Show how changes in sales, expenses and assets affect an organization's ROI
4   Compute residual income and understand its strengths and weaknesses
5   Compute economic value added (EVA) and other value management metrics

Concepts **in Context**

Quaker Oats provides an example of how the use of a specific performance measure can change the way a company operates. Prior to adopting EVA, 'its businesses had one over-riding goal – increasing quarterly earnings. To do it, they guzzled capital. They offered sharp price discounts at the end of each quarter, so plants ran overtime turning out huge shipments of Gatorade, Rice-A-Roni, 100 per cent Natural Cereal, and other products. Managers led the late rush, since their bonuses depended on raising operating profits each quarter ... Pumping up sales requires many warehouses (capital) to

© Andriy Petrenko

hold vast temporary inventories (more capital). But who cared? Quaker's operating businesses paid no charge for capital in internal accounting, so they barely noticed. It took EVA to spotlight the problem. One plant has trimmed inventories from $15 million to $9 million, even though it is producing much more, and Quaker has closed five of 15 warehouses, saving $6 million a year in salaries and capital costs.'[1]

Once an organization grows beyond a few people, it becomes impossible for the top manager to make decisions about everything. For example, the managing director of the Novotel Hotel chain cannot be expected to decide whether a particular hotel guest at the Novotel in Sheffield should be allowed to check out later than the normal checkout time. To some degree, managers have to delegate decisions to those who are at lower levels in the organization. However, the degree to which decisions are delegated varies from organization to organization.

Decentralization in organizations

A **decentralized organization** is one in which decision making is not confined to a few top executives but rather is spread throughout the organization, with managers at various levels making *key operating decisions* relating to their sphere of responsibility. Decentralization is a matter of degree, since all organizations are decentralized to some extent out of necessity. At one extreme, a strongly decentralized organization is one in which there are few, if any, constraints on the freedom of even the lowest-level managers and employees to make decisions. At the other extreme, in a strongly centralized organization, lower-level managers have little freedom to make a decision. Although most organizations fall somewhere between these two extremes, there is a pronounced trend towards more and more decentralization.

Advantages and disadvantages of decentralization

Decentralization has many benefits, including:

1   Top management is relieved of much day-to-day problem solving and is left free to concentrate on strategy, on higher-level decision making, and on co-ordinating activities.
2   Decentralization provides lower-level managers with vital experience in making decisions. Without such experience, they would be ill-prepared to make decisions when they are promoted.
3   Added responsibility and decision-making authority often result in increased job satisfaction. It makes the job more interesting and provides greater incentives for people to put out their best efforts.
4   Lower-level managers generally have more detailed and up-to-date information about conditions in their own area of responsibility than top managers. Therefore, the decisions of lower-level managers are often based on better information.
5   It is difficult to evaluate a manager's performance if the manager is not given much latitude in what he or she can do.

Decentralization has four major disadvantages:

1   Lower-level managers may make decisions without fully understanding the 'big picture'. While top-level managers typically have less detailed information about operations than the lower-level managers, they usually have more information about the company as a whole and may have a better understanding of the company's strategy. This situation can be avoided to some extent with the use of modern management information systems that can, in principle, give every manager at every level the same information that goes to the managing director and other top-level managers.
2   In a truly decentralized organization, there may be a lack of co-ordination among autonomous managers. This problem can be reduced by clearly defining the company's strategy and communicating it effectively throughout the organization.
3   Lower-level managers may have objectives that are different from the objectives of the entire organization. For example, some managers may be more interested in increasing the sizes of their departments than in increasing the profits of the company.[2] To some degree, this problem can be overcome by designing performance evaluation systems that motivate managers to make decisions that are in the best interests of the company.
4   In a strongly decentralized organization, it may be more difficult effectively to spread innovative ideas. Someone in one part of the organization may have a terrific idea that would benefit other parts of the organization, but without strong central direction the idea may not be shared with and adopted by other parts of the organization.

Decentralization and segment reporting

Effective decentralization requires *segmental reporting*. In addition to the company-wide profit and loss account, reports are needed for individual segments of the organization. A **segment** is a part or activity of an organization about which managers would like cost, revenue or profit data. Examples of segments include divisions of a company, sales territories, individual stores, service centres, manufacturing plants, marketing departments, individual customers and product lines. As we shall see, a company's operations can be segmented in many ways. For example, a supermarket chain like Tesco or Sainsbury can segment their businesses by geographic region, by individual store, by the nature of the merchandise (i.e., green groceries, canned goods, paper goods), by brand name, and so on. In this chapter, we learn how to construct profit and loss accounts for such business segments. These segmented profit and loss accounts are useful in analysing the profitability of segments and in measuring the performance of segment managers.

Cost, profit and investment centres

LO 1

Decentralized companies typically categorize their business segments into cost centres, profit centres and investment centres – depending on the responsibilities of the managers of the segments.[3]

Cost centre

A **cost centre** is a business segment whose manager has control over costs but not over revenue or investment funds. Service departments such as accounting, finance, general administration, legal, personnel and so on, are usually considered to be cost centres. In addition, manufacturing facilities are often considered to be cost centres. The managers of cost centres are expected to minimize cost while providing the level of services or the amount of products demanded by other parts of the organization. For example, the manager of a production facility would be evaluated at least in part by comparing actual costs to how much the costs should have been for the actual number of units produced during the period.

Profit centre

In contrast to a cost centre, a **profit centre** is any business segment whose manager has control over both cost and revenue. Like a cost centre, however, a profit centre generally does not have control over investment funds. For example, the manager in charge of an amusement park would be responsible for both the revenues and costs, and hence the profits, of the amusement park but may not have control over major investments in the park. Profit centre managers are often evaluated by comparing actual profit to targeted or budgeted profit.

Investment centre

An **investment centre** is any segment of an organization whose manager has control over cost, revenue and investments in operating assets. For example, the managing director of the Truck Division at General Motors (one of the companies that pioneered decentralization in the last century)[4] would have a great deal of discretion over investments in the division. The managing director of the Truck Division would be responsible for initiating investment proposals, such as funding research into more fuel-efficient engines for sport-utility vehicles. Once the proposal has been approved by the top level of managers at General Motors and the board of directors, the managing director of the Truck Division would then be responsible for making sure that the investment pays off. Investment centre managers are usually evaluated using return on investment or residual income measures as discussed later in the chapter.

Responsibility centres

A **responsibility centre** is broadly defined as any part of an organization whose manager has control over cost, revenue or investment funds. Cost centres, profit centres and investment centres are all known as responsibility centres.

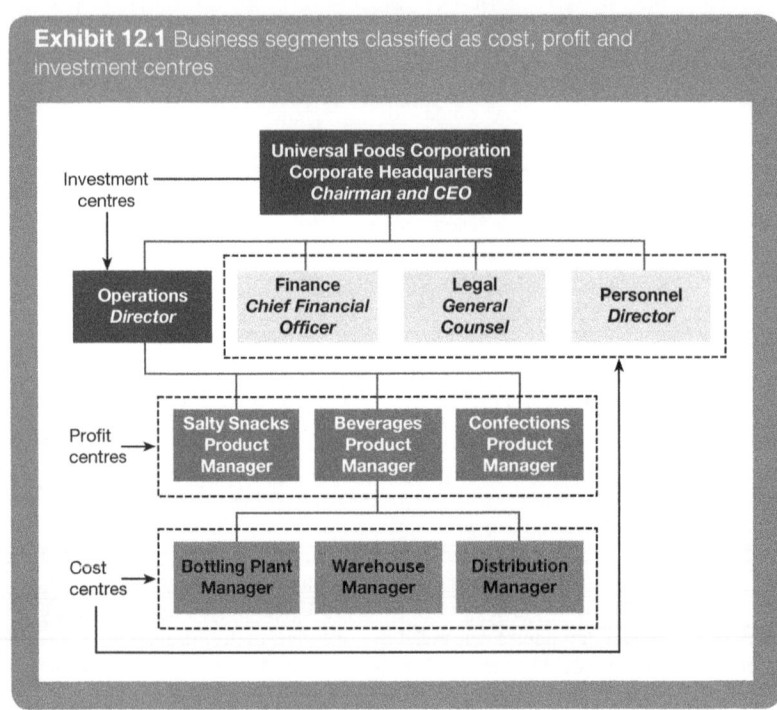

Exhibit 12.1 Business segments classified as cost, profit and investment centres

A partial organization chart for Universal Foods Corporation, a company in the snack food and beverage industry, appears in Exhibit 12.1. This partial organization chart indicates how the various business segments of the company are classified in terms of responsibility. Note that the cost centres are the departments and work centres that do not generate significant revenues by themselves. These are staff departments such as finance, legal and personnel, and operating units such as the bottling plant, warehouse and beverage distribution centre. The profit centres are business segments that generate revenues and include the beverage, salty snacks and confections product segments. The managing director of operations oversees allocation of investment funds across the product segments and is responsible for revenues and costs and so is treated as an investment centre. And finally, corporate headquarters is an investment centre, since it is responsible for all revenues, costs and investments. In this chapter we are going to focus on the management of investment centres.

LO 2 Rate of return for measuring managerial performance

When a company is truly decentralized, segment managers are given a great deal of autonomy. So great is this autonomy that the various profit and investment centres are often viewed as being virtually independent businesses, with their managers having about the same control over decisions as if they were in fact running their own independent firms. With this autonomy, fierce competition often develops among managers, with each striving to make his or her segment the 'best' in the company.

Competition between investment centres is particularly keen for investment funds. How do top managers in corporate headquarters go about deciding who gets new investment funds as they become available, and how do these managers decide which investment centres are most profitably using the funds that have already been entrusted to their care? One of the most popular ways of making these judgments is to measure the rate of return that investment centre managers are able to generate on their assets. This rate of return is called *the return on investment (ROI)*.

The return on investment (ROI) formula

The **return on investment (ROI)** is defined as net operating profit divided by average operating assets:

$$ROI = \frac{Net\ operating\ profit}{Average\ operating\ assets}$$

There are some issues about how to measure net operating profit and average operating assets, but this formula seems clear enough. The higher the return on investment of a business segment, the greater the *profit generated per pound invested* in the segment's operating assets.

Net operating profit and operating assets defined

Note that *net operating profit*, rather than net profit, is used in the ROI formula. **Net operating profit** is profit before interest and taxes and is sometimes referred to as EBIT (earnings before interest and taxes). The reason for using net operating profit in the formula is that the profit figure used should be consistent with the base to which it is applied. Notice that the base (i.e., denominator) consists of *operating assets*. Thus, to be consistent we use net operating profit in the numerator.

Operating assets include cash, debtors, inventory, plant and equipment, and all other assets held for productive use in the organization. Examples of assets that would not be included in the operating assets category (i.e., examples of non-operating assets) would include land held for future use, an investment in another company, or a factory building rented to someone else. The operating assets base used in the formula is typically computed as the average of the operating assets between the beginning and the end of the year.

Plant and equipment: net book value or gross cost?

A major issue in ROI computations is the monetary measure of plant and equipment that should be included in the operating assets base. To illustrate the problem involved, assume that a company reports the following amounts for plant and equipment on its balance sheet:

Plant and equipment	£3,000,000
Less accumulated depreciation	900,000
Net book value	£2,100,000

What amount of plant and equipment should the company include with its operating assets in computing ROI? One widely used approach is to include only the plant and equipment's *net book value* – that is, the plant's original cost less accumulated depreciation (£2,100,000 in the example above). A second approach is to ignore depreciation and include the plant's entire *gross cost* in the operating assets base (£3,000,000 in the example above). Both of these approaches are used in actual practice, even though they will obviously yield very different operating asset and ROI figures.

The following arguments can be raised for using *net book value* to measure *operating assets* and for using *gross cost* to measure operating assets in ROI computation.

Arguments for using net book value to measure operating assets in ROI computations:

1 The net book value method is consistent with how plant and equipment are reported on the balance sheet (i.e., cost less accumulated depreciation to date).

2 The net book value method is consistent with the computation of operating profit, which includes depreciation as an operating expense.

Arguments for using gross cost to measure operating assets in ROI computations:

1 The gross cost method eliminates both the age of equipment and the method of depreciation as factors in ROI computations. (Under the net book value method, ROI will tend to increase over time as net book value declines due to depreciation.)

2 The gross cost method does not discourage replacement of old, worn out equipment. (Under the net book value method, replacing fully depreciated equipment with new equipment can have a dramatic, adverse effect on ROI.)

Managers generally view consistency as the most important of the considerations above. As a result, a majority of companies use the net book value approach in ROI computations. In this text, we will also use the net book value approach unless a specific exercise or problem directs otherwise.

LO 3 Controlling the rate of return

When we first defined the return on investment, we used the following formula:

$$\text{ROI} = \frac{\text{Net operating profit}}{\text{Average operating assets}}$$

We can modify this formula slightly by introducing sales as follows:

$$\text{ROI} = \frac{\text{Net operating profit}}{\text{Sales}} \times \frac{\text{Sales}}{\text{Average operating assets}}$$

The first term on the right-hand side of the equation is the *margin*, which is defined as follows:

$$\text{Margin} = \frac{\text{Net operating profit}}{\text{Sales}}$$

The **margin** is a measure of management's ability to control operating expenses in relation to sales. The lower the operating expenses per pound of sales, the higher the margin earned.

The second term on the right-hand side of the preceding equation is *turnover* which is defined as follows:

$$\text{Turnover} = \frac{\text{Sales}}{\text{Average operating assets}}$$

Turnover is a measure of the sales that are generated for each pound invested in operating assets.

The following alternative form of the ROI formula, which we will use most frequently, combines margin and turnover:

$$\text{ROI} = \text{Margin} \times \text{Turnover}$$

Which formula for ROI should be used – the original one stated in terms of net operating profit and average operating assets or this one stated in terms of margin and turnover? Either can be used – they will always give the same answer. However, the margin and turnover formulation provides some additional insights.

Some managers tend to focus too much on margin and ignore turnover. To some degree at least, the margin can be a valuable indicator of a manager's performance. Standing alone, however, it overlooks one crucial area of a manager's responsibility – the investment in operating assets. Excessive funds tied up in operating assets, which depresses turnover, can be just as much of a drag on profitability as excessive operating expenses, which depresses margin. One of the advantages of ROI as a performance measure is that it forces the manager to control the investment in operating assets as well as to control expenses and the margin.

Exhibit 12.2 Elements of return on investment (ROI)

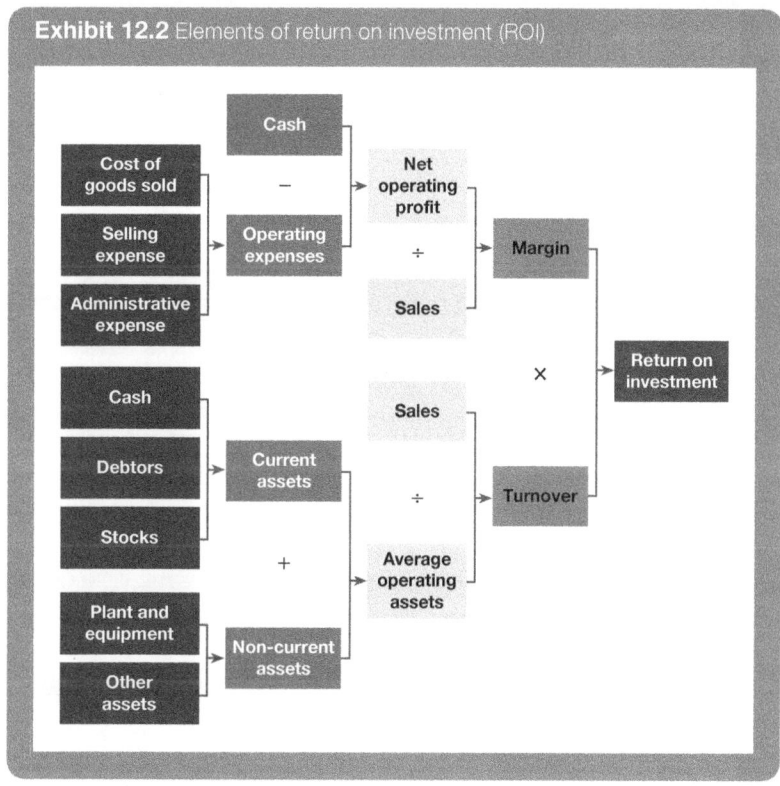

Du Pont pioneered the ROI concept and recognized the importance of looking at both margin and turnover in assessing the performance of a manager. The ROI formula is now widely used as the key measure of the performance of an investment centre. The ROI formula blends together many aspects of the manager's responsibilities into a single figure that can be compared to the returns of competing investment centres, the returns of other firms in the industry, and to the past returns of the investment centre itself.

Du Pont also developed the diagram that appears in Exhibit 12.2. This exhibit helps managers understand how they can control ROI. An investment centre manager can increase ROI in basically three ways:

1   Increase sales
2   Reduce expenses
3   Reduce assets.

To illustrate how the rate of return can be improved by each of these three actions, consider how the manager of the Raffles Burger Grill is evaluated. Burger Grill is a small chain of upmarket casual restaurants that has been rapidly adding outlets via franchising. The Raffles franchise is owned by a group of local surgeons who have little time to devote to management and little expertise in business matters. Therefore, they delegate operating decisions – including decisions concerning investment in operating assets such as inventories – to a professional manager they have hired. The manager is evaluated largely based on the ROI the franchise generates.

The following data represent the results of business activity for the most recent month:

Net operating profit	£10,000
Sales	100,000
Average operating assets	50,000

The rate of return generated by the Raffles Burger Grill investment centre is as follows:

ROI = Margin × Turnover

$$\frac{\text{Net operating profit}}{\text{Sales}} \times \frac{\text{Sales}}{\text{Average operating assets}}$$

$$\frac{£10,000}{£1,000,000} \times \frac{£100,000}{£50,000}$$

10% × 2 = 20%

As we stated above, to improve the ROI figure, the manager can (1) increase sales, (2) reduce expenses, or (3) reduce the operating assets.

(1) Increase sales

Assume that the manager of the Raffles Burger Grill is able to increase sales from £100,000 to £110,000. Assume further that either because of good cost control or because some costs in the company are fixed, the net operating profit increases even more rapidly, going from £10,000 to £12,000 per period. The operating assets remain constant.

$$\text{ROI} = \frac{£12,000}{£110,000} \times \frac{£110,000}{£50,000}$$

10.91% × 2.2 = 24% (as compared to 20% above)

(2) Reduce expenses

Assume that the manager of the Raffles Burger Grill is able to reduce expenses by £1,000 so that net operating profit increases from £10,000 to £11,000. Both sales and operating assets remain constant.

$$\text{ROI} = \frac{£11,000}{£100,000} \times \frac{£100,000}{£50,000}$$

11% × 2 = 22% (as compared to 20% above)

(3) Reduce assets

Assume that the manager of the Raffles Burger Grill is able to reduce operating assets from £50,000 to £40,000. Sales and net operating profit remain unchanged.

$$\text{ROI} = \frac{£10,000}{£100,000} \times \frac{£100,000}{£40,000}$$

10% × 2.5 = 25% (as compared to 20% above)

A clear understanding of these three approaches to improving the ROI figure is critical to the effective management of an investment centre. We will now look at each approach in more detail.

Increase sales

In first looking at the ROI formula, one is inclined to think that the sales figure is neutral, since it appears as the denominator in the margin computation and as the numerator in the turnover computation. We *could* cancel out the sales figure, but we do not do so for two reasons. First, this would tend to draw attention away from the fact that the rate of return is a function of *two* variables, margin and turnover. And second, it would tend to conceal the fact that a change in sales can affect both the *margin* and the turnover in an organization. To explain, a change in sales can affect the margin if expenses increase or decrease at a different rate than sales. For example, a company may be able to keep a tight control on its costs as its sales goup, with the result that net operating profit increases more rapidly than sales and increases the margin. Or a company may have fixed expenses that remain constant as sales go up, resulting in an increase in the net operating profit and in the margin. Either (or both) of these factors could have been responsible for the increase in the margin percentage from 10 to 10.91 illustrated in (1) above.

Further, a change in sales can affect the *turnover* if sales either increase or decrease without a proportionate increase or decrease in the operating assets. In the first approach above, for example, sales increased from £100,000 to £110,000, but the operating assets remained unchanged. As a result, the turnover increased from 2 to 2.2 for the period.

Reduce expenses

Often the easiest route to increased profitability and to a stronger ROI figure is simply to cut the 'fat' out of an organization through a concerted effort to control expenses. When margins begin to be squeezed, this is generally the first line of attack by a manager. Discretionary fixed costs usually come under scrutiny first, and various programmes are either curtailed or eliminated in an effort to cut costs. Managers must be careful, however, not to cut out muscle and bone along with the fat. Also, they must remember that frequent cost-cutting binges can destroy morale. Most managers now agree that it is best to stay 'lean and mean' all the time.

Reduce operating assets

Managers have always been sensitive to the need to control sales, operating expenses and operating margins. However, they have not always been equally sensitive to the need to control investment in operating assets. Firms that have adopted the ROI approach to measuring managerial performance report that one of the first reactions of investment centre managers is to trim their investment in operating assets. The reason, of course, is that these managers soon realize that an excessive investment in operating assets reduces turnover and hurts the ROI. As these managers reduce their investment in operating assets, funds are released that can be used elsewhere in the organization.

How can an investment centre manager control the investment in operating assets? One approach is to eliminate unneeded stock. Just-in-time (JIT) purchasing and JIT manufacturing have been extremely helpful in reducing stocks of all types, with the result that ROI figures have improved dramatically in some companies. Another approach is to devise various methods of speeding up the collection of debtors. For example, many firms now employ the lockbox technique by which customers in distant states send their payments directly to post office boxes in their area. The funds are received and deposited by a local bank on behalf of the payee firm. This speeds up the collection process, since the payments are not delayed in the postal system. As a result of the speedup in collection, the Debtors balance is reduced and the asset turnover is increased.

Criticisms of ROI

Although ROI is widely used in evaluating performance, it is not a perfect tool. The method is subject to the following criticisms:

1 Just telling managers to increase ROI may not be enough. Managers may not know how to increase ROI; they may increase ROI in a way that is inconsistent with the company's strategy; or they may take actions that increase ROI in the short run but harm the company in the long run (such as cutting back on research and development). This is why ROI is best used as part of a balanced scorecard. A balanced scorecard can provide concrete guidance to managers, make it more likely that actions taken are consistent with the company's strategy, and reduce the likelihood that short-run performance will be enhanced at the expense of long-term performance.

2   A manager who takes over a business segment typically inherits many committed costs over which the manager has no control. These committed costs may be relevant in assessing the performance of the business segment as an investment but make it difficult fairly to assess the performance of the manager relative to other managers.

3   As discussed in the next section, a manager who is evaluated based on ROI may reject profitable investment opportunities.

Focus on Business Practice
Performance management at Deere & Company

© BanksPhotos

Deere & Company is a world leader in providing advanced products and services for agriculture, forestry, construction, lawn and turf care, landscaping and irrigation. They also provide financial services worldwide and manufacture and market engines used in heavy equipment. In recessionary times, a firm like Deere & Company would be expected to experience declining performance as investment in new equipment declines and construction halts. And Deere & Company has lived up to these expectations with a 45% drop in construction equipment sales and a 15% drop in agricultural equipment sales in 2009. Despite this, Deere & Company still posted profit of $873 million for the year. This strong performance is due in some part to a tight focus on costs and lean manufacturing processes, and may also be in part to the needs of developing economies like China and India where increasing food output means greater agricultural equipment sales. The solid performance may also be attributed in part to a novel 'profit driver' introduced by former CEO Bob Lane. All managers at Deere & Company must 'pay' a 1% per month (12% per annum) charge before reporting any gain. Or in other words, Lane regarded a 12% annual profit as breakeven (see also the later *Focus on Business Practice* on EVA).[5]

Exercise: Assuming the above 12% charge is the minimum return on investment required by Deere & Company, would they proceed with investments which yield a lower return? Why or why not?

LO 4 Residual income[6] – another measure of performance

LO 5 Another approach to measuring an investment centre's performance focuses on a concept known as *residual income*. **Residual income** is the net operating profit that an investment centre earns above the minimum required return on its operating assets. **Economic value added (EVA)** is a similar concept that differs in some details from residual income.[7] For example, under the economic value added concept, funds used for research and development are treated as investments rather than as expenses.[8] However, for our purposes, we will not draw any distinction between residual income and economic value added.

When residual income or economic value added is used to measure performance, the purpose is to maximize the total amount of residual income or economic value added, not to maximize overall ROI. For purposes of illustration, consider the following data for an investment centre – the Scottish Division of Alaskan Marine Services Corporation.

Alaskan Marine Services Corporation
Scottish Division
Basic data for performance evaluation

Average operating assets	£100,000
Net operating profit	£20,000
Minimum required rate of return	15%

Alaskan Marine Services Corporation has long had a policy of evaluating investment centre managers based on ROI, but it is considering a switch to residual income. The finance director of the company, who is in favour of the change to residual income, has provided the following table that shows how the performance of the division would be evaluated under each of the two methods:

Marine Services Corporation
Scottish Division
Alternative performance measures

	ROI	Residual income
Average operating assets	£100,000 (a)	£100,000
Net operating profit	£20,000 (b)	£20,000
ROI, (b) ÷ (a)	20%	
Minimum required return (15% × £100,000)		15,000
Residual income		£5,000

The reasoning underlying the residual income calculation is straightforward. The company is able to earn a rate of return of at least 15% on its investments. Since the company has invested £100,000 in the Scottish Division in the form of operating assets, the company should be able to earn at least £15,000 (15% × £100,000) on this investment. Since the Scottish Division's net operating profit is £20,000, the residual income above and beyond the minimum required return is £5,000. If *residual income* is adopted as the performance measure to replace ROI, the manager of the Scottish Division would be evaluated based on the growth from year to year in residual income.

Motivation and residual income

One of the primary reasons why the chief accountant of Marine Services Corporation would like to switch from ROI to residual income has to do with how managers view new investments under the two performance measurement schemes. The residual income approach encourages managers to make investments that are profitable for the entire company but that would be rejected by managers who are evaluated by the ROI formula.

To illustrate this problem, suppose that the manager of the Scottish Division is considering purchasing a computerized diagnostic machine to aid in servicing marine diesel engines. The machine would cost £25,000 and is expected to generate additional operating profit of £4,500 a year. From the standpoint of the company,

this would be a good investment since it promises a rate of return of 18% (£4,500/£25,000), which is in excess of the company's minimum required rate of return of 15%.

If the manager of the Scottish Division is evaluated based on residual income, she would be in favour of the investment in the diagnostic machine as shown below:

Marine Services Corporation Scottish Division Performance evaluated using residual income			
	Present	New project	Overall
Average operating assets	£100,000	£25,000	£125,000
Net operating profit	£20,000	£4,500	£24,500
Minimum required return	15,000	3,750*	18,750
Residual income	£5,000	£750	£5,750

*£25,000 × 15% = £3,750.

Since the project would increase the residual income of the Scottish Division, the manager would want to invest in the new diagnostic machine.

Now suppose that the manager of the Scottish Division is evaluated based on ROI. The effect of the diagnostic machine on the division's ROI is computed below:

Marine Services Corporation Scottish Division Performance evaluated using ROI			
	Present	New project	Overall
Average operating assets (a)	£100,000	£25,000	£125,000
Net operating profit (b)	£20,000	£4,500†	
ROI, (b)/(a)	20%	18%	19.6%

†£25,000 × 18% = £4,500.

The new project reduces the division's ROI from 20% to 19.6%. This happens because the 18% rate of return on the new diagnostic machine, while above the company's 15% minimum rate of return, is below the division's present ROI of 20%. Therefore, the new diagnostic machine would drag the division's ROI down even though it would be a good investment from the standpoint of the company as a whole. If the manager of the division is evaluated based on ROI, she will be reluctant even to propose such an investment.

Basically, a manager who is evaluated based on ROI will reject any project whose rate of return is below the division's current ROI even if the rate of return on the project is above the minimum required rate of return for the entire company. In contrast, any project whose rate of return is above the minimum required rate of return for the company will result in an increase in residual income. Since it is in the best interests of the company as a whole to accept any project whose rate of return is above the minimum required rate of return, managers who are evaluated based on residual income will tend to make better decisions concerning investment projects than managers who are evaluated based on ROI.

Divisional comparison and residual income

The residual income approach has one major disadvantage. It cannot be used to compare the performance of divisions of different sizes. You would expect larger divisions to have more residual income than smaller divisions, not necessarily because they are better managed but simply because of the bigger numbers involved.

As an example, consider the following residual income computations for Division X and Division Y:

	Division	
	X	Y
Average operating assets (a)	£1,000,000	£250,000
Net operating profit	£120,000	£40,000
Minimum required return: 10% × (a)	100,000	25,000
Residual income	£20,000	£15,000

Observe that Division X has slightly more residual income than Division Y, but that Division X has £1,000,000 in operating assets as compared to only £250,000 in operating assets for Division Y. Thus, Division X's greater residual income is probably more a result of its size than the quality of its management. In fact, it appears that the smaller division is better managed, since it has been able to generate nearly as much residual income with only a quarter as much in operating assets to work with. This problem can be reduced to some degree by focusing on the percentage change in residual income from year to year rather than on the absolute amount of the residual income.

ROI, RI and the balanced scorecard

Simply exhorting managers to increase ROI is not sufficient. Managers who are told to increase ROI will naturally wonder how this is to be accomplished. The Du Pont scheme, which is illustrated in Exhibit 12.2, provides managers with some guidance. Generally speaking, ROI can be increased by increasing sales, decreasing costs, and/or decreasing investments in operating assets. However, it may not be obvious to managers how they are supposed to increase sales, decrease costs and decrease investments in a way that is consistent with the company's strategy. For example, a manager who is given inadequate guidance may cut back on investments that are critical to implementing the company's strategy.

For that reason, when managers are evaluated based on ROI, a *balanced scorecard* approach is advised. And indeed, ROI, or residual income, is typically included as one of the financial performance measures on a company's balanced scorecard. The balanced scorecard provides a way of communicating a company's strategy to managers throughout the organization. The scorecard indicates how the company intends to improve its financial performance. A well-constructed balanced scorecard should answer questions such as: 'What internal business processes should be improved?' and 'Which customer should be targeted and how will they be attracted and retained at a profit?' In short, a well-constructed balanced scorecard can provide managers with a road map that indicates how the company intends to increase its ROI. In the absence of such a road map of the company's strategy, managers may have difficulty understanding what they are supposed to do to increase ROI and they may work at cross-purposes rather than in harmony with the overall strategy of the company. Other critics of EVA are also concerned that a single top-down metric will not be enough to guide the generation of corporate wealth.[9]

© gaspr13

GEC was an example of a company that seemed to thrive while it used ROI but then collapsed as it adopted value-based management/residual income. Yet a more sophisticated analysis might suggest that it was the choice of strategy rather than the adoption of a particular metric that led to problems. The company focused on telecoms just at the height of the so-called Dotcom bubble – when many other companies also decided to focus on that industry. As a consequence, there was overcapacity in that industry and a fall in profitability.[10]

Exercise: Perhaps GEC should have paid more attention to actions of its competitors as suggested by the principles of SMA?

The problem of single period metrics: the bonus bank approach

The problem with ROI, RI and EVA is that they are all single period metrics. Thus, although it can be shown that under certain assumptions the capitalized value of residual income equals the net present value of the company,[11] a one-period measure cannot capture the economic value of a division or investment. From this point of view, investment decisions based on these techniques will not be identical to those based on the 'correct' NPV rule.

Advocates of EVA have tried to respond to this problem by basing executive remuneration on a 'bonus bank' system. The aim of this approach is that bonuses are not just based on a single year's performance but may be accumulated over a number of years. The aim is to discourage managers who may be able to boost EVA in the very short term, take a bonus and then leave the company. In fact, one of the distinguishing features of EVA over RI is the great care that is devoted to designing managerial compensation schemes that are aligned with shareholder wealth objectives.[12]

© Dmitriy Shironosov

At *Allianz*, the company explains the principles behind its use of EVA®. They calculate EVA® as normalized profit minus capital charges, where capital charges are defined as a measure of the company's capital multiplied by the cost of capital. New investment in each division is based on their risk-return profile and their strategic position. Using this process, the divisions can only ensure that they receive growth capital if they:

- operate in a profitable market or business;
- transform their market position into sustainable creation of value and a leading market position;
- maintain an orientation and competency that fits within the long-term strategy of the *Allianz Group*; and
- are able to generate distributable earnings in an amount that is at least equal to their cost of capital.

The requirement to meet the cost of capital is just the minimum. Over the medium-term, the objective is to generate a return of 15% or more on the capital employed. Therefore, companies must determine what business activities will increase their value and concentrate their efforts and resources on these activities. Further, new value drivers must be created, for example, through new products, more cost-effective processes and optimized distribution channels. Local management must also prevent value being destroyed along the complete **value chain**. If value diminishes, countermeasures must be implemented immediately. Because EVA® is an important factor in managing the business, senior management compensation is based on this measurement to a significant extent.[13]

Exercise: Consider what issues might be neglected by a company that uses ROI rather than EVA as a key performance metric.

Summary

- Segment reports can provide information for evaluating the profitability and performance of divisions, product lines, sales territories and other segments of a company. Under the contribution approach to segment reporting, only those costs that are traceable are assigned to a segment. Fixed common costs and other non-traceable costs are not allocated to a segment. A cost is considered to be traceable to a segment only if the cost is caused by the segment and eliminating the segment would result in avoiding the cost.

- Costs that are traceable to a segment are further classified as either variable or fixed. The contribution margin is sales less variable costs. The segment margin is the contribution margin less the traceable fixed costs of the segment.

- For purposes of evaluating the performance of managers, there are at least three kinds of business segments – cost centres, profit centres and investment centres.

- Return on investment (ROI) is widely used to evaluate investment centre performance. However, there is a trend towards using residual income or economic value added instead of ROI.

- The residual income and economic value added approaches encourage profitable investments in many situations where the ROI approach would discourage investment.

Key terms

Cost centre A business segment whose manager has control over cost but has no control over revenue or the use of investment funds (p. 281).

Decentralized organization An organization in which decision making is not confined to a few top executives but rather is spread throughout the organization (p. 280).

Economic value added (EVA) A concept similar to residual profit (p. 288).

Investment centre A business segment whose manager has control over cost and over revenue and that also has control over the use of investment funds (p. 281).

Margin Net operating profit divided by sales (p. 284).

Net operating profit Profit before interest and profit taxes have been deducted (p. 283).

Operating assets Cash, debtors, inventory, plan and equipment, and all other assets held for productive use in an organization (p. 283).

Profit centre A business segment whose manager has control over cost and revenue but has no control over the use of investment funds (p. 281).

Residual income The net operating profit that an investment centre earns above the required return on its operating assets (p. 288).

Responsibility centre Any business segment whose manager has control over cost, revenue or the use of investment funds (p. 281).

Return on investment (ROI) Net operating profit divided by average operating assets. It also equals margin multiplied by turnover (p. 283).

Segment Any part or activity of an organization about which the manager seeks cost, revenue or profit data (p. 281).

Turnover The amount of sales generated in an investment centre for each pound invested in operating assets. It is computed by dividing sales by the average operating assets figure (p. 284).

Endnotes

1 Tully (1993).

2 There is a similar problem with top-level managers.

3 Some companies classify business segments that are responsible mainly for generating revenue, such as an insurance sales office, as revenue centres. Other companies would consider this to be just another type of profit centre, since costs of some kind (salaries, rent, utilities) are usually deducted from the revenues in the segment's profit statement.

4 See Johnson and Kaplan (1987).

5 Deere's Harvest, *Time*, May 24, 2010 – also at http://www.time.com/time/magazine/article/0,9171,1971431-1,00.html

6 Since residual income was developed in America, the term 'income' rather than 'profit' is used.

7 The basic idea underlying residual income and economic value added has been around for over 100 years. In recent years, economic value added has been popularized and trademarked by the consulting firm Stern, Stewart & Co.

8 Over 100 different adjustments could be made for deferred taxes, LIFO reserves, provisions for future liabilities, mergers and acquisitions, gains or losses due to changes in accounting rules, operating leases, and other accounts, but most companies make only a few. For further details, see Young and O'Byrne (2001).

9 See, for example, Mouritsen (1998).

10 Seal (2010).

11 O'Hanlon and Peasnell (1998).

12 See, for example, Young and O'Byrne (2001).

13 www.allianz.co.uk

When you have read this chapter, log on to the Online Learning Centre for *Management Accounting for Business Decisions* at **www.mcgraw-hill.co.uk/textbooks/seal**, where you'll find multiple choice questions, practice exams and extra study tools for management accounting.

Assessment

Questions

connect

12–1 What is meant by the term *decentralization*?

12–2 What benefits result from decentralization?

12–3 Distinguish between a cost centre, a profit centre and an investment centre.

12–4 Define a segment of an organization. Give several examples of segments.

12–5 What is meant by the terms *margin* and *turnover*?

12–6 What are the three basic approaches to improving return on investment (ROI)?

12–7 What is meant by residual income?

12–8 In what way can the use of ROI as a performance measure for investment centres lead to bad decisions? How does the residual income approach overcome this problem?

Exercises

connect

E12–1 Time allowed: 15 minutes

Selected operating data for two divisions of Outback Brewing Ltd of Australia are given below:

	Division	
	Queensland	New South Wales
Sales	£4,000,000	£7,000,000
Average operating assets	2,000,000	2,000,000
Net operating profit	360,000	420,000
Property, plant, and equipment (net)	950,000	800,000

Required

1 Compute the rate of return for each division using the return on investment (ROI) formula stated in terms of margin and turnover.

2 As far as you can tell from the data, which divisional manager seems to be doing the better job? Why?

E12–2 Time allowed: 15 minutes

Provide the missing data in the following tabulation:

	Division		
	Alpha	Bravo	Charlie
Sales	£?	£11,500,000	£?
Net operating profit	?	920,000	210,000
Average operating assets	800,000	?	?
Margin	4%	?	7%
Turnover	5	?	?
Return on investment (ROI)	?	20%	14%

E12–3 Time allowed: 20 minutes

Meiji Isetan Corp. of Japan has two regional divisions with headquarters in Osaka and Yokohama. Selected data on the two divisions follow (in millions of yen, denoted by ¥):

	Division	
	Osaka	Yokohama
Sales	¥3,000,000	¥9,000,000
Net operating profit	210,000	720,000
Average operating assets	1,000,000	4,000,000

Required

1 For each division, compute the return on investment (ROI) in terms of margin and turnover. Where necessary, carry computations to two decimal places.
2 Assume that the company evaluates performance by use of residual profit and that the minimum required return for any division is 15%. Compute the residual profit for each division.
3 Is Yokohama's greater amount of residual profit an indication that it is better managed? Explain.

E12–4 Time allowed: 30 minutes

Selected sales and operating data for three divisions of a multinational structural engineering firm are given below:

	Division		
	Asia	Europe	North America
Sales	£12,000,000	£14,000,000	£25,000,000
Average operating assets	3,000,000	7,000,000	5,000,000
Net operating profit	600,000	560,000	800,000
Minimum required rate of return	14%	10%	16%

Required

1 Compute the return on investment (ROI) for each division using the formula stated in terms of margin and turnover.
2 Compute the residual income for each division.
3 Assume that each division is presented with an investment opportunity that would yield a 15% rate of return.
4 (a) If performance is being measured by ROI, which division or divisions will probably accept the opportunity? Reject? Why?
   (b) If performance is being measured by residual income, which division or divisions will probably accept the opportunity? Reject? Why?

P12–5 Return on investment (ROI); comparison of company performance   Problems

⏱ Time allowed: 30 minutes

connect™

Comparative data on three companies in the same industry are given below:

	Company		
	A	B	C
Sales	£600,000	£500,000	£?
Net operating profit	84,000	70,000	?
Average operating assets	300,000	?	1,000,000
Margin	?	?	3.5%
Turnover	?	?	2
ROI	?	7%	?

Required

1 What advantages can you see in breaking down the ROI computation into two separate elements, margin and turnover?

2 Fill in the missing information above, and comment on the relative performance of the three companies in as much detail as the data permit. Make specific recommendations on steps to be taken to improve the return on investment, where needed. (Adapted from National Association of Accountants, Research Report No. 35, p. 34)

P12–6 Return on investment (ROI) and residual income

⏱ Time allowed: 20 minutes

Financial data for Joel de Paris plc for last year follow:

Joel de Paris plc
Balance sheet

	Ending balance	Beginning balance
Assets		
Cash	£120,000	£140,000
Debtors	530,000	450,000
Stock	380,000	320,000
Plant and equipment, net	620,000	680,000
Investment in Buisson SA	280,000	250,000
Land (undeveloped)	170,000	180,000
Total assets	£2,100,000	£2,020,000
Liabilities and shareholders' equity		
Creditors	£310,000	£360,000
Long-term debt	1,500,000	1,500,000
Shareholders' equity	290,000	160,000
Total liabilities and shareholders' equity	£2,100,000	£2,020,000

Joel de Paris plc Profit and loss account		
Sales		£4,050,000
Less operating expenses		3,645,000
Net operating profit		405,000
Less interest and taxes:		
Interest expense	£150,000	
Tax expense	110,000	260,000
Net profit		£145,000

The company paid dividends of £15,000 last year. The 'Investment in Buisson', on the balance sheet represents an investment in the shares of another company.

Required

1 Compute the company's margin, turnover and ROI for last year.
2 The board of directors of Joel de Paris Inc has set a minimum required return of 15%. What was the company's residual income last year?

P12–7 Return on investment (ROI) and residual income

🕐 Time allowed: 30 minutes

'I know headquarters wants us to add on that new product line', said Dell Havasi, manager of Billings Company's Office Products Division. 'But I want to see the numbers before I make any move. Our division has led the company for three years, and I don't want any letdown.'

Billings Company is a decentralized organization with five autonomous divisions. The divisions are evaluated on the basis of the return that they are able to generate on invested assets, with year-end bonuses given to the divisional managers who have the highest ROI figures. Operating results for the company's Office Products Division for the most recent year are given below:

Sales	£10,000,000
Less variable expenses	6,000,000
Contribution margin	4,000,000
Less fixed expenses	3,200,000
Net operating profit	£800,000
Divisional operating assets	£4,000,000

The company had an overall ROI of 15% last year (considering all divisions). The Office Products Division has an opportunity to add a new product line that would require an additional investment in operating assets of £1,000,000. The cost and revenue characteristics of the new product line per year would be:

Sales	£2,000,000
Variable expenses	60% of sales
Fixed expenses	£640,000

Required

1 Compute the Office Products Division's ROI for the most recent year; also compute the ROI as it will appear if the new product line is added.

2 If you were in Dell Havasi's position, would you be inclined to accept or reject the new product line? Explain.

3 Why do you suppose headquarters is anxious for the Office Products Division to add the new product line?

4 Suppose that the company views a return of 12% on invested assets as being the minimum that any division should earn and that performance is evaluated by the residual income approach.

5 (a) Compute the Office Products Division's residual income for the most recent year; also compute the residual income as it will appear if the new product line is added.

   (b) Under these circumstances, if you were in Dell Havasi's position, would you accept or reject the new product line? Explain.